## The Complete Book of Love a

*Dr Philip Cauthery* MB, CHB, DPH firs
psychosexual aspects of adolescent me
started working as a Student Health physician after 16 years as a medical officer in the Royal Air Force. In 1967 he participated in the creation of contraceptive services for the unmarried in Birmingham and he has always been a pioneer for women's rights to contraception and abortion. Author of *Fundamentals of Sex* and *Student Health*, he has worked as a psychosexual adviser and as a participant in many radio and TV programmes, as well as contributing regularly to the medical press on psychosexual topics. For six years he was editorial adviser on psychosexual medicine to *Parents* magazine, writing and answering letters about sexual problems.

*Dr Andrew Stanway* MB, MRCP practised medicine on the Professorial Medical Unit at King's College Hospital in London before leaving to edit medical journals for doctors. In 1973 he started a medical film company making educational and documentary films for doctors, dentists, health care professionals and TV around the world. He has written thirty books including *Overcoming Depression*; *Infertility – A Guide for Infertile Couples*; *Alternative Medicine – A Guide to Natural Therapies* including four titles with his wife, Dr Penny Stanway, about family life and childhood problems including *The Baby and Child Book*. His books on depression and infertility took him further into the area of sexual problems and their effects on people's lives and he has since become increasingly active clinically in this field. He has a practice in Surrey that deals with personal, psychosexual and marital problems.

*Dr Penny Stanway* MB, BS worked in two hospitals and spent a year in general practice, where she saw mostly women and children. She then spent several years working in child health in the community. She is an international adviser on breast-feeding and she is author, with her husband, of the bestseller *Breast is Best*. At one time she wrote widely for mother and baby magazines and answered letters for Britain's *Parents* magazine. Now she writes books on health (including *the Mothercare Guide to Child Health*, and *Diet for Common Ailments*) and practices as a counsellor for emotional problems.

The Complete Book Of

# LOVE & SEX

*Dr Philip Cauthery and*
*Drs Andrew and Penny Stanway*

Arrow Books

Arrow Books Limited
62–65 Chandos Place, London WC2N 4NW

An imprint of Century Hutchinson Limited

London Melbourne Sydney Auckland
Johannesburg and agencies throughout
the world

First published in Great Britain by Century 1983
Revised edition first published by Arrow Books 1989


Illustrations by Barrie Thorpe, Lydia Malim and Ann Savage



Photoset by Rowland Phototypesetting Limited
Bury St Edmunds, Suffolk
Printed and bound in Great Britain by
The Guernsey Press Co. Limited, Guernsey, Channel Islands

ISBN 0 09 963550 X

# Contents

# Introduction

Sexuality is a vast subject covering many fields of study. Genitality, with which it is usually confused, is only a small part of it, yet sex books and sex education tend to concentrate on this aspect of it.

This is understandable because the anatomical differences between the sexes, and especially the genital differences, are the subject of endless fascination and interest from childhood onwards. In our western culture we put so many prohibitions on interest in our genitals and genitality that there is a danger of becoming absorbed with the topic to the exclusion of the more important aspects of sexuality in our relationships and lives.

Men and women are highly complex physical, emotional and psychological beings and to ignore the love, the feelings and the relationships that go hand in hand with genitality is like driving a car with only one wheel. The result is the same – a dangerous imbalance. For many people the sexual aspects of their lives are less fulfilling than they should or could be and they end up passing on their hang-ups, wrong perceptions and misunderstandings about sex and sexuality to their children.

As a culture we try to overcome our natural interest in but unnatural emphasis on the genitals by talking a lot about love and most readers would agree that if men and women could love each other perfectly the world would be a very different place. In a sense if we can love another human being perfectly we are half-way towards loving everyone, and the world needs love more than ever before. The sort we need is not the vague love that teenagers feel for all mankind but rather a mature, practical and real love for another real human being.

Real love is in short supply and many people, because of their upbringing, do not love themselves enough to be able to love another person. Yet others are so obsessed with themselves that they are unable to allow another person to intrude in any significant way. Men and women in all kinds of relationships often feel they do not love each other very much and some even hate each other. Some men dislike all women and some women, all men. What a terrible state of affairs to have got ourselves into in a so-called Christian society that should be based on love.

Unfortunately, the man-woman relationship has many enemies. To the extent that the state or religions demand that their interests be given prior consideration and that the man-woman relationship itself should be governed by them, they intrude on and may even damage the relationship. Both, of course, do so 'accidentally' under the guise of trying to further the relationship.

In fact, for a supposedly caring society based on Judaeo-Christian morals, we seem to be doing rather badly in this area. Premarital pregnancies and sexually-transmitted diseases are on the increase in spite of efforts to curb them; over a third of marriages end in divorce; one in eight children live in one-parent families; most parents have problems in dealing with their teenagers' emerging sexuality; and depression, the most widespread psychological illness of our society, is not only commoner than ever but often has a psychosexual basis. There is certainly no room for complacency. But what can the average family hope to do to redress the balance?

Obviously a way to change things is to shield our children from the negative cultural influences that we suffered, but this is not easy because we as parents are steeped in them.

What we shall do in this book is to look at love and sex from the cradle to the grave and, with the benefit of knowledge of both family and psychosexual medicine, weave a picture of interlinking complexity that shows how a child grows up to become a sexual person. We then follow this person through life and look at other major milestones along the way. The subject is enormous and we have drawn on research from all over the world to add to our own clinical experience. After all, no one person can have seen it all and, in the final analysis, everyone is different.

We have tried to make the book comprehensive rather than encyclopaedic and each chapter could easily have been extended to a book in its own right. In this completely revised edition, we have brought all the facts and figures up to date and have taken the AIDS epidemic into account. Because we have had to be brief on very important subjects we have tried to concentrate on what families most want to know and have tried to be as practical as possible. After all, unless you have had a wide experience of teenagers and talked to them about their intimate fears, problems, loves, hates and aspirations you can't really know how your own child fits into the picture of 'normality'. Many parents end up feeling hopelessly confused, especially in our fast-changing world.

Being a parent is probably more difficult today than ever before because the conflicts within society are so great, and the last thing that most parents need is yet another sex manual to tell them and their family how to behave genitally. Clinical experience repeatedly confirms that although genital sex *can* help cement a relationship in troubled times, sex nearly always looks after itself in a good relationship. Many people with so-called sex problems have personality or interrelationship problems deep down – the sex problem is simply the obvious symptom of which they complain.

## *Why another sex book?*

Because many sex books concentrate on people as if all that mattered were their genitals. This is ill-advised. Physical sex has been greatly over-emphasised in modern Western Society. The mood is now right for a book that looks at sex and sexuality in a wider context and this involves concepts of reason, loving, caring and togetherness. Far too many books have emphasised the 'I'm the most important person in the world' approach to the subject. Love and sex in reality involve other people's lives and do so very intimately.

With the coming of AIDS more and more people are looking to their existing relationships to answer their needs for love and sex rather than throwing in the towel and starting again. This book helps make this possible by encouraging understanding, tolerance and flexibility.

## *Why a 'family' book of love and sex?*

Because our individual sexuality starts to express itself the day we are born. We need to understand the sexual components of life from birth to old age so that we can be more effective, happy and fulfilled human beings and parents and prevent our children from suffering from many of the problems we have as adults. We all want what is best for our children yet which of us is equipped to provide it in today's changing and complex society?

## *Surely there's enough talk about sex already?*

Yes, there is but there is far too little talk about the way the modern family can cope with its *sexuality* in a *genitally*-obsessed society and how parents can stop *talking* and get on with *doing* when it comes to steering their children's sexuality. We hope that this book will not simply change the way parents think but will also change the way they act – both between themselves and towards the rest of the family. Actions are what really matter. We are judged in this world more by our behaviour than our thoughts.

## *With AIDS around isn't it best to forget about sex?*

No, it would be dangerous. AIDS is discussed later but the arrival of this new disease, for which there is yet no cure, underlines more than ever the need for information about sex to be widely available. AIDS can *only* be prevented at the moment and *only* knowledge, not ignorance, can achieve this. This knowledge amounts to much more than just how to use a condom.

## *Is this another book telling me how to bring up my children?*

No. It's a book that, by increasing your insight and understanding of the whole subject of sexuality and love, should help you understand your own and your children's complex emotions and feelings in situations as different as birth and breastfeeding; dealing with your pubertal daughter; influencing your teenage son; wondering what to do about your child living with his or her boyfriend or girlfriend; reassessing marriage in general and your own in particular; sex problems within your marriage; worries about old age; and much, much more.

No one has the right to tell people what to do when it comes to bringing up their children *but* there are many errors that people make in this area. Clinical experience of dealing with these problems enables us to help the reader because he or she can learn from thousands of other people's mistakes – hopefully before they make them themselves. It's easy to say that there are no absolute rights or wrongs about family sexuality and that whatever you do your children will turn out all right but this simply isn't true. None of us can hope to bring up perfect human beings but we can do our very best to reduce negative influences by a little informed thought – and care. Whatever happens in the formal world of sex education the majority of influences on a child (and therefore on that person as an adult) come from his or her parents. Because of this we owe it not only to our children but also to their spouses and children to get things as right as we can in the first twenty years or so of their lives.

## *Why on earth should I read about this? Surely sex is natural, healthy, fun and normal?*

Unfortunately sex is none of these things for a lot of people at some stage of their lives. We all have a sex drive of some kind, whether it's weak or strong, indulged or ignored and our perceptions of ourselves as sexual beings vary enormously according to our upbringing. To copulate then is natural – it can be undertaken with anyone and not necessarily even in the context of an interpersonal relationship. However, we can do a lot better than simply copulate because we are highly elaborate verbal and emotional creatures and even genital sexual expression is a very complex business.

## *Does anything go then?*

That's entirely up to you. As doctors seeing people with real problems we don't condemn anyone for what they are or what they do but you will have to decide how you interpret and react to the book for yourself and your family. The book is non-judgemental and we have tried very hard not to let our personal preferences and prejudices come across. Each family will apply the contents of this book differently according to its race, religion, economic state, level of education, level of expectations, personalities, their care for each other and their family, and so on. For this reason we have included chapters on homosexuality, prostitution and several other areas not immediately and obviously to do with the family. However, the majority of parents worry about homosexual influences on their young teenagers at some stage; and the majority of the clients of prostitutes are married men, so an understanding of even these subjects is of considerable importance to an understanding of family love and sex.

We have written a book with no clear beginning and no end because sexuality has no beginning and no end. The baby who has just been born is at one and the same time at a starting point (for him) but an end point for his recently pregnant mother. One's first love-affair is a vital milestone along the path of life yet will, however important it seems at the time, fade away and be displaced by more mature love. Our life experience in love and sex do not go with us to the grave – they live on in our children and their children.

So, in conclusion, what we hope will come out of this book is a better future based on improved man-woman relationships. This comes down to real, live individuals relating to and understanding each other, and not to religious, political, philosophical or medical theories and rules. The world is in a rather troubled state but there is hope for the future if only the basic unit of society, the family, can be made to work better. This it can only do if its members understand each other better and live in this increased knowledge and understanding.

Having said this, there is no such thing as perfection and few people's lives are 'ideal' in this or any other area. But this does not mean that we should not or cannot have some notion of what is worth striving for.

*Chapter 1*

# Baby and childhood sexuality

To many people in our culture any concept of childhood sexuality seems totally unwholesome and many find it impossible to think of children as sexual beings at all. This is because most people think of sexuality as being inextricably linked to genitality. This is not true of adult sexuality and is even less so when it comes to children.

Babies and children *are* sexual creatures and it is only in a sex-repressed culture such as ours that credence would be given to any alternative suggestion. In the vast majority of cultures in the world children witness adult sexuality as part of their everyday life experience. Things are different here where children are required to be 'innocent' and are seen as empty slates on which anything can be written, so that they are in need of protection. Of course children do need protecting, but to protect them against sex – one of our basic appetites and means of expression – is strange, to say the least.

If it could be proved that, by allowing children to gain a knowledge of sexuality naturally as they grow up, we would be harming or damaging them in any way, we would of course, be against it – but there is no such proof. On the contrary, work done by Margaret Mead and others suggests that in societies in which children are not repressed sexually, as happens in the West, the children show no preoccupation with sex and grow up far better balanced sexually than ours do. In such cultures, perversions and deviations are rare and the sexes get on well together as adults.

The problems when discussing baby and childhood sexuality come about because for adults – as we have said – sexuality is often wrongly equated with genitality. There is evidence that the two are not so closely linked in babies and young children, who get just as much enjoyable and intense physical pleasure from other pursuits and experiences, as we adults do from intercourse and other genital behaviour.

At the risk of putting readers off it is probably useful to consider what Freud said about sexuality at this stage, if only because his theories have not been greatly improved on in nearly a century. Freud suggested that a child goes through several well-defined stages of sexual or, more correctly, psychosexual development from the cradle to sexual maturity in the teens. The first stage is the *oral* one in which most pleasure is centred around the baby's mouth; the second is the *anal* one in which pleasure mostly comes from excreting (urinating and opening the bowels); the third stage is the *phallic* one during which the child discovers his penis or her clitoris as the best source of pleasure; the fourth is a period of *latency* during which psychosexual development more or less marks time; and lastly, with puberty, the child becomes *genital* and obtains the majority of his or her sexual and sensual pleasures from genital sensations.

Most children progress from one stage to the next at a fairly predictable pace but can, because of problems in upbringing, stop at a particular stage; go awry, or go back a stage or two after having successfully negotiated one stage. It is clearly seen in clinical practice that adults can move around the scale from a major preoccupation with the adult (genital) stage. At any one stage in a person's life one of these phases is dominant in his or her sexuality but regression is possible to any of the previous stages. We shall look at all of these stages in more detail as the chapter progresses.

These stages in psychosexual development are under the control of the genetic 'blueprint' as are intellectual, physical, emotional and personality development. But genes are not the whole story because external circumstances affect the outcome too. The physical 'blueprint', for example, may specify a 6 foot individual but poor nutrition or a bad emotional environment may hamper this so that only 5 feet 8 inches is finally achieved. Similarly, the responses from parents and others to each stage of psychosexual development influence whether the stage progresses 'normally', becomes fixed or even makes the child regress to an earlier stage. The pattern of the blueprint is basically the same in both sexes but there is a considerable difference in the way our culture treats the emergent sex drive of girls compared with that of boys.

Although Freud was by no means the first person to discuss infant sexuality he was blamed for opening up the subject by people who preferred to talk of the innocence of childhood. Such people believe in the sinfulness of adults, that sex is sin, and therefore that children should be protected from it.

## **The stage of the mouth** (The oral stage)

Once it is realised that sexuality and genitality are not the same thing it becomes possible to discuss infant sexuality without impugning a baby's 'innocence'. The notion that a baby's lips and mouth are sources of intense pleasure is acceptable to almost everyone, especially anyone who has watched a baby feed at the breast. Later, following the blueprint, other areas become the focal point of peak pleasure, the mouth remaining pleasurable but not primarily so as in a baby.

The phase of development when the mouth is the primary source of pleasure is called the *oral* stage. We know that the oral stage starts before birth because foetuses have been seen both on X-rays and scans to suck their thumb *in utero*. The bliss and contentment a baby displays on sucking after birth, if all goes well, is very plain to see. Mothers usually hug their babies to their bodies, talk soothingly and rock them. In doing so they are giving the child much more than milk. They are building up a sense of trust and confidence and are laying the foundations for the child to see itself as a person who is loved and valued. Provided the baby is not allowed to become too frustrated when he or she needs food or maternal attention, he or she will slowly begin to experience feelings which eventually lead to a sense of optimism, self-assurance and perhaps even self-esteem.

If the mother repeatedly leaves the baby to scream untended she will lay the foundations for self-doubt, depression and distrust of the world. It is quite possible to see that repeated and severe frustrations of the baby's oral drives and needs, even at this early stage, could result in their excessive persistence in later life. They may not remain primary but they may remain so strong that they influence both sexuality and other behaviour. It is certainly widely held that babies that do not enjoy and fulfil this oral stage as they should are more likely to want 'oral' gratification in adulthood. This can manifest itself in cigarette smoking, in certain cases of alcoholism, in persistent eating (especially under stress), or even in an unusually high level of interest in oral sex.

Although sucking at the breast or bottle relieves a baby's hunger it is also pleasurable in its own right and children, when they can control the movement of their muscles effectively, suck their thumbs if no other source of oral pleasure is available. Later still the child learns to suck, or at least to put in his or her mouth, almost anything appealing in the environment. These are self-pleasuring or autoerotic activities and may, without stretching the imagination too far, be seen as a forerunner of masturbation. The opposition that thumb sucking, especially in older children, often encounters from parents, presumably recognises this fact, no matter how unconsciously. Of course at the conscious level the parents' fear is that others will think the child is babyish, unloved or that his teeth will be displaced.

This can be used to illustrate a point of general importance. Although we all want pleasurable experiences, the ways in which we obtain them most naturally may not necessarily be socially acceptable. Because of this, restraint is taught in childhood. For example, an adult man sucking his thumb would be considered very odd but sucking a pipe is quite acceptable.

To generalise further, many of our pleasure drives are opposed, at least in part, by cultural conditioning and are, as a result, displaced on to other activities which gratify a particular need in a way that is, perhaps, less satisfactory but more socially acceptable, thereby possibly leading to a mild degree of frustration. These displacements are taken to be the mark of civilisation and the process is thought to account for many great achievements in the area of creative thinking, writing, painting, music, sculpture, and so on.

In a humbler form the displacements probably enrich our lives and comfort in many ways. For example, a woman's displacement of pleasure drives to her home, social life and children usually improves life for all concerned. Men, or some men, may, perhaps for a genetic reason, be capable of more distant displacements and this may account for male supremacy in areas of achievement. This is not to deny that women are capable of more distant displacements or men of displacements closer to the family and home; it is simply to say that the main focal points for such displacements may be slightly different for the two sexes, so enabling each to contribute slightly differently to civilisation. Men, on balance, tend to push society forwards and women to keep it there.

To return to the oral stage, parents, of course, make use of the oral drive to pacify their baby in the early stages of life. Giving him or her something to suck will lead to pacification even if no milk or food is involved.

Two further points should be made. Presumably the infant is, at first, incapable of realising that it is the mother who relieves the tension of hunger or who provides the comfort of cuddling and rocking. At first the baby must think that it is the breast that does these things. Eventually, he or she realises that the breast is part of his mother and, if all is well, the baby starts to develop the capacity to love. A newborn baby expresses love through the mouth, and attachments between the mother and child develop which build up a capacity to form stable, affectionate relationships later in life. If this stage is not happily achieved the child's later relationships may be less than full. Sexual and emotional development are first linked in this way. Through constant contact with the mother's body and her various attentions to his or her needs, a baby becomes aware of his or her own body and its pleasures. Self-exploration of the body follows and much later the exploration of other people's bodies.

When an infant boy is at the breast he may have an erection. He may also have one during urination, nappy changing, bowel emptying, or as a result of any excitement. Similarly, girls may roll their thighs and, according to some mothers, even lubricate vaginally. Children learn to touch their genitals fairly early and babies have been observed to stimulate themselves to orgasm. At this stage, however, the genitals are not the baby's primary source of pleasure. The mouth ensures survival and is still the main source of delight.

## The potty training stage (The anal stage)

Provided all goes reasonably well with the oral stage, the child progresses to the next phase at around the middle of the second year. This is the *anal* (excretory) phase, in which the baby's excretory functions become the primary source of interest and pleasure. As bowel and urinary control become possible, usually in the second or third year, the child experiences pleasure in expelling and retaining bowel motions and urine. The child's mother is involved because of starting some form of toilet training. Boys are taught to hold their penis and to direct the stream whereas girls are expected to remove clothing and to crouch or sit down.

In ancient Egypt, where the sexes were treated equally, the reverse was the case and the women often urinated standing and men crouching. Some experts in this field believe that female feelings of inferiority start at this point of child development because of the urination postures taught to girls. Certainly, for many adult women who are otherwise totally open about their sexual behaviour, urination can be a source of considerable embarrassment. Urination, too, seems to have an erotic significance for at least some women, some of whom can masturbate to orgasm by simulating their urethral opening or with the muscular efforts required to hold back their urine. Emotional upsets in later life can be psychosomatically expressed as disorders of urination by women, in whom urinary problems are vastly more common than in men.

It has been observed that little girls of about a year often laugh as they urinate and this has been attributed to the tickling sensation that urine causes in the vulva. If this is true, urination will serve further to draw a girl's attention to the pleasurable sensations she can get from her vulva, whereas a boy is impressed more with his urinary stream and the actual performance of the act.

Either because they develop sooner than boys or because they are intrinsically more affection-dependent and want to please, or both, girls learn to control their bladders earlier than do boys and are also less prone to bed-wetting. The ability to feel shame develops around the age of one and a half years and many mothers use this to help their children gain control over their bowels, and bladder. Moral development starts with toilet training as it is the first time a baby's parents control his or her bodily desires and pleasures to bring them into line with society's accepted norms.

Once children have learned to control their bowel movements they have some power over their mothers, depending on whether they choose to perform or not, and many children use this power very effectively. The child's bowel motions thus become the first gift he or she has to give or withhold. His or her motions, including their smell and appearance, can fascinate and excite the child.

Although a mother expresses delight as her child performs on the potty she nevertheless controls his or her interest in the result by saying it is 'dirty' or has 'germs' and flushes it away. Later, when the child is in full control of his or her bowels, he or she may play with or collect the motions and hide them away. Old people whose interest in sex has waned often return unwittingly to this anal stage and become preoccupied with their bowel functions, just like a developing child.

If the anal stage progresses well it is an impetus towards creativity and productivity but frustrations can, it is thought, lead to the character traits of obstinacy, stinginess, compulsiveness and over-orderliness. These are seen as a defence against a desire to return to the pleasures of the anal stage. Obsessionalism may be a more extreme defence. On the other hand frustrations may be expressed later as untidiness, disorderliness and even destructiveness. Anal pleasures may continue to be over-represented, relative to other pleasures, later in life, and some individuals require additional anal stimulation during masturbation or intercourse to get their best orgasms. Many prostitutes tell of how they are asked to insert a finger into the anus of a client experiencing ejaculatory difficulties. Some women claim to have orgasms only from anal intercourse and a persistence of anal eroticism is obviously a possible basis for some cases of receptive homosexuality.

Interest in the anus and anal area spills over to the buttocks at this stage. Adult fantasies about beating or being beaten on the buttocks may start here and may be reinforced by parents actually or playfully smacking or threatening to smack their child's bottom. Prostitutes say many men like to be beaten before intercourse or even that being beaten is enough in itself to produce an orgasm and ejaculation. Some women too, say they enjoy being smacked on the bottom prior to intercourse. Perhaps they have been brought up to think that sex is so naughty that they can only get pleasure from it if they are punished first.

The anal stage, then, has many implications and probably the best advice to parents is to take potty training very gently, consistently and slowly, and to stop the potty training for a while if the child doesn't seem ready.

## **The clitoris/penis stage** (The phallic stage)

If all goes well with the anal stage, anal interests and pleasures slowly become secondary to phallic pleasures, around the age of three years. This is the *phallic* stage. In this stage the clitoris or penis increasingly becomes the predominant source of body pleasure. More or less deliberate masturbation usually starts now. Most parents say either that their child did not masturbate or, if the child did so, that they accepted it. Clinical evidence suggests that this is usually not true.

The phallic stage is in one sense the start of heterosexual love and an early childhood step towards independence from the parents but it is nearly always suppressed, if not by direct prohibition and punishment then by disapproval and distraction. Very few parents are sufficiently at ease with their own sexuality to be able to watch their young child play with his or her genitals. In some families the genitals are never mentioned or even acknowledged as existing. Anything without a name probably does *not* exist for a child of this age, so simply by not talking about a child's genitals as you would about any other part of the body you are expressing a negative attitude which undoubtedly influences the child's future feelings and behaviour. This is *unmentionable sex* and girls particularly suffer in this way.

In most families the genitals are given names – often of a comic type. Playing with the genitals can be condemned in the same way as was the interest in bowel motions and sex then becomes *dirty sex*. Religiously inclined families may suggest that God does not like this genital play and sex becomes *sinful sex*. Direct punishment can associate the phallic stage with fear and so sex becomes *fearful sex*. Some children are still warned of physical ill effects from genital touching and so sex can become *unhealthy sex*. Girls especially are rebuked on the basis that such practices are not 'nice' in girls and so sex becomes *nasty sex*.

Similar techniques are sometimes used to turn sex into a matter of shame, extreme privacy and embarrassment. This is *shameful sex*. To a greater or lesser extent everyone in our culture encounters all these reactions, if not from their parents then from other sources, and if not in the phallic stage, then later. These attitudes are continuously reinforced, however unconsciously, throughout childhood and adolescence in most families.

Somewhat surprisingly, clinical evidence strongly suggests that most of these suppressions are put over to the child in unconscious ways by parents, who are therefore not being consciously untruthful when they say they did not suppress their child's sexuality. What was taught to *them*, the parents, in this way in childhood they in turn pass on to the next generation. The child stores the information away, mainly in the unconscious mind, so the transaction is between the unconscious of the parents and the unconscious of the child. This accounts for our cultural conservatism over sexual matters.

The results of sexual suppression in the phallic stage seem to be more serious for girls. This may be because they are more heavily suppressed. Mothers are generally much more indulgent towards genitality in boys than in girls. This subject is considered in more detail in Chapter 2. Here it suffices to say that clinical experience seems to prove that the difficulties of a wide section of the adult female population in experiencing full sexual pleasure originates at this stage.

Before the phallic stage is reached a child has learned to distinguish between mummy and daddy and later between women and men. When very young he or she will have seen both parents and any brothers or sisters naked because few adults think such matters register on a young child. The young child may even have been present in the room when his or her parents were having intercourse and if so, according to some people, his or her behaviour over the next few days may show signs of disturbance. Later, witnessing or hearing intercourse can lead to the notion that sex is an aggressive and sadistic act and many children fear that their father is hurting their mother, especially if she is noisy when she has an orgasm. This is why it is probably best in our culture not to let children of any age see their parents having intercourse. Some phobias are thought to be triggered off in susceptible children who repeatedly witness or overhear parental sexual acts after the age of about two or three.

Parental nudity, which has always been more widespread amongst the better educated, is of much less significance, especially if the child's friends are being reared in the same sort of way, though a few psychosexual experts think that it is best for a boy not to see his mother naked after the age of four or so and for a girl not to see her father naked from about a year. Children whose friends are used to seeing their parents naked will probably be unaffected but children can be very cruel, even this young, and will tease children who seem to be brought up in ways that are contrary to the way they know. As children discuss this sort of thing at school it is probably best not to subject your child to experiences at home that will make them feel odd among their friends. They may believe that they have odd parents if their friends say so and this could be harmful to them.

A practical aspect of this stage in relation to boys is that only about 4 per cent of boys have a fully retractable foreskin at birth and 50 per cent by one year. Forcible attempts at retraction by some mothers, to clean underneath, to see whether circumcision is necessary or just to stretch it, may account for some late adolescent boys and men with tight foreskins who react with great alarm at any attempt at retraction. Their reluctance leads them to masturbate with the foreskin in the forward position and its development does not keep pace with the increase in size of the penis at puberty.

Little boys' penises need nothing done to them at all. If the foreskin will not pull back completely by the age of five, see your doctor for advice.

As children begin to look at the genitals of children (and adults) of the opposite sex, boys may come to see girls as being boys who have had their genitals removed, perhaps as a punishment for touching them. Some fear a similar punishment themselves. Girls sometimes conjure up the idea that they really have a secret penis or seem, perhaps, to blame their mothers because they have not got one. The difficulty in such speculation is that children rarely say how they feel and their reactions can only be guessed at from their behaviour.

## Gender identity

The processes by which a child eventually comes to feel with certainty that he or she is a boy or a girl – so-called gender identity – proceed slowly and with confusion. (The process can go awry and this is discussed later under transsexualism.) One process which affects the issue is the one of identification with the same-sex parent. Whether it is instinctive or whether they are identifying with and copying their mothers, many young girls display marked femininity in their behaviour. Many are like miniature women and by three or so have developed social skills which many a young man would like to have.

Girls also seem to be able to discern the sex of another individual earlier and more reliably than can boys. When a girl discovers the genital differences between the sexes, or even before, she pays more attention to her father than before, and where her relationship with both her parents is good the change is marked. She wants to attract her father's attention and to involve him in her life. In an elementary way she may compete with her mother to take trouble on his behalf and be of service to him. She may want to get into his bed and drive her mother from it. Later she may say she is going to grow up and marry daddy. Clearly her father is her first heterosexual love and in some way she is involved with him physically. She wants him to kiss and cuddle her and may show signs of jealousy at any attention her mother receives. Many a little girl uses her feminine skills effectively to get her own way with her father. If he is really cross with her it can emotionally disturb her for hours or even days, but maternal displeasure has much less effect. If she learns from him that she is attractive, lovable and valuable she will have confidence in herself as a woman later in life. Nevertheless, if the father is over-close, as some are, perhaps out of a latent fear of adult women, she can later have difficulty in leaving him psychosexually for another man. The balance, as in so much to do with sexuality, is a fine one.

A part of a girl's mind may in one sense hate and fear her mother, because she thinks that her mother realises that she wants an exclusive relationship with her father. She fears her mother will retaliate. However, she also loves her mother and realises that her mother is her care-giver. As a result she remains attentive to her mother, to see if her secret has been discovered. It is thought that the greater empathy that women have compared with men comes from this developmental stage, as does a woman's skill at concealing her true feelings.

A boy does not have to make the same switch from his mother, but his feelings about her and his father are similar to, but the reverse of, those of a girl. The intensity of such feelings tends to increase during the phallic stage. Physical contact with his mother may lead to an erection and his interest in her body may intensify. Many men who say they find partially dressed women more arousing than naked ones may have started this notion at this stage because they are more likely to have seen their mother partially, rather than wholly undressed. A mother may be unconsciously provocative to her son of around the age of five but at the same time sharply rebuke him for his sexual interest in her. Simultaneously his increasing fear of retaliation by his father leads to this so-called *Oedipal* interest in his mother being controlled rather than given free rein.

From clinic work with adult men it seems that two important consequences follow from this. The first is the establishment of a notion of female sexlessness. This view of women is, of course, reinforced by our culture which declares that girls are 'sugar and spice and all things nice'. The second consequence is that the boy enters the world of men. Females and their interests are spurned as inconsequential. The view develops that girls are best avoided and they are often banned, to the chagrin of many of them, from boys' games. Identification with the father, or another, available male person, proceeds more rapidly and the boy strives for mastery over male pursuits. One reason why boys identify with their fathers later than girls do with their mothers is that mothers are more continuously available as models for girls than are fathers for boys. In any case a boy probably first identifies with the mother as it is she, rather than his father, who first outlines the conventional male role for a boy. Women teachers may later continue the process which rewards boys for masculine behaviour and disparages them for feminine interests.

Most boys stop masturbating as the phallic stage ends and gives way to the stage of latency which roughly corresponds with the infant- and junior-school years. Curiously, adult men seem to have no conscious recollection of childhood masturbation and its later rediscovery at puberty is regarded as a new acquisition. This is in contrast with women, about a third of whom say they cannot remember a time when they did not masturbate.

Girls do not resolve the problems of the Oedipal stage in the same brisk fashion in which most boys do. Their interest in their father continues although perhaps in a weakened form. Sometimes it is later displaced on to horses, which may symbolise masculine power, although, no doubt, there are other reasons for a girl's love of her horse.

## **The quiescent stage** (The latency stage)

During the latency stage of sexual development, a child's early interest in his or her parents widens out to other adults such as teachers, and interest in the mysteries of sex enlarges into interest in other mysteries and learning generally. Although Freud and others thought that little by way of psychosexual development occurred at this stage few modern experts would agree. Things might slow down a little but the child certainly does not shut down on sex.

Curiosity about sex may lead to the use of dictionaries, other available books and newspapers to learn about sexual matters. In this way general curiosity and learning can be promoted. Investigations of the genitals of friends of the opposite sex, which may have started as early as three or so, may continue until seven or eight. Children who have seen their parents having intercourse may pretend to do it with others, girls sometimes undertaking the male role, but it has no sexual significance in adult terms. Sex play between brothers and sisters up to and including the latency stage of psychosexual development (which ends at puberty) is innocuous, as is any other heterosexual play, but if continued it can fix the children on each other in such a way that their subsequent ability to relate effectively to members of the opposite sex is impaired.

## The pre-adolescent stage

Hormonal changes occur as puberty approaches. Girls who stopped masturbating at the end of the phallic stage often start again around the age of nine or ten. It is still an 'innocent' activity which the girl may feel little guilt about unless she was criticized or punished for earlier masturbation or sex games. This increase in eroticism may be reflected in an increasing interest in portrayals of nude adult females and the father who was previously welcome in the bathroom is now banned.

Dreams or fantasies of appearing partially or wholly nude occur and are exciting. Sex games are undertaken now only with other girls and under the guise of dressing-up games or sexual enactment games such as kiss-me-like-a-boy-would and mutual genital inspection and bottom smacking may occur. The phase is a sort of 'homosexual' one and is perfectly normal. Girls rarely teach each other to masturbate – unlike boys. The reason may be that sexual skills are more innate in girls whereas in boys, as in higher primate males generally, there is a larger learned component to sex. Girls can seem to be very mature just before puberty and often take a special interest in relationships between the sexes, both human and animal.

Boys tend to gang together even more strongly in pre-adolescence and although there may be mutual showing of genitals it is not really a homosexual stage. They tend at this stage to denigrate women, presumably because of residual fears of them from earlier childhood arising from encounters with them in the form of mothers and teachers, and they also tend to regress towards the anal stage. Talk about excretion and breaking wind, making noises, eating crudely and failing to wash adequately are signs of this regression.

At this point, the end of latency, the first half of childhood is complete. The child has largely been reared within the small world of his or her own family with its particular combination of advantages and disadvantages. Any harm done in the process of psychosexual and other development will, from now on, become increasingly evident. It is this long incubation period between cause and effect which makes it so difficult to be sure about the significance of earlier events. The distortion of memory, the inaccessibility of the unconscious and the repression of painful thoughts and family myths make it hard to disentangle the facts. The most important lessons in life, the very early ones, do not even register in the conscious memory. And yet, in spite of the problems, it is possible to use the information given briefly in this chapter to understand what lies behind the difficulties experienced by adolescents and adults in their relationships with others and themselves. From what they say and avoid saying, from the way they say it and their associated emotional changes, from their dreams and fantasies, from their preferences and practices, and in other ways, it becomes possible to know what happened to them and how they felt, even unconsciously, during childhood. Sometimes repressed material is retrieved from the unconscious and the person then relives it as vividly as if it had occurred only an instant before and all the emotions originally associated with it return.

Of course everyone is different, but three patterns constantly recur in clinical practice though they appear in many guises. The first is a poor relationship with the self, involving excessive self-criticism, excessive self-consciousness, self-detestation or depression and excessive self-blame. The two main causes are disturbed parental relationships, the child perhaps having been at least partly unwanted or believing himself or herself to be, and poor child spacing. The second is the suppression of sexuality, resulting in the child being frozen at some particular stage, perhaps making him or her regress to an earlier stage or deviating him or her from 'normal' development. The third is a persistent attachment to the opposite sex parent which can arise, amongst other reasons, if that parent was over-close or over-rejecting. The consequences can be profound not only for the individual's future sexuality but for his or her emotions, personality and inter-personal relationships.

Although this brief account of baby and childhood sexuality can be verified by the average observant person, it is still not universally accepted. Some people find it hard to believe that events in childhood can exert such a profound effect on such matters as the ability to enjoy intercourse later in life. If it is accepted that infant and childhood sexuality and the way it is handled are the foundation for what comes in adulthood, then its enormous importance can be readily appreciated. To argue that childhood experiences have no bearing on events in later life is contrary to all the available evidence and also to common sense. After all, we happily accept such reasoning on non-sexual matters.

A more subtle and difficult criticism arises in the question of why children who are treated in virtually the same way with regard to sexual and emotional matters display totally different sexualities and sexual problems in adulthood. One answer lies in the fact that apart from one-egg twins no two individuals are genetically the same. Another answer is that no two people can really be subject to exactly the same influences and therefore any two people will respond differently to similar experiences. How secure children feel in their place in the family also affects their vulnerability to experiences. Also, the child's own perceptions of what is happening may be different from those of a brother or sister who is going through the same experience. For these, and no doubt other reasons, the long-term consequences of a similar upbringing can vary enormously. Parents too are not static personalities – they change as the years pass and react differently to, and therefore have a different influence on, each of their children.

All of this makes the study of childhood sexuality a minefield but an understanding of the processes outlined in this chapter can put problems into some sort of perspective. We are a product of all our yesterdays as well as of our genetic blueprint.

*Chapter 2*
# Adolescence

Early adolescence starts with puberty in both sexes. Why puberty starts when it does is uncertain but hormonal changes begin to occur a year or two beforehand and there is evidence that these affect behaviour.

Puberty is often thought of as starting at the same age in both sexes but there is little doubt that the changes occur earlier in girls. A boy's adolescent spurt in height occurs, on average, two years after that of a girl, so for a time girls are, on average, taller than boys and may be stronger. This may partly contribute to the avoidance of girls by boys which characterises this stage. The unusually early onset of puberty is much commoner in girls than in boys and, when it occurs in boys, unlike girls, the cause is usually a disease or disorder. The late onset of puberty, in contrast, is of less medical concern in boys because perfectly normal boys may be late just as perfectly normal girls may be early.

## The early-adolescent girl

The first sign of puberty is nearly always the development of the breasts, often one, the left, before the other. At about the age of eleven but sometimes as early as eight or as late as thirteen, mounds appear and the areola, the pigmented area around the nipple enlarges. Up to this time the sensitivity of the area is roughly equal in boys and girls but in girls it now begins to increase. Full breast development takes about two and a half years. Depending on her personal and family attitudes and those of her friends, a girl will either welcome or conceal these changes.

Pubic hair development normally starts a few months after the breasts begin to develop but can start before. A few girls, perhaps because of guilt about masturbation, believe that hair growth is a sign of abnormality or even a sign of changing sex and so may cut it or shave it off. Around this time the vagina starts to produce an increased amount of whitish, acidic fluid.

Coinciding with, or just before, these changes, the girl experiences a physical growth spurt. This reaches a peak soon after the pubic hair begins to appear, and then the rate of growth begins to slacken. About two and a half years after the first signs of breast development, menstruation first occurs.

Many women say they were never warned in advance about their periods starting, but most mothers say they prepared their daughters. This apparent contradiction can be explained. Because the subject concerns sex and because the mother has unwittingly inspired anxiety in relation to sex over the childhood years, her daughter does not want to know and banishes the information from her consciousness even though she has in fact been given it.

Whatever the explanation, a girl's first period can be a shock which leads to fears of injury or illness. Depending again upon environmental attitudes some girls welcome their first period while others are ashamed. All girls probably worry to some degree about their lack of control over the event. Earlier, hard-won mastery over the other body functions in childhood now seems to be partly lost and many worry about the shame they might feel if they ever leaked blood, making their period obvious to others.

The average age at which a girl's first period occurs is probably one measure of the affluence of a society, and in the West it has been falling for centuries. The link with affluence is food. The better nourished a population the earlier the girls start to menstruate. In fact girls that are over-nourished start even earlier. This is a good case for staying slim. The decline has reached its lowest limit so far in the generation of girls born in the years immediately after the Second World War. The first period now usually occurs at about thirteen years, but may be as early as eleven or as late as fifteen and still be quite normal. Various factors can affect the age of onset, blind girls tending to start early, whereas girls living at a high altitude or those who have younger brothers usually start late.

A girl can become pregnant before her first period but most girls are infertile for the first year or so of having periods because they are not yet ovulating (producing eggs). After this there is a slow build-up towards maximum fertility in the early twenties.

Early periods may be prolonged, heavy or irregular. Signs that a girl is becoming fertile are regular and predictable periods, especially if they are accompanied by premenstrual symptoms such as breast tenderness or pain and painful periods.

Hair usually begins to appear in the armpits at about the time of the first period. The onset of all these changes of puberty varies from girl to girl and any one girl may not follow the usual sequence. The whole process can take from one to five years to complete.

Along with these specific sexual changes, fat is deposited under the skin, making a girl's contours more plump and rounded. This makes her body sexually attractive to men. At this stage many girls are confused by their feelings. They have impulses both to show and to conceal their bodies but by the end of early adolescence they have usually come to terms with their emerging sexuality. Under hormonal influences their interest in sex heightens. A girl's desire to grow up and be treated as a woman is exciting to her but also fear-inspiring, giving her a simultaneous desire to remain in, or regress to, childhood as a form of escape from the realities of impending womanhood. Other contradictions arise from the fact that she has a need to be seen by males as desirable whilst at the same time fearing she might not be acceptable to them or that she may appear brazen or cheap.

As a result of these feelings early adolescence is often stressful for a girl. Unlike the early adolescent boy, her entry into the sexual arena is dramatic and swift. Because her biological drives are so strong, her parents are often concerned and this can lead to family conflict towards the end of early adolescence. Her earlier good relationship with her father may worsen as he tries to control her comings and goings but the cruellest battle is often fought with her mother. In some families these rows can become very bitter with the father physically punishing the girl and the mother accusing her of being a whore.

Many, perhaps most, girls openly rebel at some stage and tell their mothers that they hate them. If the parents 'win', the girl's subsequent development may be impaired, but the greater danger is that the girl may feel she can win by running away or having early intercourse simply to spite her parents. Many experts in this field believe that girls who behave like this are simply seeking love from a man to replace the parental love they have lost but others believe that much more often it comes about because a girl wants to punish her mother.

So the answer for parents of early-adolescent girls is to try to understand their desires and fears and to do all they can to cope with the situation without reaching a stage of open warfare. The best plan is simply to keep the channels of communication open.

With her many conflicts and bodily changes it is easy to see why the early-adolescent girl can be so moody and changeable. It is also fairly obvious why many girls fail in the tasks of early adolescence. The origins of a lot of mental ill health in women can be traced back to early adolescence as can an inability to cope with the female role.

The making of a woman: *Pre-pubescent girl (left) and fully mature woman (right).*

Some girls opt out by becoming fat or by developing anorexia nervosa, thus regressing, Peter Pan-like, to childhood, ceasing to menstruate and losing their breasts. Others become over-devoted to academic work, to religion, or to animals. Some girls act out their distress and become sexually delinquent and other try to seduce an older man who is sometimes the exact opposite to their father. Others, especially those who had a poor relationship with their mothers in early childhood, may secretly wish to return to childhood and 'solve' the problem but over-react in the opposite direction and rush into 'adult' pursuits such as sex and drink.

Early adolescence is the time when a girl accepts, or fails to accept, that she is a sexual being. This involves much more than simply realising that she will eventually have intercourse and possibly babies. She has to accept that she has sexual interests, wishes, desires and pleasures and that her life will never be the same again. She has now entered the sexual arena and has to take her chances with the rest of us.

Her sexual fantasies change during early adolescence from being relatively impersonal to being more explicit and more excitingly personal. Usually the fantasies of early adolescent girls are of a fairly vague nature, frequently involving situations such as stripping, prostitution and rape. Girls of this age may search for newspaper items and books about these things and then discuss their findings with their friends at school in the hope of understanding what they are about. It is a paradox that a girl of this age is likely to assume that she is a sex expert and may reject sex information from her parents and teachers. This is perfectly normal.

Fantasies may be suppressed because they are seen as disgusting and any that involve her father or a father-like figure are nearly always severely suppressed. A girl's behaviour may, however, be the exact opposite of what she really wants because of her attempts to control herself. For example, it is common for girls who unconsciously want to be close and loving to their fathers to consciously avoid all contact with them at this stage.

During early adolescence masturbation usually increases in intensity and frequency but does not change much in form. Any bad masturbation habits a girl has already acquired tend to become further entrenched and fixed at this stage. Girls who rub their vulvas to have an orgasm usually further refine their own particular pattern of stimulation but new features often emerge. One technique, for example, is to clasp the whole vulva when arousal has reached a certain stage and then to count to ten before resuming stimulation.

Very guilty girls who want to get it over with as quickly as possible do not use delaying tactics such as these, often to the detriment of their ultimate enjoyment of sex.

The other change that occurs is a considerable increase in shame as the full sexual significance of masturbation dawns on a girl. This comes about because her sexual experience seems to contradict all that she has previously supposed to be 'nice' in a girl. Some girls accept the situation easily but others have more difficulty. Some repress their sexuality so completely that they actually give up masturbation in early adolescence. Others struggle against it and try to keep it under strict control. For example, some girls promise God they will never do it again. Some reinforce their control by telling themselves that they are doing themselves harm or that they will change sex as a result. This last fear arises from the fact that until the last forty years or so masturbation was spoken of as being essentially a thing boys did. Many a girl therefore used to believe (and some still do) that she was the only girl who did it, and even if she asked her friends (which was rare), to try to get reassurance, they too denied masturbation because they had been made to feel guilty about it.

This rise in shame about masturbation can lead to changes in behaviour and some of these can be annoying. Common examples are frequent hand-washing for fear – amongst other things – that others may be able to detect that she has been masturbating, and a neurotic over-concern about spots. A girl may become even more secretive about her sexual interests and is often easily embarrassed when sex is mentioned by adults. Her mother's sexuality can also lead to embarrassment and even frank hostility. If her mother becomes pregnant, for example, she can feel compromised and ashamed.

Of much more concern though are those early adolescent girls who somehow dissociate themselves from their sexuality and try to find ways to indulge it whilst denying to themselves that they are doing so. The deception does not take the form of straightforward lying – it is really an internal self-deception based upon a psychological trick. Examples are endless. One is to separate fantasy from its associated masturbatory activity – in this way it is possible to deny to oneself the sexual nature of the act. On the other hand, fantasy alone may be used as a masturbatory act or the fantasy may be highly symbolic and apparently non-sexual. Another way is either to deny that an orgasm has occurred or to experience it only after the physical act is complete. Yet another is to displace the orgasm from the genitals to some other part of the body, especially to the oesophagus (gullet) or the stomach. Some incidental activity such as rope climbing or cycle riding may be utilised to produce an orgasm. These and many other ways may be used, both at the time and in adulthood, to deny that there is (or was) a sexual content to the early-adolescent stage. This denial has poor implications for the girl's future.

Although early-adolescent girls talk about sex to each other, it is usually in a non-personal way. It is rare for girls, unlike boys, at this stage to involve their own sex physically in their sexual activities, although they often develop emotional crushes on admired older girls or school-mistresses. A helpful way of thinking of this is to understand that the girl usually thinks of the older person as being successful in an area of concern to her. This is often in sophistication and attractiveness to men. The girl wants closeness, partly to learn the secret of success and partly to be held in esteem, almost as a friend, by someone she admires. True lesbian activity at this age is very rare indeed and parents need not fear that crushes will mean that their daughter will become a lesbian.

The majority of girls are keen to test out the effectiveness of their changing bodies in attracting male attention. Most girls first experience kissing and perhaps breast fondling during this stage. Some relate wildly exaggerated stories to their friends with the aim of emphasising their desirability.

Although some girls display little or no open interest in boys at this stage, for a variety of reasons, most of which need cause no concern, others become over-involved. Apart from rebellion, other motives for early intercourse include the inability to face up to masturbation. Unless she renounces sex altogether and regresses to childhood, the only other course is to seek sexual stimulation from others, usually boys. Such a girl may well intend to go no further than allowing the boy to masturbate her but since these girls usually go for considerably older, more experienced boys, intercourse is likely to result.

However, very few girls of this age experience intercourse in any adult way, and the danger is that this pattern of inadequate and unsatisfactory response to intercourse becomes fixed. Girls should be advised, not warned, against too early intercourse for this reason. Experience shows that the vast majority of girls are not ready for intercourse at this stage of their development.

## The early-adolescent boy

The first sign of puberty, occurring somewhere between the ages of ten and fourteen, is in the scrotum, which enlarges and becomes reddened. At around the same time there is an increase in the size of the testes. This latter change is under the immediate control of a pituitary hormone called the follicle-stimulating hormone (in women the same pituitary hormones control the menstrual cycle). The secondary sexual characteristics that then develop, such as the increase in the size of the penis, beard and body-hair growth, the voice breaking, muscle development and so on are brought about by the testosterone produced by the enlarging and functioning testes.

Largely under the influence of testosterone, erections increase in frequency, as do sexual fantasies and eventually at around the age of twelve to fourteen, most boys start to masturbate. The starting point is often hearing about masturbation from slightly older boys or seeing someone else masturbating. Most normal boys promptly turn into ardent practitioners. For many boys, the start of their interest in masturbation occurs slightly before ejaculation is possible and their orgasms are of the so-called 'dry run' variety. Friendships with other boys usually intensify and mutual genital display, comparison and masturbation are fairly common. This reduces the sense of guilt boys feel, because they know other boys are doing it as well. Although this developmental phase is frequently 'homosexual' in this way, it is completely normal and should not really be thought of as homosexual at all.

Although a few boys may be seduced by older girls or women at this stage, most are unable to handle heterosexual advances even from girls of about their own age.

Old erotic interests in his mother (from the Oedipal stage of development) re-emerge and the process of finally growing away from her begins, so eventually freeing the boy to love and to make love to a woman outside the family. His father and 'extensions' of his father in other admired men are usually idealised and used as models. They usually inspire his day-dreams of achievement. In some cases old rivalries and fears of his father may surface again, sometimes leading to depression and, rarely, to suicide.

The reawakening of his attraction to his mother is the starting point of the boy's interest in heterosexuality. Although his outward attitudes may not show it, his notions about girls begin to change sharply. Girls become increasingly desirable and of fascinating interest. This can lead to blushing and social unease when he is in contact with them. He very often uses 'girlie' magazines, however guiltily, to stimulate his sexual fantasies. Discussions about, and definitions of, pornography are endless but a practical way of looking at the subject is to distinguish it from erotica on the basis that pornography promotes incorrect sexual learning. Obviously adolescents, and particularly early-adolescent boys who are in a stage of rapid sexual learning, need to be shielded from pornography. Whether 'girlie' magazines are erotica or pornography is debatable. If they teach boys that only girls who have bodies like those of the models are desirable then they promote incorrect sexual learning. But in that they encourage an admiration for the female body and an interest in heterosexuality, they are undoubtedly helpful.

On average, boys begin to understand the mechanics of intercourse two or three years later than do girls and are frequently well advanced into early adolescence before they get a grasp of the subject. As a result, their sexual fantasies are vague and voyeuristic.

Early adolescence is the time of dirty jokes. Although these may be entertaining, they inspire performance fears because they usually involve accounts of a huge penis or prodigious sexual feats. Misinformation about women, their functions and their fatal powers is also rife.

In all this, the standards and attitudes of a boy's group of friends – for which the psychological jargon term is 'peer group' – exert a powerful influence on his own sexuality. In the main this is superficial because his basic standards were set years before by his parents. Matters as unimportant as hairstyle and style of dress are common causes of conflict with parents but all that is happening is that the boy is conforming to the requirements of his peer group. Most boys are not overtly rebellious, unlike many girls, probably because they are given more freedom anyway. In many families a form of amused and mutual tolerance becomes established between a mother and her son from early adolescence onwards, and she exerts influence by persuasion rather than by any direct attempt to impose her authority.

Early adolescence is the stage at which teenagers start to take the initiative in forming relationships with others outside the family. If they have not got the social skills necessary to form friendships they become increasingly isolated. Where such skills are lacking, they can be taught. Usually, with boys, the friendships are with members of their own sex. Boys of this age have more friends than do girls and confide in them less but worry more about their ability to make friends. They tend to be more concerned with competitive striving and with establishing themselves in the eyes of other boys, whereas girls are more concerned about their relationships and looks. For adolescents of both sexes people in the peer group function as testers, models and mirrors outside the family.

Genital anomalies, delayed puberty, delays in one aspect of development (such as the voice breaking) or a display of feminine interest or traits can lead to teasing from the peer group, which is not unfriendly if the boy is likable but can result in self-imposed isolation if he reacts badly.

Many early-adolescent boys are concerned about nocturnal emissions (wet dreams) and also about breast development. The first nocturnal emission usually occurs between the ages of thirteen and fifteen and in some families the subject is totally ignored. A few boys not only display no concern about it but also leave evidence of masturbation for their mothers to find. Such boys are thought by experts to have difficulty in breaking away from their mothers.

The breasts (or often just one) enlarge in around a third of all boys during early adolescence and this can produce embarrassment if it is conscious. The vast majority regress spontaneously.

Early adolescence, then, is the stage at which girls and boys learn to accept their body changes and emerging sexuality as the start of their progress from childhood to adulthood. Although it is a time of considerable change for both sexes, boys, in general, face a less complicated situation than do girls. In general, early adolescence is not a particularly stressful time for boys but it can disorganise and distress a girl.

## Mid-adolescence

Middle adolescence, or adolescence proper, starts at around the age of fourteen or fifteen in girls and fifteen or sixteen in most boys. By the end of early adolescence boys are still mainly homosexual in a social sense but an interest in girls has started to develop. Nevertheless the boy is still looking towards boys rather than girls for approval and friendship. Any social contacts with girls are usually undertaken along with other boys. Although for most girls the main friendship is with another girl, a girl's heterosexual drive and interests have been much greater than those of boys throughout early adolescence. A girl with a boyfriend is likely to think of him as her best friend.

A recent survey of nearly 800 fifteen-year-olds revealed that girls, compared with boys, were more concerned about their personal safety, their 'looks', criticism from others, arguments with their parents, confusion about life, speaking-up in class, the health of their mothers, obtaining a job eventually and their ability to do it well. The concerns of girls are thus more mature and adult than those of boys at the same age. Worries about their mothers' health may reflect the tendency of mothers generally to use emotional blackmail to control older girls by making remarks about the consequences of the girls' behaviour on their health. The phase of conflict between mother and daughter can become ferocious and may result in the girl running away or becoming pregnant to punish the mother. If a girl feels she receives only criticism instead of help and understanding she may think these or other dramatic acts are necessary.

A lot of this kind of trouble could be avoided if parents recognised that most girls are in a conflict over their desire to please their parents but also to grow up and fulfil their own needs. Adolescents, both boys and girls, criticise themselves enough and require little in the way of external help in the matter! Approval and success at home increase their self-confidence and protect them from excessive peer-group pressures and also from flagrant rebellion.

Survey evidence shows that the majority of mid-adolescents get on well with their parents and respect and admire them. A survey of 1000 teenage boys revealed that most felt understood by their parents, regarded their discipline as reasonable and were proud of them. Nevertheless, mid-adolescence is the time when the instinctual sex drive is finally withdrawn from the direction of the opposite-sex parent and is invested in the adolescent him- or herself. Masturbation rates tend to rise, as does a preoccupation with the self and the body. The capacity for abstract thinking which starts in early adolescence increases and results in mid-adolescence being a potentially creative period. Girls may begin to keep diaries recording their moods and activities. Emotional and romantic feelings can be inspired by things such as literature and landscapes. Poetry writing may start. Although mid-adolescents can be savage, more in the way of mindless violence than for any purpose, the stage is usually one in which inner feelings of tenderness and beauty develop.

Sexual fantasies keep in step and, although they may include unusual or even 'deviant' elements, active involvement with the opposite sex begins to emerge in fantasies. Although girls may have earlier explored their vaginas and many may have used tampons, the vagina becomes more significantly incorporated into the body-image at this age. Earlier, unsophisticated fantasies give way more to fantasies of 'making love'. Psychosexual history-taking from a spectrum of girls and women, not just those with sexual problems, shows that by the age of sixteen something like three-quarters of girls have included vaginal activity both in their fantasies and their masturbatory practices. The physically relatively insensitive vagina now becomes psychologically valuable and can give her physical pleasure.

Thoughts of using her vagina to show her emotional feelings to a boy, and the pleasure he will obtain from it, become exciting.

Mid-adolescents may be involved in heterosexual relationships and intercourse is common. A 1987 study of 6000 readers of a UK woman's magazine found that the average under-20 had lost her virginity at 15.8 years. This is also a time of sexual rehearsal in fantasy and self-generated romanticism which may be placed on a member of the opposite sex though almost always in a play-acting way. This is not to deny that, for example, a sixteen-year-old girl can love a boy, but it must be said that she can only love him to the extent to which a sixteen-year-old is capable. Although mid-adolescents may wax lyrical about their boyfriend or girlfriend, when seen a year or two later, they not infrequently have some difficulty in recalling their names. Early and pre-intercourse heterosexual experimentation may arise in this stage and fondling of the breasts and vulva may occur, but most girls are too shy and most boys too ignorant for this to progress to mutual masturbation. Most girls do not handle their boyfriends' penises during this stage. However, many mid-adolescent and some early-adolescent girls behave provocatively, not so much with the intention of having intercourse but more to reassure themselves that they can attract male attention. Such behaviour can be misunderstood by boys and men and rape, or something close to it, may be the result.

Mid-adolescence is the true turning point from childhood to adulthood. As well as sexual, emotional, social and personality development taking place, career choices are usually being explored. It is a time of expansion but the mid-adolescent still relies heavily on his or her parents. Moods can change rapidly from feelings of despair to exaltation and day-dreams are common. Everything and yet nothing seems possible.

## Late adolescence

Late adolescence starts around the age of seventeen or eighteen in girls and about eighteen to twenty, or later, in boys. It is basically a time of changing relationships, even with the self. It represents the last days of childhood.

Independence from parents increases, although some late adolescents cling to their families or their families to them. As at all stages boys are given more freedom than are girls and usually still feel comfortable at home. Girls can be very conscious of their need to escape: into work away from home, into higher education, and even into marriage. When they do escape they often pass through a phase in which they want to reduce contact with home to a minimum whilst maintaining a friendly relationship.

Parental criticism or disappointment still hurts the late adolescent but most consult their parents about important decisions and sooner or later do accept their advice. Some parents are excellent at giving approval and support to late adolescents without interfering but others try to exert total control. The latter court the risk of open or covert rebellion or, if the child submits, of changing his (more frequently than her) future growth. Open rebellion can take the form of delinquency or, in girls, unsuitable relationships, a premarital pregnancy and so on. Covert rebellion is sometimes expressed in failure of one form or another. Late adolescents are not fully realistic about their parents, but the old idolisation of the parents that was present in childhood is usually overthrown in mid-adolescence. The emotional feelings withdrawn from the parents (and especially the opposite-sex parent) into the self by mid-adolescence are available in late adolescence for investing in significant relationships outside the family.

From mid-adolescence the child increasingly creates his or her own social life independent of his parents, but in late adolescence the emphasis is on opposite-sex relationships. Progressively throughout adolescence the individual becomes increasingly cynical about friendships and by late adolescence, in contrast with early adolescence, feels that the chances of finding a new, good friend are increasingly remote. At this stage many girls say they dislike other girls but boys still mainly function in same-sex groups of one kind or another. Boys often see a girlfriend only as someone with whom they share sexual, but few other, intimacies.

Emotional development along adult lines proceeds rapidly but in girls, on average, it occurs two or more years earlier than in boys of the same age. Girls are more ready to commit themselves to a relationship, perhaps partly motivated by guilt over their sexual activities and sometimes regard their boyfriend as being more committed to them than he really is. By the late teens some boys still look upon girls either as medals or as game to be tracked down. This is not so much the result of their insensitivity but rather reflects the more rapid progress of girls and poor education on sex and emotions for boys. Misunderstandings are rife and more girls think of themselves as being engaged, to a greater or lesser degree, than do boys. Suicidal gestures can be the result of the rejection which ensues. Although adults can be very impatient with such gestures it is important to remember that the girl is really saying that if she cannot be loved she does not even want to live.

Girls, much sooner than boys, can become preoccupied with thoughts of loving and being loved, and they may cry themselves to sleep thinking about it. Late adolescence can be a harrowing time for a girl and bouts of depression are common. At this stage some girls become more or less passive, being chosen rather than choosing. Older and even married men can seem very attractive, not only because of their resources and experience but because ultimately the girl knows there is little hope of an enduring relationship, so thoughts of ending the liaison distresses her less. Paradoxically, with older men she feels she is doing more of the choosing and is more in charge. As she becomes more self-confident her sights usually become set on men more of her own age.

Boys reach the same stage of emotional development later (at around twenty-three to twenty-five) than girls, but because women tend to marry men a few years older than themselves, most men do not have to experience rejection distress. This is not to say that boys have less anxiety than girls: it simply takes a different form and is more concerned with approaching girls and, eventually, with sexual performance fears. Some late-adolescent boys conceal their anxiety behind callow behaviour towards girls.

The average girl today first has intercourse around or before her sixteenth birthday, and probably more than 95 per cent of girls first have intercourse between the ages of fifteen and twenty, whereas the range amongst boys is much wider. Male virgins of twenty-three to twenty-five are not uncommon. As a result, many young women today have had several fairly intense relationships before they finally marry. If this helps them to deal better with sex and any guilty feelings and so frees them to choose a partner based on personality factors rather than being swayed by an obsession with genitality, then this is beneficial.

Although most earlier sex education has been too little and too late, there is an intense practical interest amongst late adolescents and young adults about the establishment and maintenance of relationships. Many really do want to know how to understand and please the opposite sex, and not just physically. They want to know if anything is wrong with them and if so how to correct it. Minor defects can be sources of agonising worry. In spite of being nearly adult they can easily be disorganised by anxiety and often need parental support.

Various strands of their previous development now begin to be knitted together, for good or ill, but change, even dramatic change, is still possible. Although what happens in childhood has immense consequences, it is not necessarily permanent. New attitudes, perspectives and insights are possible and late adolescence is the last chance before the relatively fixed attitudes of adulthood overtake the individual. A lot of preventive work can be undertaken with late adolescents, but the majority have no readily available service to help them, unless they are in extreme distress. As a result, maladaptive attitudes towards the self and others are carried forward into adulthood where they ultimately cause trouble either for the individual or those around him or her.

Like most people, late adolescents need success but, because they are at the starting-line of adult life, their needs are particularly great. Although some may seem self-assured and even arrogant, typically under-confidence and self-doubt are never far away. They are in a difficult situation because they are becoming increasingly aware of their need for a relationship with a member of the opposite sex. This is more than a genital need, although men reach their lifetime peak of sex drive during this period. This is before many of them have had intercourse.

## Young adulthood

Late adolescence ends around the age of twenty to twenty-one in girls but not until twenty-three in boys and for some well beyond that. It is succeeded by young adulthood. In this stage young women usually become less apprehensive about themselves, probably because of the confidence gained as a result of earlier successes (even if the relationship did not last) with men. They appear, in general, to be more philosophical and more capable of taking a long-term view of the future. In general, too, their relationship with their mother improves and most mothers appear willing to accept their daughter as an autonomous person.

Poor relationships between a father and his son can reach crisis proportions in late adolescence and early adulthood, as the son begins to feel more self-assured. Where it continues at a vicious level it is often found that Oedipal factors are still at work in the son and that his relationships with women are often disturbed.

As a part of the late-adolescent process, the individual changes his or her relationship with society. Criticism and idealism may find expression in political or religious activity but also in good works towards others. The childhood tendency to divide the world into goodies and baddies still recurs and may cloud judgement, but it recedes throughout adolescence except in the politically disturbed fraction of late adolescents and young adults. In the main there seems to be a working out – or not working out – of childhood grievances which are usually unconscious and elevated to some point of political principle which then has to be imposed on the whole community if possible.

Romanticism is still rife in late adolescence but it is to be hoped that it is tempered a little by reason in early adulthood. Equally, it is to be hoped that it is never lost.

*Chapter 3*

# Sexual attraction

## Physical considerations

What happens normally is that boys and girls think about the things that interest or excite them while masturbating. The pleasant sensation of masturbation reinforces the enjoyment of the fantasised person, situation or object and the adolescent takes this image or fantasy 'on board' as part of their growing sexual personality. How and about what the adolescent fantasises depends to some extent on his or her personality and several studies have been done in this area. In one, ninety-five men were shown silhouettes of female figures which had various breast, buttock and leg sizes. The researchers found that different types of men emerged according to their preferences for the silhouettes. The 'breast men' tended to be *Playboy* readers, extrovert and masculine in their interests, and those who liked small-breasted women tended to be inward-looking and submissive, drink little and hold fundamental Christian beliefs. Men who liked large buttocks were also keen on neatness and order and those who liked small ones were work-centred and uninterested in sport. The most remarkable characteristic of those who preferred large legs was that they drank little and were shy in social situations. Men who preferred small legs drank very little but they smoked, and read sports magazines rather than *Playboy*. In general, a preference for large women was linked to ambition and a high consumption of alcohol whereas men who preferred smaller women were persevering and of a higher social class.

Similar studies of women looking at male outlines show that they prefer 'V's rather than 'pears' in male body shape. Women who liked large men were more likely to be interested in competitive sports. Smaller women preferred large men and so did those raised in fatherless homes.

There are definite class differences in likes and dislikes. In one study which involved psychiatrists, psychologists, porters, maintenance men and soldiers being shown fifty colour photographs of women, some women were found to have almost universal appeal regardless

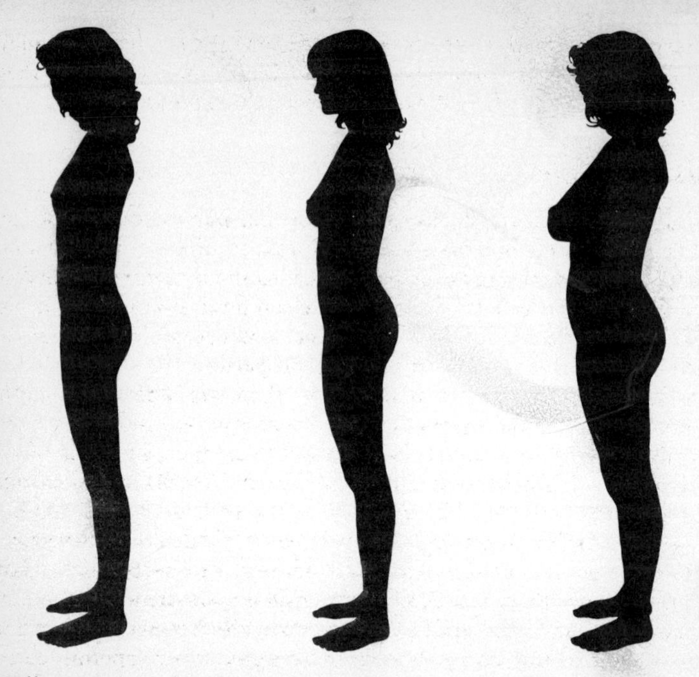

Different male preferences for the female body: *Silhouettes used in one of the studies mentioned in the text to seek out male preferences for different female body shapes. Some of the findings were surprising but, rather predictably, Playboy readers tended to like big-breasted women.*

of the age, social class or marital status of the men. There were some interesting differences too. The porters and soldiers preferred the photos of naked, large-breasted women who were being sexy, and the psychiatrists preferred young, clothed girls who were 'unconventional' or 'provocative'. All the men tended to choose attractive and dressed women when asked to select a possible wife from the photos and they avoided those women shown in provocative or sexy poses. This and other work suggests that what a man finds attractive in a woman depends upon her age, social class, personality and to some extent on what he wants of her.

Research done with women looking at pictures of men shows that the professional and educated positively disliked the muscle-man type and preferred conventional, dressed men who were slim, dark and sensitive looking. Many men think that all women like muscular, hairy-chested, broad-shouldered men with large penises, but studies have shown this not to be true. Women overall like men with small buttocks and a tall, slim physique and many in one survey said they were actually put off by the features men thought women liked.

## *Body odour*

Our body's natural smells are an essential part of our attraction system, yet our culture has become obsessed with cleanliness and we seem to be intent on destroying or masking them. Certainly it makes sense and is pleasant to keep oneself clean but it is not necessary to overdo the deodorant or the perfume, because our own personal odours can have very powerful sexual properties.

As well as our obvious body odours there are other more subtle 'odours' called pheromones. These are chemicals produced by the body of an animal which have an effect on the behaviour of its fellows, as a form of communication. They are 'smells' which are not consciously recognised by the brain but nevertheless affect the behaviour of others. Pheromones have been widely described in various animal species and research has confirmed, not surprisingly, that humans have them too. A substance called androstenone occurs in male sweat and urine and has an attractant effect on women. Similar substances in women are the vaginal pheromones or copulins which attract men. These are produced in increased amounts around the time of ovulation and arouse men most then.

There are other fascinating pheromone phenomena. For example, women living together (in women's halls of residence, nurses' homes and convents, for example) tend to menstruate at the same time. Even though their menstrual cycles are different when they enter the community they tend to synchronise in time. One researcher spread male pheromones on the pillows of nuns' beds and found that those nuns' periods were disrupted from the 'norm' of the other nuns. This has now been called the 'strange male effect'. It has been found that telephones sprayed with male pheromones are used more by women than adjacent ones that are not sprayed; and that theatre seats sprayed with male pheromones attract women. Even children can detect the sexual odour of adults and around the age of three sometimes have a distaste for the smell of the same-sex parent.

## *Faces*

There is evidence to suggest that there is a widely held notion of the 'ideal' face. In one study people were shown photos of twelve young women between the ages of twenty and twenty-five and there was marked agreement as to which faces were the most attractive. The only people who disagreed to any extent were the over fifty-five-year-olds and some members of the unskilled occupations.

As so many people agreed about what is attractive they must clearly be making their judgement using certain shared standards. People shown photographs of physically attractive people readily assign them more socially desirable attributes than they do photos of unattractive people. On balance, we also assume that attractive people will be more likely to hold top jobs, be better parents, be more happily married and have better lives generally. It also seems that we are more likely to trust physically attractive people on a first meeting than the physically unattractive. This confers a tremendous advantage on the attractive because by definition almost all contacts are one-offs and will never get any further if there is no immediate attraction. There is a greater chance that this immediate attraction will happen with attractive people.

### *Height*

As a man's height increases so does our expectation of his socially desirable personal qualities. People tend to guess the height of authority figures and attractive people as taller than they actually are and one researcher has noted that every American president elected since at least 1900 has been the taller of the two major candidates. Women almost everywhere invariably prefer men who are taller than themselves.

## Love at first sight

Many of us have been brought up to believe that the 'ideal' relationship starts with a glance across a crowded room. The eyes meet, it's love, and the couple live happily ever after. This can in fact occur, depending on how one defines 'love', because we can train ourselves to make up our minds about people on the slimmest of information. Almost all of us stereotype people and, using the flimsiest of information, make instant judgements about their personalities and characters. We meet many people in everyday life and we cannot get to know them all in depth. We therefore have to use some kind of quick sorting method.

Unfortunately, stereotypes can be harmful and can make us miss a good opportunity to get to know someone. This is especially true when it comes to occupations. Some men assume that women in certain occupations or jobs are promiscuous, so that the large numbers who are not either have to act up to their image or wait for a man who does not believe the stereotype and finds the woman attractive in herself. We have all heard that 'gentlemen prefer blondes' but in fact dark men seem to prefer brunettes and blond men's preferences spread equally between blondes and brunettes. The majority of young women say they prefer dark men, with the exception of artificial blondes, who, according to one survey, do not care what colour hair a man has.

Once over our visual stereotypes we start judging people on their personalities. We tend to believe that people who get on well with others are intrinsically more attractive (or whatever we feel is important in life). In this way we link personal attributes to each other so as to build up a comfortable picture we think we can live with. So we arrive at suppositions such as 'a man who is this kind to children must also be . . .'. Add to this a list of personal theories about people from past acquaintance (I once went out with a girl with long fingernails and she was awful, so this one with long fingernails probably will be too), and the field of choice one gives oneself soon begins to narrow. Some studies have shown that certain men assess women according to how similar or dissimilar they are to their own mothers.

Our reliance on judgements based on stereotypes can have unfortunate negative effects because we tend to behave in a way which fulfils our prophecies (and we all like that to happen). Studies have found, for example, that lovely clothes enhance women's social and sexual status. Even other women imagine well-dressed women to be more passionate, free, romantic, thrilling, approachable, adventurous, flirtatious and sexy than unfashionably dressed women. Media advertisements showing women in glamorous settings with attractive men, confirm their view. One survey found that wearers of fashionable clothes were thought to have different dating patterns, sexual morals, and smoking and drinking patterns. But this can mean that unfashionable or unattractive women can find it very difficult to behave sexily, adventurously, romantically and so on simply because the rest of us do not see them in that sort of role. So the unattractive and the unfashionably dressed are not encouraged to behave in these ways, and so they do not, which is then seen as proving that they are all the things they are generally held to be. This sort of self-fulfilling prophecy approach kills off perfectly possible partners at the starting post before we really know what they are like.

## Getting to know your choice

Now let us assume that we are past the initial impression stage and things are beginning to progress. Based on first impressions a woman might think, 'He's a bit thick but I fancy him, so I'll pretend to be thick too so he won't be put off'. Armed with the 'knowledge' that Western men do not like their women to be brighter than they are themselves, she puts herself down because *he* seems unintelligent. The man will unconsciously alter *his* behaviour to come into line with what he feels she expects and the charade gets off the ground.

Many men think that women most respect and enjoy the company of dominant men and one survey found that girls certainly are attracted to competent men. But if men tried to overcome their incompetence by being dominant, the women found them more *un*attractive. The most appealing men were those who were competent and dominant. It does seem to be the case that men who have power and are good at what they do are very attractive to women.

So now our two individuals are talking and eyeing each other up. The main thing they are doing is making character and personality judgements, but they are also trying to find out if the other likes them. Similarly, nods, eye-to-eye contact and positive body language all help to build up a positive or negative picture. Some people are good at reading these tell-tales and build on them at once but others are very bad at it. If a girl finds a boy attractive there are common give-aways. She may, for example, tend to look into his eyes momentarily and then look away, she may blush, or she may giggle at the slightest joke or teasing.

The way we interpret these signs varies according to our mood from day to day. Studies have shown that aroused men (who had just read some sexy material) were more likely to see a girl as sexually attractive and receptive than were unaroused men. So we could meet someone on one day and be unaffected by them and then meet them again in a different and more receptive mood and really hit it off.

## What you can tell by looking

In addition to possible physiological setbacks, which can include illness, family and money problems, there can be misunderstandings all through relationships but particularly at the beginning. Studies of what male college students wanted on a first date compared with what they thought the girls wanted show that they misunderstood each other right from the beginning. Whereas only half the men and women actually wanted or expected to kiss on this first occasion, three-quarters of them thought it was expected. Even studies of engaged and married couples show tremendous areas of misunderstanding, so obviously there is room for a good deal more openness if relationships are to be successful and enjoyable.

Even if the level of communication between two individuals is not all that great there are certain things that one can learn from research and other people's experiences that help decide on a person's sexual availability.

Women of all ages are less permissive than men, but up to the age of twenty there is a slight rise reaching a peak then and declining thereafter, especially in those who have children. Women with girls in their late teens are least permissive of all and are only exceeded by the deeply religiously committed.

The way people talk about sex can be revealing but it is a mistake to go entirely by what a person says on the subject. One study, for example, found that attractive girls were more likely to have premarital intercourse but that the attitudes to intercourse they expressed were no different from those expressed by unattractive girls. Similarly, studies of girls from religious families tend to show that they have intercourse younger than girls from non-believing homes yet their upbringing and outward signs would tend to point in the opposite direction.

Kinsey found that women living in urban areas were more sexually experienced. About 60 per cent of American men aged twenty to twenty-two admit to having had premarital intercourse (according to one survey), and the figure is about the same in Germany, Canada and Norway, rising to 75 per cent of English men. The English also lead this chart in 'one-night stands', especially among women, a third of whom claimed to have experienced one-night stands as opposed to fewer than 10 per cent in the other countries. The fear of AIDS may have reduced such behaviour recently but probably not to a large extent.

Once we get away from groups of people and consider individual *personalities*, things become more interesting. For example, studies have found that submissive girls are almost without exception virgins whereas only about one third of dominant women are. Extroverts, hardly surprisingly, have intercourse much more often and do so at an earlier age, with more people and in a greater variety of positions. The differences are quite large. For example, 45 per cent of extrovert men in one study had had intercourse at the age of nineteen compared with only 15 per cent of the introvert men. The difference in women was even more startling – introvert women had intercourse three times a month whereas the extroverts experienced it on an average of seven and a half times a month.

Psychologically ill people tend to be promiscuous, have more premarital sex and have more 'hostility' and 'lack of satisfaction', according to one study. Very sensitive people tend to experience more impotence (men) or frigidity (women) – that is, men failing to erect or ejaculate and women failing to have orgasms. People with so-called 'hysterical' personalities were found in one study to be sexually very experienced but highly guilt-ridden.

Social give-aways that reveal sexual activity are fairly useful when assessing the field. For example, smoking and drinking are good clues to a teenager's sexual activity. Sexually inexperienced teenagers rarely get drunk and in one study sexually active teenagers smoked more than would be expected. Teenage girls who smoked more than twenty cigarettes a day were almost never virgins.

Girls who live away from home are more likely to be sexually experienced and girls living by themselves are least likely to be virgins. The lowest level of teenage sexual activity is found among girls living at home with both natural parents.

We have seen that attractive girls have more boyfriends but it does not stop there – they also have more intercourse. Attractive girls provably have a more active sex life and research shows that they have twice as many male friends and have been in love more often. Attractive girls say that more of their friends have had intercourse but perhaps all of their friends are attractive!

The subject of *virginity* comes high on the priority list of sexual attraction for many people and many men still want to marry a virgin. Very little is known about why boys remain virgins but some have religious scruples or other moral objections. It looks as though the vast majority simply have not had the opportunity.

In one survey of late-adolescent boys 58 per cent said they wanted to marry a virgin or, more exactly, to be the only sex partner the woman they marry has had.

The majority of girls (more than ninety per cent) are not virgins on their wedding day. About two thirds claim in surveys to have slept only with their husband-to-be but all such evidence must be taken with a large pinch of salt. Clinical experience suggests that this is much too low a figure and that many have had other sexual partners but dare not admit it – even to themselves on occasions.

## What do you want in a relationship?

Even if on first meeting two people find they are attracted to each other, it is essential before pursuing the relationship further that they sort out their ideas of what the purpose of the hoped-for relationship is. In other words, they should have realistic and mutually acceptable goals or they will end up wasting each other's time and even exploiting one another. Obviously, if either is thinking seriously of marriage as the end point, he or she will be looking for different things from someone who wants a short-term partner with whom to go to a social event or have sex.

So when a couple meet and start getting to know each other they have to make some rather quick and basic assessments of what each other's goals are. There are problems here because girls are occasionally misled by men – or even mislead themselves – into believing that the men want a long-term relationship and that they are in love when really all they want is sex (though not necessarily intercourse). A survey of what makes men and women unwilling to have intercourse at this stage of a relationship found that men said that fear of pregnancy and the inability to persuade the girl were top of their list, whereas women said that they did not have intercourse because they were not in love, because they would feel guilty afterwards, or because it was against their principles. The fear of AIDS is tending to be an inhibiting factor in some people.

There is a lot of misunderstanding between the sexes. Men think women refuse to have sexual intercourse because of fear of pregnancy and for fear of losing their reputation rather than through shame or because they are not in love. The problem obviously lies in trying to assess such a delicate situation before embarking on the chase at all, and most of us try to do this along the lines described in this chapter.

Perhaps the last thing we should look at in the sexual attraction a girl has for a boy at this stage is the concept of love. Many youngsters, especially girls, find themselves 'in love' quite early in a new relationship. The most obvious thing about people who are in love is that they are blind to the faults of the loved-one even though these are pointed out by caring friends and relatives.

The infatuation stage of being in love is important in the context of sexual attraction because it can seriously impair one's ability to make reasoned decisions. There is no doubt in our minds, from clinical experience, that many girls of this age who feel sexually aroused by a man unconsciously generate feelings of love so as to 'permit' themselves to go further sexually. Boys may also protest love because they hope it will obtain sexual favours. The sad thing is that such episodes debase the true concept of love between a man and a woman and make it even more difficult for people to recognise love when they see it in a potentially permanent relationship. On the other hand, if valuable lessons have been learned, all experience is useful.

## *Early experiences of intercourse*

A critical review of the evidence suggests that the age at which intercourse starts is mainly governed by the genetic blueprint as modified by earlier sexual and emotional experiences. Personality development and social skills have to be sufficiently well developed to attract a partner but their availability for sex and emotional exaggeration are also important ingredients.

On balance girls think they are looking for a romantic relationship and boys for a physical one. Girls generally are hoping for their search to end in security, while boys are looking for adventure, but there are probably more girls around today in an adventurous frame of mind and boys in a romantic one.

Emotional and sexual attraction are complex issues of which we know only a few dimensions. Variations in taste between individuals ensure that almost any man or woman will be attractive to someone of the opposite sex. Hairy women, for example, often believe themselves to be unattractive but some men prefer them. Physical differences and even disabilities can be attractive to others. Physical attractiveness is the most important factor to young adolescents and to adults looking for brief affairs. Distinguishing emotional attraction from the physical is mainly an adult skill.

For women particularly, how attractive they *feel* greatly influences how attractive they *are*. A good morale is vital to one's sense of attractiveness.

*Chapter 4*
# Selection and courtship

Some individuals misuse intercourse, or rather, copulation. Some men, for example, whether married or unmarried, seek sex with almost any woman, to prove their virility, attractiveness, potency, or to boost their ego. Thus, a company director, might, after a boardroom row in which he felt beaten by the other directors, seek intercourse with any woman in order to restore his self-esteem. This enables him to function again. A woman prone to depression may seek to ward it off by attracting a man into intercourse, or one with lesbian anxieties may try to prove to herself she is heterosexual by constantly seducing men. Yet other individuals remain fixed in permanent adolescence and do not emotionally mature – their capacity for love is impaired in some way.

Most people, unlike these, are by early adulthood seeking more than just sex in relationships. They genuinely want to love and be loved. The reduction in their obsession with genitality alone may be accompanied by the thought that virtually any penis will go into any vagina so it cannot be all that special. This realisation is a justification for the acquisition of sexual experience and a protection against inappropriate marriage based only on sexual desire and availability.

Of course, all attractions are initially sexual attractions, however unconsciously, but with increasing maturity something more is required and flirtation now is not so much aimed at seduction but at establishing real contact with the individual underneath. Hopefully, with increasing experience, more accurate assessments of the real personality can be made and compatability judged. Personality features, communication, and a capacity for shared happiness become more important than just the physical features mentioned in the last chapter. Hopefully too, romanticism will be kept in the background so as not to obscure the situation. In fact even a degree of scepticism can be healthy. In this way the old adage 'marry in haste and repent at leisure' can be proven wrong. The great lesson to learn is that man-woman relationships are between personalities, not between genitals. A good relationship can survive nearly all problems, including genital ones. Happy and unfettered genital expression within the relationship is a considerable assistance but in the last analysis, apart from its reproductive aspect, it is icing on the cake – not the cake itself. Happy sex, if only for a short spell, is possible with many members of the opposite sex but an enduring, happy relationship is possible with far fewer.

So choice and selection based mainly on personality is one secret of success but even if we have learned to be good at selection how much choice do we really have and on what basis should we, or do we, make it?

Some people still regard their choice as very restricted and talk of the one-in-a-million partner, Mr Right (or Miss Right). One expert took the other extreme view when he claimed that 75 per cent of the men and women in the population were good all-purpose spouses and could marry any other and make it work. There is a particle of truth in both views but if the aim is to encourage happy, fulfilling relationships neither is more than part of the answer.

The first problem is how to meet people. Nearly 60 years ago an American researcher found that of 5,000 couples in Philadelphia 17 per cent married someone who lived within one block of each other and almost a third married someone within four blocks. Only a fifth

Day dreams: *Most people have some idea of what type of person they would like as an ideal partner and sometimes even fantasise the ideal type of relationship with them. One aspect of maturity is adapting to the realisation that there is no such thing as 'ideal' in this world.*

had lived in different cities. Although people travel more widely now, this tendency to marry someone local is still with us. Most people do not look far and still tend to marry individuals they meet at work or in their major leisure pursuit. Apart from explaining the local effect it could be argued that our choice of work and play to some extent reflects our personalities so we are more likely to meet people similar to ourselves there. Two practical points emerge. First, clubs, pubs, discos and such places are not particularly good places to search for a long-term partner, and second, the selection of social recreations in which both sexes indulge, such as tennis, sailing, climbing, dramatics, music etc, and which facilitate an expression of one's personality are likely to be more fruitful. A further point is that men and women who see each other regularly have a tendency to come to like each other.

With these considerations in mind it can easily be seen that choice is wider for the young, if only because the majority of their peers are unmarried, than it is for older individuals. To maximise choice it is sensible for older people to use bureaux and advertise or respond to advertisements either in the local press, specialist magazines reflecting their interests or, in specialist singles magazines. The notion that such courses of action are 'infra-dig' because 'I should be sufficiently attractive to find a partner myself' are self-defeating because the aim is to increase your choice, not simply to find a partner.

## What influences choice?

Some say that opposites attract. Whilst this may be true, it is not often the basis for a good long-term relationship. For example, a woman whose whole pleasure in life is centred around the home and her relationship with her husband will be unlikely to be happy for long with a man to whom achievement at work and advancement are the main pre-occupations in life. No two people are exactly similar in personality but gross fundamental dissimilarities are no prescription for a happy marriage.

However, some women who regard themselves as having some serious physical or psychological defect say they are attracted to men with the opposite characteristic and it sometimes crosses their mind that if they ever had a baby by him it would, with luck, inherit his and not her characteristics or at least cancel out her 'defects' in the child.

Another view is that many people seek to marry a replica of their mother or father. This hypothesis makes sense if the childhood relationship with the opposite sex partner has gone well and been

Choice: *Obviously there is more to partner choice than the man's occupation—intelligence, appearance, personality, height, sexuality and availability are some of the other factors which will influence our choice. These in turn tend to influence the way we seek out our potential partners.*

happy or if it has been a failure. In the latter case the individual may unconsciously seek to return to childhood and 're-work' the relationship in the hopes of a happier outcome. Also the child receives half its genes from the opposite sex parent and so is similar to him or her to some extent. Therefore choosing a partner who is similar in adulthood may involve choosing someone who is similar to our opposite sex partner.

Although it does not seem that there is any noteworthy tendency for people to marry partners who look the same as their opposite sex parent the effect could be more subtle. One's defences, so to speak, may go down more readily when someone is encountered who, no matter how unconsciously, is seen to have a similar smile, gesture, manner of speaking and personality style of a much-loved and much wanted opposite sex parent. Such a person may be seen almost from the outset as particularly exciting sexually, desirable and loveable. The fact that the first deep relationship of many young men is with an older woman and of many young women with an older man suggests that such an effect exists but it must be stressed that it is not worked out in the conscious mind.

Similarly, for some individuals, a much-loved brother or sister seems to be the unconscious basis of choice and in such cases physical similarities can be important. Some such couples look as if they could be brother or sister. In fact it has been found that men with younger sisters who married women with older sisters were happier than in the reverse situation.

Age is another consideration. Most women marry men one to five years older than themselves. Since boys mature more slowly than do girls this makes sense since they are likely to be equally mature at marriage. However, in the longer term it would make more biological sense for women to marry men about seven years younger than themselves given the longer life-span of women. In fact the happiest marriages have been found to be between women with husbands four to ten years younger than themselves. However, this may be an unsafe guide in general since it is possible that such women are more maternal than average and such men more immature than most or they may have a special need for a mother-like woman.

Since relationships are between personalities and these are independent of age it follows that large age disparities are not necessarily fatal to a happy marriage. In fact if chronological age were disregarded and only the psychosexual (or mental, or emotional, or maturational) age of the partners considered then some couples with very discrepant chronological ages would be found to be the same age

'Come on, we're supposed to be there at 8.00': *How do you rate their future together?*

psychosexually. Even where the psychosexual ages are discrepant the relationship can still make sense. For example, a mature man with a weak male ego can have a happy relationship with a psychologically immature woman since she badly needs a daddy and to have an adoring and devoted woman boosts his ego. Of course, such a mutually beneficial relationship still needs similarities in the basic personalities if it is to prosper.

Social class also matters if only because attitudes and aspirations are partly governed by class. In consequence people tend to marry in the same social class but men tend to marry 'down' more often than do women.

What the available scientific evidence shows is that the more similar people are in background, rearing, attitudes, beliefs, education, intelligence, ambitions, prejudices and so on, the more likely are they to be happy together. Obviously such couples tend to understand each other easily and communication between them is relatively free. This state of affairs is called homogamy. Dealing with someone who has a different cultural or social background to ourselves can be very difficult when it comes to partner selection. Their backgrounds and values are sufficiently different to make it especially difficult, without considerable effort, to understand precisely the feelings their speech and behaviour are intended to convey. For this reason inter-racial marriages can be fraught unless the partners have been brought up in similar cultures. However, for some individuals, marriage to a foreigner is an advantage for reasons which may often ultimately spring from sexual guilt; that is to say, the foreign partner is very different from the opposite sex parent and in consequence unhampered sexual and emotional inter-action is possible with them even if they find it difficult to have sex with a partner of the same race.

## Courtship

Once a choice has been made this is hardly the end of the matter. The chosen partner should be explored and the potential for longterm happiness further assessed. At this stage the best advice, based on the evidence, is to avoid copulation. Anybody can be happy, for a spell at least, in bed. Women, particularly, seem to need a word of caution here. When asked how many occasions you should go out with a man you like and who seems to like you before allowing full sexual activity the majority of young women say at least three! There is some evidence that the threat of AIDS is making people slightly more cautious.

A woman first meeting a man who excites her will use him in her masturbation fantasies from the start. As we point out elsewhere, it seems natural for women to express their emotional feelings by close body contact and sex. All that is required is that she likes the man and that sufficient time has elapsed for her to feel a relationship exists and that she is not a whore. But is this approach wise?

In a relationship which is not intentionally casual the period between first meeting and first intercourse could be called courtship. If a long relationship is hoped for then slow progress needs to be the policy. This is where the scepticism mentioned earlier comes in. The idea can be expressed in a question to one's self along the lines 'Can I really believe my luck – after all this time can I really have met someone who understands me and yet still loves me and whom I understand and love more than ever?' Courtship should be a time for exploration, testing and the establishment of genuine communication. If, at any stage, the relationship is seriously not right, and cannot be made right, it should be abandoned. This is not to say that at the first difficulty it should be given up but rather that the ability to overcome the difficulty should be tested.

At this stage progress is best made out of bed. The point is not that sex is off the menu but that it is taken slowly and gently, stage by stage. In itself it is one test of compatibility and ability to communicate and proceeds whilst the personalities and capacity for mutual interest and happiness are explored. Those who have been in many previous relationships may consider that courtship is unnecessary but it is more essential than ever if a real relationship with the real person is to be established and not just an image of one based on past experiences. Everyone, after all, is different and it is unfair to apply generalisations to others.

So, running in parallel with the social, emotional and psychological development of the relationship, the sexual relationship unfolds. It is part of the learning about each other which goes on in courtship. Progress may take weeks or months and first intercourse may be deferred until marriage but the stages fall into a pattern which recapitulates psychosexual development.

First there is kissing and cuddling. Some people find kissing very exciting but others are indifferent or even dislike it. Now is the time to find out about your partner's preferences. Deep kissing early on in a relationship may, these days, give rise to anxieties due to the fear of AIDS. Many women love their necks being kissed and their ears nibbled. For others, of both sexes, kissing is a whole body activity and they like the bodies to be pushed together while kissing. Cuddling is probably an under-rated activity. Virtually all women say they love to be cuddled and that cuddling alone can make them feel happy and content. Many men too like cuddling but fear to ask for it or promote it in case they come across as being less than 'manly'.

The next stage is stimulation over clothes, especially of the woman's breasts, back, bottom and thighs. She may similarly stimulate the man. Now the special erogenous values of each area to the partner can begin to be learned. Since the relationship is deepening it is best to be open and unashamed about what is required from now on. If such revelations are unacceptable to the other, now is the time to find out. In the same way it is best to be open about your personality and not to try and conceal features which it might be feared are unacceptable. 'Glasnost' should be the policy followed. It is foolish to pretend to be something we are not.

The stage which follows is partial, and eventually perhaps total, nudity. No sensible person regards their body as perfect or expects anyone else to be so. Nevertheless women often seem all too keen to draw attention to the real or imagined imperfections of their bodies even before they have shown them to the man. This is a mistake.

Those women who complain that men are interested only in their bodies for sex underestimate the extent to which Mother Nature has made men susceptible to the beauties of the female body. Tastes vary, as we said earlier, but men have an appreciation which most find hard to express in any adequate language, and which goes far beyond the genitals. Men too have their anxieties about their bodies which an understanding woman can do a lot to allay. One aspect of love is mutual admiration. At this stage further investigations of erogenous zones and how the partner most likes them to be stimulated is possible.

Some moralists may object to the next stage, which many people, even today, still avoid out of shame, and yet its benefits are enormous. It is the stage of mutual masturbation. It powerfully assists the growth of trust if this stage can be negotiated successfully. The young especially are, due to the influences of their upbringing still exerting a large effect, often very shy and secretive about this aspect of themselves and even more so where a member of the opposite sex is involved.

Ideally the couple should show each other how they like to be stimulated and teach one another to be expert with their genitals. All women masturbate differently so no matter how many previous partners the man has masturbated he knows nothing of the present one until he finds out. Having found out he now has a reliable way of producing an orgasm for her. This increases his confidence and decreases his performance anxiety thereby making penile failure in the future less likely. Eventually the skill can be used before, during and after intercourse to enhance the woman's pleasure and make orgasm for her more likely. Many men worry about their ability to produce an orgasm for their lover.

Similarly, the woman learns to masturbate her man as well, or better, than he can himself. He becomes used to and confident about erecting and ejaculating in front of her and, if she does not want or cannot have intercourse in the future, she can still relieve him. In effect she tells him that she accepts his masturbation. This is helpful because many men stop or reduce masturbation when they meet a woman who they know is going to be special. All this involves much more than simply inducing an orgasm, it has to do with learning to do it really well based on the needs of a particular partner.

Even more embarrassing for many, and in many ways even more important, is the uninhibited and honest communication of masturbation fantasies and special needs. This involves deep intimacy and considerable love. Secrets are shared now and used to the benefit

**Stages of courtship**
ACROSS A CROWDED ROOM
*Attraction, Approach, Acceptance.*

**Stages of courtship**
EXPLORATION
*Communication, Contact, Consummation.*

of one another. Such revelations are liberating and the gratitude felt towards the partner for accepting and indulging the 'shameful' needs is often enduring and life-long. If this level of communication can be achieved nothing is likely to be more difficult in the future.

Finally, when the penis first penetrates the vagina it is not going to be copulatory contact with a stranger but true intercourse with someone loved and understood who loves and understands in return. Most importantly of all it makes the woman and the man real friends and powerful allies. Some people find this level of intimacy and sharing intimidating or even disgusting but in reality it is beautiful. To fail to go through the stage in full means that assumptions are made about the sexuality of the other and this diminishes real love.

Courtship can be a beautiful process too. The couple learn how to behave gracefully, politely and happily with each other, often to the vast relief of agonised parents who see an oaf of a son or a rebellious, moody daughter blossom into the attractive person they always hoped for. As the partners enthuse the other with their interests new horizons begin to open.

During courtship the emphasis should be more on reality than romance. Faults in the other should be perceived realistically and decisions taken as to whether these departures from notions of an 'ideal' partner can be overlooked or even turned to advantage. People can, within reason, be as loveable for their faults as their virtues. Courtship too is a time of confession but it is best not to be too detailed for fear of provoking later jealousy.

If at any time courtship fails and the relationship ends it is very sad. However, the partners should know much more about themselves and the opposite sex than they did before. They may even realise their choice was incorrect, learn the lesson and do better next time.

*Chapter 5*

# Engagement and premature marriage

Courtship is an intensely personal business but after a time, if the couple feel fairly sure that they are right for each other, they will want to start making long-term plans for being together. This will usually mean getting married. The bridge between courtship and marriage is engagement. Ideally this is a public declaration to the world that the two like each other greatly, are basically well adapted to one another, have done their 'homework' during courtship and are setting out to make a life together.

Of course, not every courtship, nor even every engagement, ends in marriage and it is helpful to know what the commonest reasons for 'failure' are, so that a couple can see these worrying signs in their relationship.

## Reasons for failure

1 One (or both) of the individuals is too immature in his or her personality development and simply is not ready to settle down. Such a person finds that he or she resents the thought of becoming linked to one person exclusively, talks a lot about the loss of freedom and wants to continue to play the field.
2 Often, a person will say, 'I love her (or him) a lot and we'd make a good couple, but do I really want to be married to him or her for years and so lose my freedom?' Such doubts are probably universal but fleeting. When they persist the couple are not keen *enough* on each other to want to make an exclusive commitment and should not get engaged.
3 Not uncommonly, because boys mature later and more slowly, the girl is ready, willing and able to go ahead with the serious commitment involved but the boy is not.
4 Unfortunately, some potentially very good relationships fail at this stage because they are unrealistically based from the start on romantic, instead of realistic, notions.
5 Some people are so indecisive that they simply cannot make

important decisions of any kind and so back away from engagement.

6 Often one or other of the couple feels that the relationship is nearly right but is not quite good enough in some ways. This is a real dilemma because no one is perfect, and this goes for the person doing the agonising. There are two useful questions to ask yourself. The first is, 'Given that I'm not perfect, have my faults and am certainly not "ideal", have I the right to demand that someone else is all these things?' The second is, 'Given that I know of these faults and shortcomings in the relationship, am I sufficiently flexible to be able to adjust?' In other words, 'Can I love him or her, warts and all?'

7 Engyesis ('marriage sickness') is a medical term used to describe a cluster of symptoms (anxiety, depression and doubt) about one's partner which occur during courtship and engagement. When it was first described in 1888 it was thought that it was the sexual tensions of this group of people that caused these very real psychological problems. The main symptoms are inability to sleep, loss of appetite, weight loss, headaches, a feeling of tension and a lack of concentration. Almost all such people are insecure about their proposed marriage. Some people become suddenly struck with one or more of these symptoms on making specific wedding arrangements. The ill one then often says, 'You can see how ill I am, it wouldn't be fair to go on with the marriage', to which the well partner says, 'I love you, I'll stand by you.' At this point the ill one becomes worse and goes to a doctor. The idea that sexual tensions are the cause of these problems is probably not true because in one survey at least half such couples were having intercourse. This same survey found that about half the patients had had a previous psychiatric ailment or illness for which they had sought medical advice.

The question is what to do in such cases. One survey found that the illness subsided more or less completely with the breaking of the engagement or on marriage but that about a third continued to have symptoms after marriage. Medical opinion differs as to what should be done. Some doctors say that any relationship that produces illness must be basically unsound in some way and so should be abandoned and others that given that two-thirds seem to do well after marriage, perhaps it is simply a way of reacting to the common stresses of courtship and engagement, which go once the couple settle down together.

8 Parental opposition is, and always has been, a factor in the

breaking off of courtship and engagements. Very often in our experience, parents *do* know best and usually have their child's future at the heart of their suggestions. Of course, by no means all such advice *is* lovingly given and some parents have all kinds of motives for wanting to put their children off marrying *anyone*, let alone any one particular person. It really is up to the individual to decide. Parents, it seems from research, approve of over 80 per cent of all engagements, so this is not a widespread problem.

## Preparation, planning and final commitment

In spite of all these possible set-backs engagement is still very much the norm though the form it takes can vary. Only about 4 per cent of those who marry have never been engaged at all but there are 'shades' of engagement between this and marriage. Engagements can be formal, with a notice in the newspapers, a party and substantial family involvement; semi-formal with only close family being told; or informal, the couple arranging to marry but telling no one, or few people, about it.

In one survey of those who were engaged, 8 per cent married within six months; 29 per cent married in six months to one year; and 28 per cent married within one to two years. Eighteen per cent of the men and 30 per cent of the women in this survey had seriously considered marrying someone else at some time.

Engagement then is a time of preparation and planning. It is a time for putting practical meat on to the bones (the plans and intentions) that developed during courtship. It is the couple working together in social ways, for example, planning housing, furnishing, wedding arrangements and so on. All these activities may reveal stresses, differences and difficulties not revealed or apparent in courtship. If such problems are great the relationship should end. After all, a perfect courtship is all very well but living together as a couple in society is a *social* business, not just a private one.

Because of this it follows that a successful engagement proves that the couple can work together in double harness and tests the similarity of their attitudes towards the social management of their relationship. As a result, a successful engagement makes it more likely that the couple will have a happy marriage.

Engagement obviously tests another set of adaptive capacities in the two families. With real luck friendships spring up with the prospective parents-in-law and the two families cooperate to help their young.

**Stages of Engagement**

THE EARLY STAGES

*A time for meeting each others' parents and friends and starting to become a part of each others' social lives. Most couples have a formal party or some kind of celebration to which the friends of both are invited. This is often the first time 'both sides of the family' get together formally.*

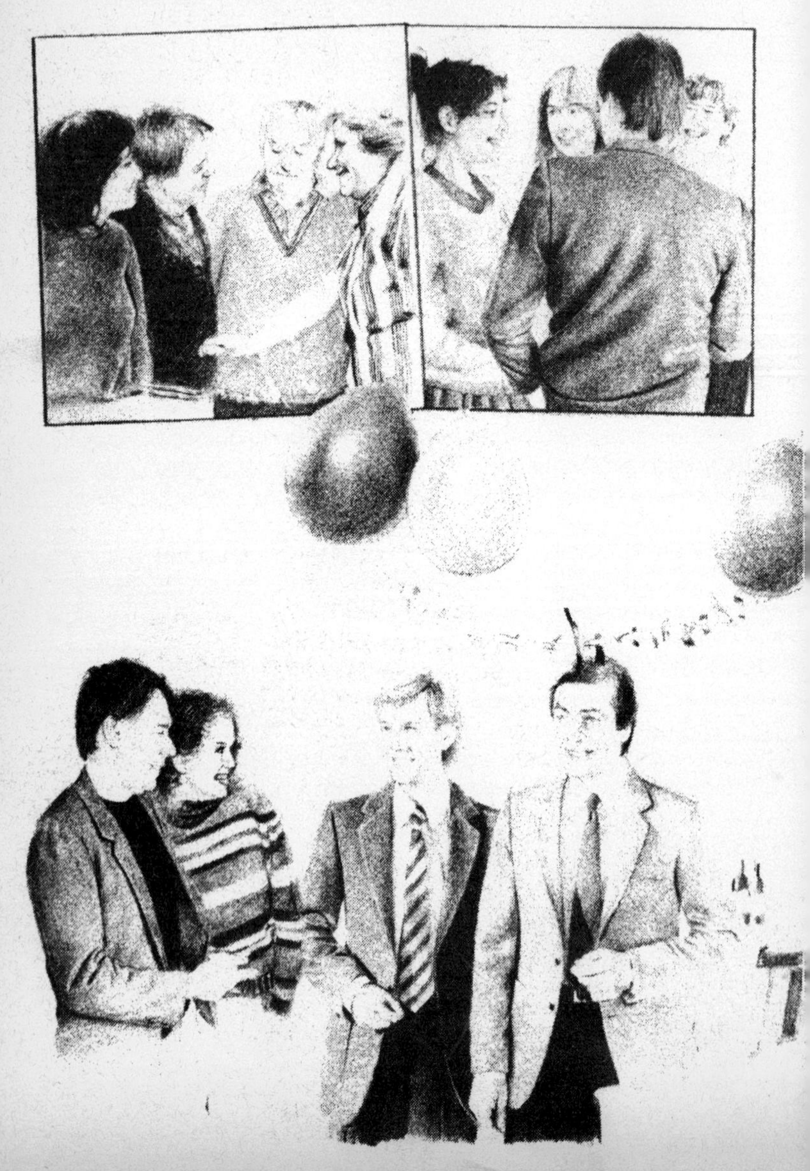

**Stages of Engagement**

THE LATER STAGES

*This is a time for solving practical problems. Choosing a ring, a place to live and preparing for the marriage itself.*

Engagement also tests the capabilities of the parents to let go of their young. A mother who is emotionally over-dependent on a son may be unreasonably hostile to his fiancée and may even create situations in which her son is tested to see if his love for her is greater than that for his fiancée. If a problem like this becomes apparent the son will usually try to side-step the issue but it is a problem which is unlikely to go away. The capacity of the couple to recognise and cope with the problem in a way which does not involve making the mother unhappy is a test of their skill in managing relationships with others.

Similarly, a father may, out of unconscious jealousy, wonder what his precious daughter sees in her lout of a fiancé. This is usually less of a problem than that of the hostile mother but it is still a test of the social skills of the couple.

Many youngsters report that they can get on better with their parents-in-law (prospective or otherwise) than their own parents. This is probably helpful. By no means do all families side with their own child in difficulties which arise between engaged and married couples and such balances probably have a considerable stabilising effect on the relationship.

An increasing number of couples live together with no immediate intentions of engagement or marriage. It could be argued that all the purposes of courtship and engagement can be achieved within such a framework just as well as outside it. Unfortunately, this often turns out not to be true in practice and it can short-circuit the highly important phases of adjustment, communication and testing.

It is not uncommon, even in good, steady relationships or engagements, for one or even both partners, especially if they are young and inexperienced, to have doubts about the relationship. This sometimes occurs because they have very little against which to judge the value of their partner and the relationship. Temporary separations can help by reinforcing the relationship.

Sometimes engaged partners, both men and women, involve themselves in bursts of promiscuous behaviour. The unconscious or even conscious purpose may be to discover what sex with others is like before making a final commitment. Although this can eventually be seen simply as bad behaviour, and it may certainly suggest that the sexual aspects of the courtship have not been correctly managed, it is far better than sexual experimentation with others *after* marriage. However, someone who has a continuing need for such promiscuous activity should be assessed with the utmost scepticism by the other partner because, despite claims and promises to the contrary, this sort of behaviour often continues after marriage.

## How to cope with rejection

Where, during courtship or engagement, the relationship is seen to be wrong or unsuitable, it is best to end it in a straightforward way with a rational discussion of the reasons. However, having said this, not everyone is capable of dealing with rejection and tactics for ending the relationship may have to be modified. Threats and blackmail have to be resisted because an unsuitable relationship will only become more unsuitable as time goes by. Women especially may make suicidal gestures on such occasions and men may behave unsociably and even violently. In such cases they may need medical help. If you are rejected, here are some helpful thoughts:

1 Considering how rotten a bad marriage can be, you have had a lucky escape.
2 You should be wiser and more clever in choosing your next partner and managing the relationship; after all, if you have learned nothing of value to help you next time, you have only yourself to blame.
3 It is unrealistic but all too common to pick out one feature, physical or psychological, about yourself and blame it for your 'failure' – this almost never applies.
4 Even thinking about the situation in terms of 'failure' is wrong since relationships are about mutual compatibility and not about estimates of the eternal or absolute worth of the participants.
5 You are free for all the thrills and excitements of making another choice and testing it in courtship.

Having said all this, it has to be admitted that the abandonment that is involved, especially if the partner has left the relationship for someone else, and the sense of loss, exposes the individual to depression, mourning, self-criticism and a temporary loss of self-confidence and esteem. Women seem, on average, less able to cope with this kind of set-back than men and being rejected in this way *can* sometimes alter their self-esteem for the rest of their life.

## Premature marriages

Lastly, in our brief look at engagement, let us take a look at premature, that is, immature marriages because the seeds for these usually disastrous relationships are sown during the courtship and engagement phase of a couple's development.

By immature marriage we mean one entered into under the age of twenty. However, many much older people are so immature that they also have disastrous marriages for the reasons we outline here.

All the available statistics show that marriages entered into where the woman is twenty or under have very high failure rates indeed. Not only do at least one in three of these marriages fail but they still have an above-average failure rate as long as twenty to thirty years after the marriage. So why do youngsters do it?

One of the commonest reasons is that the immature man has a poor sense of his own masculinity and by marrying tries to prove something to himself and society. Girls tend to marry this young for many reasons including an over-romantic desire to 'be married' – one which is almost totally unfounded on reality; to escape from the sexual or other restrictions of their parents; to go along with their friends who have married young; because they desperately want a baby; because they desperately want sex and cannot have it outside marriage; because they are so immature that they cannot make a realistic choice between the options that are open to them in life and marriage seems a good way out of the dilemma; and because they can simply think of nothing they would rather do unless it is to become a single parent.

Because most young marriages are entered into for the wrong reasons and because the personalities of the couple are immature, they are almost doomed before they begin. Young couples think that difficulties and differences (often apparent, even to them) will be smoothed out as the years pass, but this rarely happens because all too often their personality developments do not bring them together but separate them further. Many such marriages end within five years and leave the couple free to try again, hopefully wiser and better equipped to do it better second time around. The tragedy is that many young couples in this group have a child as soon as they get married and quite a few are actually forced into marriage because the girl is pregnant. Young couples having children immediately may do so because in their immature way they see it as a way of proving to the world that they are really grown up. It is a sad fact that many of these couples are not at all adult and often have to live with in-laws or parents because they are so poor. This is yet another nail in their marital coffin and things quickly go downhill. Young men in this situation are often very restrictive and jealous of their young brides and yet often become involved with other women. The marriage slowly, and – inevitably – painfully, drags to an end.

Any of us who are parents or have responsibilities for the young will want to see such young marriages discouraged wherever possible. But handling the situation can be very difficult because parental friction is often at the heart of the problem anyway. If you as parents feel things are going this way for your under-twenty-year-old, it is best to get outside help unless you have such a good relationship that you can have a frank two-way discussion about the subject. The problems are, ironically, much more serious when immature thirty-year-olds want to marry and no one but an expert in this field would recognise the reason why.

Immature marriage and all its dangers can be minimised by going through all the stages of courtship and engagement in the way we have suggested. The golden rule must be that if anything you have read in the last few chapters makes you unsure about your intended marriage – don't go ahead with it. Wait, think about it, discuss it with your parents, if you can, or with a friend or even a doctor or other professional who understands the problems.

*Chapter 6*
# Romance

The very words romance and romantic are tricky ones. A romance can mean a good story or even an elaborate lie to impress the gullible. A woman who is fanciful about her relationships, regardless of the facts, may be described as romantic but so may a taciturn, tall, dark and handsome man on the basis of his appearance alone. In reality he may be an Arab Sheikh more bothered about his billions from his oil well. Landscapes, buildings, furnishings and so on may be described as romantic as may such acts as giving a woman red roses, serenading her or even, according to TV adverts, risking a broken neck to deliver a box of chocolates to her boudoir! Elements of sacrifice for love may be involved as when the Duke of Windsor acted romantically by giving up the throne for his beloved.

Judging from the sales of romantic literature to women, which parallel the sales of girlie magazines to men, it is evidently something women yearn for and find difficult to obtain in real life. However, most such literature has, until the recent AIDS' scare, been more sexually explicit than before.

So does it all come back just to sex? Possibly. It could be viewed as an expression of the deepest need in many women which is to be loved, not just for their bodies but for themselves. Certainly even the smallest personalised and thoughtful gift or action can be a great source of delight. When she feels loved in this special way it liberates a flood of emotions and feelings, including sexual ones.

Romance is important to men too but they often see the situation the other way round. Since they believe that women have sex only with men they love, they then over-value a woman's sexual behaviour as a sign of her love for him. Although consciously a man may well know this is untrue, unconsciously he often reacts as if a sexual refusal by the woman he loves is a statement that he is not loved. As a result of this the word romantic to men tends to mean an ever-loving, ever-willing, perpetually faithful woman who loyally and excitingly devotes all her efforts, her emotions and her sexuality towards him. For women, the connotation seems to be involved much more with a set of events such as the music, the wine, the meal, the man, the attention . . . In some circumstances it may even be used as an 'excuse' for her sexual behaviour, especially, perhaps, on holiday.

## A learning phase

Probably the need for romance and the search (or hope) for romantic love is best thought of as a stage in the development of the capacity to love in a mature, adult way. It emerges strongly in late adolescence when the love which used to be self-centred (in mid-adolescence) begins to be available for direction towards others. It would be extraordinary if people went from their self-loving, mid-adolescent phase straight to an 'other-centred' type of love without some sort of intermediate learning phase. Romantic love is this phase in adolescence. Romantic love is a way in which we learn to bring together our sexual and loving feelings and to 'aim' them at the same person for the first time.

This phase of romantic love, which many young people experience more in fantasy than in fact and which others never grow out of, is still very much concerned with the self – it is almost entirely a preoccupation with one's own feelings. This might seem strange at first sight because romantic love is, on the surface, very much concerned with the other person.

Both in literature and in fact, this phase of romantic love can also be associated with bouts of anxiety and depression. The loving feelings may even be experienced as a form of agony and yearning. Romantic writers very often talk of 'the agony of being in love' and in a sense suffering and tragedy are often an integral part of romance. Some women unfortunately never grow out of this phase and remain tragedy queens, as it were, all their lives. They have perfectly acceptable and enjoyable relationships yet spoil them by creating traumas and tragedies which they feel are necessary to their concept of romantic love.

So, it can be seen that the phase of romantic love is a learning one. Learning to love is much like learning any other skill; just as adolescents have to learn social skills, they have to learn the skill of love. Because it is immature love, it is often described as 'calflove' or 'puppy love' but this misses its importance. Unless one uses this stage as a foundation, one cannot build the love structure an adult needs. Parents should never make fun of or put down their teenagers in this stage of puppy love – the teenager needs to go through it.

Most people, however, progress to other relationships and, it is to be hoped, begin to get some idea as to what sort of partner would really suit them. Such a relationship once again releases romantic feelings, but now they are simply one component of the more complex emotional and sexual reactions of the chosen partner. Ideally the romantic portion of the relationship should be encouraged to emerge slowly so as to allow realistic assessments to be made. Romantic love then becomes increasingly added to the relationship rather than being its starting-point. In this way the objection that love is blind can be overcome.

## Romance in marriage

Usually, the romantic portion of love declines as a marriage continues. Some people (especially women) interpret this as meaning that love itself has gone from the relationship and this can start a search for a new lover or even a divorce. In other cases the woman who feels this may meet the deficiency she is experiencing partly by addiction to media accounts of romance (in romantic novels, for example) and partly through her children in whom she invests over-romantic feelings. Men often try to ignore their disappointment about the loss

*Spontaneous displays of affection and romance can occur anywhere at any time in a loving and co-operating relationship.*

of romance and either become involved in affairs of the 'my-wife-doesn't-understand-me' type or take up compensatory pursuits such as absorbing hobbies or more work. Each partner may attempt to punish the other, using sex as the weapon, and the ultimate consequence can be that the real love in the relationship is in fact eroded, even though it was still there at the beginning of the problem. More couples should understand the link between romance and sex and how to put it in perspective so that its natural decline is not blamed unrealistically.

As we have said elsewhere, a well-developed man-woman relationship consists of several roles. One, and an important one, is the lover role. The romantic-love portion of their love for each other can easily be kept alive when they are functioning in the lover role. When a loving couple are making love they can recapture this late-adolescent phase of emotional development and again immerse themselves temporarily in the intense and passionate expressions of feelings of love, valuation of the other and commitment. We shall see later how important this is. After all, each time we make love we go back in time to our courtship days when romantic love played an important part in our lives. Regular top-ups of romance during love-making can be all that most couples need to keep romance alive in their lives.

Many married women complain of the lack of 'warmth' in their relationship, and many men wonder where the girl who loved them so intensely and of whom they have so many happy memories has gone. Obviously, talking can resolve the problem but deeply romantic feelings cause many people embarrassment after adolescence and in any case if one partner has to tell the other what to do to show romantic love, they may feel that the very fact of having to tell shows that it was absent.

Surprising though it may seem, *too much* romance can be a problem. The excessive expression of romantic loving feelings can mean that the individual is more in love with love (as are the characters in the late-adolescent phase of romantic love) than their partner. As we said earlier, some people never develop emotionally beyond this phase and this severely limits the love they can feel. It is a shame but a fact that these so-called romantics never really enjoy a natural, loving relationship and suffer accordingly.

So what are the answers? Perhaps the most important is for the partners to avoid assuming thoughtlessly that their notion of romantic love is identical with that of their mate. If each pays attention to what really gratifies the other in this area then they can build up an accurate impression of their individual needs. In this sense post-marital romantic love is not quite identical with the late-adolescent type, which is based purely on the notions of the individual. Post-maritally it needs to be adapted towards the needs of the partner.

*Chapter 7*

# Marriage

## As a relationship

It is probably true to say that with a few exceptions any marriage has the potential to be good. How marriage actually works out for any one couple is probably not so much governed by circumstances (which is what most couples believe) but by lessons learned in childhood and applied later. For example, a fear of the opposite sex, no matter how unconscious, can be learned early in life from indifferent or hostile parents or brothers and sisters of the opposite sex. Quite often a dominant, critical and punitive mother who wants (unconsciously) to take revenge on men generally for distress suffered in her own childhood brings up a son to be afraid of women. His male ego may be weak but he compensates by bullying his wife. She may even have been attracted to him in the first place by his 'masterful' personality without realising that it was really a disguise for weakness. By the time she finds out the truth the marriage is often on the rocks. Such a man dare not give in to a woman because in doing so he sees himself as being submissive to his mother. Such men often batter their wives.

## Wife battering

The main feature of wife battering is that the husband thinks he is unable to control certain issues in the home without resorting to violence. Such a man is usually a poor employee, poor partner, earns little and supports the family very inadequately. All of these are interlinked, of course, and an improvement in any one area makes battering less likely. Such couples have no talk 'safety valve' – they cannot discuss their problems. This often results in the wife nagging the husband until he gets so furious that he lashes out. Because communication is so poor the problem easily escalates to violence with other members of the family. Being brought up in this kind of home virtually ensures that the children are likely to copy it within their own marriages. The answer to wife battering is to get help straight away. Things rarely get better by themselves. There are refuges for battered wives all over the country now and the local Samaritans or Citizens Advice Bureau can help you find one.

Not every inadequate man need end up battering his wife. Many do very well if their wives understand the situation. A helpful wife will boost her husband's confidence and build him up at every opportunity, so undoing the damage his mother did. The strong can afford to be gentle whilst the weak have to be vicious to achieve their goals. A couple who have such problems often find that their whole relationship is enriched if one can modify the other's personality in this way.

From this rather dramatic example we can draw a general principle which holds good for marriage in general: that is that a couple should do everything they can to boost each other's ego (self-esteem) and never do anything that attacks the other's personality. Marriages are made between personalities and if they are attacked there may be nothing left.

## How to cope with rows

Many a woman says that her husband will not row with her and that as a result she cannot clear the air. This often happens because women tend to have superior verbal skills and, along with their female logic, defeat men, who then choose not to argue. There must have been a failure of communication somewhere along the line for things to have got this bad, and many a woman complains that her husband simply does not talk (or listen) to her enough. So great is her desire to clear things up that she provokes arguments. As a result she scares her husband off. Women are far better at assessing the underlying feelings in a relationship than are most men. Often a man does not see a problem as important and may not even see it *at all*. This does not mean that it does not exist. If one partner in a marriage has a problem, they both have it.

Women also tend to link problems to the whole relationship. For example, a woman may say that if her husband loved her he would not do or say a certain thing. It may be a simple misunderstanding of the ways in which he believes he should demonstrate his love, and once again this is usually conditioned by what he learned in childhood.

In such rows the woman, because she feels hurt or neglected may, because of her greater verbal skills, say more wounding things than she really feels simply to provoke a serious response from her

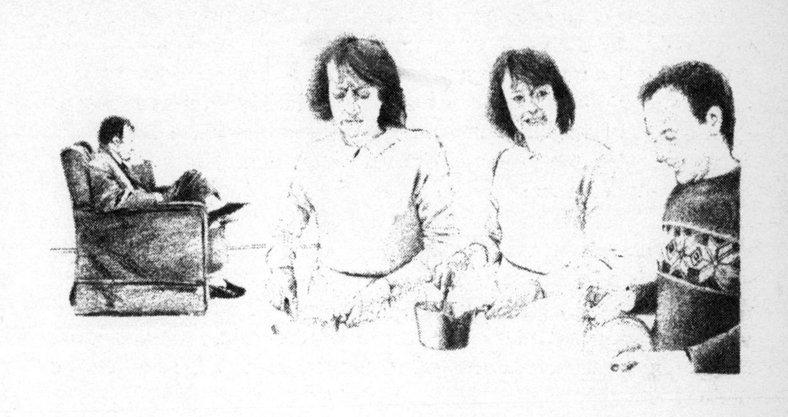

*A small change in attitude and behaviour can make a world of difference.*

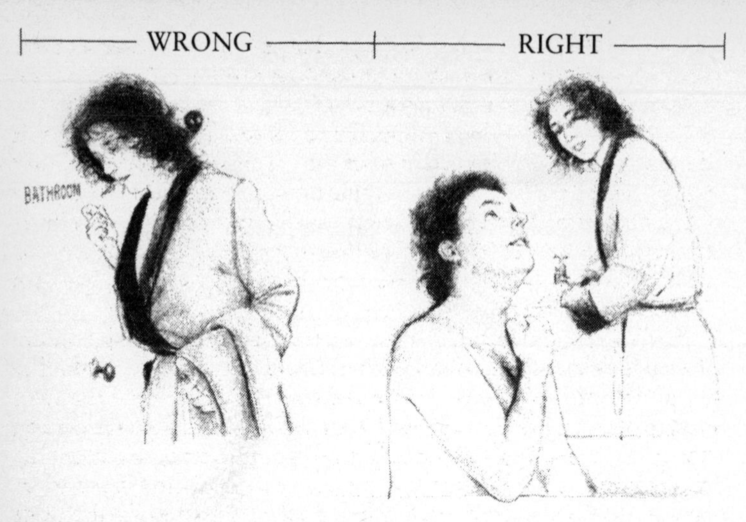


husband. Such over-dramatising of the argument would not be necessary if men were more sensitive to their wives' needs.

Many a man reverts to childhood when his wife becomes aggressive or seems to be provoking a row and responds as if she were a hostile mother. He sulks, mooches around the house, or goes out to escape. This does nothing to help because the woman still has not had her say and still feels scorned, overlooked, unloved, treated as worthless or whatever sparked off the row in the first place. She needs loving care and understanding but her husband, by behaving like a young boy, cannot hope to provide it. The underlying problem is thus not resolved. The next time a problem area is aired the couple, already on a plateau of tension, spark each other off more readily.

Often such hostility arises over 'no-go' areas within the marriage. Subjects as diverse as children's schooling, the woman's weight, his drinking friends, religion, oral sex and so on are out of bounds, skirted round and never actually discussed. One partner (or both) harbours strongly-held views, yet cannot get the other to discuss them or come to an agreement at all. Slowly these 'no-go' areas within the marriage grow in size and number until the couple are relating only in the most superficial way, skimming over the surface of life. As soon as any discussion gets valuable it hits a 'no-go' area and hostility or silence breaks out. Eventually such a couple end up saying little to each other.

Clearly no two people will agree on everything, but a loving friendship can withstand a fair amount of disagreement. There are usually no absolute answers to the problems being discussed and one person's views are worth about as much as another's. Many 'no-go' areas are not really serious anyway.

Once 'no-go' areas begin to intrude on a couple's life, sex often is the first casualty. Professionals working with marital problems never accept sexual problems at face value because they are so rarely the cause of marital disharmony. Sex is usually the injured bystander as the marriage crashes but in a society so over-concerned with sex it is understandable that people who go for professional help often complain of a sexual problem first.

Rows and an extension of 'no-go' areas within the marriage reduce the tenderness each feels for the other, and usually a woman is the first to go off sex. As a consequence the man progressively withdraws from the relationship, 'deloves' his wife and escapes into gardening, 'the boys', a time-consuming hobby away from home, or a considerable increase in work. The woman's fears that she is no longer loved, appreciated and wanted are confirmed for her too and the marriage spirals downwards.

By understanding how things can go wrong one can more easily find answers to prevent and cure the problems. At the first sign of emotional dis-ease within a marriage the 'unaffected' partner should say, 'Let's sit down and you tell me about it. You're obviously upset, I'll try to help.' The listener then allows the 'complainer' to get the problem off his or her chest without interruption and then negotiations start with real care and warmth. Such behaviour tackles troublesome situations early and major 'no-go' areas never get a chance to take root. Each person sees the other behaving in a way that is compatible with the way they think someone who 'really loves me' ought to behave, and such tolerance breeds tolerance in return. Quite quickly in a marriage run along the lines just described a fund of goodwill builds up and the couple can make concessions to each other on certain matters (that could easily have become 'no-go' areas), can overlook peccadilloes and can even delight in each other's shortcomings. In general, women are better able (or perhaps more prepared) to adapt to men in this way than vice versa but obviously there are exceptions.

If this course of action is not followed another category of rows may then emerge which is not primarily brought about by the apparent cause, which in turn becomes concealed and unresolved. It is at this stage that many couples seek professional help or see a solicitor about divorce. It takes a really skilled professional to find where the problems lie in such cases and all too often couples have the

## No-go Areas

*The growth of 'no-go' areas within a marriage can ruin even the best relationship.*

wrong (more superficial) problem treated only to return home to continue their unhappy lives. Often such professionals attach blame to one of the partners involved, but this can be very unfair because the answers are rarely clear-cut and the obvious 'offender' in the marriage is often the weaker and needs help more than (even implicit) condemnation.

Men and women have very different ideas as to which faults are killers of marriages. One survey found that women thought that selfishness and inconsiderate behaviour were the most important faults in their husbands and that men rated nagging and moaning top of the list. The old fears of sexual incompatibility, too many or no children, drunkenness and lack of trust, so commonly found to be problems in the past, have now virtually disappeared in favour of selfishness, money problems, conflicting personalities and jealousy among wives of husbands paying attention to things other than them.

But rather than simply rowing about these areas couples can use the technique known as 'shaping-up'. The idea behind this concept is that rather than falling out over minor areas of disagreement one makes a conscious effort deliberately to ignore them or to treat them neutrally. When the 'offending' partner behaves in a way which the other wants to encourage he or she is rewarded by signs of pleasure, affection, flattering comments and even sexual favours. This technique can also be used to modify sexual behaviour which a partner does not like.

## Sensual massage

When the communication system has broken down and sex has been abandoned, an attempt by one partner to resume sexual contact in order to try to get the marriage on its feet again is often sulkily rejected. Any trivial physical contact may then be viewed as an attempt to initiate sex and so also be rejected. The rejection is resented and the spiral continues downwards.

A possible way out of this that sometimes works is to try sensual massage. Because intercourse is not involved it can be accepted and can be a real bridge builder. In effect, it amounts to a return to the middle stages of courtship.

It is basically a type of massage performed first by one partner on the other and then the other way round. There is only one rule – the partner who is being massaged has to tell the other exactly what feels nice and what does not. The only goal is for the massager totally to devote him- or herself to pleasing the other, whatever it is that he or she asks for. Sensual massage is not genital. In fact we suggest that nipples, breasts and genitals are avoided.

The massaging is done in a warm room with both partners completely naked and baby oil or warmed massage oil perhaps containing an aromatic essential oil can be used. Take the phone off, put on some music you both enjoy and put a sheet on the floor. The key to really good sensual massage is that there must be constant feedback – at least for the first few times, until each knows exactly how to please the other. In a couple who massage each other several times a week, the needs or desires of one partner may change and, again, the change should be picked up and acted upon by the one who is massaging. Be careful that you do not fall into the trap of one partner always being the 'giver' and the other the 'receiver'. The one who finds it more difficult to 'receive' often needs help more than the other partner. It is very pleasant just to cuddle up together afterwards and go to sleep.

A couple doing this several times a week are making time for each other, caring about each other's responses and talking to each other more and, as a result, find it harder to be angry, especially over little things. Their quality of life is improved greatly as a result.

## Shifting roles

Marriage is more difficult to manage well than other situations in life because there are many roles involved in any one marriage and because the nature of the relationship keeps changing. Unlike many other social situations where roles are clearly defined, within marriage the roles are often shifting and confused. Which role is played at any one time depends both on deep internal needs and desires and on the circumstances operating in the marriage at the time.

Four basic roles are seen in most marriages. The first is the *mother-son role.* It seems to be a feature of female behaviour from childhood onwards for a woman to want to care for the things she loves. She expresses her love in very practical, often domestic, ways and wants to be loved in return for her efforts. If her caring and loving activities are ignored or rebuffed then she fears she is being taken for granted and bad emotional tensions build up. She interprets her husband's lack of appreciation as a lack of love for her. This caring she needs so badly to express is a form of mothering. Some men, as we have seen, cannot allow themselves to be dependent and they thereby deprive their partner of a major source of satisfaction. In reality all men need *some* mothering from their wives, but if this behaviour oversteps the mark and becomes bossy and overbearing as opposed to loving and caring, many men cannot cope, and they rebel. Such marriages often take on a new lease of life if the man is ill or has a coronary, for example. Now his wife is really needed in her mothering role. She comes into her own and her husband loves her for it. Even when her husband is dead and her children gone, many such women channel their mothering role into caring for others or for animals.

The arrival of children disturbs the mother-son role in many marriages and this is why so many problems arise around the time of a first baby. Many a woman is quite happy mothering her husband in the early years of marriage. Once a baby comes along though he has to share this mothering with someone else and many men become jealous. They may become depressed, have an affair, or indulge in other disruptive behaviour. However if both partners become involved in caring for the child whilst making an effort to maintain their own relationship the marriage is actually enriched.

The other side of the mother-son coin is the *father-daughter role.* Some women do not believe in the worth of this role – asserting that it simply amounts to men being dominant and paternalistic. This view unfortunately deprives their men of a vital function they feel the need to fill in relation to their wife, that of pleasing, protecting and providing for her. Many marriages work for a good deal of the time in this role without friction, and the father-daughter role-play is implicit rather than obvious. This works well because the man is not endlessly dominant and the woman endlessly submissive – there is a shifting dominance within the overall roles. Some women, once they have children, start to call their husband 'Daddy' along with the children. Such women have reverted to the blissful stage of their own lives when they are happy to be loved unconditionally by their father, whose rules and regulations they accepted, but within the confines of which they knew they could get their own way most of the time. They flirt with their husbands continuously, whilst at the same time regarding them as someone whom they can trust always to love them unconditionally.

Some women find such a picture quite disgusting but most of those who adopt this role find that it suits them best. In this role they boost their husband's self-confidence and he in turn feels strong and behaves better both to them and to their children.

The third, and probably most basic, role is the *friendship role.* This is discussed later.

The fourth role is the *lover role.* The emotional aspects of loving are discussed elsewhere as are the physical aspects but here we ought to look at the damage that is done even before the couple meet and marry. We saw in Chapter 1 how Western child-rearing tends to make sex out to be rude, nasty or even dirty, and then we wonder why it is that teenagers start on their careers as lovers with negative ideas. It is important because the way we behave in the lover role greatly influences the way we behave as parents, and the vast majority of married couples have children.

A lot of research has proved beyond doubt that a woman's sexuality is inextricably tied up with her mothering abilities and vice versa. A woman who is at ease with her body, who is orgasmic, and enjoys intercourse and her relationship with her husband, also finds childbirth, breastfeeding and the rearing of babies easier and more enjoyable. This all has deep implications for the way she thinks of and cares for babies. A woman who is a good lover is almost always a good mother, so it makes great sense for couples to work together to ensure that the woman enjoys all aspects of her sexuality so that her confidence and enjoyment of them are boosted. Researchers have shown that some women experience clitoral enlargement whilst giving birth and may consciously experience birth and breastfeeding as sexually arousing. A woman's sexuality is not simply manifested by her intercourse performance; it is a continuous facet of her personality, expressed by her clothes, the way she walks and sits, her hairstyle, the way she cares for and feeds her babies and what she does with her husband. To confine the concept of a woman's sexuality to her performance in bed is to misunderstand the whole subject and to underestimate women as highly sexual creatures in everyday life. Most men are guilty on this count, at least to some extent.

So, being good lovers and encouraging each other in the lover role is very important, not only for immediate pleasure but also as a rehearsal for and reinforcement of the parenting role. A woman who is a good lover often behaves in a loving, motherly way towards her husband before and especially after intercourse and a man who is a good lover practices his powers of tenderness and affection, which can then be shared with his children.

## As a way of life

Marriage, or the close man-woman relationship that exists whether or not it has been dignified by the marriage ceremony, can be an enormously strong bond. It can withstand long-term illness, mental and physical disabilities, sexual deprivation, addiction to alcohol in one partner, unemployment in the breadwinner and so on. All of this suggests that a good marriage is much more than simply a long-term commitment to sexual exclusivity. We see marriage much more as an enduring friendship – an alliance between a man and a woman who work together as friends – in a self-contained team of two.

Unfortunately, the concept of a husband and wife being each other's closest friends seems rather odd to many, so it is hardly surprising that once the romantic feelings of the first year have died away, some couples complain that they have little left. There is evidence that where a woman sees her husband as her best friend, she feels understood and says that things get better year by year. She finds she can tell him anything, even things she cannot relate to her closest woman friend. No direct similar evidence exists in respect of men but what men are known to think of a good relationship leads us to assume that they see things in much the same way as women.

As in any close alliance there are bound to be 'frictions of association' – troubles caused by being together for much of the time, but in a good marriage these are kept to a minimum by a sensible division of labour between the sexes which is roughly the same in all cultures. Although many of us curse the lot of our own sex from time to time, wishing we were the opposite sex, in a good marriage the tasks that have to be done are divided up according to who does them best and the marriage not only survives but thrives.

Once we start to think of the man-woman relationship as a kind of super-friendship it begins to alter the whole subject of sex. It is possible to have sex with anyone but there are very few people who could be life-long friends.

Once a friendship is formed it is in the interests of the couple to please each other and to respect the interests and feelings of the other. So, for example, the husband of a woman who does not like fellatio (oral sex with a man's penis) respects this restriction and does not use it to 'prove' that she does not love him. If, then, one day she decides to try it with him, yet cannot go through with it, the 'loving friend' type of husband is not angry but would see her effort as endearing and, for her, a sign of love.

## Affairs

Affairs are said to be increasingly common, though all the statistics about their prevalence are misleading because affairs tend to be under-reported in surveys. The impression of clinicians working in this field, however, is that women are as likely, or nearly as likely, as men to be, or to have been, in such relationships and that possibly by the age of, say, fifty-five around three-quarters of married individuals will have been involved in one or more affairs, although they may not have gone as far as intercourse. In fantasy, if not in fact, virtually everyone will have had several.

A few people find a kind of sexual refuge in marriage and have little practical sexual interest in other members, of the opposite sex, but for most marriage does not reduce the attraction of others. This attraction may be expressed only in fantasy, friendship, or mild flirtation with limited sexual aims, but it is still there. A few immature people are incapable of making serious attempts at sexual commitment in *any* relationship, and so affairs continue regardless of marriage. Some people, by divorce and remarriage, perhaps several times, 'legalise' their affairs in a way that would not really have been possible in the past, except for rather special cases such as Henry VIII.

A few couples who feel they cannot tolerate the sexual restrictions of marriage reach an agreement which specifies that extra-marital relationships are acceptable provided that the partner be informed, although many people are inclined towards the opposite in that they do not mind their partner having such a relationship as long as they do not know of it. Either way, it is perhaps a better alternative to repeated divorce, especially if the individuals believe that their relationship is worth preserving.

Today, the true mistress or lover is a rare creature but many men (and increasingly women) who find one sex partner for life insufficient, look outside marriage for variety. It is scarcely surprising that affairs are as common as they are in the absence of any culturally acceptable way of coping with a need for sexual adventure, given that so many couples are reluctant or unable to increase the amount of sexual adventure in their relationships. The 'hole-in-the-corner affair' is intrinsically dishonest because of the deception it involves. Such deception, especially if maintained over a long period, must destroy something in the marriage. Whatever some people may wish, most individuals find it impossible to sustain a solely one-to-one relationship for the whole of their (increasingly long) married lives, but so far society has not found a better way of coping with this reality other than the rather shabby system that is reluctantly accepted today.

For most people an affair is simply an adventure and is never meant to replace their marital relationship – in fact, most individuals involved in an affair, when asked, say that they want *both* the new partner *and* their spouse. Of course a few of those having affairs *are* on the look-out for new partners because of underlying dissatisfaction with their marriages or they even hope to find their ideal.

This puts the finger on the real difficulty. In our culture marriage carries the implication, and even the promise that the relationship will be sexually exclusive. In an age of efficient contraception old objections about reproduction (and inheritance) confusion which could result from extra-marital sex have lost some of their validity. Increasingly marriage is being seen as a relationship which does not necessarily confer exclusive ownership rights on the partners and this freedom to 'be oneself' emotionally and in other ways has brought with it the dangers of too much sexual openness. This may well change as AIDS affects us all.

A related aspect is the view that if a man marries a woman she has the right to be maintained by him for the rest of her life, regardless of separation or divorce. Views on this are also slowly changing. Although many people will find these changes unacceptable for themselves and will try to run their marriage on traditional lines, which is fine if they have a like-minded partner, the changes in attitude which are now occurring could actually strengthen marriage as an institution because extra-marital sex would not be seen as a mortal blow to the relationship. In the past such an event often meant that the marriage was brought to an end by the wronged partner. Greater toleration may be good for marriage overall.

Conventional attitudes are perhaps harmful in another way to some good marriages. Many people (especially women) are brought up with the belief that it is wrong to have sex with more than one member of the opposite sex. This leads to what is termed serial monogamy; that is, over a period of time a woman will have intercourse with several partners, abandoning one before starting with the next. Combined with the belief that you can have intercourse only with someone you love this paves the way for unnecessary divorce.

The motives lying behind affairs are many. They include the search for ideal love, sex or romance; curiosity, especially in those who had little or no experience before marriage; confirmation of attractiveness in women or masculinity in men; poor sexual self-esteem for whatever cause; sexual boredom; experimentation; revenge on the partner (even if the affair is not made known to him or her); the sudden opportunity to fulfil a fantasy; and testing to see if a sexual problem in the marital relationship is due to the partner or oneself. Promiscuity as such is not a frequent cause although an unfilled sexual need is commonplace. Travel, holidays, being away from home ground, alcohol and parties all have the potential for leading to affairs, but these are often brief. With increasing numbers of women working there are more opportunities for intimacy with the opposite sex to occur.

More permanent affairs are a greater threat to marriage because of the possibility that the relationship could become more than sexual and might turn into a full-blown love-affair. Here, a woman, to reduce her guilt about her sexual activities, often emphasises the love aspect of the relationship and, if she believes (as is common) that it is possible to love only one person, then divorce may be the end result. In such cases the original relationship (or relationships if both are married) may be destroyed, only to be replaced by one which is not much better and may even be worse. If both parties were to make their intentions clear to each other at the start of the affair such situations could often be avoided. In these circumstances men may mislead women by initially displaying more emotion than they really feel so as to get them to agree to sex and women may mislead men by behaving more sexually than they really feel so as to establish an emotional relationship. As in most facets of man-woman relationships, greater honesty between the sexes could avoid unhappy outcomes.

Most affairs are probably kept secret, unless they are discovered, and the realisation that the marital partner may be involved in an affair can lead to destructive suspiciousness even in a good relationship. In some instances, however, a partner who cannot have intercourse for one reason or another may, out of consideration, urge the other to have an extra-marital relationship. In other instances the reason is sexual weariness with one partner on the part of the other; an attempt to reduce guilt about having had an affair; the desire on the part of one partner thus to obtain justification for an affair they intend; or, occasionally, to have the partner reveal in minute detail what happened as a form of vicarious sexual pleasure.

More uncommonly, one partner wants to be present and participate as an additional stimulation. This leads to troilism in which an additional man or woman may be added to the couple's sexual relationship. A man, for example, may be aroused by watching his wife undertake lesbian acts with another woman, and may then want to have intercourse with them both. However, sometimes it is the wife who enjoys watching her husband have sex with another woman or vice versa.

An extension of this is into wife-swapping on a casual or permanent basis. This could be called a joint affair if it is permanent, since the husband and wife are both involved. Oddly, such openness can lead to jealousy; for example, the husband may become jealous because he believes, or even sees, that his wife is more sexually aroused by the other man than by him. It is not therefore surprising that 'swinging' as it is called, is in decline and is destructive to relationships. AIDS too has altered the picture.

For some people the very secrecy of an affair is part of its attraction – they say they find 'naughty' sex more satisfying than 'legal' sex. This is understandable because 'naughty' and 'sex' are notions which are commonly combined during childhood. It is also understandable in those who have been brought up in the belief that they will not be loved if they behave sexually. So they subsequently behave (with the person they love) in an inhibited way because of the fear that they will no longer be loved if they reveal their real sexual needs. For some people sex with a stranger is infinitely more gratifying, since they are more uninhibited.

Perhaps the biggest single dilemma facing the person who is having an affair is whether or not to tell. There are no easy answers to this but it is probably wise to err on the side of *not* telling. 'Coming clean' may make you feel good (or even 'self-righteous'), but it can have a devastating effect on your partner who, especially if it comes as a surprise, may react more dramatically than you imagine. Some people tell in order to take revenge on their spouse or in an attempt to jolt them into better behaviour. As we have said, telling is rarely the best course. Few people really want their spouse, once told, to accept the situation with equanimity – simply because this would show that he or she does not care about the relationship. A massive over-reaction with talk of divorce or even suicide is not uncommon and can permanently damage the relationship. Discretion, secrecy, lying and subterfuge then are the prices one has to pay to keep an affair from one's spouse and for many these outweigh the advantages of the affair itself.

The discovery that one's partner is, or has been, involved in an affair is usually a shattering blow – sometimes more to one's self-esteem than anything else. However, calm discussion should reveal whether it resulted from a real dissatisfaction within the marriage or was simply an adventure. If it is the former, it may be an opportunity to sort the marriage out, perhaps with professional help; if it is the latter, there would seem to be little point in any extreme reaction.

Apart from the suspiciousness, jealousy, distrust, anger, divorce and unwanted pregnancy which may result from an affair, the most solid objection is probably that of sexually transmitted disease (STD).

If everyone followed the traditional pattern of no sex before marriage and no sex with anyone else afterwards then STDs would die out in the heterosexual community.

For all the hurt and harm they can cause affairs continue now as in the past. Changing attitudes towards marriage and affairs, no matter how unacceptable to some, are, at least, one answer, even if not the complete one, to the problem of divorce. That the acceptance of affairs could reduce divorce is a total reversal of the traditional view of marriage but for some it works.

## Sexual difficulties

See Chapter 13.

## Marriage in name only

Some marriages, of course, endure for the sake of the children, for financial reasons, or because of strongly held religious views. The couple have, to all intents and purposes, secretly divorced or agreed to get a divorce at a later date. Such a couple usually maintain a façade of friendliness but satisfy their needs for love, companionship and sex elsewhere. This sort of marriage is remarkably common. Clinical experience suggests that only about a third or a quarter of marriages are what most would call successful. However some research indicates that the proportion of totally satisfactory marriages may be as low as a tenth.

A large number of unsatisfactory marriages continue for very obscure reasons. The partners remain involved with each other but bitterly and almost all areas of conflict remain unresolved for years. Possibly these are good marriages that have simply moved in the wrong direction as we described in the previous chapter. People involved in these marriages have a most unsatisfactory way of life and often have physical or psychosomatic illnesses as a result. Many are on drugs that alter the mind and many are frankly depressed. Psychosexual and marital counselling can help. Having said this though, there is no doubt that a few couples actually seem to thrive on friction as a way of life.

This brings us to the subject of the 'good' and the 'poor' marriage. A marriage is good if the couple think it is, even if it seems poor by comparison with others. A good example is the marriage between two sexually inhibited people. Such people please each other yet may never have discussed their attitudes towards sex. Before marriage they do little (if anything) sexually and afterwards intercourse may well be infrequent and of poor quality. In some cases these couples hardly ever have intercourse at all, yet are quite happy. This way of life suits them and that is all that matters.

## The phases of marriage

Marriage, like all human endeavours, never stands still; it evolves with time.

### *Phase one*

This first phase lasts until the couple start a family. Changing homes, friends and life-styles to accommodate the marriage can be difficult. However, for many, the first few years spent together – with the wife working and no children – providing themselves with a home and preparing for a family, can seem, in retrospect, to have been the best years of their marriage. Sex is usually frequent and experimentation commonplace, but sexual difficulties arising from sexual inexperience and the lack of a will to learn are widespread. Many young women complain that their husbands do not do what they like most, that they are too rough and that they are selfish. In spite of all this most young couples at this stage say that they are happy sexually and that they look forward to their problems disappearing as they mature and get used to each other. The fact that the divorce rate is highest in this phase of marriage would appear to contradict what we have just said but, as we shall see, this is not as surprising as it at first seems.

Ideally, during this phase of married life the couple are learning to resolve conflict and should be getting used to communicating with each other before children come along. If the couple cannot sort out the problems of living together, tensions arise and anger, resentment, and misunderstandings are common.

During this stage some young people become ill physically or mentally, and depression is not at all uncommon. Once things begin to go bad, sex, rather than being the cause of the trouble as many couples think, becomes the victim. Provided the basic relationship is good, nearly all these early problems can be resolved by the couple themselves or with professional help.

All these adjustments take a long time and it is essential to allow plenty of time between getting married and having a first baby. Far too many couples have a baby so soon after marriage that they have hardly had time to get used to each other as partners, let alone as parents. In most couples it is the woman who starts putting on the pressure for a baby.

Whether this pressure comes about because of the intrinsic biological yearnings of women or whether it is the result of our apparently baby-centred culture is hard to say but the result is the same. The couple, who hardly know each other have to take another human being into account and have to adapt to quite different roles too soon.

Some young couples imagine, quite wrongly, that once the wife becomes pregnant all sex should cease. This is bad enough in a long-established relationship but in the first few years of marriage it can lead to trouble. After the birth, the nights of broken sleep and new-baby routines can stress even the mature married couple but they particularly take their toll on the recently married. The new mother needs plenty of help but the young husband, still seeing himself as a grown-up boy with a permanent live-in girlfriend, often is not ready or able to cope with new burdens. The woman, fearing that the baby will change her body for the worse (the vagina, stomach and breasts are now irrevocably altered in many women's views), fear that after only a few years of marriage her husband will go off her.

Is it surprising with all this going on that couples in their first seven years of marriage are so prone to divorce?

## *Phase two*

This lasts about twenty years, covering the period during which the children grow up and leave home. In general, dissatisfaction with marriage increases during this period and most couples tend to draw apart. Earlier problems that were not resolved are aggravated, intercourse rates fall, and experimentation declines. Ironically, sex now rears its head in a rather unexpected way. The man who, in the first years of marriage, felt he was getting less sex than he thought he needed (because his wife was inexperienced or reluctant), is now amazed to discover that she wants more than he can supply at a time when he is under increasing pressure at work and at home.

As the last sexual inhibitions are shed many women really come into their own sexually in their late thirties and forties. Some begin to worry about the menopause and what it will do to their attractiveness. Some women have a mad fling at this stage for fear that it will be their last chance before their charms fade. Often such women do so with their husbands, but others look elsewhere. Of course, there is no evidence that women are less sexy after the menopause – on the contrary, many blossom as never before although others feel that with their fertility gone they have no right to sexual pleasure.

Two useful signs that a woman of this age is looking outside her marriage for sex are the onset of effective dieting after many years of unsuccessful efforts and suddenly finding endless fault with their husbands. The latter is a commonly used way of 'de-loving' him because in our culture, if she still loved him she would not be 'free' to fall in love elsewhere.

A common factor that links the first two phases of marriage is that the two partners may not see themselves as equal in attractiveness and value. The more attractive spouses can come to see themselves as under-benefiting from the relationship and the less attractive ones as over-benefiting. Either way, couples often start to count the cost and this is a bad sign. The relationship no longer seems to be a good bargain, benefiting each equally. The under-benefited one becomes less willing to please and eventualiy starts having affairs, scarcely caring about the effect on the other partner. The over-benefited partner is less likely to object for fear of losing the (too good) spouse and is unlikely to have an affair to retaliate for fear of being totally abandoned. This is another reason why couples should be as nearly equal as possible in attractiveness as in all else.

## *Phase three*

This lasts from about the age of fifty until the death of one of the partners. It is usually a phase of togetherness and increasing satisfaction. The couple have no fear of pregnancy and their sex lives often improve. Unfortunately, some older couples still feel that sex is for the young and so do not enjoy sex nearly as much or as often as they could. Thankfully things are changing in the right direction as far as this is concerned. It is worth taking care not to lose the habit of intercourse if one partner has to go into hospital or is ill for a long period. It is also interesting to see that evidence suggests that an active sex life is linked to a long life. People of this age often have grandchildren who bring pleasure with few responsibilities (a rare combination in life) and no longer have to worry about being competitive at work. The man will have got as far as he is going to and is either settled in his career or is running up to or already in retirement.

Throughout all these three stages of marriage there is a biological need for attachment. In the good man-woman relationship this attachment grows, particularly at times of stress when the couple think about each other, want to be with each other, communicate distress to each other, and are comforted by one another. The bond that forms between long-married couples can be formidable. They tend to think along the same lines and seem to be 'one body' as described in the Bible.

## Types of marriage life-style

When two people live together for a long period, married or not and even if they are of the same sex, they need to work out some kind of structure which will enable them to function as a unit. Many marriage 'experts' have classified such relationships within marriage in great detail but because of shortage of space we will look here only at the four commonest types.

### *The patriarchal marriage*

This is the most common marriage structure today, even with the tremendous growth of women's power and influence. In this the woman looks to the man to be the stronger, the breadwinner, the leader (most of the time), the major decision-maker, and so on.

Surveys show that most women want (or have been conditioned into wanting) this type of marriage. Many women go about their lives very much as it suits them for most of the time whilst avoiding direct challenges to their husbands so that they feel patriarchal enough of the time to be happy. Undoubtedly many marriages thrive on this form of behaviour in the woman.

### *The board-of-directors marriage*

This type is increasingly common and is seen to some extent in all good marriages. In such a marriage there is a sensible division of labour (often in fact dictated by convention) and by and large decisions are made jointly after discussion. The person best at a particular task does it. There are certain areas of married life which men seem to tackle better than women and vice versa. This, of course, does not mean that women cannot mend cars or that men cannot make dresses but, on balance, given the way we are made and brought up, certain jobs remain culturally attached to each sex.

**Marriage Styles**

*Although the marriages shown here and on the next two pages look very different the couples may (or may not) be equally happy and fulfilled.*

PATRIARCHAL MARRIAGE.

BOARD OF DIRECTORS.

## *The marriage of equals*

In this the woman and the man are completely interchangeable in daily-living terms. Biological sex differences (except, of course, for reproductive functioning) are ignored. Couples who adopt this form of marriage seem to have more problems than others but, with careful arrangements for outside child care to enable the woman to work as an equal to her husband, a good working arrangement can be achieved. Such a marriage can work exceptionally well for child-free couples or the childless.

## *The role-reversal marriage*

With the increase in unemployment and the high earning potential of some women, it is occasionally economically necessary or sensible for the man to be the person who looks after the children and the home. Research shows evidence of social strain in this arrangement, but it can be made to work.

## *Alternating roles and dominance*

A good marriage is one in which the partners adopt the roles to which each is best suited, irrespective of whether they are traditionally deemed to be 'male' or 'female' functions. No conflict arises because such a couple adopt their respective roles in a reflex fashion.

None of this means that either party is intrinsically inferior or superior – when one partner is away or ill the family continues to run smoothly because the remaining partner can fulfil the role of the absent one with ease.

But given that our society has somewhat ingrained views about male and female roles in marriage and family life this changing around can be tricky to achieve, especially if either or both have problems accepting their 'opposite sex' characteristics. A man may, for example, be a better 'mother' on occasions than the woman, and she might be a better provider for the family. In a successful relationship such notions are easily coped with because neither sees the other as having won or lost in the value and worth stakes. Sometimes, of course, both may try to be dominant or passive and this reciprocity fails. This calls for considerable care in sorting out or power struggles ensue that can be damaging to even the best relationship.

Having said this, there are times when we have to allow our partner to be dominant or passive, even if it doesn't suit us ideally at the time.

ROLE REVERSAL.

This generosity of spirit is the hallmark of the couple who are sufficiently well balanced to be able to give and not count the cost.

In a well-balanced relationship no one keeps the score but the partners work together in tandem, building up each other's self-confidence and sharing the benefits equally. Such a couple's marriage, based as it is on mutual respect and friendship, improves as the years go by.

In whatever way society changes, it is extremely unlikely that marriage will go away. We sincerely hope it does not because experience suggests that it is the only hope for a sane future in our culture. The natural unit of humankind is a woman and a man complementing each other's skills, talents, resources – and happiness.

## Functions of marriage

Marriage, or any other close man-woman relationship, offers a whole range of wonderful options as a way of life. Provided expectations are not set too high and the couple keep their feet firmly on the ground, marriage can be a friendship; a source of attachment; an alliance against a hostile world; a source of companionship; a mutual admiration society; a therapy group of two; a work group with each member specialising in jobs they do best; a source of tender, loving care; a means of keeping adolescent romance alive; a secret society with its own language and history; a child-rearing group; and a means by which we can increase the love we feel for ourselves indirectly by putting someone else first in life.

Although marriage is a personal contract between two people it is also a social act because it is the way in which society chooses to organise men and women in family units to bring up children. Around the world different cultures have very different ways of organising family life but in the West we have arrived at the nuclear family in which, typically, two adults live alone with their children. The heart of this type of family structure is the parents, not only because they are the starting-point but also because they are the only consistent source of adult company for the children. The vast majority of people still think that children should ideally be raised within the context of marriage. Many young couples throughout the Western world live together, but once they decide to have children they usually get married.

There is no need to 'sell' marriage. It is as popular as ever even at a time when its failures are so apparent and seemingly inevitable. Of all those of marriageable age in the UK 95 per cent will be, are, or have been married at some time in their lives. Marriage is, unfortunately, still portrayed as some kind of fairy-tale ideal rather than the reality of two people living together and sharing their lives for a very long time. The thing is that today, with age expectancy rising all the time, a couple married in their twenties can expect to be together for fifty years or longer, which is more than twice as long as they would have only a hundred years ago.

Statisticians and analysts looking at the mid-life peak in divorces (second only to the first-five-year peak) suggest that it could be a sort of natural break point for many people. After all, they argue, had they lived a few centuries ago they would have been 'divorced' by death.

Many, if not most people, (and especially girls) go into marriage with expectations that are far too high. What most people do not realise is that by idealising marriage as an institution they trivialise the man-woman relationship. This comes about because it is intrinsic in our culture to regard marriage as the *ideal* manifestation of the man-woman relationship. Until recently it was the only social structure within which men and women could enjoy each other's company *and* have intercourse. Reliable contraception and the women's movement have changed all that, probably for ever, and now most people don't get married *solely* to have intercourse or to have a close, meaningful relationship with someone of the opposite sex. Even so, most people still see marriage as their preferred life-style, even if children are not involved. The one in ten couples who live together in the UK (many with children) as if they were man and wife without in fact being so go to show how conventional we all are, even in these so-called enlightened times.

## Why marriages go wrong

Marriage has many enemies today. The politicians and legislators formalise it and constrain it; the churches impose rules to try to regulate it yet few adherents to their faiths live by them; and so on. The greatest of all enemies of marriage is society itself. In a world in which we change our cars every couple of years and move home every seven, is it surprising that we have come to look at life through 'disposable' spectacles? Of course there were bad marriages in the past but most partners stayed together, sometimes in a state of armed neutrality but often simply because they realised that the grass would not necessarily be greener on the other side of the hill. Easier divorce has undoubtedly ended a lot of very unhealthy marriages, but it has also given a couple, with too high an expectation of marriage as an institution and of each other as individuals, a way out which is sometimes too easy.

Research shows that most people are no happier once they are divorced than they were within an unsuitable marriage and the best thing to do is almost certainly to patch up existing marriages whenever possible. After all, presumably the couple must have had a certain amount going for them at some stage or they would not have got married at all. Having changed or having fallen out of love are not necessarily good reasons for divorcing. Professional help to keep them together (especially when children are involved) is the best prescription in our view but, of course, better education for marriage is the best preventive.

If there are no children, the couple is freer to split up but even so there are very real pains caused by the loss of someone one has loved and been loved by. Divorce may be *technically* easier today, but in human terms it is every bit as hard and probably worse, especially for women. A century ago, one third of women of marriageable age were not married and had no opportunity to be. Today, over 90 per cent of women are married (or have been). Life is far from a bed of roses for the unmarried older women – at the very least there are considerable social and personal disadvantages.

When one considers the tremendous amount of goodwill, excitement and appreciation of the opposite sex there is in the teens, it seems incredible that things should go so disastrously wrong for so many marriages. The truth is that the trouble starts much earlier than this. All through childhood we are rather poor as a society at helping the sexes enjoy and understand each other.

Wherever the blame lies we need to change things for our children and their children. We need to reappraise for ourselves the long-held views of the man-woman relationship and question them logically. If the long-held beliefs and prejudices do not stand up they should be rejected, just as one rejects other illogical facets of life. We cannot fight Nature, which intended that men and women should get on well together and form bonds to give children a stable and loving environment in which to grow up.

When looking at marriage as a social institution we have, unfortunately, no way of defining 'good' marriages. Divorce is a measure of failed marriages, but in between the extremes of these and the good marriages are countless millions of ailing marriages. It has been estimated that for every divorce (about one in three marriages) there is a similar number of poor marriages which are sick but not terminally ill. Even though the divorce rate is so high, there is evidence that many so-called 'good' (not divorced) marriages are less than ideal. This is in itself a cause for real concern.

People's attitudes vary according to when you talk to them. Many people are desperately unhappy with their marriage one month or year and content the next. One survey found that over 80 per cent of women said that given their time again they *would* marry the same man. In another survey 75 per cent of married people said they had seriously thought about divorce at some time. These two supposedly contradictory findings are, in fact, not incompatible. Contact with young couples suggests that the numbers of good marriages among the young are rising, so perhaps the divorce rate will fall soon.

## What to do when marriage goes wrong

Probably about two out of three marriages have serious problems at some time although, as we have seen, only half of these will end in divorce. So what can someone who is worried about his or her marriage do?

### *Talk it over between yourselves*

If you have bought this book and read this far you will already have learned enough to have answered some of your main problems (we hope!) and throughout the rest of the book you will find answers to many others, which you will be able to discuss with your partner. Ignorance of the facts is only one area of trouble, albeit an important one. Feelings are the biggest problem when things go wrong and often one cannot share one's feelings about someone else with them. At this point a third party becomes almost essential.

### *Talk to a close, trusted friend*

Don't go around sharing your marital and relationship problems with just anybody or you will receive so much conflicting and unprofessional advice that you will be even more confused. Also, it may feel embarrassing for you and your partner when things improve. Seek out a trustworthy friend and talk things over rationally and confidentially. Bear in mind that a friend will tend to take your side because he or she likes you and will not want to offend you. A true friend will tell you the bad news along with the good, but such discussion can put intolerable stress on the friendship and may even kill it completely. Because there are so many problems with all this, lots of people do not confide their marital problems to friends or family but go straight to professionals.

## *Talk to a professional*

Unfortunately, in the UK we do not have a tradition of specialist care for marital and sexual problems. Those who can help professionally are:

**Your general practitioner**
He or she will probably have no specialist training in this field but should be quite helpful as a result of dealing with similar problems time and time again. A general practitioner can rarely spare much time but can sometimes refer you to other people who are more expert and have more time.

**Marriage guidance counsellors**
The worst thing about these otherwise helpful people is their name. The word 'guidance' is an historical quirk, but today they do little 'guiding' in the old-fashioned sense. Partly to recognise this fact the UK Marriage Guidance Council has changed its name to Relate. They are not in business to save marriages come what may, but to offer a realistic service to the married, the single, the divorced and separated, homosexuals, and anyone who needs personal counselling. These counsellors are all trained but are not specialists in the medical sense of the word. Their training is fairly restricted, and they are taught not to tell clients what to do. They work in forty-to-fifty minute time slots, which many people find too short to be really useful. Most marriage guidance counsellors are middle-class women and this puts some people off going to them. Having said this they do see every class of society and nearly as many men as women. Many of the commoner and uncomplicated marital and sexual problems can be dealt with by them and Relate Marriage Guidance also has centres which can offer more specialised sex therapy and group sessions. Marriage guidance counsellors charge very modest fees indeed. The address of Relate Marriage Guidance is listed at the end of the book.

**Psychosexually trained doctors and psychiatrists**
Psychosexual medicine is a fairly new branch of the medical profession in the UK and at the moment has attracted very few practitioners full time. The majority of 'experts' working in this field are consultant psychiatrists who, because of their understanding of psychological

and emotional problems, tend to deal with sexual problems too. Many do not particularly want to deal with sexual problems and their patients share their reluctance. Few people with sexual or marital problems *are* mentally ill, and psychiatrists are doctors who deal mainly with mental illness. Going to a psychiatrist still has something of a stigma attached to it and there is always the suggestion (not from the doctor, of course) that one might actually have something 'wrong' with one's personality. A few psychiatrists offer psychoanalysis for such problems but only a tiny fraction of 1 per cent of all marital problems need or receive true psychoanalysis.

**Self-help and voluntary organisations**

Many of the self-help organisations that offer counselling services are listed at the back of the book. You will see that many of these specialise in specific areas; so be careful which one you contact so as to be sure of getting the best possible help. Many such organisations have trained psychologists (who are not doctors but are trained in the normal workings of the mind) on hand. Psychologists can actually be more helpful than doctors in many cases because more often than not individuals with sexual or relationship problems are not *ill* and do not need a medical mind to sort them out. The strength of the non-medical specialist is that the individual does not go along thinking that there is a magic operation or bottle of pills to answer his problems.

**Sex therapists**

These are rare creatures in the UK although some of the above groups offer some kind of sex therapy in a limited way. The vast majority of the 'treatment' of marital and sexual problems is done by talking and listening and by the partners discussing things they have learned when they go home. All professionals can hope to do is dispel some ignorance, get the couple talking again, help give them insight into their problems, show that they are not alone (millions of others have been down the same path before) and that they, the professionals, care enough to listen and really to try and help. Once they have recognised at least some of these things most couples are ready to work hard between consultations to rebuild their marriages.

A small percentage of couples (or individuals) need more specific physical help with sexual problems. A woman who has never had an orgasm, for example, can, by having the blocking anxieties instilled in childhood removed, have her inherent capacity to do so restored to her; an impotent man or one with premature ejaculation can be helped; and couples with similar problems can be shown how to overcome them. Sex therapy is often highly effective and results can be obtained remarkably quickly for most problems.

None of these helpers can work miracles for a marriage. The couple has to want the treatment or counselling to work and they have to be prepared to put a lot of themselves into it. Results can be quick but rarely are – it usually takes several sessions to make any impact on a problem and progress is then dependent upon the willingness and ability of the partner to change and adapt to the suggestions made by the counsellor. The best time to catch any marital or sex problem is in the early stages.

## The truth about divorce

Divorce rates have been increasing since the end of World War II – as divorce laws have eased. The rate increased by three times in Britain between 1965 and 1975 and by two and a half times in the US over the same period. The troubles that wreck marriages, it has been found, usually start early. One study found that the problems became apparent in the first year in well over a third of marriages even though the couples struggled to save the marriage.

In the US there is an impression that divorce is a lower-class 'disease' that has been caught by the middle classes, but in Britain it is thought to be a middle-class 'disease' that is spreading down. Today divorce is seen equally across all the socio-economic classes.

In the US in 1970 the average length of marriage at divorce was six and a half years, but in Britain the average time has remained stable since 1965 at about thirteen years. The countries with the highest divorce rates are the USSR (where an enormous number of marriages end in the first year) the US, Hungary, Egypt and Denmark. England now leads Europe in the divorce league tables.

Those who divorce very early and very young (because they have made a 'mistake' or fallen for someone else) usually fare well and by their late twenties cannot remember much about their previous partner. These really cannot be called marriages in the true sense of the word. Strange as it may seem, marriages that have gone on for forty or fifty years can sometimes also be painlessly dissolved because the couple have spent such a long time drawing apart and 'de-loving' each other.

Between these two extremes lie the vast majority of divorces –

those between people who have lived and loved for some years and have children, usually still at home. In Britain, 75 per cent of divorces involve families with children under eighteen, and in the USA during the years 1972–5 a quarter of a million children were living in families affected by divorce. This figure is much higher now. It is impossible accurately to assess the harm done to the millions of children around the Western world affected by divorce but several surveys show that it is often very severe, as we shall see.

A few people experience an enduring feeling of elation at being rid of their troublesome and unsatisfactory relationship but these are rare. For the vast majority divorce is extremely painful and many describe it as a sort of living death.

Many studies have shown that people do not realise how awful divorce really is. Perhaps the most universally experienced feeling is one of overwhelming *loneliness*. There are class differences here. The lower social classes, with their independent substructure of friends and more relatives living close by, usually suffer less because these continue after the divorce. The middle-class couple works and plays as a couple more and their friendships outside tend to collapse after a divorce.

Long marriages are usually the most painful to break and many such couples feel exactly the same as if they had been bereaved. *Suicide* and suicide attempts are not at all uncommon. One US study found that suicide rates among divorced people were three times higher in women and four times higher in men than in their married peers. If the separated are added to the divorced as they should be, at certain times the suicide rate for the divorced can be ten times those of the marrieds. Young and middle-aged married men have the lowest rate of suicide in society but divorced men have the highest.

The divorced and separated are also a very illness-prone group. Of course there are the psychological and emotional problems including a sense of rejection, despair, loneliness and feelings of failure, protest, anger, guilt, anxiety and depression, and all of these can be bad enough to need treatment. One study found that marital problems were the factor most commonly associated with psychiatric illness and that women were more often affected than men. Many wives seek help for such problems within their marriage because they want professional reassurance that their husbands' claims that they are 'going mad' are wrong. All kinds of physical symptoms, including headaches, abdominal pains, painful periods, bouts of diarrhoea, palpitation, and very many others, can also be seen in those who are in the early phases of divorcing or separating.

One of the earliest casualties of all this disruption is sex. The pain of divorce extinguishes or impairs the sex drive, often for months.

Some individuals seem to give up interest in the opposite sex, perhaps thinking 'once bitten – twice shy'. Others live in passive hope that a new and perfect partner will come along, but others become frantically involved in the search for a partner. Rebound relationships may be formed which are worse than the original marriage. Perhaps all divorcing individuals should be offered counselling to help them avoid repeating earlier mistakes or committing new ones.

But marriage, as we have seen, is also a social act and it is the loss of this component that is extremely hard to bear. There is a lessening social stigma attached to divorce but, whatever society thinks, it will never be possible to extinguish all the sense of failure and shame. Much of the social stigma comes from the long-held view that divorce lets women down and somehow threatens marriage as an institution. To some extent these are valid points but they have been over-stressed and in today's world are no longer nearly as true as they were. The Church of England has the option to refuse, and the Roman Catholic Church actually refuses, to remarry divorcees in church – and this too further condemns and shames those involved. Clinical experience suggests that of the 50 per cent of marriages that are solemnised outside a church, many would like to have had a religious ceremony but could not because of the Church's ruling.

On a day-to-day basis things are not easy either. Married friends tend to fall away and on occasions even the divorced person's parents drop them. Just when people most need advice, help, support and company they often find these most difficult to come by. Add to this the conflicting feelings of love, hate, loneliness, missing the partner, efforts at reconciliation and so on and one can see how destructive and disruptive divorce is to the personalities involved.

Children can greatly add to the emotional problems. They provide endless excuses for the partner who did not want the break to phone with questions and problems about the children. This often keeps the wounds open longer than would otherwise be the case. The parents communicate through the children and learn about each other in this clandestine way.

All of this is so awful an experience for many couples that they pull back from the brink – about a quarter of all divorces filed are withdrawn. Of those who do go through with it one in ten say they would remarry their ex-spouse. Fewer than half of such remarriages are happy, according to one survey.

There are also the many practical problems of housing, money, moving, and child care. Divorce affects the pocket just as much as the heart and everyone involved is financially worse off. The basic problem is clear. Two households have to live on the money that previously supported one. The man will usually pay maintenance to his ex-wife. The amount will depend on the particular circumstances of the two parties and whether or not there are children involved. Because of the recent change in the law and the pressure to reduce the amount of time a man should be expected to support his ex-wife, it is advisable to consult a lawyer who can take individual circumstances into account before giving advice.

In our apparently child-centred society, many people worry about the effects of divorce on the children involved. It is quite difficult to find these out precisely because there are no really long-term studies. About 80 per cent of delinquents come from broken homes and a follow-up study comparing children from divorced families with those from non-divorced families found that four times as many boys and three times as many girls from the divorced-family group had to go to reform schools; 20 per cent of the men were convicted of a felony by the age of fifty (compared with 9.9 per cent of the rest of the population); and that alcoholism was three times higher among women from divorced parents. In the USA, researchers feel that the

*All too often the 'deserted' partner fantasises about the idyllic life the other must be leading. Realities are often harshly different.*

poverty caused by divorce is as much to blame for the delinquency rates as the divorce itself. What seems to be more important for the delinquency figures is the after-care by parents. One study found that delinquency rates were related to a lack of visiting by the father and showed the importance of good relationships with the stepfather.

The conclusions of all the research are not clear-cut. Is an unhappy home with fighting parents worse for children than one in which the parents get divorced? A 'bad' after-divorce is most upsetting; a 'good' after-divorce perhaps has no serious long-term effects; and the effects of a conflict-filled home are no doubt worse than a good divorce. Unfortunately, it is often very difficult to organise a good divorce, even with the best will in the world.

Things are very difficult for mothers who run a family single-handed and one study found that in one third of such families total chaos was the norm. Anything from 50–60 per cent of children from one-parent families are, or have been, in the care of local authorities – a terrifying figure. Children of the recently divorced tend to have more tantrums and school problems, cry a lot, wet their beds, go back to early childhood behaviour, run away and so on. Children hate divorce and most say that their homes were happy before the divorce. They yearn for the departed parent and probably never get over the

loss. Children of divorced parents are far more likely to get divorced themselves than are normal children.

## Second time around

Because there are now so many people around in the remarriage market a whole new industry has arisen to cope with them. Marriage bureaux are, of course, not new but they are increasing in numbers and some deal with specialised groups of the population. Computer-dating is popular and singles clubs and those for the divorced and separated are commonplace. The middle-aged, once single again, have particular problems because, although the media often portrays them as having all the advantages of being single, the reality is very different. Confidence may have been lost and, as they are older, adjusting to a new potential partner is harder. Divorced women are often seen as a threat by married women and so may have difficulty in meeting suitable men.

However, it appears that about half of divorced people find their second partner through informal sources (friends and relatives) and half through formal ones. The sex lives of the divorced vary greatly – some abstaining because they feel so wretched about it all (though their feelings change over the months and a normal sex drive returns in most people) and others for religious and moral reasons. Those who can have sex only in the context of romantic love often remarry very quickly to legitimise their need for sex.

About 60 per cent of remarriages are to other divorced and separateds. This is probably no bad thing since they recognise the problems and pitfalls and can understand each other's situation better. They reassure each other that they are not unique in their problems, or unstable, and a bond is more likely to form as a result. Unfortunately, most people are unaware of the real reasons for their marriage failure and so make exactly the same mistakes again. Nearly half of all remarriages fail, mainly because people choose those who are similar to their first spouse (although this may not necessarily be obvious to those involved). Those who have been married twice have a divorce rate five times the norm.

*Chapter 8*

# Some sexual anatomy

Although many sex books seem to put too great an emphasis on the basic plumbing of sex, it helps to understand at least a little of the basic anatomy (structure) and physiology (working) of the sex organs, if only because so many men, women and adolescents worry so much about things that really need cause them no concern at all.

## The male sex organs

A man's sex organs seem at first sight to be rather simple, lying as they do mostly outside the body where they can be seen and handled. This is an advantage to boys who can easily see how they are made and do not have any concern about what is inside them in the way women do.

Basically a man's sex organs consist of his penis and his scrotum, which is a bag hanging from below the penis containing the testes that produce sperms and male hormones. These emerge from a mound of

*Cross section of male pelvis to show both internal and external sex organs.*

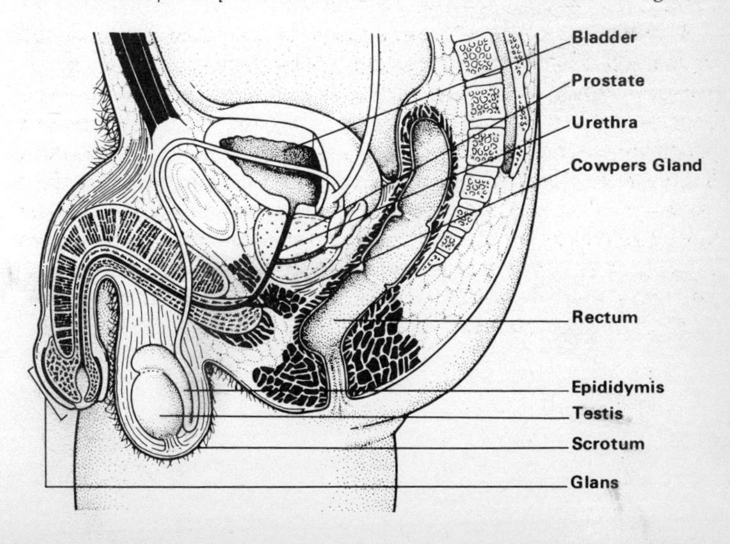

pubic hair that extends up to the navel. There are 'hidden' parts of the sexual anatomy – the prostate gland, for instance, which lies deep in the pelvis – but most men are not even aware that they have such a gland unless it begins to give trouble in old age.

The penis is a man's most obvious and talked about sex organ. Most men at some time or another have worried about the size of their penis, just as women concern themselves with their breast size. Surveys of women who have had many sex partners show that a man's penis size really does not matter when it comes to sexual satisfaction, but even though most men know this, about a third still wonder whether things wouldn't just be that little bit better if they had a longer or thicker penis. The size of an un-erect penis does not seem to matter very much because, apart from very small and very large ones (which are somewhat uncommon), the majority of penises erect to about the same length and circumference. Just as we cannot possibly say how often a couple 'should' have intercourse, we cannot say how long a penis 'should' be. Men's erect penises in fact vary in dimension less than other parts of their bodies.

There are all kinds of myths connecting penis size with the size of a man's body, his race, his amount of sexual activity, and so on but careful research has shown that all such old wives' (or husbands') tales are based on hearsay. There is no definite correlation between penis size and body size, and black men do not have longer penises than white men. One of the many clever things about the vagina is that it can adapt to a penis of any size and can do so painlessly and pleasurably. So the same woman can get exactly the same level of vaginal pleasure from a five-inch and a seven-inch penis.

The penis is a tube-like structure, but although it looks like one tube, it is in fact three. As you look down on the penis from the top there are two tubular masses of tissue under the skin called the *corpora cavernosa.* They are called *cavernosa* because they are cavernous in structure and can swell to accommodate large volumes of blood. The third cylindrical structure in the penis lies on the under surface and is called the *corpus spongiosum.* It ends in a bulbous swelling (the glans) which is the sensitive tip of the penis.

The corpora cavernosa swell when a man becomes sexually aroused and an erection occurs because more blood flows into the penis than is allowed to flow out. The penis has to swell and become rigid to fulfil its sexual function – that of placing semen high up in the vagina near the cervix.

The *urethra* is the tube that carries urine from the bladder to the outside. It terminates at the tip of the penis in a thin, slit-like opening.

Semen comes out of this same opening, so the urethra has a dual urinary and sexual function in men. During ejaculation the muscle at the base of the bladder, which is normally contracted except during urination, compels the semen to travel down the penis instead of entering the bladder. Certain medical disorders and some drugs can so alter this muscular mechanism that the man ejaculates semen into his bladder instead of down his urethra.

The shaft of the penis is covered with dark, loose skin which looks rather delicate and thin, and this skin continues below over the scrotum as a more wrinkled, thicker and hairier covering. The skin protrudes over the tip of the penis as a loose fold called the foreskin.

The *scrotum* is a bag of skin. The position of the testes in the scrotum is controlled by the cremasteric muscles which contract to pull the testes up towards the body when cold and relax to lower the testes into the scrotum when hot. By adjustment in the height of the testes their temperature is kept slightly lower than that of the rest of the body. This is important because normal sperm development can occur only if the testes are maintained at a temperature of about 2–3°F lower than that of the core of the body. Both fear and cold cause the cremasteric muscles to contract and so draw the testes nearer to the body. A mass of veins surround the artery that supplies the testis on each side, producing a heat-loss system which also helps to reduce the temperature of the testes. In this way the testes receive blood at a lower temperature than that supplied to the rest of the body.

Each testis is composed of several hundred little lobes, each of which contains a number of highly convoluted semeniferous tubules. These eventually straighten out and converge to form the five or seven ducts that open into the epididymis. The testis produces not only sperms but also makes hormones, the latter in special cells called Leydig cells. Testosterone is responsible for a man's sexual characteristics (his penis, his muscular body, beard growth, distribution of body hair, deep voice and aggression), affects his metabolism and his psychological behaviour, and also stimulates the formation of various chemicals in his reproductive tract, that ensure the production of sperms.

The formation of sperms takes about two weeks. When they are first produced they are not motile (do not move). After passing through the tubules that form the testis, the sperms are collected in the epididymis where they are stored. While they are here they mature further and become motile. From the epididymis the sperms enter the vas deferens, a fine, muscular tube, and travel along this up out of the scrotum and into the abdominal cavity. It is the vas deferens each side that is tied off in a man undergoing vasectomy. The vasa deferentia gently milk the sperms along by muscular action to their upper ends where they widen to form the ampullae. Most sperms are stored in the epididymis, as we have seen, but the ampullae act as secondary storage sites. Beyond the ampullae are two blind bags off the vasa deferentia called the seminal vesicles. They are important because they produce a fluid containing a sugar called fructose which is the fuel sperms need to enable them to live on their journey to fertilise an egg.

The prostate gland, which makes about 10 per cent of the seminal fluid (semen – the ejaculated fluid that contains the sperms), lies at the base of the bladder and surrounds the first part of the urethra. The prostate produces substances which act as a vehicle for the sperms, supply them with nutrients and buffer them against attack from the acid vaginal secretions. It is because it needs to counteract acid vaginal secretions that semen is so alkaline.

Beyond the prostate is a pair of small glands called Cowper's glands. These produce a small amount of lubricant which is added to the seminal fluid before ejaculation takes place. Rather less than 10 per cent of the volume of any ejaculate is composed of fluid from the testes and epididymes; about 80 per cent comes from the seminal vesicles; and the remaining 10 per cent from the prostate.

The whole process of maturation of a sperm from the day that it starts in the testis to the day it is ejaculated takes about three months, most of which is spent in the epididymis. Once a man becomes sexually excited, his penis enlarges and the vasa deferentia increase their muscular milking action and send more sperms into the ampullae. A combination of muscular contractions of the pelvic structures produces an ejaculation of the semen and when this happens the seminal vesicles and the prostate add their secretions to the sperms which are discharged as semen via the penis. Sperms form only 5 per cent of the volume of semen and a normal man ejaculates between two and five millilitres (or even more) of semen after a day or two of abstinence. Men who have large volumes of semen are not necessarily more fertile than those who do not, but volumes of less than 1 ml are sometimes associated with infertility because there is not enough fluid to maintain contact with the cervix.

Controversy rages on the subject of circumcision and its effects on a man's sex life, so it is worth a mention here. Circumcision is an operation carried out to remove the foreskin and so leave the penis head uncovered all the time. Circumcision is now a rare operation and is usually only carried out for medical or religious reasons.

Routine circumcision is a thing of the past, but its decline has been accompanied by a rise in cases of urinary infections in boys. There is absolutely no problem in having a foreskin left intact when it comes to sexual functioning provided that the man keeps the head of the penis underneath the foreskin clean. This is not only more pleasant for the woman who may want to kiss or suck the penis, but is also thought to be safer because it has been found that the wives of uncircumcised men are more likely to get cancer of the cervix than those who are married to circumcised men.

When it comes to sex and circumcision, men vary greatly in their views on the subject. Some uncircumcised men claim that because the head of the penis is covered all the time it is more sensitive and so gives them more pleasure and some circumcised men claim that because their penis head is rubbing against things (underpants usually) all the time it becomes de-sensitized and so allows them to enjoy longer vaginal stimulation before they reach orgasm. Clinical experience shows that whether or not a man has a foreskin seems to make very little, if any, difference to his enjoyment of sex. Obviously if the foreskin is so tight that it cannot be pulled back and it hurts him, it would make sense to discuss it with a doctor. However, medical views about circumcision are also very varied. If the foreskin can easily be pulled back at five (do not fiddle with it before) and boys are taught to pull it back to wash underneath, this is all that is needed for health and future sexual pleasure.

Sometimes an uncircumcised man can find that his foreskin becomes trapped behind the head of the penis if it is tight. This can be painful and distressing but it is possible to try a DIY treatment before seeking medical help. Soak a large handkerchief in very cold water and apply it to the affected area. Hold it in place tightly for a few minutes. Then pull the foreskin forwards using the hanky held firmly in place. If this doesn't do the trick after one or to goes get medical help.

## Sex play and a man's sex organs

When it comes to handling a man's sex organs there are a few hints that might help lovers. First, a man's penis can be very small at times, especially if he is cold or anxious or not feeling at all sexy. There is no need for concern because the penis will come back to its normal size as soon as it is stimulated. Similarly, a man's scrotal contents appear to vary greatly in size and still be perfectly healthy and normal. If one side swells up or is tender, even on gentle handling, get medical advice.

Once a man is aroused sexually, his genitals can stand quite a lot of fairly vigorous handling, but be guided by him as to what he likes. Many men complain that their women are too gentle and do not, for example, rub hard enough when masturbating them.

Although a man's penis is the most obvious part of the sexual anatomy he will enjoy being stimulated along the whole length of his sexual tract too. Many men enjoy the root of the penis (between the penis base and the anus) being rubbed and massaged as there is a large amount of erectile tissue there. Some men like their prostate massaged by the woman inserting her finger into the anus (beware of long fingernails and be sure to lubricate the anus well first or it will be uncomfortable). This can be especially pleasant when a man is being masturbated. The prostate is easily felt as a small, hard, rounded object at the base of the penis inside the man's rectum.

Apart from putting things inside the urinary passage, squeezing the testicles too hard or biting the penis there is really no harm that can be done during love-play or intercourse. All men are fairly similar in the way they prefer to be stimulated but individual variations do occur.

## The female sex organs

A woman's sex organs are rather more of a mystery than a man's because many of the important parts lie inside the body and so cannot be seen, and even those that are outside are not easy to look at. As a result some women have some very strange notions about their sex organs. In addition to these problems a woman's vagina lies only a matter of centimetres away from her anus (back passage) and so may become mixed up in her mind with dirt and stools. Also, of course, girls in our society are brought up to be more ashamed of their genitals and this is another reason why many claim never to have looked at their vulvas even though they very much wanted to. A woman who has irrational fears and suspicions about how she is made will not function well sexually and her partner will not be allowed or encouraged to enjoy her body as he should.

### *Breasts*

In other societies other parts of the body are considered to be a greater 'turn-on' but the breasts have eclipsed almost all of these in the West, and a woman's most easily observed signs of sexual arousal take place in her breasts.

Whilst about one third of men have some kind of hang-up about their penis size, about three-quarters of all women are, according to one survey, dissatisfied with their breasts. This has come about partly because of the advertising world's emphasis on a rather particular type of breast. Whilst it is probably true that men tend to prefer (and probably have been conditioned to prefer) large-breasted women, the variety of taste is wide and, anyway, no thinking man judges a woman solely by her breast size. There is no evidence that big-breasted women enjoy sex or breast-play any more than do their smaller-breasted sisters.

Interestingly enough, it seems that society's ideal breast image is slowly changing anyway. The ideal woman as currently portrayed by the media is neither very slim nor very curvy. Her breasts are neither particularly big nor particularly small.

Breast pain is very common indeed among women of all ages. One UK study found that about two thirds of women had had it at some time in their lives and that about one third had their daily and sexual lives disturbed by it.

More than half of sufferers don't seek medical help because they think that they'll be treated as neurotic women but the condition is real enough and causes a lot of unnecessary suffering.

There are three types of breast pain. The first occurs cyclically, gets better with the menopause and does quite well with hormone treatment. The second is non-cyclical, tends to go on after the menopause and can be difficult to treat. And the third is really a type of cartilage problem in the chest underlying the breast and simply mimics breast pain.

Many women who have breast pain worry that it might be a cancer but it very rarely is and the vast majority can be reassured fairly easily on this point.

Stopping the Pill can help some women, as can stopping smoking and cutting right down on the amount of fatty foods they consume. Evening primrose oil is a proven cure in about half of all cyclical cases and a combination of this plus changes in life style listed above can greatly enhance this success rate.

## *Breasts and sex*

During the earliest phase of sexual arousal the first visible sign that anything is happening is that the nipples become erect. This comes about as the tiny smooth muscles in them contract. One nipple often erects before the other and erection can occur without physical stimulation. Stimulation either by the woman herself or by her partner usually hastens erection but is not essential. The nipples increase in length and diameter as the woman becomes more excited and blood collects in and around them. This mechanism is rather like that which causes the penis to become erect. As the woman becomes more aroused the whole breast swells and she may have a measles-like rash on them and over her chest and neck.

## *A woman's genitals*

The pubic hair covers all the vulva (the outer part of the sex organs) and forms a fairly neat triangle with its base just above the pubic bone. The extent of the spread of the hair is very variable and some women's hair grows on to the tops of their legs and even up the abdominal wall a little. Both are perfectly normal. Some women like to keep their pubic hair trimmed. A few shave their pubic hair completely. If a couple enjoy oral sex the woman's pubic hair will have to be kept fairly short or it will get in the way of oral stimulation of her clitoris. Under the pubic hair the pubic bone can be felt.

Between the legs there are two fairly thick, fleshy lips, the *labia majora*, which are covered with hair. There are two inner lips inside. Sometimes one lip is longer than the other and the inner ones sometimes hang down more than the outer ones. The inner lips are much thinner than the outer ones and come together at the top around the clitoris. At the bottom the lips separate to go around the vagina. Three structures can be seen between these lips. First the clitoris, a little knob-like structure covered with a hood of tissue; second, the urinary opening (very small and closed off except when passing urine) which lies in the front wall of the vagina; and third, the opening of the *vagina* itself, an opening that will admit a finger tip even in a virgin. There is a veil of thin skin almost closing off the vaginal opening in a virgin. This is called the *hymen* and can come in lots of different shapes. Many girls today use tampons and some put things inside their vaginas when they masturbate so, even if they have not had intercourse, they may not have much in the way of a hymen left. Usually in such girls and all women who have had intercourse, all that remains are a few tags of pinkish skin around the vaginal opening. Almost all hymens break (or the hole stretches) with heavy petting or on first intercourse, but if there is any difficulty consult your doctor.

The vagina, contrary to many people's belief, is not a rigid tube inside a woman's body but is a flattened cylinder with an S-bend in it whose walls touch each other all the time unless something is inside.

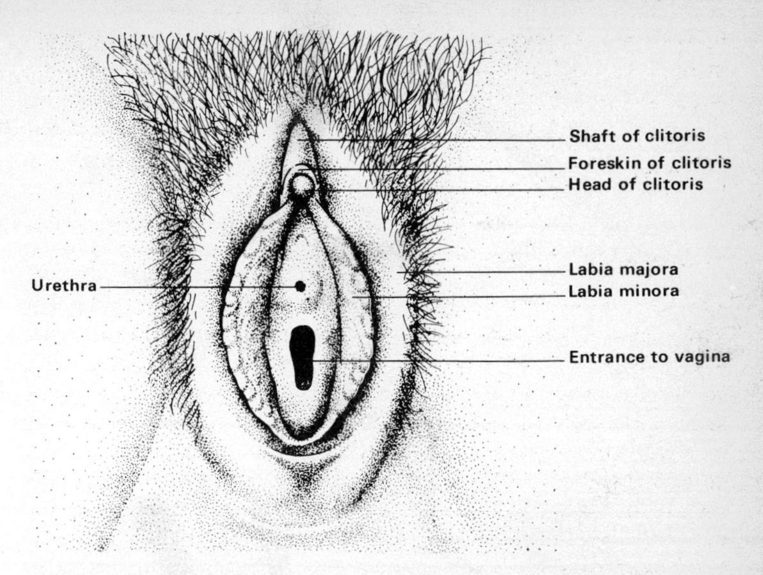


The parts of the female external genitals. *This diagrammatic representation should be used for general guidance only because as we saw on page 122 there are very variable appearances which are all perfectly normal, for example in this drawing the urethra is some distance from the vaginal opening, but this is not a universal feature of female anatomy.*

The vagina is about three or four inches long but during sexual arousal it lengthens and widens at the top. To all intents and purposes no woman's vagina is too small to accept a penis. If a penis cannot go in, either the woman has a tight hymen that has not been broken; has a condition that causes pain on attempted intercourse; or is suffering from a condition called vaginismus.

Unbelievable as it will seem to many, there are women who, due to childhood inhibitions, aversion or special fears, have never explored the vagina themselves. The following instructions are designed to help them do so. Others, also, may benefit from a planned expedition around the organ.

Whilst lying, sitting or squatting put your middle finger and/or index finger inside your vagina and feel the walls (damp and moist) and the direction in which your vagina goes (upwards and backwards). Also find your G-spot (see page 150 for details). When you have a finger inside contract the vaginal wall muscles around your finger. At first you will not be able to do this well, so it will need some practice. Start by sitting on the lavatory and pass a little urine. Then in mid-stream stop the flow – and practice this until you can do it at will easily. Now with two fingers inside the vagina contract these same muscles around your fingers. If you have had a baby there are good reasons to learn to do this because it will help strengthen the pelvic floor muscles and it will make intercourse more pleasurable for you and your partner. Some women routinely use these muscles during foreplay and intercourse to increase their partner's pleasure.

Next put your finger deeper inside till you can feel the cervix – the part of the womb that lies in the top of the vagina. This feels a bit like the tip of your nose and is rather firm with a dimple in the middle.

At the top of the vagina the ovaries can sometimes be felt through the vaginal walls on each side. Some women enjoy having their ovaries stimulated.

This is all that you can actually feel but inside there are other parts of the reproductive system. The *uterus* is a pear-shaped, muscular organ about three inches long and two inches across at its widest part (the fundus). The pointed part of the pear shape points down into the top of the vagina and the body of the 'pear' lies above the vagina in the pelvis. In most women the uterus is angled slightly forwards but in about 20 per cent it is tipped backwards (retroverted). It used to be thought that women with retroverted uteri were more likely to be infertile but this is now known not to be so.

The uterus has a cavity lined with a special type of cellular tissue called endometrium. The narrow canal leading from the vagina to the cavity through the cervix is normally plugged up with mucus. Suffice it to say on this subject that when a woman is most likely to conceive (around the time of ovulation) her cervical mucus is most encouraging to sperms and that when this mechanism fails in some way, her partner's sperms, however plentiful, may not get past the cervical mucus barrier.

At the sides of the top of the wide end of the uterus two tubes enter. These are the fallopian tubes that run from the ovaries to the uterus. Each fallopian tube is about four inches long and is thinner than the lead in a pencil. The tubes have very muscular walls lined with hair-like projections. Both walls and projections move in such a way as to waft ova (eggs) progressively along from the ovaries to the uterus. Cells lining the tubes produce substances that alter sperms so that they can fertilise an egg – indeed, fertilisation of an egg by a sperm occurs in one or other of the fallopian tubes. The open ends of the tubes are a collection apparatus which ensures that eggs are caught and channelled down into the fallopian tubes. There are numerous nervous, hormonal and chemical mechanisms at work in normal

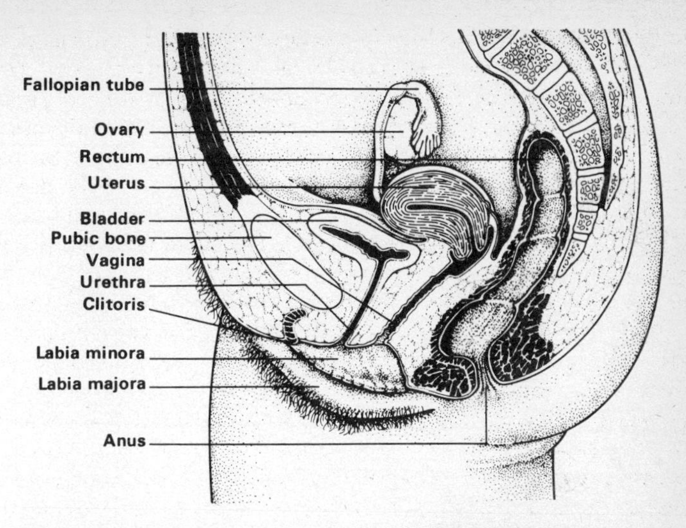


*A highly diagrammatic cross-section through a female pelvis. The pads of fat and tissue between the pubic bone and urethra, urethra and vagina, and vagina and rectum have all been deliberately exaggerated so that all these organs can be more clearly seen. In many women the vagina is not a straight tube as shown here but curves backwards in an S-bend.*

fallopian-tube functioning and we still know very little about exactly what goes on. But just as the structure and physiology of the fallopian tubes is vital to the downward passage of an egg, it is also important for the upward progress of the sperms. For one of many possible reasons an egg may remain in a fallopian tube once fertilised and the pregnancy develops there. This is called a tubal or ectopic pregnancy. An operation is needed at which the affected tube and the foetus are removed though surgeons try if possible to conserve the affected tube.

Perhaps the commonest condition affecting the uterus that we should consider in a book such as this is uterine fibroids. Although no one knows what causes them about one in five women suffer from them, even though they may not be aware of them. Common problems include heavy periods including flooding; painful periods; and infertility. The anaemia that the heavy periods cause may have to be treated, and operations include removing the fibroids themselves or even the whole uterus. Sometimes nothing need be done except to watch what happens over some months.

The ovaries are paired organs about the size of walnuts lying one each side of the pelvis. They have two functions. First, they release a ripened egg each month and, second, they produce progesterone and oestrogen – two important female hormones. The ovaries are remarkable organs – when a baby girl is born she already has all the eggs (30,000–40,000) in her ovaries. After puberty the eggs begin to ripen or mature under the influence of complicated hormonal changes that occur cyclically. This usually happens every month (unless the woman is pregnant or on the Pill; nor does it happen for some of the time she is breastfeeding) until the end of her reproductive life, the menopause, intervenes. In practice, several eggs begin to mature each month but for some unknown reason only one usually ripens. The average woman has 400–450 cycles in a lifetime. The ripening and release of an egg each month is called ovulation.

A woman's body functions in a cyclical way, each cycle lasting about a month. It is important to remember that this is only an average and that there can be large variations in cycle length that are still quite normal. In a classical 'text-book' cycle the events run as follows. The first day of the cycle is taken as the first day of menstruation. This is the day when the lining of the womb, now that it is not going to be needed for pregnancy, starts to be shed in the form of clots, cells and blood. The brain (particularly the hypothalamus)

*Schematic representation of various events during a woman's menstrual cycle.*

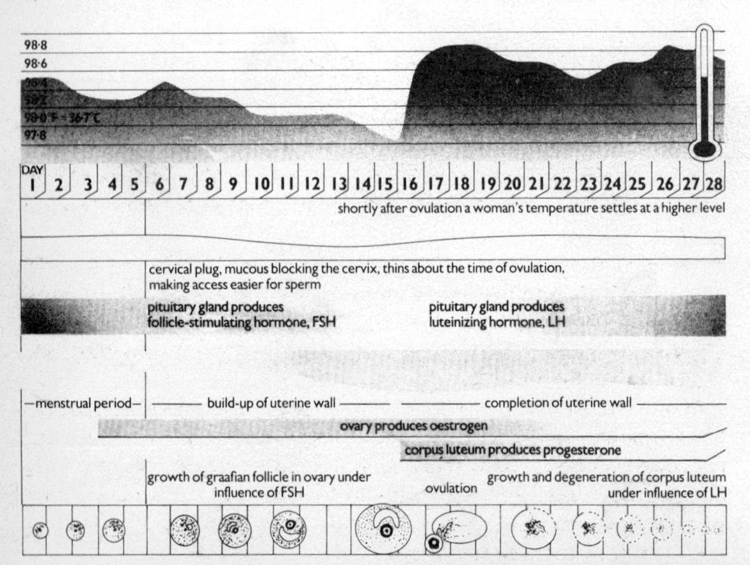

influences a tiny gland that lies near it (the pituitary gland) to produce a hormone called follicle-stimulating hormone (FSH) which stimulates the ovary to ripen an egg that month. Another hormone, luteinizing hormone, (LH) is produced by the pituitary during the whole cycle. A surge of LH is produced around the middle of the cycle (day 14) which helps release the ripened egg. This release of the egg is called ovulation and it is at this stage that a woman is most likely to conceive. Some women experience abdominal discomfort at this time.

Each month, then, an egg is released from one of the ovaries and is 'collected' by the tube. It takes at least three days for an egg to pass along the tube. While this is going on, the ruptured egg sac on the ovary turns into a functioning gland called the corpus luteum which produces another hormone called progesterone. Progesterone, together with oestrogen, acts on the lining of the uterus. Oestrogen produced in the first half of the cycle primes the endometrium and encourages growth. Without it, progesterone produced in the second half of the cycle could not act properly to ripen the endometrium ready to receive the fertilised egg. If the egg is not fertilised, the corpus luteum which has a lifespan of only about fourteen days, begins to cease functioning. Progesterone and oestrogen levels then fall, causing the lining of the womb to shed thereby starting a menstrual period.

## *Premenstrual Syndrome (PMS)*

This collection of mental, physical and emotional syndromes occurs in about a third of all women of child-bearing age. More than a hundred signs and symptoms have been reported in the medical literature but this very woolliness has made many men suspicious of the whole subject.

To those women who suffer from PMS things are all too real. The most common complaints are anxiety, nervous tension, and mood swings, irritability, weight gain, breast tenderness, and headaches. Some women are depressed and a few actually suicidal. A loss of sex drive is not at all uncommon either.

It is not known what causes PMS but hormone changes are thought to be responsible. Whether these changes are made worse by nutritional deficiences as a result of a poor diet is open to debate but clinical experience shows that this is likely to be true, if only because so many women greatly improve or are completely cured by taking the right nutritional supplements.

Most women with PMS say that it gets worse as they age, as they have more babies, if they are under stress, if they are worried, and if they do little physical activity.

If you are a sufferer, try keeping a PMS diary, noting down your signs and symptoms month by month. This can help your partner and your family to understand what is happening.

Find a PMS club or group where you can share experiences.

Keep a note on the family calendar so that they can see at a glance that it is a time for them to be more understanding.

Try the following self-help methods for the ten days before a period, stop smoking; drink no alcohol; stop adding salt to your food; cut right down on tea and coffee, eat six small meals a day rather than three ordinary ones; take evening primrose oil as directed on the pack; eat brewer's yeast tablets as directed on the pack; take some daily exercise, preferably out of doors; and try to cut down the stress in your life.

## *Periods (menstruation)*

From puberty until the menopause women have a period each month if an embryo has not implanted. There are many reasons for periods not appearing in normal women, the commonest of which by far is pregnancy, but others include an emotional shock, physical or mental ill-health, a change of time zones, a woman's fear that she might be pregnant and all kinds of stress.

Periods can vary greatly in their duration and in the heaviness of the blood loss. Normal periods can last for anything from two to eight days and the amount of blood loss is usually between five and six tablespoons. It seems a lot more because blood spreads over surfaces easily. If you ever have bleeding between your periods, see your doctor.

One of the earliest practical considerations is sanitary protection. Sanitary towels or tampons have to be used to absorb the menstrual blood. Sanitary towels are pads of highly absorbent material – often paper. Today's slimmer pads are unobstrusive even under tight clothes and many come with a waterproof backing film to prevent leaking.

Tampons are more convenient and comfortable for many girls and women. These are small plugs of absorbent material about the size of a finger that are inserted into the vagina where they expand and absorb the menstrual flow. If a girl is a virgin she may find it difficult to push the tampon into her vagina at first but most hymens already have a large enough hole to make it fairly easy. On first inserting a tampon the girl may actually break or stretch the hymen and this can cause some soreness for a day or two. It may be helpful to use a mirror at first. For the first few times a tampon is used it can help to smear its tip with KY jelly or something similar. Follow the instructions on the packet as these vary according to the type of tampon you are using. The most helpful thing of all when putting a tampon in the first few times is to relax. It cannot get lost inside. It is relatively easy though to forget that it is there, especially when the period ends and there is no leakage. All tampons have a string attacked to their base which, when pulled, brings them out of the vagina. Tampons very rarely get stuck but if they do don't worry. Just ask your mother to help you or go to your doctor.

Whether a tampon or a sanitary towel is used it should be changed several times a day and more often if the flow is heavy. Lots of girls and women put a stick-on 'pant-liner' inside their pants to mop up the inevitable occasional leak.

Many girls and women wonder about sex and their periods, but even though many cultures have a taboo on sex with menstruating women there is no reason to avoid intercourse. Of course, some women or their partners use periods to avoid having sex for a quarter or more of the month. An orgasm can help to reduce some of the symptoms of premenstrual tension and the cramping pains some women have in the first couple of days of their period. Research has proved that many women are most interested in sex around the time of a period and actually during it, and again at around ovulation (in the middle of the month), so clearly there is no reason to believe that nature meant sex to be a no-go area because of a period.

Although there is an ancient Jewish notion that menstruating women are unclean, no medical evidence has ever been found to support this, though some doctors persist in talking about menstrual 'toxins', the existence of which has never been proved. In spite of the advertising world's suggestions, and many women's suspicions, that menstruating women smell and that men are likely to find them unattractive, this is not true if reasonable rules of hygiene are observed.

Having periods affects women in many different ways. Some are completely unchanged physically and mentally and others are tired, grumpy, irritable, have a lot of lower abdominal pain and back pain, and feel bloated. Considerable research shows that women are more likely to be ill, to be admitted to hospital, to have acute medical and psychiatric illnesses, to crash the car, to hit their children, to be off work, and a host of other things, around the onset of their period. Men (including male doctors) for years thought that these problems were in the mind but research has now proved that the signs and symptoms are indeed very real. Explaining all these premenstrual troubles to children can be a problem and should be done in a way that does not make them think of menstruation as an illness. Girls raised to think in this way often end up with intolerable premenstrual symptoms themselves because they expect to be *ill* when they have a period.

Obviously having periods can be messy and some women consider them a misery and call periods 'the curse'. Today's Western woman will have 400–500 periods in a lifetime, but her ancient ancestors would only have had about thirty cycles, partly because of a later onset of periods and an earlier menopause and partly because most of the others would have been suppressed by having many pregnancies and breastfeeding on a prolonged basis.

Endometriosis is worth a mention here because it is found by chance during laparoscopic examination (see page 207) in up to 5 per cent of women whereas the condition is said to be present in up to half of subfertile ones. Endometrial cells (cells that normally form the lining of the uterus – the endometrium) are found outside the uterus in this condition, especially in the ovaries, bowels and behind the vagina. Such cells escape from the open, outer ends of the fallopian tubes during mensturation and are usually mopped up by the body's defences. Defects in these defences possibly prevent the cells being scavenged and so endometriosis results. Women between 30 and 45 are most vulnerable and whilst many have no symptoms others suffer from heavy periods, abdominal and back pains, painful periods, and painful intercourse. Surgery, or a male-type hormone called Danazol, which induces a temporary false menopause, can be used to relieve the condition. Any blockage of the cervix which may encourage menstrual blood to flow along the tubes must also be cleared.

*Chapter 9*

# Sex differences

## 'Measurable' differences between men and women

When one starts looking at men and women and comparing them, the first thing that becomes apparent is that man is a more vulnerable creature.

At every age from conception onwards more males die than females and to compensate for this more males are conceived. Male babies are more likely to be miscarried, to be stillborn, to have birth injuries and to have congenital disorders. Even so, about 105 boys are born to every 100 girls.

Throughout life about 4 per cent more males die at any given age than females, and whilst our life expectancy has been rising the most striking advantages have been to women, who are living longer than men (currently on average seventy-five years to men's sixty-seven). Men are more likely to die younger because they have more illnesses, more diseases and more accidents than women. Men are more prone to ulcers, heart attacks, virus infections, cerebral palsy, bronchitis, sex-linked diseases (such as haemophilia), various infectious diseases, lung cancer, successful suicide, mental retardation, autism, speech defects, visual and hearing defects, truancy, delinquency, alcoholism, anti-social behaviour and many other conditions. Ironically, although men spend less time in the home they have more domestic accidents!

From birth, and even before, boys and girls are constitutionally different. Male foetuses grow faster than female ones and at birth boys are on average longer and heavier than girls. Boys grow faster up to the age of about seven months after which girls grow faster to the age of four years.

Boys eat more food than girls and at all ages females have a greater proportion of fat to muscle than do males. Males have a higher blood pressure, perhaps linked to their greater physical strength and capabilities. But although boys start off larger at birth, girls are always more mature up to and past adolescence. Girls' bones and teeth mature earlier and they experience puberty earlier.

As well as these developmental differences there are sensory ones that are well proven. Girls are more sensitive to touch and pain stimulation (right from birth)! They can also hear and smell better. Boys tend to do better at visual 'tasks'.

Of course there is a considerable overlap of all of these characteristics between males and females but on balance the differences are measurable and meaningful.

Most people are happy enough to accept that such physical differences exist but it is when it comes to less tangible things such as differences in intelligence that the controversy really begins. For our purposes this is not important and is discussed no further.

Personality is another area to look at when comparing men and women. There are undoubted differences between boys and girls even very early on. Boys are more active (could this be because their mothers are more active with them?) and more liable to explore in play and girls are less active and sit still for longer. Boys run, jump, push, pull and are rougher, whilst girls tend to choose cutting-out, modelling drawing and other sedentary pursuits. A mass of personality-difference studies come basically to the same conclusions. Women tend to be 'inward looking', more concerned with people and relationships, more sympathetic, more tearful, more easily disgusted, more helpless, more emotional, more passive, moodier, more suspicious and more susceptible to social pressure than men. Men, on the other hand, tend to be more aggressive, more adventurous, more assertive, more exhibitionist and boastful, more rebellious and revengeful and more tough-minded. However at the level of the individual there are many exceptions to these generalisations and we all have a mixture of classical 'masculine' and 'feminine' personality traits.

Men and women *are* measurably different but that does not make either sex better or worse. In certain circumstances a woman's intrinsic personality traits are particularly valuable and in others a man's are needed. In raising a family both are *essential* because it has been proved time and again that balanced children need an adult of each sex to bring them up as they will have to live in a world populated by males and females and the characteristics of the sexes are unlikely to change dramatically one way or the other inside a few generations.

## The biological approach

If inadequate studies such as intelligence and personality tests cannot convince us about the differences between men and women, perhaps the truly scientific world has the answers.

Biologists differentiate between males and females in seven main ways: 1 the chromosomes; 2 the sex organs; 3 the sex hormones; 4 the internal reproductive organs; 5 the secondary characteristics; 6 the gender role; and 7 sexual identification.

### *Chromosomes*

All living organisms are made up of cells, each of which has a nucleus which contains chromosomes. These carry the genes which contain the blueprint which defines every detail of each organism's structures and function. These genes are inherited, thus explaining how it is that physical and psychological characteristics can be passed from generation to generation. Genes control the myriad of complex enzyme systems in the body, some of which are responsible for brain and hormone metabolism – both of which probably affect behaviour to some extent. Every cell in the human body contains twenty-three pairs of chromosomes, each of which in turn carries thousands of genes. The exception to this rule are the sex cells (sperms and eggs) each of which contains twenty-three *single* chromosomes. When an egg is fertilised by a sperm the two sets of twenty-three link to form a complex double set which is essential for the development of a new human being.

One pair of the twenty-three pairs of chromosomes is responsible for determining the sex of the individual. Generally each chromosome matches its partner in the pair, except for the sex chromosomes in males which are different. One is called the X chromosome and the other is very small and is called the Y chromosome. A woman has two X (normal-sized chromosomes) and a man an X and a Y. So women are XX and men are XY in sex-chromosome structure. Sperms carry either an X or a Y chromosome. The sex of the baby is decided by which reaches the egg first. If this is a Y-carrying sperm, the baby will be male. An absence of a Y chromosomes produces a female even if one of the chromosomes is missing (as sometimes occurs) with an XO pattern.

Because the Y chromosome is so small it is obvious that females have more genetic material than males right from the start. There is now evidence that one of these Xs is repressed and that only one is really operative. This would make sense in that both sexes would thus tend to have roughly equal amounts of chromosomal material.

But Nature plays some odd tricks from time to time and as a result teaches us some interesting things about males and females. Many of these lessons go to prove how difficult it is to be dogmatic even about something as seemingly straightforward as whether a person is male or female.

## *Hermaphrodites*

True hermaphrodites (a very rare condition) are individuals with both male and female chracteristics. Sometimes they have two XX chromosomes (as in a female) and normal female internal reproductive organs but with the external genitals being composed of male *and* female organs. Such people can thus have both ovaries and testes. Because such babies cannot easily be 'sexed' at birth they have been valuable in studying sex difference, because a biologically male infant can be brought up as a female and a female reared as a male. Sometimes the illogicality of the rearing is not apparent until puberty when the biological sex and the gender role clearly do not match up. Research has found that a change of gender role before the age of two and a half years is easily tolerated by the child and no harm is done. After that age there are increasing emotional and psychological disturbances which can last into adult life. So this type of evidence suggests that sexual identity is firmly established in the first three years of life. First signs begin to appear as early as one year old.

In hermaphrodites there seems to be a considerable preference for the gender role that they have been given at birth and by which they have been brought up – even when this goes against the obvious physical sexual identity.

**Turner's Syndrome** is a condition that arises when the baby's cells have only one sex chromosome instead of two. The cells are chromosomally XO (instead of XY or XX). Such children are female but fail to develop or to mature sexually and may be mentally retarded. One study of thirteen such girls showed that although they had no sex hormones they all had 'typically feminine' day-dreams, fantasies of marriage, romance and heterosexual eroticism. So in spite of having only one X chromosome they behaved in certain ways like females with two. This and other work seems to suggest that biological sex is much more important than gender allocated sex.

**Transsexualism** occurs when a person feels that he or she belongs to the opposite sex in spite of perfectly normal physical evidence to the contrary. No one has any certain idea why this occurs and it is nothing to do with either transvestism (dressing up in clothes of the opposite sex) or homosexuality. Parents treating a child as if it belonged to the opposite sex may be important.

## *Sex hormones*

From the sixteenth day after fertilisation of an egg a female embryo is detectably female as determined by the presence of Barr bodies (the repressed X chromosomes mentioned earlier). By the seventh week ovaries or testes are beginning to develop, and in the male testosterone, the main male hormone, is produced. Hormones are complex chemical messengers produced by one part of the body to be active somewhere else. The release of such chemicals is under the control of an area of the brain called the hypothalamus.

In the foetus the hypothalamus is cycled. That is, its activity switches on and off spontaneously for some as yet unknown reason. In females this cycling continues and controls many body functions, including ovulation and the menstrual periods during their fertile life. The male hypothalamus becomes uncycled at some stage, probably under the influence of testosterone.

So it is the absence of testosterone that makes a foetus female. In a condition known as *testicular feminisation* the genital tracts and external genitals are female and breasts appear at puberty. The person is genetically a male, with XY chromosomes, but looks like a female. The same thing can occur in reverse with 'women' who look like men.

All of this begins to raise some very fascinating questions. If, as we have seen, the brains of male and female foetuses are behaving differently (one cycled, and the other not) might there not also be other differences in brain function? It is already known that certain brain centres are influenced by sex hormones as well as influencing them and micro-anatomical research has shown that some areas of the hypothalamus are larger in women than in men, and that the connections between the cells of this area of the brain and the brain itself are different in the sexes.

It is interesting, before leaving the subject of hormones, to look at a rare condition called the adrenogenital syndrome. Girls with this condition are exposed to abnormally high levels of male hormones right from foetal life, because their adrenal glands over-produce these particular hormones secondary to an inborn error of metabolism. These girls have an enlarged (penis-like) clitoris and, compared with their sisters, spend more time in rough-and-tumble play, are athletically orientated and less interested in playing with dolls. In other words, they are tomboyish in every respect. This (and parallel animal work) seems to prove that levels of male hormones from birth affect the developing brain in a way that changes a child's behaviour.

*Chapter 10*

# Copulation

What is copulation? The word is the scientific term used to describe the act of putting the penis in the vagina. As any penis will go into any vagina there is nothing very special about being able to copulate. Any man who can have an erection and any woman who can open her legs can copulate. Most people learn to copulate in their teens or early twenties, then some progress to intercourse and making love, as we shall see. Unfortunately, many couples stop at the copulation stage, where they remain for the whole of their married life.

The amount of sex anyone has depends on the balance struck at any one time between the anti-sex attitudes of society and their upbringing, on the one hand, and the pro-sex drives of Nature on the other. Take the brakes off the anti-sex mechanism (by falling in love, getting drunk, going on holiday, or whatever) and the real sex-interested self emerges to enjoy itself as it could have all along. So cultural conditioning in a sex-negative culture such as ours is a starting-point in determining how often people have sex.

Although cultural conditioning is by far the most important factor and is obviously infinitely variable between people and even within any one person from time to time, there are many other factors that control the frequency of sex. Availability of someone to have sex with is an obvious factor. Many – those in prison and some single, divorced, separated and widowed people (not to mention priests, nuns and monks who choose celibacy) – simply do not have a sex partner and may seek sexual release through masturbation. Tiredness is a common cause of – or excuse for – a poor sex drive. This comes about most commonly because of the pressures of work and of caring for young children. Illness (physical and mental), a fear of rejection, a poor view of oneself (because of being fat, for example), living with in-laws and scores of other reasons can all determine the amount of sex any one couple has.

Some couples are perfectly happy copulating once a month or less and others need to do so several times a day. Both frequencies are normal for them and, provided they are both happy, who is to say they should not be? Within the lives of any one couple the picture can change dramatically. A young couple, just married, may well have intercourse every day, or even several times a day. They then have a baby and may have intercourse a few times a month or less during the early years. In middle age their intercourse rates will possibly rise again as the woman becomes keener and in old age they may have more sex than they did as youngsters in their twenties and thirties.

The concepts of 'highly sexed' and 'undersexed' are harmful and silly. There is an infinite variation in people's drives for intercourse and these change. A man's 'needs' for copulation seem to be linked only to one measurable thing in his past: his masturbation rate during adolescence. Similarly the terms 'frigid' or 'nymphomaniac' are redundant. These are words used by men to describe women who have a lesser or greater sex drive than they (the men) think they should. A 'frigid' woman in the arms of one man can become a 'nymphomaniac' with another. Having said this it can be very frustrating and can create serious physical and emotional tensions in an individual or a couple who are used to a certain frequency of sex if for some external reason their intercourse rate falls, especially suddenly. Often it is the imbalance between the drives and needs of one partner and those of his or her spouse that causes problems, but even when this appears to be a real problem the underlying trouble usually lies elsewhere. Most loving, friendly couples, even if they have very different needs for intercourse, cope perfectly well and develop a pattern of mutual masturbation or find other methods of sexual release that are satisfying to them both. Even in less 'ideal' marriages women may agree to sex more often than they say they would really like, to please their husbands.

*Different types of sexual release in men under 40. According to Kinsey.*

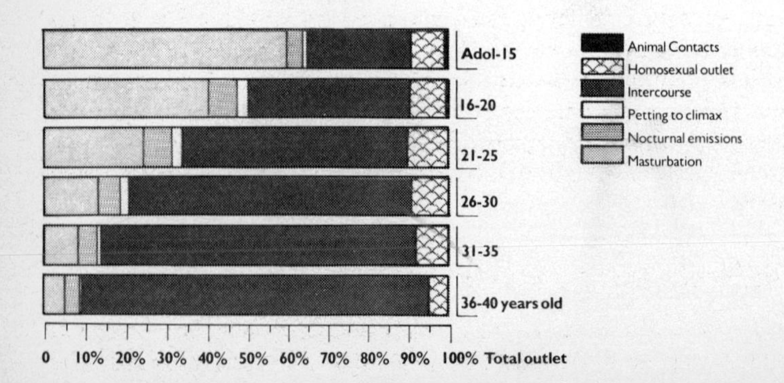

Which partner controls the copulation rate within any one couple is difficult to prove. Women are classically thought to do so because they can say 'no' at any time and men are popularly supposed to be forever keen to get at their wives. Clinical experience shows that this is far too simple and rarely true. Many women never refuse their husbands sex and research has shown that many wives are unhappy because their husbands do not want to have sex nearly often enough.

It has long been suggested that sex is 'good' for you. It can enhance the sense of well-being of most people but some seem perfectly all right without it. Some tentative medical evidence is beginning to accumulate that suggests that people with a good sex life tend to live longer. Also, there is strong evidence that women who have a satisfactory sex life are less prone to heart attacks.

Certainly sex makes most people feel 'good' as opposed to 'bad' but even this (because of long-held cultural views that intercourse and masturbation weaken a man) raises problems. Of course, certain types of intercourse (such as extra-marital sex) can make people tense and guilty. Many men quite consciously, if unwillingly, abstain from intercourse before activities such as important business meetings or sporting events as a result of these fears. Some men, fearing that sex will weaken them so much that they will be unable to function in the world, often abstain from intercourse or masturbation so as to have 'enough energy' to put into their careers and other activities. There is no evidence that sex in itself is weakening or damaging, although guilt after masturbation can make men feel off-colour.

Couples copulate for many different reasons. Sometimes it is purely to release sexual tension, on other occasions to show their love and affection, on others deliberately to try to conceive, on others to punish the partner in some way, and on others to reward. Sex can even be used as a weapon in a bad marriage.

In summary, copulation is a highly complex business. The act itself is simple – nearly anyone can do it – but the reasons people do it and the implications for the couple are not so simple. Whether, when, how and why a couple copulate depends on their upbringing, their needs, their drives, their partner's needs and drives, external factors, the behaviour of their friends and acquaintances, and many other things.

## Understanding the mechanics

Our knowledge of the detail of what really happens during sexual arousal was, until about twenty years ago, very patchy indeed. The

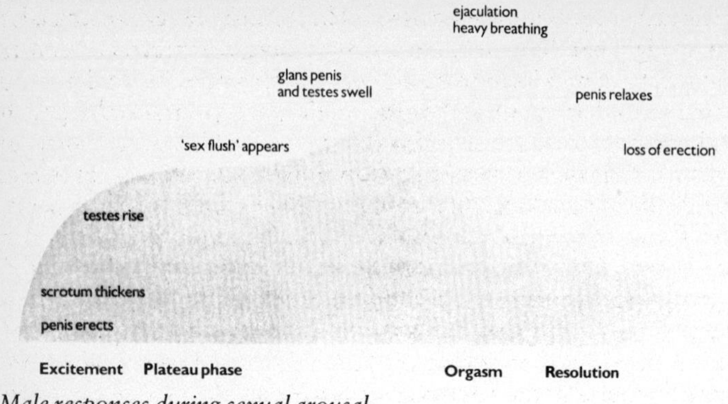


*Male responses during sexual arousal.*

pioneering work of Dr William Masters and Dr Virginia Johnson in the USA changed all that and now many other researchers have repeated and extended their work.

## *In a man*

A man usually starts to become sexually aroused in his head. He is 'turned on' by something erotic (either in reality or fantasy) and this mental change sends nervous impulses down his spinal cord to his genitals. In response the spongy tissue of his penis becomes filled with blood, causing the organ to stiffen and change from the limp, downward-hanging organ it usually is to a protruding, rod-like one. This is called an erection. During these changes the man's heartbeat quickens, his pupils enlarge, his blood pressure rises, his breathing quickens, his nostrils flare, his muscles tense, he sweats a little and he feels sexually excited. This is called the excitement phase of his sexual response. His scrotum becomes tenser and thicker and the testes themselves are drawn up tightly against the body.

It is possible for all these changes to occur and the man then to go back to his normal pre-excitement phase. Apart perhaps from feeling somewhat let-down, he will return to normal within minutes. Most often though, having got this far, he will go further either by masturbating or by copulating.

The penis now swells even more and its tip (the glans) becomes purplish blue and the contents of the scrotum increase in size. This is the plateau phase and it is more difficult to return to normal from this than from the earlier excitement phase.

The next stage is the orgasm itself. The intensity of sexual arousal is now so high that the man *has* to ejaculate. Surges of nervous impulses now run back and forth from his nervous system to his genitals and the passages that run from the testes to the penis contract (along with local muscles) to squirt semen out of the end of his penis. Once an orgasm is near there is nothing a man can do to stop it – it takes him over. At ejaculation a small quantity of semen shoots out of the penis, often for some distance, and is associated with a wonderful sensation deep in the pelvis as the prostate gland (previously swollen with fluid) discharges its contents. A series of four or five contractions follows at a rate of about one every 0.8 of a second, each producing a smaller volume of semen than before until the tubes carrying the semen are empty. Eventually the contractions cease and the man relaxes. His erect penis returns to its normal size and he feels relaxed and even sleepy. The colour and consistency of semen varies a lot with how long he has been continent. There is no way of judging the quality of semen by its appearance or its volume. Each ejaculation (about a teaspoonful) contains millions of sperms, any one of which could make a woman pregnant.

Once the man has ejaculated, he may take several hours to become arousable again. Younger men have a shorter refractory period and are arousable again sooner than older men. Some boys can have repeated orgasms just like most women. There is absolutely no harm or danger in ejaculating several times a day but it can be tiring. There is no truth at all in the notion that men have only a certain fixed amount of semen which can be ejaculated – every healthy man can ejaculate semen many times a day for the whole of his life and still suffer no adverse side-effects.

The whole male cycle can be achieved very quickly, especially in teenagers and young men who become aroused and ejaculate in a few minutes. Things are rather different in women.

## *In a woman*

In many ways the body-changes that occur in a woman are very similar to those in a man but the whole cycle usually takes longer to get going, lasts longer and is capable of near-instant repetition – which a man's is not. Some women say that under certain circumstances they become aroused and have an orgasm very quickly indeed.

During the excitement phase in a woman her nipples erect, her breasts swell and the veins in her breast skin become more readily

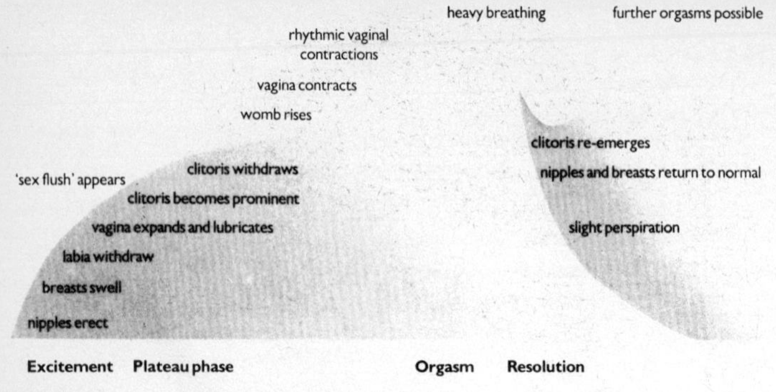


*Female responses during sexual arousal.*

visible. The skin of the whole body becomes slightly dusky because of an increased blood flow and there may be a sex flush – a faint measles-like rash over her stomach, chest and neck. This rash disappears at orgasm.

During the excitement phase the woman's genitals become engorged with blood. The inner lips of her vulva (labia minora) and clitoris swell and become darker in colour. As the clitoris is stimulated it becomes erect (like a miniature penis) but usually does so very slowly compared with a penis. Some women's clitorises swell to over twice the size of the resting state but others, even when fully aroused, are much the same size as before stimulation began. If stimulation is continued a 'plateau' phase is reached in which the shaft and the tip of the clitoris go back under the protective foreskin. This makes it appear that the clitoris has disappeared. The tip and the shaft reappear if stimulation stops and the process is repeated if stimulation stops and starts. After orgasm only about ten to fifteen seconds are required for the clitoris to return to its normal resting position and size.

The outer lips (labia majora) swell and pull back so as to open up the vulva a little. The vaginal walls start to 'sweat' and the fluid lubricates them and appears at the vaginal opening in some women. At this stage the woman feels moist inside as her sexual tension grows. The vagina now relaxes and becomes 'tented' at its top end. The womb (uterus) is pulled upwards and makes the vaginal cavity larger. Further breast-swelling occurs, the areolae around the nipples swell so much that sometimes the nipples seem to disappear and the woman may begin to twitch all over her body. Sometimes this

The missionary position: *This position for copulation or intercourse is often frowned upon in sex books but nevertheless remains the favourite of the majority of women.*

twitching starts in a toe or a leg, or her abdominal muscles may give fluttering twitches. Her pulse rate, breathing, pupil size, and so on all change and she is ready for an orgasm. As she has one, her body arches, her muscles tense, her face may draw into a grimace and her vagina and uterus contract rhythmically along with some of her pelvic muscles. Her body may be thrown into spasms of violent contractions or she may sense very little. Some women scream, cry out or bite their lips as they climax – the response depends almost entirely on the personality and experience of the woman, her early masturbation practices and the circumstances in which she finds herself during that particular orgasm. Once the intense contractions of the vagina and uterus are over, the woman quietens down to her plateau phase.

Most women are capable of having several orgasms one after the other but many say that one is quite enough and that they feel perfectly satisfied and have no need for more. Some women can have twenty or more orgasms one after the other but between one and three is the most common number. How many a woman has depends on her masturbation practices in her teenage years, her in-built sexual inhibitions, her partner's ability and willingness to continue stimulating her and, of course, her own desire to have more.

This then describes the basic mechanics and we shall see later what can go wrong. Overall, it is probably fair to say that in our teens we experience intense, quick onset orgasms and that as we mature arousal takes longer, lasts longer and produces better quality orgasms. This is certainly true up to old age for most of us and continues well into old age for many. Young boys and even some girls tend to be trigger-happy and to climax quickly. This is acceptable during early masturbation practice but is not so welcome when one has a partner to consider. Orgasms vary in intensity and quality from person to person and even within any one person. If a woman has a series of orgasms, any one of them can be the best. As in any other sphere of life, practice makes perfect. Only by sharing with each other what they like best can a couple hope to enjoy high-quality orgasms most of the time. But this takes us out of copulation into intercourse.

By our definition copulation may not involve the full spectrum of female arousal – though some women have orgasms when copulating. A man, on the other hand, has to be fully aroused in order to penetrate a woman.

One of the bridges that convert pure copulation (which one can have with anyone) into intercourse (which is a loving, caring and sharing of one's sexual personality) is foreplay.

A knowledge of sexual arousal mechanisms can be helpful to enable both partners to know that each is properly aroused and excited by what they are doing during foreplay and intercourse. For example, a man skilled in his partner's sexual response can tell by feeling her nipples or clitoris exactly where she is in the cycle and so knows how best to caress her or whether to go on to intercourse. Obviously a preoccupation with bodily changes at such a time is unhealthy and unloving but a little knowledge, practically applied, can improve the quality of one's foreplay and intercourse enormously.

*Chapter 11*

# Foreplay (pleasuring)

This is a highly personalised and enjoyable behaviour that takes place between a man and a woman often before penetration occurs. It is an extension of the love-making that ideally goes on throughout their everyday lives, as discussed later.

A lot of nonsense has been written about foreplay. The received wisdom perpetuated from sex manual to sex manual is that the secret of good sex is preparation. Unless, it is claimed, a man spends hours preparing his woman's genitals (and the rest of her) she will have no orgasm, poor orgasms, or will not even want sex at all.

Many women sometimes like to enjoy extended love-play before having intercourse and at other times enjoy a 'quickie' in which the man simply thrusts his penis into her straight away. This sort of 'kitchen-table', unpremeditated sex can be thoroughly enjoyable for both partners, yet it involves little or no foreplay.

Most couples though do not practice this kind of 'quickie' sex every time and usually enjoy some form of foreplay before they have sex.

Foreplay has many functions. It makes the couple relax; it gives them an opportunity to talk 'sweet nothings' to each other; it makes them aroused; it prolongs the pleasure of intercourse (which would otherwise be over quickly); and it makes the pleasure of intercourse more intense. It is a time when a couple can lose themselves totally in each other, forgetting the rest of the world entirely. Foreplay also postpones the onset of intercourse, which is a good idea on the basis that something lovely is always better if you have waited for it.

The term foreplay is rather unfortunate in many ways because it gives the impression that it is always a forerunner to penetration. This is not so and gives the erroneous impression that such pleasuring must end in penetration. For many couples this is a nonsense. They kiss, cuddle and pleasure one another as an end in itself or as a prologue to masturbation or some other sexual delight. The pressure on many people to have intercourse just because they start to pleasure one another is at the heart of much goal-centred sex and does some couples a lot of harm.

There are, however, some exceptions. Due, probably, to severe punishment for touching in childhood, some women dislike foreplay, especially genital stimulation. A woman who does not really want sex with her partner, or who is always unsatisfied, may also reject foreplay because she does not want to become aroused only to be let down.

Men who have difficulty erecting often want to proceed to penetration when it occurs for fear that it may be lost. Also, men who have a tendency to premature ejaculation may also try to keep foreplay to a minimum so as not to become sexually over-aroused.

Any couple who have followed the advice in the chapter on courtship should have no difficulty in gauging their partner's mood and adjusting foreplay accordingly.

## Some useful hints

There are, needless to say, no absolute rules in foreplay, but the following hints might be useful, at least on some occasions and to some couples.

1 Most foreplay begins with kissing and cuddling and progresses to petting and it can be very arousing to undress each other slowly or to strip in front of each other. Some couples like to prepare for foreplay on their own, each bathing or washing and then presenting themselves 'ready for action', while others enjoy the preparatory stages as part of the love-play itself.

2 Have a bath or shower together (or separately). You may choose to use perfume as a sexual turn-on but it is not necessary to use anything at all. This frees your body's natural scents to turn each other on. Don't be obsessional about washing your sex organs but make sure they are clean and fresh. Their natural odour is designed to excite the opposite sex, so don't destroy it.

3 Make the surroundings as relaxing and arousing as possible. If you like music, put on some that you enjoy; dim the lights (love-play in the total dark reduces the enjoyment because you cannot see your partner's pleasure). Spend time massaging each other and simply lie down together, naked or lightly clothed, and talk or drink a little alcohol. Take the phone off and lock the door if the children are likely to come in and disturb you.

4 Tell each other what you feel – praise little things about one another and kiss, especially parts of the body you know your partner is embarrassed about (a scar, a fat abdomen or whatever).

Be gentle, tender and affectionate and share each other lovingly. Don't rush; give yourselves time and don't touch each other's sex organs until you are both ready.

5 Be unashamedly romantic – go back to your courting days and relive the romantic love you felt for each other. Tell each other that you love each other (if it is true). Being told you are loved is a great sexual turn-on. If you enjoy using coarse sex language, and some couples do, go ahead. Anything you want to do that you both enjoy is all right. It is at this stage that many couples talk to each other in their private language and praise each other's bodies in endearing terms.

This first stage of love-play should not be genitally centred; it should have no goals other than sharing each other's company and luxuriating in pleasuring one another.

## Things that women like

Obviously women's likes and dislikes are very personal and individual when it comes to love-play and the caring man finds out what pleases his partner most by asking her to tell him and by experimentation. We cannot stress enough how different women are one from another in what they like, so don't go by your previous experience of women. What she does to you may be a clue as to what she likes done to her.

### *Kissing and caressing*

Almost all women like being stroked and caressed and kissed all over their body. Usually it is best to start furthest away from her sex organs and work towards them slowly. Find areas of the body which she especially likes having stimulated and concentrate on these. The feet, behind the knees, the insides of her thighs, the shoulders and the ear lobes are areas that many women find arousing. The nearest you should get to genital stimulation at this stage is to run your fingers over and through her pubic hair.

Next, go on to caress other more specifically erotic areas such as her breasts, mouth and bottom. When kissing these, or indeed any areas be careful not to tickle your partner because this can break the relaxing spell. Breasts need to be approached gently at first. Many women complain that men are too rough with their breasts before they are aroused. Kissing and sucking is what most women like best

**Male and Female Erogenous Zones**

*Note how much more of a woman's body is erotically sensitive than that of a man's.*

and stroking is pleasant too. Never bite the nipples (especially when a woman is highly aroused) because you could easily hurt or damage them. As you caress and kiss the woman's breasts, her nipples will stand out and become hard and her breasts will swell slightly. About half of all women say that they enjoy their breasts as erotic centres during love-making. Of the remainder, some are excited more by their partner's obvious enjoyment of them than they are by the direct stimulation he gives them. Many a woman's breast sensitivity changes in the course of her menstrual cycle and what can be very arousing at one time of the month can be annoying or even painful at others. It is therefore important that men learn about their partner's breasts and vary their love-making techniques to take these changes into account.

A woman's buttocks are also very sensitive and arousing for her during foreplay. Most women like their buttocks caressed and squeezed. This also gives the man an opportunity to get very near her vaginal area with the woman face down and this can be very arousing because of the promise it brings. Some women enjoy gentle smacking on their bottom. This is not necessarily related to the sado-masochistic pursuits we will consider later.

When caressing your partner you may find you get carried away and that you bite or suck her so hard that she is marked. Be sensitive about this. First, never bite too hard but keep it playful and, second, don't bite her where it will be seen by others, which will embarrass her.

By now your partner should be very relaxed and pleasantly aroused and her excitement phase will be well under way. The time all this takes varies enormously from couple to couple and even within any one couple, depending on the circumstances. When you both feel ready, let your hand go down to her vulva and start to caress her clitoris. Some women are so aroused by what has already happened that they will guide your hand to their pubic area. The whole area should be fairly moist from the woman's vaginal fluids which are produced as she becomes aroused, but KY jelly can be useful if the woman lubricates slowly. If she is still dry, use some saliva so that as you caress her clitoris your finger does not feel rough but slides more easily. What you do to your partner's clitoris depends entirely on what she likes and you should ask her, but most women like the pressure to be gentle and the movements slow at first, building up to harder and more vigorous movements as they near orgasm. What any one woman likes is based on her unique masturbation method.

Now as the clitoris responds dip your fingers into her vagina to keep the vulva moist with vaginal fluid. You really should not need any lubricant other than saliva or the woman's natural fluids. Once she is very excited don't delay but bring her to a climax and be sensitive to her needs for this. Many women want their partner to put his penis into their vagina while continuing to caress their clitoris; others need manually produced orgasms before the man enters; and others like to have one orgasm without the penis inside and then to have others with it inside with either the man or the woman herself caressing her clitoris.

Either before caressing the clitoris or even after an orgasm (depending on what your partner likes or asks for) you can use your fingers to stimulate her vagina. Always make sure that your nails are well cut and that you have not got any obvious infections on your fingers before doing any of this.

Many men assume that because they enjoy their penis being stimulated by hand that women will also enjoy vaginal stimulation best. This is by no means true and some women dislike fingers inside them. If your partner *does* like to be stimulated in this way, and most do, don't thrust several fingers in at once or do it when she is dry. Get her well lubricated as we have described above, then lick your middle finger and gently insert it in with your palm upwards. You may be able to feel the neck of the womb (cervix) as a hard knob with a dimple in the middle. Some women like their cervix stimulated when they are very aroused or like the finger to sweep around inside the vagina. Some like their ovaries stimulated (at the sides of the top of the vagina). Some women like their partner to use his fingers in a sort of thrusting (penis-like) movement and others like the fingers simply inserted and kept nearly still.

Many women use two fingers inside their vaginas when they masturbate and so may well want more stimulation than one finger can give, especially if they have had a baby. Find out how many fingers your partner most enjoys: though it may be different from one time to the next. A few women like their vaginal opening stretched with several fingers. Some women, once sufficiently aroused, can have very enjoyable orgasms from being stimulated using the fingers alone but many enjoy the combination of fingers inside and other things such as cunnilingus (oral stimulation of the clitoral area).

## *The G-spot*

Recent research has confirmed what many women have known all their lives, that the front wall of the vagina can be very sexually

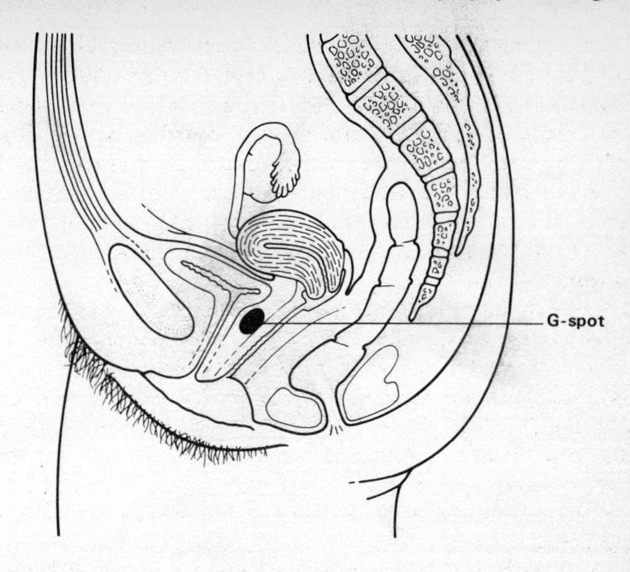


*Highly diagrammatic representation of the female pelvis to show the approximate location of the G-spot.*

sensitive and can even produce orgasms when stimulated in the absence of clitoral stimulation. This area of the vaginal wall has been called the G-spot after the German gynaecologist, Ernst Grafenberg. It was he who suggested that there might be orgasmic centres other than the clitoris and many women know he was right – in fact some women can have pleasurable intercourse only in positions in which the penis stimulates the front wall of the vagina vigorously.

The G-spot is probably composed of a complex network of blood vessels, nerve endings and the tissue surrounding the bladder neck and the urethra. When a woman is unaroused it can hardly be felt but once excited it can be felt as a hard area with defined edges. If the woman is very aroused this transformation takes place very rapidly. Although not all women have a G-spot, it appears, the majority do.

A woman can find her own G-spot, though, and so can her lover. When a woman lies on her back this is difficult because gravity tends to pull the internal organs down and away from the vaginal entrance, so she would need a very long finger and a short vagina. The best position is sitting or squatting. Insert one or two fingers into your vagina and experiment with stimulating the front wall. The first sensation is usually one of wanting to urinate and it is sensible to try your first experiments with the G-spot whilst sitting on the lavatory. Explore the front part of your vaginal wall, perhaps even applying some pressure with your other hand on the lowest part of your abdomen just above the pubic bone. As the G-spot begins to swell you will feel it as a small lump between the two sets of fingers.

To the finger the G-spot feels like a small bean, but when swollen it can be an inch across. The size of the spot varies from woman to woman, as one would expect, and women vary in their enjoyment of the G-spot.

As you continue stroking the area you will probably notice some pleasurable contractions in your uterus. Experiment with this area, just as you did with your clitoris in the past, until you learn what is best. You will probably need greater finger pressure on your G-spot than on your clitoris to produce the same pleasant sensations and the sensations will be felt deeper inside you than when you masturbate clitorally.

As you get beyond the sensation of wanting to urinate you can move to a bed or somewhere more comfortable. Continue stimulating the spot while kneeling or sitting on your feet with your knees apart. Some women ejaculate a clear fluid from their urethra as they have an orgasm from stimulating their G-spot.

Of course you can share the discovery of your G-spot with your partner. The best position for doing this is with you lying face down, legs apart and your hips up on a pillow. Ask your partner to insert two fingers (palm down) and explore the front wall of your vagina with a firm touch. You can move your pelvis to enable his fingers to get the best possible contact with your G-spot. He can later insert his penis and stimulate the spot this way too. Another good position for finding the spot is to lie on your back and then have your partner insert two fingers palm up. He will feel the spot about half-way between the back of the pubic bone and the end of the vagina where the cervix is. Putting his other hand above your pubic bone at the very bottom of your abdomen, and pressing firmly can also help him find and stimulate the spot more easily.

Incidentally, it is probably worth remembering that many women who use a diaphragm as a means of contraception lose sensitivity of their G-spot as a result, because it cannot be adequately stimulated through the rubber dome. If you want your partner to stimulate your G-spot, wait until the last moment until inserting your diaphragm – just before he puts his penis into you. For the woman who greatly enjoys stimulation of her G-spot during intercourse another method of contraception will be more suitable.

## *Oral stimulation*

This is extremely pleasant for both partners and many women who cannot have an orgasm in any other way often do so with their partner caressing their clitoris with his tongue. There is absolutely nothing revolting or dirty about kissing a woman's genitals. Either lie between her open legs with your head coming from below or crouch over her with your penis on her upper chest or face and kiss her vulva like this. It helps to have a pillow under her bottom to raise the whole area slightly and to prevent you from breaking your neck! Lick the whole of the vulval area with your lips and tongue and dip your tongue into the vagina and stroke it upwards towards her clitoris.

Cunnilingus: *Not all men enjoy doing this to a woman and not all women enjoy having it done, yet it is an increasingly popular type of foreplay. Some women can have an orgasm with a man only in this way.*

Caress the clitoris with your tongue as if you were using a finger and keep doing what she likes until she climaxes. Most women who have orgasms in other ways, and many who otherwise would not have had one, have extremely good orgasms from such oral caresses. There are lots of other positions (such as sitting on a chair or kneeling on all fours) in which you can kiss your partner's vulva, so experiment and find what you both most enjoy.

In spite of this a word of caution is necessary since oral sex is a common area of conflict. Some women regard their vulvas as smelly, germ-ridden and revolting, and do not like their man to use his mouth there. Even if they do go ahead, a sign that this is so is that they dislike him kissing them on the mouth afterwards. Some men have a similar view. Some women feel the same about sucking the penis, especially if she suspects the man of wanting to ejaculate in her mouth.

Oral sex with a casual partner about whom there is uncertainty is potentially dangerous because, contrary to earlier opinions, it is now thought AIDS can be transmitted this way. There is an increased chance of AIDS being transmitted in this way from an HIV-positive man if the woman has recently cleaned her teeth because there will be tiny abrasions on the gums through which the virus can enter her bloodstream.

Apart from this the only danger in cunnilingus arises from blowing air into the vagina. Several women have died as a result due to the air reaching the bloodstream.

## *Anal stimulation*

Many women enjoy having their anus stimulated, especially as they near orgasm. How you do this will be dictated by what your partner wants, but a finger (or tongue) encircling the anus can be very stimulating. Some women like to have a finger tip inserted into the anus itself and others like a lot of anal sensation with several well-lubricated fingers. Whatever you do, be sure not to put the same fingers into the vagina after having been in the anus, as this can cause an unpleasant infection. Anal stimulation such as this cannot cause AIDS – unless of course your partner has the disease or is HIV-positive when there is a real danger. Anal play in faithful, healthy couples is perfectly safe.

## *Vibrators*

Something else enjoyed by some women is to have a vibrator or dildo used on their vulval area generally or inside their vagina as part of foreplay. Most women, once proficient at having self-induced clitoral orgasms, are not very keen on the orgasms produced by a vibrator but there are exceptions to every rule and some enjoy their partners using a vibrator on them whereas they would not particularly like to do so themselves.

## Things that men like

Women are luckier than men in that the whole of their bodies are highly erotic, especially as they get aroused. A man's erotic areas are fewer in number and his most erotic zones by far are his genitals. Many women can and do have orgasms by having their feet, ear lobes, ankles, anus and many other areas kissed or stimulated, but a man will usually become aroused and ejaculate only if his genitals are stimulated. This is not to say that men do not also enjoy having their bodies caressed and kissed – they do. Some men, for example, enjoy having their nipples sucked.

Women need to know just as much about how to please their partners, partly because it turns their men on, which is nice for them, but also because doing arousing things to their partner is highly arousing for the woman herself. A woman who lies back and lets it all happen in loveplay is missing half the fun! Men today expect women to play at least some part in love-play and the commonest complaint about wives in this context is that they are too passive. Unless the woman wants to be taken forcefully, there is no reason for this to continue. Sex is not something a man does *to* a woman; it is something they enjoy *with* each other, trying to make it pleasurable for each other every time. This by definition becomes teamwork, not a solo performance.

We think that every woman should learn to excite and arouse her partner just as he should learn to please her. This is especially true as the man gets older when he will need increasing amounts of stimulation to become aroused but his erection will last longer and be more satisfying for the woman. Once a man has an erection he is raring to go, so your activities should not be aimed at arousing him physically by bringing him to ejaculation too easily or you will be disappointed. Of course sometimes you will want him to climax quickly and so will not hold back his progress. What will turn him on most is seeing that you love him and want him.

## *Caressing*

As we said at the start of this section, although a woman can be turned on by almost anything if she is in the mood, a man is mainly turned on by having his mind and genitals stimulated. This means that he will want his partner to get to his penis as soon as possible. Don't be hurried but tantalise him and make him wait.

## *How to handle a penis*

The most sensitive portions of the penis are the lower rim of the head and the bridge of skin connecting the foreskin to the head on the underside. The shaft is relatively insensitive – like the outer lips of the vulva. Casually watching a man masturbate may give the impression that he holds his penis in his hand and more or less pumps it. This is not quite so. Usually his thumb and index finger are used to encircle and stimulate the lower rim in a to-and-fro massaging movement. His other fingers surround the shaft but as the skin over the shaft is so mobile it simply moves backwards and forwards with the hand and contributes little to the sensation.

Watching him closely whilst he masturbates and then practising whilst he gives advice on how firmly to hold the penis and the rate of movement required should allow his technique to be learned rapidly. Anointing the penis with baby-oil can help overcome any slight imperfections in technique.

In some men the foreskin is too tight to retract so direct stimulation of the rim is impossible. To masturbate they usually massage the whole head through the foreskin using the tips of the fingers.

Although some men hate it, most like to have their scrotum and testes held, or even squeezed, as they are masturbated by their partner. This can be easily achieved by squatting between his open thighs as he lies on his back.

Just as woman can be driven wild by oral caresses of their vulvas, most men love to have their penis kissed and gently sucked. 'Oral sex' has become enormously commonplace in the last thirty years but is not, of course, new. Some women enjoy this oral intercourse, but most find they choke if the penis goes to the back of their throat, or they do not like the taste of the semen. Some women are perfectly happy if their partner ejaculates into their mouths but do not like swallowing the semen. They keep a tissue handy or go to the bathroom to spit it out and rinse their mouths. You cannot get

Fellatio: *As with cunnilingus, not all women are keen to do it (especially to ejaculation) and not all men are keen to have it done to them. Fellatio is, however, increasingly fashionable.*

pregnant from swallowing semen; and there is no proven health hazard, unless the man has a sexually transmitted disease.

Most women use oral stimulation as part of foreplay and not as a type of intercourse. A very substantial proportion of men going to prostitutes ask them to kiss and suck their penises, clearly having an unfulfilled need that any woman can cater for with her partner.

Start off simply licking and kissing his penis lightly and gently, and then slowly take the head of the penis into your mouth. Keep your mouth wide open, keep your teeth out of the way and then start to run your tongue around the rim of his penis and all over the tip. Put it into the opening a little and do whatever the man enjoys. Push your head up and down so that the penis goes in and out of your mouth, first deeply and then more shallowly. Use your tongue to stimulate the little ridge on the underside of the tip of the penis – most men find this very exciting. Although many women think they should be sucking when doing this, it is not necessary or even desirable though a gentle suction can be pleasant. Never, ever, blow down the penis.

If you sense that your partner's breathing is getting heavy and you feel that he is about to ejaculate, take his penis out of your mouth and caress him to orgasm (perhaps over your breasts) or slip his penis into your vagina. Most men get an enormously powerful erection when stimulated in this way, and a man who has problems obtaining an erection may very well not be able to get one at all without oral stimulation. Older men often respond very well to oral stimulation.

## Unusual love games and foreplay

Let us make no bones about it: Nature meant a man and a woman to have intercourse with a penis going into a vagina. Unfortunately, due to unconscious anxieties, some people find that they cannot get sufficiently aroused to have intercourse unless they do things beforehand which many people would consider 'odd' or 'kinky'. These include sado-masochistic practices (hurting and being hurt); dressing up, for example, in leather, sexy outfits or furs; and having to have intercourse in strange locations. Many couples flirt with things like this on the odd occasion but they never become compulsive or an essential part of their love-making.

Foreplay, by definition, usually leads to intercourse and is not an end in itself. Unfortunately, some people get hung up on the sorts of practices mentioned above and substitute foreplay for intercourse almost all the time. Sex now becomes totally out of balance – the pleasure comes mostly from the furs, the dress, the place, or whatever and not from the person. Such people do not enjoy the pleasures of intercourse for its own sake and can also experience two other problems. First, they seriously reduce the numbers of partners they can hope to find and second, some such practices can actually be dangerous if they get out of control. Many of the people who need such turn-ons during their foreplay are very inhibited. They are not 'sex maniacs', as people generally think, but they get more pleasure from their particular turn-on than from intercourse.

The picture here is changing though as AIDS affects people's sex lives. Some couples who are unsure of their partner's sexual health use pleasuring or foreplay as an end in itself – perhaps followed by masturbation. This is certainly a form of safer sex.

# *Chapter 12*
# Intercourse

## What intercourse is all about

Anyone can copulate with a willing member of the opposite sex, as we saw earlier, but the act is not necessarily based upon an intimate knowledge of the sexuality of the partner and, although it can be exciting and gratifying, in reality it amounts to no more than masturbation using the genitals of the opposite sex. A lot of couples, married or not, spend much of their sexual lives copulating with one another and not having intercourse, let alone making love. They have never communicated about their sexual needs and preferences. This can come about because of shyness, inhibition, lack of courage, or a lack of knowledge or imagination.

For most couples the desire to please and to give pleasure, along with the desire to experiment, leads to the elaboration of simple copulation into intercourse. This elaboration expresses the needs and the sexual personalities (sexualities) of that particular couple. As they develop and grow together as a couple they develop a pattern of sexual behaviour which is unique to them. Copulation at its most basic is almost entirely a physical experience but intercourse is much more. It involves the personalities and intimate needs and desires of the people involved. Love is certainly not a prerequisite for enjoyable and fulfilling intercourse – but it helps. Some people, however, find it difficult to express themselves sexually with someone they love. This is one of the many ironies of sexual dysfunction.

Some women are so excited by the thought of intercourse that they have an orgasm at or soon after penetration. Many men have the same experience but if they can develop an attitude of mind which thinks of penetration, at least initially, as being a continuation of their foreplay techniques, they find they can make intercourse last as long as they or their partner wishes. It is possible to do this by accepting the pleasurable sensations in the penis and, instead of trying to suppress awareness of them by thinking of something non-sexual, trying to focus attention on the partner and her responses. When they finally decide to 'let go', perhaps on some mutually agreed signal from the woman such as, for example, her stroking him in some particular way, they can unleash their sexual desires and start to move in a way which produces maximum penile pleasure. At this stage the man often becomes relatively unaware of the woman's reactions because his own pleasure is so intense. On the other hand his mounting passion, tension and vigour may be more than sufficient for his partner to obtain an (or another) orgasm. Trying to obtain a simultaneous orgasm by any other means can all too easily reduce what should be a spontaneous pleasure to a series of predetermined goals which have to be worked hard for. Most people find this takes the fun out of sex, even if on occasions it results in them climaxing together.

From the point at which he 'lets go' the man is no longer concerned with how long he lasts, and the time it takes him to have an orgasm is likely to be somewhere between a half to three minutes. The average man on the majority of occasions ejaculates within two minutes or less, unless he learns to control the situation. Exceptions are those men who suffer from a form of impotence known as retarded ejaculation. Any man can teach himself to establish ejaculatory control and there are several well-tried techniques available. These include the determination of a frequency of ejaculation reasonable for the individual man (if he goes too many days between orgasms he will be too 'trigger-happy'); the rehearsal in fantasy of the technique we have just described when he masturbates; and the practice of semi-masturbation in which he rubs his erect penis with accompanying fantasies but does not allow himself to reach orgasm. By doing these things the average man can easily get used to maintaining an erection for long periods without ejaculating and can then ejaculate at will. Most experts would agree that being able to do this is valuable because most, if not all, women enjoy some prolongation of the act and many complain that their men are too quick. Premature ejaculation as such is a somewhat different problem and is discussed later.

Women too can train themselves through masturbation to develop attitudes and practices of value in intercourse. For many women their desire for intercourse rises with the amount they masturbate. Through masturbation and appropriate fantasy a woman can train herself to increase her excitement during intercourse and so reduce the time it takes to have an orgasm. As far as we know, those women who have a capacity for multiple orgasms establish it first by masturbating. The ability to masturbate well is basic to intercourse, just as learning to talk is the basis of the ability to converse. In a way successful and enjoyable intercourse could be described as two masturbators comparing notes and then making it perfect for each other. In fact, unless you know exactly what your partner likes when masturbating you will not get the best out of intercourse.

But this view of intercourse reveals a common difficulty. For reasons discussed elsewhere in the book, some men find that they perpetually prefer to adopt a passive role in intercourse. This may be one reason why prostitution is popular – the man can pay a woman to do things to *him*. In some cases all that can be done to help such couples is to suggest that they each take it in turns to be active and passive. Most men have occasional masturbation fantasies of the woman taking charge and most women have occasional fantasies of being in charge. So most couples are likely to enjoy occasional role reversal in intercourse and this of course doubles their repertoire. Some women, on the other hand, have a need to be totally passive, since to behave in any other way would raise their sense of guilt to a point where they can no longer enjoy themselves. Such women can often be unsatisfactory partners, especially for the older man who needs prolonged stimulation from the woman if he is to function well.

To some degree we are all reared with inhibitions about intercourse. One effect this has is to raise anxiety, which in turn tends to make men ejaculate earlier than would otherwise be the case and to delay orgasm in women. Good masturbation can help to master and dispel these inhibitions but both sexes also need their partner's help to abolish them. So, a woman who understands her sexuality and the needs of her body should educate her partner, and her partner, by encouraging her to develop her capabilities, can liberate her from her inner inhibitions. After all, between the two of them there should be complete openness and a willingness to do what the other wants.

The trouble with inhibitions is that they tend to increase one's awareness and vigilance. The individual, so to speak, 'watches' him or herself for any infringement of the unconscious 'rules', and this is exactly the opposite to what is needed for good intercourse. What we need to do is to cut off our earlier taught restraints so that we can totally lose conscious control of what we are doing during intercourse. In this sense, good intercourse is a kind of regression to babyhood and this may be the reason why some couples indulge in baby-like talk and noises when making love. After a certain point in the proceedings rational talk reimposes awareness of the real world and undermines the other-worldiness so vital for good intercourse. Some people, especially women, fearing total sexual abandonment, continue to talk, as a defence against this loss of control. The same end can be achieved if a woman self-consciously concentrates on having an orgasm instead of relaxing and letting it happen. An inhibited man too may over-concentrate on the state of his penis, his partner's physiological responses, or the mechanics of intercourse. Although he achieves his unconscious inhibiting aim of pleasure reduction by doing these things, the consequence is likely to be poor performance and early ejaculation with a poor-quality orgasm.

So much for the background factors so vital to success in enjoyable and fulfilling intercourse. Realising they exist, recognising them and dealing with them can help a man and a woman help each other. *The overwhelming principle, contrary to what most sex books would have you believe, is that attitudes are more important than techniques.* The most powerful sex organ of the body is the brain. Too many 'experts' have put far too much emphasis on genital technique and positions during intercourse. The vast majority of couples with good, enjoyable and lasting sexual relationships do not spend their lives changing techniques but eventually learn to make love in a few tried and tested ways that they find mutually enjoyable and satisfying.

Having said this, it is helpful to be aware of some of the many ways in which it is possible to have intercourse, because most couples want to experiment from time to time and need to be aware of the alternatives there are at special times of life, for example, during pregnancy.

## What about positions?

There is nothing magical about the choice of position for intercourse. There is no virtue whatsoever in experimenting for the sake of it if you are both happy with the way things are. Problems arise when one partner is happy with the status quo and the other wants more variety. There is only one way out of this dilemma and that is to talk it over.

Any positions in which the penis and vagina can be brought into approximate alignment can be used. Rather than catalogue all these positions it is probably more useful to consider the various central factors involved. These can be summarised as the alignment of the penis; its penetration; body contact; the movement of the penis in the vagina; and special methods of stimulation.

Obviously the easiest way to put the penis into the vagina is straight in, so that the length of the penis goes in parallel with the woman's vaginal walls. This will mean the couple getting into one of various positions which become obvious when you try them out. In some positions the penis does not go straight up the length of the vagina but goes in at an angle. Inserting the penis at an angle to the line of the vagina is usually uncomfortable, but some women enjoy it because of the greater distension it produces of the vaginal opening or even because of the slight pain. It is important to bear in mind that the only part of a woman's vagina that is at all sensitive is its opening and a little way inside – the depths of the vagina are virtually unable to sense anything, apart from movement. Deep inside, the vagina is probably even less sensitive than the skin of the shaft of the penis. It is because of this that the size of the penis does not matter to a woman. Forward angulation so that the tip of the penis presses hard on the front wall of the vagina produces sensations in the urethra (urinary passage) which can lead to orgasm in some women. This comes about because it stimulates the G-spot. In many others it is unpleasant because it makes them want to pass water. Backward angulation so that the rear wall of the vagina is jabbed by the penis can be uncomfortable or even painful if the woman is constipated, but such a position brings the base of the penis into closer proximity to the clitoris and so is more likely to stimulate it. When the man is in a position in which he controls the angle of his penis, such as when he is on top of the woman, he is unlikely to make much use of it but when the woman is on top she can stimulate the front wall of the vagina by leaning backwards, or the clitoris by leaning forwards.

Most, if not all, men like deep penetration, especially as they reach orgasm. If a woman is nervous of deep penetration the couple can use a position in which she controls it. Man-below, woman-on-top positions are good for this. If her partner is on top, a woman can also control penetration at any time, by closing her thighs. Because of the tenting effect which occurs at the inner end of the vagina during peak excitement, the tip of the penis probably receives less stimulation in deepish penetration, provided the to-and-fro motions are not too great. This can help men with ejaculatory control problems.

The deepest penetration is possible in positions in which the woman's thighs are bent towards her chest. Positions such as these with the woman on her back with her knees on her breasts, or on all fours (particularly if her forehead is on the bed) allow the penis to be deeply inserted into the vagina. The more her thighs are in line with her body and the more they are closed, the less the penetration. Men who masturbate by clasping their penis between their thighs usually have difficulty in getting sufficient stimulation from the vagina to reach orgasm. They, and men who tend to lose their erection after penetration, can be helped by having the woman beneath them with her legs out straight. After the penis has been inserted, she then closes her legs and the man places his thighs outside hers. Some men say they

# Intercourse positions

| Man's position | Woman's position | Woman's legs | Vaginal entry from | Advantages disadvantages recommended for |
|---|---|---|---|---|
|  Standing | standing | apart | front | A/C/F/G/J/L/N |
|  Standing | legs wrapped around his waist | widely apart | front | B/F/J/P/R/d |
| 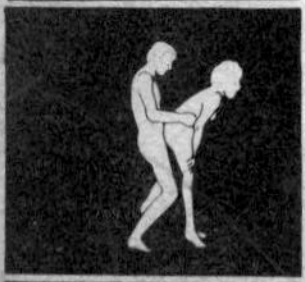 Standing | standing, leaning forward | slightly apart | behind | B/E/G/J/N/S/T/a |
|  Standing | facing away on all fours on bed | widely apart | behind | B/E/G/J/L/N/P/S/a |
|  Standing | on all fours with straight legs, hands flat on floor | widely apart | behind | B/P/S/a |
| 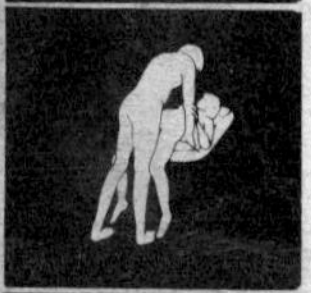 Standing | lying on back on table | widely apart | front | B/C/D/E/F/G/H/N |
| 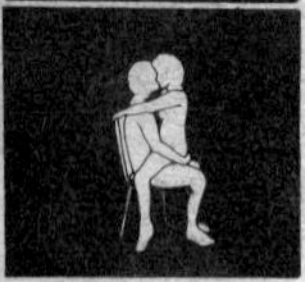 Sitting on chair | sitting on penis facing him | widely apart | front | A/B/F/G/J/P/b/c |

| | Man's position | Woman's position | Woman's legs | Vaginal entry from | Advantages disadvantages recommended for |
|---|---|---|---|---|---|
| 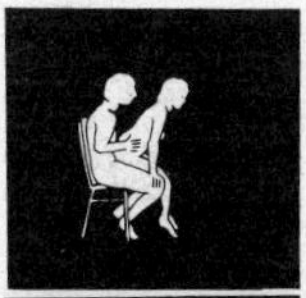 | Sitting on chair | sitting on penis back to him | apart or together | behind | A/B/E/G/J/L/M/N/b |
|  | Sitting on chair | sitting across his lap with one leg over chair arm | apart | front | C/E/F/G/J/L/M/R/b/d |
|  | Sitting in narrow armchair | sitting facing man | widely apart, knees resting on arms of chair or on seat | front | B/F/G/J/N/a/c |
| 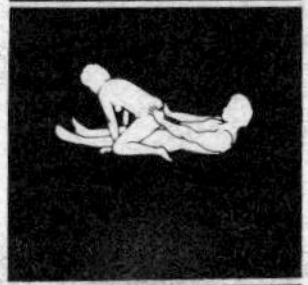 | On back, legs straight and together | Kneeling over penis facing his feet | widely apart, knees or feet on bed | behind | A/C/D/J/M/P/d |
| 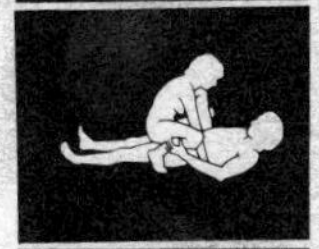 | On back, knees bent or straight | squatting over penis facing him | widely apart, feet on bed | front | A/B/E/F/G/H/J/M/N/R/c |
| 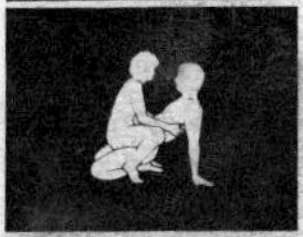 | Kneeling, leaning back on hands for support | she sits on his penis facing him | apart, astride his closed legs | front | A/B/F/H/J/M/N/R/c |
|  | Kneeling, facing woman | flat on back on edge of bed or low table or sitting in a chair | apart, feet flat on floor | front | B/D/F/G/H/K/M/N/O/a |

| | Man's position | Woman's position | Woman's legs | Vaginal entry from | Advantages disadvantages recommended for |
|---|---|---|---|---|---|
|  | Kneeling, facing woman | sitting in a chair or on edge of bed | pulled up to chest, heels on man's buttocks | front | B/D/G/H/K/M/N/O/a |
|  | Kneeling, facing woman | lying flat on back on edge of bed or low table | apart, ankles locked behind his back or neck | front | B/G/H/K/M/N/O/b |
|  | Kneeling, behind woman | kneeling, facing away from man, trunk supported, on bed or table or simply on all fours | together or apart | behind | B/N/G/J/P/a |
| 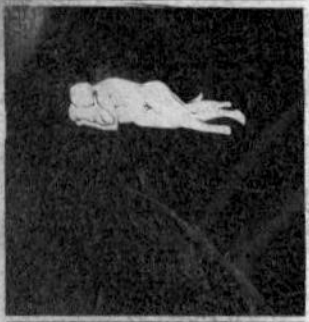 | Face down, body weight mainly supported on knees and elbows | flat on her back | apart, flat on bed | front | B/F/K/N/O/Q/b |
|  | Face down, body weight mainly supported on knees and elbows | flat on her back | together | front | F/K/N/O/Q/b |
| 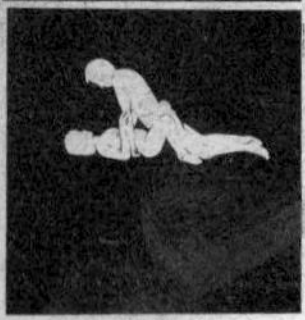 | Face down, body weight mainly supported on knees and elbows | flat on her back | widely apart, feet flat on bed, bent thighs | front | B/F/K/N/O/a |

| | Man's position | Woman's position | Woman's legs | Vaginal entry from | Advantages disadvantages recommended for |
|---|---|---|---|---|---|
| 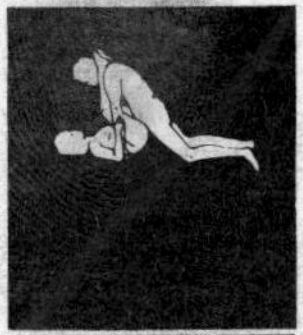 | Face down, body weight mainly supported on knees and elbows | flat on her back | knees on breasts, ankles over his shoulders | front | B/K/N/S/a |
|  | Face down lying on top of woman, supporting weight on elbow | face down | wide apart | behind | C/S/T/a |
|  | On side | on side, 'moulding' into his body contours, facing away from him | together, parallel | behind | B/D/E/G/N/b |
|  | On side | facing away from him, bending top leg and resting foot flat on man or bed | apart, with top leg raised | behind | B/D/E/G/L/M/N/O/T/b |
| 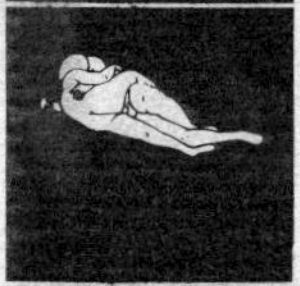 | On side, thighs bent upwards | on side facing him, legs apart, man lying between them | apart | front | F/M/N/P |
| 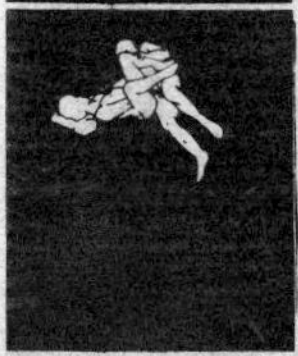 | On side at right angles to woman's body | on back, legs drawn up, feet flat on bed or held up by woman grasping behind knees | apart | behind | B/D/E/G/J/K/L/N/O/Q/T/d |

**Key to symbols used in intercourse position chart**

- A Woman can move
- B Allows deep penetration
- C Shallow penetration only
- D Good during pregnancy
- E Allows access to clitoris
- F Couple can kiss
- G Man can caress partner's breasts
- H Man can see vulval area
- J Needs little undressing
- K Good for conception
- L Woman can reach scrotum
- M Stimulates G-spot
- N One partner can stimulate body of other
- O Good for learning sex with a new partner
- P Anus accessible in woman
- Q Anus accessible in man
- R Tiring
- S Stimulates back wall of vagina
- T Good for female orgasms in some inexperienced women

**Movement**

- a Allows full stroke movement
- b Full penetration with slight movement – also allows control of speed to orgasm
- c Woman can move – can greatly assist women with orgasm problems during intercourse
- d Neither can move much – woman stimulates man using pelvic muscles
- e Both can move well

---

need general muscle tension if they are to obtain a good orgasm. Rear entry with both partners standing but the woman bending forwards is an example of how this can be achieved, especially if he has to stand on tiptoe to bring the penis level with the vagina, perhaps because she is wearing high-heeled shoes.

For those who get a lot of pleasure from cuddling and close physical contact, the man-on-top and the 'spoons' positions are best. Rear entry, woman-on-top, and the left-lateral positions involve less body contact, as does that with the woman sitting with her legs apart and the man kneeling between them.

## Movement

A common notion in Victorian times was that '*ladies* do not move'. This may well be true but only *women* can have intercourse. However, a man with difficulties in controlling the time of ejaculation can find that passionate movements by his woman destroy his control. On the other hand an older man or a man with a tendency to slow ejaculation or a loss of erection may benefit from his partner's movements. A woman can move most freely in positions in which her body is free. These include positions such as the rear-entry, woman-on-top, and left-lateral. Women like to move in all kinds of ways during intercourse and movements include thrusting and rotating the pelvis so that the penis is swept around the interior of the vagina. The best way to imagine this is to think of the base of a felt-tip pen inserted into the vagina. The woman then draws circles with the tip. A woman can also contract her pelvic muscles. If this is done as the penis moves inwards and if they are released as it moves outwards, it greatly enhances the sensation for both partners.

A little practice during masturbation or during intercourse pays real dividends. A variation of this is for the penis to remain motionless in the vagina and for the woman, by repeatedly contracting and relaxing her pelvic muscles, to bring her partner, and herself, to orgasm.

In positions in which the man mainly controls the movement, he usually wants to move at a speed which corresponds to the one he uses when masturbating. Some like short, rapid movements and others slow, long ones. Women have their preferences too and a communicating couple will tell each other what they want. Quick, teasing movements at the vaginal opening without full penetration and even total withdrawal from and re-penetration of the vagina, for example, can, at the early stages of intercourse, bring some women to orgasm.

## Adding to the excitement

Special methods of stimulation can add pleasure to either or both partners, but some people worry about them in the belief that they are perverted. It is commonly accepted that no sexual activity is wrong between a couple in private if it harms neither of them and they both willingly agree to it. A woman wearing special clothes can greatly please some men. Hearing their partner use words such as 'fuck', 'cunt' or 'spunk' during intercourse can bring some people to near-instant orgasm. If the woman likes to have both her breasts held this can be achieved in the 'spoons', woman-on-top and rear-entry positions. Some men like their scrotum held or their testes squeezed and this is easy in the rear-entry, the left-lateral and the man-on-top positions. Since the vast majority of women do not have an orgasm with penile thrusting alone, they will need their clitoris stimulated if they are to have an orgasm at all. This is easily achieved in the left-lateral position and to a lesser extent in the rear-entry and woman-on-top ones. The best thing is to experiment and find a position you both like.

Looking is an important source of sexual stimulation to some people and not being seen, to others. Women especially may not want to be watched and this can easily be achieved by turning off the light or using positions in which her face is turned away, such as the rear-entry, 'spoons' and woman-on-top positions where she faces the man's feet. The left-lateral and woman-on-top positions allow the man to watch his partner and this can powerfully affect some men. Watching their partner's movements and facial contortions at orgasm is intensely exciting for some women and a man who particularly likes to see his partner's bottom or to watch his penis moving in and out of her vagina will find rear entry particularly exciting. A couple who like to watch can use mirrors.

Although each couple will find for themselves the positions that give them most pleasure, certain deserve a few special comments. The missionary or man-on-top position is often condemned as unimaginative yet well over half of all women say it is their favourite. If the man takes some of his weight on his elbows and knees so as to form a bridge over her, she is not crushed. She can reach her clitoris and the man has a fine degree of control over the alignment, movement and penetration of his penis. Whilst still taking his weight on his arms he can place one behind her upper back in order to bring her (and especially her breasts) towards him, and with the other under her bottom he can control her movement and even stimulate her anus if she likes that. Kissing and biting her ears and neck, which some women find very stimulating, is possible and this position is probably best for those who like intercourse to be romantic. Women whose inhibitions prevent them from being too active or who enjoy feeling helpless particularly enjoy this position, but it is also suitable for those women who like to move – this is possible if the man bridges over her.

The 'spoons' position, in which the woman lies curled up on her side and the man lies behind her and curled around her, is a rear-entry position and therefore allows the man to stimulate her breasts and clitoris. In the 'reverse spoons' the woman faces the man on her side and the man, also on his side, lies between her legs, one of which is under her waist and the other over it. Some women have a marked preference for this position, perhaps because they masturbate on their side. If the woman sits with her legs apart on the edge of a chair and the man kneels between them this is really a 'reverse spoons' position but with the couple vertical rather than on their side.

The left-lateral position is used by right-handed men and the right-lateral by the left-handed ones. It is an excellent position for the

A variation for intercourse: *Experimentation, especially popular in the young, can greatly add to excitement and pleasure during intercourse.*

early days of intercourse and for getting a woman used to having an orgasm during intercourse. It is easiest to understand by imagining the man sitting on a chair with his penis erect and his thighs together. The woman sits at right angles to him on his lap so that his penis enters her vagina. She faces to his right and her legs are widely separated. If it is now imagined that the couple fall through a right angle to his left so that the woman is on her back and he curled around her right side and lying on his left side. Her clitoris is nicely exposed and he can easily stimulate her with his right hand. She is free to move, and control their joint movements, and can hold his scrotum and testes in her left hand. He can kiss her right breast and fondle her left one and also assess her stage in the sexual-response cycle from the changes in her nipples and breasts.

Rear entry, with the woman bending forwards, on all fours, or draped over some suitable object, allows very deep penetration and a lot of exquisite genital sensations for both sexes. Many women regard it as dog-like and so unconsciously discourage it – often by unconsciously contracting their vaginal muscles, thus causing pain.

Woman-on-top positions are often preferred by passive men; by women who like to control penetration, alignment and movement; and perhaps by women who still have unconscious childhood fantasies about having a secret penis. A woman's thrusting may activate the pleasure of her fantasy. Many women who can have orgasms only during intercourse in this position are often curiously inhibited and even tense in other positions. As a variation the man can hold the woman by her buttocks and then move himself.

Something that works well for the woman who wants to obtain an orgasm actually during intercourse but has difficulty doing so is for her to masturbate herself in her usual position and then for the man to adjust his own position as best he can so as to put his penis into her.

Studies of the fantasies of many women show that they want their men to take charge and even to order them about sexually. This is usually a way of overcoming their guilty feelings. By being 'ordered' to do something she would otherwise not do she feels freed from the responsibility for her action. If such a woman wants to have an orgasm during intercourse it is probably wise for the man always to suggest that she stimulates her clitoris (when he is not doing it for her), whatever position is used, because cultural inhibitions can make it essential for her to have a lot of stimulation if she is to overcome the barriers to orgasm during intercourse.

After intercourse many women like to masturbate – not necessarily because they are dissatisfied, as many are, but because the orgasm feels different and completes the session for them. Because so many women are shy or because they think their men will be cross or offended, some go to the bathroom to masturbate or even wait until he is asleep. It makes sense for such women to masturbate after intercourse while he helps her by fondling and kissing her. Few men are selfless enough to do this but it is well worth the effort, in the interests of the loving relationship.

Not all intercourse has to be genital to genital. It can be mouth to genital, hand to genital, or genital to anus. (Anal sex is discussed in more detail on page 319.) Most couples use these methods as foreplay techniques but they can be used right up to orgasm as well.

Location can affect the pleasure of intercourse. 'Naughty' sex pleases certain individuals, most of whom occasionally fantasise about intercourse out of doors, or in situations in which they might be discovered. Hotels and holidays promote intercourse for the same reason and because the lovers are relaxed. Intercourse whilst travelling on ships and trains can also be especially nice. Intercourse when the couple are close to others (such as under a blanket on a crowded beach) is a real turn-on to some but may verge on exhibitionism. Although people enjoying such situations appear at first to be 'oversexed' they are, in fact, often highly inhibited. They do what they do because they need more stimulus to get aroused.

Many people have a marked preference for intercourse at a certain time of day. Usually, they are also most likely to masturbate then. A couple may be out of phase on this, however, and compromises will be necessary if they are to have a successful sex life.

Some couples have intercourse on a pre-planned basis (for example every Friday night), but most simply go by their instincts and feelings at the time. There is nothing wrong with premeditated intercourse – looking forward to anything is always half the pleasure – but if intercourse becomes so stereotyped that it is forbidden (or even only unlikely) at other times, this is probably harmful to a couple's sex life. If pre-planning is tantalising, spontaneous 'quickie' intercourse is delicious. There really should be no rules – if a couple feels like having intercourse, whether the woman is pregnant, breastfeeding, having a period, ill or whatever, they should do it if it is acceptable and pleasing to them both.

Most couples have intercourse on their bed but, as we have seen, this is by no means essential. Varying the place can be far more stimulating and fulfilling than varying the position for the sake of it. If you always wait until the circumstances are 'just right' for intercourse (people's definitions of this, of course, vary considerably), you could be waiting a long time and your sex life may suffer, especially if you have young children, are ill, or have social or work circumstances that make it difficult to have intercourse as often as you would like.

## Using fantasies

As mentioned in the chapter on courtship, the sharing of fantasies is a sensible way to ensure compatibility. For those in an established relationship who have not done so previously it can present difficulties. Few people would seriously want to fulfil every fantasy even if they had the chance of doing so but talking about them communicates something of value. If the partners are self-confident and aren't on the look-out for criticism in everything, then sharing fantasies is exciting, amusing and promotes love. The whole point of the sharing is to extend understanding and cooperation. It opens up new possibilities which can be jointly explored, if only in part or in a modified form. Since fantasies used in self-masturbation change, slowly maintaining this communication is an on-going way of keeping sexual boredom at bay. As mentioned later, personal masturbation in the relationship also has another value, that of keeping extra-marital affairs in check.

A degree of apprehension and nervousness is understandable at first when sharing fantasies and one way round this is to read sexy books in bed together, especially those with readers' letters. Use the topics raised to see if they excite any response. Checking the genitals of your partner to see if they have become aroused also helps.

An interesting fact is that when partners in an established relationship eventually do reveal all they often discover that their fantasies match with, for example, the woman fantasising about a man doing to her just what her partner fantasises doing to a woman.

In clinical practice it is usually found that individuals in a good, satisfying relationship very commonly use fantasies involving members of the opposite sex other than their partner. These may be well-known figures such as film stars, friends, acquaintances or even strangers encountered in everyday life. Of course men and women also commonly have fantasies involving faceless, non-specific members of the opposite sex. This, along with occasional flirting, can be protective to the marital relationship because it is less threatening than actually having intercourse with others.

Other difficulties can arise from sharing fantasies. Some individuals, both men and women, have been brought up to be so inhibited about sex that they consciously restrict their fantasies or even abolish them from the consciousness altogether. In this way a woman may feel that prostitution, for example, is so revolting that even if a prostitution-type fantasy came into her mind she would banish it at once.

Some men's fantasies are perpetually passive – the woman always takes charge of them. Women often fantasise that they are in a passive role because they have been brought up to believe that sex is something men do *to* them. Obviously if both partners fantasise passively they cannot really satisfy each other. The best solution in this situation is for them to agree to take it in turns to have their fantasy indulged.

A similar type of difficulty can arise when one partner, usually the man, always has fantasies of activities that do not culminate in intercourse. Some individuals are inhibited about intercourse and so encourage activities close to it, such as oral sex, which avoid the act of intercourse itself. Sometimes, although intercourse is what they would like, their most arousing fantasies are about, for example, dressing in women's clothing, or the woman being tied up and/or beaten.

With these difficulties in mind, the sharing of fantasies allows the circumstances and types of intercourse to be so adjusted as to give maximal pleasure to both partners. It means that intercourse becomes unique to that couple and adds to their sense of private adventure. It also, perhaps, makes it less likely that either partner will seek adventure elsewhere, because they are both totally pleased and catered for within their sharing relationship.

Women frequently say that if they have to tell their man what to do it reduces their pleasure. This problem is solved if the man reserves some of her fantasies for occasional and unexpected use, especially if he adds a few variations of his own.

Good sex is neither exclusively of the mind nor of the body – it is a blend of both. As a result intercourse proceeds at least as much at the psychological level as at the physical level. The sharing of fantasies teaches partners about each other and this can be very important for men, who are frequently brought up to believe, usually unconsciously, that women are really sexless and have intercourse only to please a man or because they love him.

## The first time

A man, although he may not be consciously aware of it, can be disabled by a fear which probably took root in the Oedipal stage of childhood but which now emerges as fear of failure, getting his partner pregnant, or of catching VD or AIDS. Consciously he may think he is just over-excited but he may experience difficulty erecting; a loss of erection; ejaculation prior to penetration or as soon as it is accomplished; an inability to penetrate; and so on. One way or another intercourse is thus avoided. The only sensible advice is not to worry, to accept that such problems are commonplace, and to keep on trying. Prior masturbation to orgasm steadies the nerves of some and, given that a young man can erect again quickly, he can have a second attempt.

Similar apprehensions sometimes afflict girls. If a girl is too tense the muscles around the entrance of her vagina contract making penetration difficult, painful, or even impossible. The techniques mentioned for dealing with painful intercourse in the 'Sexual Difficulties' chapter will be useful at such times.

Girls can help themselves before first attempting intercourse by using tampons, thereby breaking or stretching the hymen. Some use their fingers (or similar objects) in the vagina as a part of masturbation, accompanied by fantasies of being penetrated. The entrance to the vagina can be very tight in an inexperienced female but, unless she is unduly afraid, stretching the area is usually a pleasurable sensation.

Fears of intercourse can be so excessive in some women that penetration is never achieved. Any attempt leads to closing the thighs, arching the back and screaming. Such women often marry men who have their own anxieties about intercourse and after many years of marriage the women are still virgins. Usually it is their desire to become pregnant which brings them to the notice of the medical profession.

These are extreme cases with underlying serious psychosexual problems which do not affect most women. The perfectly normal apprehensions and fears of virgins about to undertake intercourse can be overcome by the techniques of adjustment mentioned earlier under 'Courtship' and by setting the scene suitably. For example, contraception should be sorted out prior to first intercourse; a location where disturbance is unlikely should be selected; sufficient foreplay to induce copious lubrication should be undertaken (or KY jelly used to reduce friction); and the woman should be so sure she wants to do it that she is eager and excited about it. If these 'conditions' aren't met or nearly met it is best to remain at the level of mutual masturbation for a further period of time.

The young can be very disappointed with themselves and their early intercourse experiences. Although intercourse may be natural it is, like everything else in life, also a skill which needs mastering. Due to the anti-sexual nature of our western culture it takes most couples time to overcome their underlying fears and embarrassments. On average it seems to take about five years to become proficient at sex, even with a helpful partner.

## Perpetual intercourse

Where the partners are in a happy, loving, communicating and understanding relationship, intercourse, in the widest sense of the term, is a continuous activity. After all, intercourse is more than just the penis being placed in the vagina. Loving and sexual talk, affectionate behaviour and erotic contacts such as kissing, breast fondling and brief genital manipulation indulged in frequently throughout a couple's daily life build up sexual tension in both. Looking and showing, especially in the case of the woman wearing underclothes which her partner finds erotic, all help to add to it. In these, and a hundred other ways more particular and personal to themselves, the couple build up one another's desires to a point where genital expression becomes urgent.

Well adjusted couples do not even have to ask – they know when they are ready. Then they can read each other's mood and adjust foreplay as required. For example, the man can tell if the woman is in an 'I want to be forced' mood and so after a chasing game he will take her with irresistible passion. Alternatively, she can tell if he wants to be seduced and can then put on her best 'mistress' behaviour followed by intercourse, perhaps with her on top. On other occasions they both know they would like a prolonged encounter with plenty of foreplay, romance, gentleness and tenderness. This sort of relationship has an element of 'natural morality' in it since no sensible person with such a partner would want to bother with anyone else, they would simply take too long to train or might even be untrainable.

All this contrasts sharply with those men who, for example, when their partner hears them clean their teeth before coming to bed knows she is for it. When he squeezes and sucks her breasts hard, which she may dislike but she has never said and he has never asked, it confirms she is to do her duty – and this with a man who, perhaps, scarcely pays any attention to her except when he wants her genitally. Although perhaps somewhat exaggerated, this scenario, or a variation of it, is so commonplace as to make one wonder why affairs and divorce are not even more common. Equivalent bad behaviour in women includes, for example, asking the man if he has finished yet whilst the act is still in progress, and so on. Such men and women are copulators and often fear the intimacy and self-exposure which true intercourse involves.

*Chapter 13*

# Sexual difficulties

It has become fashionable in recent years to talk about people's sexual problems as if we were being afflicted by a new epidemic. To some extent we may today be in the throes of a period of more prevalent sexual dysfunctioning but on the other hand, because of the publicity sexual problems now receive, people who in the past would have kept quiet about them now feel willing to discuss them or seek help. Also, the apparent increase in sexual problems may to some extent be the result of an increased level of expectation, brought about by the increased discussion of sex. However, sexual problems are not new: they have always been around.

Public awareness and the pressure of the women's movement over the last thirty years has definitely and provably increased men's anxieties about sexual performance, and many are now so concerned about their ability to give their partners an orgasm that they have impaired their ability to enjoy their own sex lives. The assertiveness of women outside the bedroom has also adversely affected many men and this is reflected in their reduced practical interest in sex. Modern middle-class men are under tremendous pressure to perform in and out of bed, at work, in the home, socially, and at play, to such an extent that sex is often pushed to the end of their list of priorities. There is evidence to suggest that intercourse rates are falling and some researchers now believe that the male population is in sexual retreat.

There are many causes, both psychological and physical, for sexual problems and more are recognised each year. In a book such as this we can give only the briefest outline of the main problem areas.

## Underlying causes

Although an increasing number of sexual difficulties are known to be the result of physical illness, the majority are probably of psychological origin. It is always possible that discoveries such as the fact that high prolactin or oestrogen production in some men can produce impotence will explain some sexual difficulties but they are unlikely to be the explanation in most cases.

It is not only an absence of hard biological evidence that leads us to say that most sex problems originate in the mind; there are other reasons too. First, when investigated, most people's sex problems show sufficient evidence of a psychosexual origin to make it worth considering this as a serious possibility. Second, psychotherapeutic techniques (talk therapy) perhaps combined with other techniques that do not involve drugs or surgery, often relieve the problem. Clearly most sexual problems have little or nothing to do with the body's basic plumbing. Evidence for this is seen in many cases. For example, the man who cannot erect for intercourse but wakes with an erection in the morning and, judged by the stains on his sheets, has night emissions too. Many people with problems are reluctant to consult a doctor, sometimes because they feel that he or she will think badly of them or does not have the time to treat them, whilst others put off seeking help because they do not believe help is available or effective.

At the heart of the psychological factors that prevent sexual success and produce sexual casualties is the anti-sexual nature of our culture. As we have mentioned elsewhere, conservatism on the subject of sex in child rearing leads to the unconscious transmission of sexual suppression from one generation to the next and sex education, at least as it is practised at present, does little to redress the balance.

Normal religious beliefs affect the situation very little except that children brought up in religiously extreme homes have more than their fair share of sexual problems as adults. As we have already explained, in the chapter on childhood sexuality, problems arising from the Oedipal complex can also disrupt sexuality in later life and result in sex difficulties. A false perception of the partner, as in the case of, for example, a man who unconsciously identifies his partner too much with his mother, may result in rare or unenjoyable intercourse.

Avoidance of intercourse, making it brief as in premature ejaculation or reducing the full pleasure by not reaching orgasm, since, unconsciously, he perceives the woman as his mother, also leads to anxiety. Along the same lines, a woman having a baby can change in her husband's eyes from a lover to a mother and he may well then see her as relatively (or totally) undesirable. He may even become impotent if they do try to have intercourse.

A loss of sex drive, or even completely going off sex, after the birth of a baby is common in women too, for reasons which include pain from an episiotomy, a birth injury, hormonal disturbances, postnatal depression, fear of a further pregnancy, tiredness, overpreoccupation with the new baby, or an unconscious identification with the woman's own mother, now that she has become a mother. Many, if not most, women perceive mothers in general as sexless.

Increasingly today, drugs, pharmaceutical preparations and chemicals also interfere with sexual performance. More subtly, unconsciously perceived chemical messengers called pheromones may also be involved. Psychological 'messages' can also be transmitted by one partner and picked up unconsciously and yet still influence sexual behaviour. Body language is one example. It is quite possible that such psychological and pheromonal messages, if negative and transmitted over a long period of time, might adversely affect the sexual capacity of one's partner.

The emotional relationship between a couple can express itself as a sexual problem – indeed most so-called sexual problems are probably the result of emotional and relationship problems. A failure to erect or lubricate, premature ejaculation, or failure to have an orgasm can be expressions of resentment, anger and many other emotions, as can the rejection of advances.

There are men and women who see themselves as sexual enthusiasts but who, when the subject is examined more deeply in therapy, are found continuously to be putting sex last on their list of priorities in life. It is not, they say, that they don't *want* to have intercourse but there is 'just no time for it' and in any case they are 'always too tired'. Also, they often add, 'sex isn't everything'. Where both of the partners want to avoid sex such a situation is satisfactory. If a woman places a low priority on sex, or at least continuously finds other things she would rather do, her man sees this as rejection and loses interest or performs badly when she does agree. Many women too measure their attractiveness, and therefore their value, by the ardour shown by their partner. If he puts everything else first she may respond by getting angry, becoming sexually uninterested or performing badly. Believing herself to be unwanted she may even fall out of love with him. A sign that this is occurring is a sudden loss of her ability to have orgasms.

Stereotyped, habit-ridden copulation and insensitivity to the needs of the other partner both sow the seeds of sexual difficulties, as do relatively minor problems such as bad breath and, for many women, the man being unshaven. Sometimes just even loving the partner can produce problems. As mentioned already, some men perceive the woman they love as sexless and put her on a pedestal. They are impotent with her but not with others. Some women are inhibited with the man they love, having been reared in childhood to believe that sexual activity leads to a loss of love (in that case from their parents) but can perform with efficiency and abandon with a stranger. Other women may overcome this by fantasising about other men when having intercourse with their partner. In any case, for reasons which are largely unknown, everyone finds certain members of the opposite sex infinitely more desirable, arousing and exciting than others. Some men and women can perform perfectly well with certain members of the opposite sex but not with others.

Many people who talk continually about how much they want intercourse are unconsciously trying to avoid it. Such people may fix on a physical event such as having a baby, a sterilisation operation or the onset of some disability as an excuse to avoid intercourse, sometimes permanently. For women who see sex as being mainly for reproduction, sterilisation can disturb them anyway. Disturbances of body-image also affect sexual performance. Women who have not accepted their vagina as part of their body psychologically do not to all intents and purposes have a vagina. Attempts at intercourse are experienced as being like a knife being pushed through an intact body surface, and they suffer from a condition known as vaginismus. These are the virgin wives mentioned earlier. A man who has fear-inspiring images of the female body can, unconsciously, think of the vagina as a whirlpool or a mouth with biting teeth. Placing his penis inside it is like putting his head in a lion's mouth, so it is avoided by failing to erect or by ejaculating before entry or soon afterwards.

So the background to sexual problems is very varied and is often time-consuming to sort out, if only because basic causes are often overlaid with conscious excuses and explanations that first have to be stripped away. Some problems are the direct result of upbringing and the potential problem existed long before that person met his or her partner. It was lying dormant but ready to bloom. In some cases an apparently normal sex life may be sustained for months or even years before a 'sexual breakdown' occurs. This happens because at the time the person's sexual desires exceed his underlying fears and he can function fairly well. Once desire wanes even a little all the inhibitory forces take over and the person develops a frank sexual problem. An unhappy example is seen in those women who have been brought up with the 'sex is naughty' view of sexuality. They function well before marriage and enjoy sex but lose orgasmic capacity and interest in sex afterwards, when it is legitimate. In other cases the problem reflects a difficulty within the relationship. Sex itself may be the primary cause of the problem or it may, so to speak, simply be knocked down as an innocent bystander.

Psychological illness, personality factors and problems with religious beliefs may or may not contribute to sexual problems. For example, a person who is prone to excessive anxiety about life generally may or may not be anxious about intercourse: sex can provide a refuge for such people. Conversely, someone who displays low levels of anxiety in the rest of his life can show signs of alarm, muscle tension and sweating as sexual contact becomes imminent. Men and women with personality disorders run the risk of retaliation through a sex problem in their partner. For example, a critical, domineering or excessively maternal woman may come to be seen by her partner as an unpleasant mother figure.

## What can be done?

Obviously, from what has been said, some sexual problems need expert handling just like any other medical or emotional problem but self-help is the obvious place to start. Discussing the subject can help and a good book can give one or both of the partners insight into their problem. At this stage the couple can often get real benefits from returning to courtship, taking the pressure off sexual performance, and favouring the non-physical side of their relationship.

If help is needed there are three main sources. Relatively untrained and well-meaning counsellors, professional or not, can help with superficial sexual problems and indeed many people find a satisfactory result in the hands of such counsellors. However, the majority of sexual problems receive only superficial first-aid when treated like this, and such 'cures' may last for only a short time. The two provably useful approaches to sexual problems that now have a track record worthy of the name are psychosexual therapy and sex therapy. Both need to be practised by fully trained professionals if they are to be effective, mainly because untrained people dabbling in these areas of people's lives can do damage – often without realising it. Those who think the answers to all sex problems are easy and quick to find simply do not understand the problems.

Both forms of therapy involve the person making changes to the way he or she behaves or thinks and this is never easy, even for a motivated and intelligent person, partly because of the complexity of the problem and because the partner is necessarily involved. This does not mean that the partner has to be involved in the actual treatment but that his or her reaction to the problem will undoubtedly affect the situation and the results of the therapy.

## *Psychosexual therapy*

This is all about searching for the contributory causes of the problem and then treating it in as precise a way as possible. Such therapy is, of course, highly personal and unique to the individual or couple being treated. Nearly always the unravelling of the problem involves uncovering layer after layer of complexity and is something like solving a detective mystery. As in the practice of medicine generally, making an accurate diagnosis is the key to success, but one difficulty is to assess the importance of the mass of symptoms and material which is produced. Almost anything *could* have contributed to the current sexual problem and, often quite unconsciously, many people whilst wanting to be helped, put all kinds of difficulties in the way of establishing the truth. The examples of the underlying causes of sexual problems we have outlined in this chapter are very elementary. They do little to show how complex the origin of all sexual problems really is. Frequently there are several contributory causes and these are further affected by interactions with the partner. The sexual problem is often the final symptom produced by a host of varied underlying currents, many of them nothing at all directly to do with sex.

## *Sex therapy*

This is much less concerned with the cause or causes but more with the actual problem itself and what can be done to overcome it. To a psychosexual therapist a sexual problem is simply a symptom of some other underlying difficulty or problem, whilst to the sex therapist it is the main focus of attention. But, although the sex therapist may think that the treatment techniques he or she uses are simply concerned with the problem, they may be successful because they unwittingly and incidentally relieve the underlying problem. So, for example, being instructed by the therapist to masturbate or mutually masturbate can undo old harm by removing guilt and anxiety from the act and thereby making it pleasurable. For this reason some psychosexual therapists 'borrow' the techniques of sex therapists and incorporate them into their overall treatment plan. Some degree of education, or rather re-education, the relief of anxiety, permission-giving, encouragement and mutual trust are common to both therapies. Both have their successes and failures.

Because sexual and psychosexual problems are often so closely bound up with the person's personality, there are no potions, magic pills or speedy therapies. Almost all sex problems need time, care, trust and confidence between patient and therapist if they are to be at all successfully treated. It is scarcely surprising that Masters and Johnson, the world-renowned couple who get such good results in the USA, are as successful as they are – they have patients in their clinic for days and even weeks at a time. Such therapy is very expensive and few people outside the USA are able to afford it. Fortunately, slightly less time-consuming adaptations of their methods are available in the UK, which bring their methods within the economic reach of most people.

## How common are sexual problems?

Very little information is available on how commonly sexual problems and difficulties occur, and there is no way of getting accurate figures on the subject. In the USA it is estimated that sexual problems affect half of all marriages at some time or another and one survey in Britain found that 57 per cent of twenty-five-year-olds had some sort of sexual difficulty – yet only 2 per cent had consulted a doctor. In a UK study of 436 women in the community it was found that one third of them had some sort of sexual dysfunction at the time of the study. Nearly one in five complained of poor sexual interest; a similar number said that vaginal dryness was a problem; very nearly as many had too infrequent orgasms; and nearly one in ten had actual pain on intercourse.

This was in a randomly selected population in two general practices in a large country town. These sexual dysfunctions increased with age with women over 50 having one or more of the problems listed. Only one third of the women with sexual dysfunctions judged themselves to have a sex *problem* and only 4 per cent said that they wanted help for their problem.

In an attempt to find out how common sexual problems were in the USA, 100 volunteer 'normal', middle-class couples who rated their marriages as happy were investigated in considerable depth using a questionnaire which was completed separately by the partners. One finding was that 10 per cent of those questioned thought that their marriages were satisfactory, without realising that their partner did not agree. Twelve per cent of the couples had received some kind of marital or sexual counselling during the marriage, but no couples who were currently being treated were included. Over 80 per cent regarded their marriages as being happy or very happy, and nearly 90 per cent said they would marry the same person again. As has been found in a number of other surveys, 10 per cent of the women but only 5 per cent of the men said they would marry someone else if they had their time again.

'Sexual problems' in this survey were defined as being disorders of erection or of ejaculation in men and disorders of arousal or of orgasm in women. 'Sexual difficulties' included such things as: an inability to relax; the partner choosing the wrong time; lack of interest; not enough foreplay; a distaste for sex; different sexual habits and practices; and so on. Each person reported not only their own problems and difficulties but also those they thought were present in their partner. Women, it turned out, knew of the existence of problems and difficulties in their men but the men seriously underestimated them in their wives. Of the men, 60 per cent said they had no problems and 50 per cent no difficulties. In contrast, only 37 per cent of the women reported themselves free of problems and only 23 per cent said they had no difficulties. As a result of the greater sexual suppression of girls and women it comes as no surprise that women have more problems than do men, but it is also likely that men are more reluctant to mention or even recognise theirs since their manliness is at stake.

As to the actual problems themselves, the most common by far in men (36 per cent) was ejaculating too quickly. Much less common were problems in maintaining an erection (9 per cent); in getting an erection (7 per cent); and in being unable to ejaculate (4 per cent). Eight per cent of men had more than one problem whereas 63 per cent of the women had more than one. These latter were problems in getting excited (48 per cent); in reaching orgasm (46 per cent); in maintaining excitement (33 per cent); and in being unable to have an orgasm (15 per cent). However, 11 per cent of women complained of reaching orgasm too quickly.

What can the average couple hope to achieve themselves if they have a sexual problem? The next section of the chapter looks at the main sexual problems with a special emphasis on self-help. Obviously this review is brief but it is a first step, before you take your problem to a professional.

# Helping yourself overcome your sex problem

## *Sex problems in men*

One way or another anxiety usually lies at the heart of a man's problems which are of psychological origin. The anxiety is usually unconscious but either way it diminishes his pleasure and impairs his performance.

**Premature ejaculation**

Sex therapists argue about the definition of premature ejaculation. Some say it is present if a man comes to orgasm in less than thirty seconds and others if orgasm is reached less than two minutes after penetration. Others say five minutes and yet others assert that the problem is present if the man cannot contain himself sufficiently to enable his partner to have an orgasm on at least half of all occasions. Another definition says that it is present if orgasm occurs with ten or fewer thrusts of the penis. Most psychosexual therapists see all this as rather pointless and instead look for psychosexual evidence of a need or wish to avoid intercourse, or intercourse with one particular partner. They also take account of the woman's orgasmic capacity before arriving at the conclusion that the man is a premature ejaculator.

As for causes, sex therapists regard hasty, early acts of intercourse – such as, for example, might occur with prostitutes or when it is feared that the girl's parents will return home – as being important, whereas psychosexual therapists concentrate more, for example, on earlier masturbation,.

A premature ejaculation is less enjoyable an experience for the man than a 'normal' one. This is probably the result of the underlying anxiety and is why so many inexperienced men suffer from it. As confidence is gained it is usually overcome, especially if the woman is reassuring. A critical woman, however, can easily convert premature ejaculation into impotence simply by helping to build up a type of secondary anxiety in the man. He becomes more anxious and so performs less and less well.

A range of treatments alone or in combination can be used for men with premature ejaculation. Men whose problem stems from the unconscious notion that intercourse is an imposition on a woman (and many women for their own unconscious reasons tend to encourage this view) can be cured simply by listening to their wives giving their psychosexual histories and talking about their masturbation and fantasies. The next step is to use this information so that the woman is near orgasm before they start having intercourse. This increases the chance (especially if stimulation of her clitoris continues during intercourse) that she will have an orgasm, which in turn increases his confidence.

Fantasies about successful intercourse when the man masturbates help, as does starting to masturbate but stopping when near to orgasm, then starting again, and repeating this cycle so that he becomes able to remain sub-orgasmic for increasing periods of time. Eventually, after several weeks of practice, he will be able to control his rate of coming to orgasm during masturbation and will be able to ejaculate at will once he is sufficiently aroused. The next stage is for his partner to do the same to him, but he has to say when she is to stop for a while because he has the early feelings which tell him that if stimulation continues orgasm will be inevitable.

When the couple have worked together for ejaculatory control, the woman can cover the man's penis with baby oil, KY jelly, or talcum powder and help him learn control with the enhanced slippery feelings these substances produce. A further refinement is for her to place her thumb on his frenum (the little vertical ridge on the underside of the tip of the penis), with her index finger on the rim of the opposite side of the penis and her middle finger just below it, and then to squeeze the penis just before orgasm is reached. This reduces the man's erection. After a while stimulation of the penis is started again and the procedure repeated until the man can 'last' for as long as they both want. This training can be successful after just a few sessions in couples in whom the underyling causes of the problem have been detected and explained. During intercourse the man – instead of ignoring the early warning feelings, as premature ejaculators do – recognises them and stops moving for some moments whilst they subside.

Other techniques which some men find useful are: avoiding

The Squeeze Technique: *This specialised form of masturbation carried out by a man's partner is useful in helping him with premature ejaculation.*

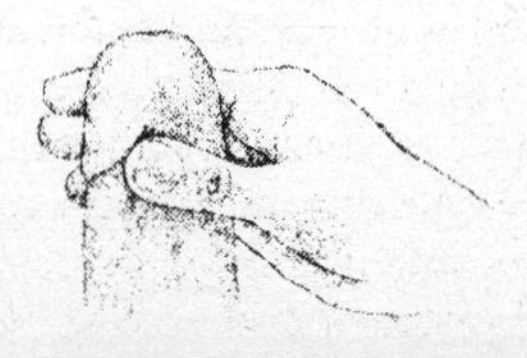

excessive stimulation before penetration; using a sheath; thinking about some non-sexual subject (although this is usually inadvisable); covering the penis with a mildly anaesthetic ointment or spray; tightening the anus by squeezing the internal muscles; and pushing the penis very deeply into the vagina so that the tip lies in the expanded upper portion, and then making only small movements. Other recommendations are to keep fairly high orgasm rates and to have an orgasm by masturbation before having intercourse.

However, the easiest way of all involves simply a change in attitude. This change is not usually difficult for premature ejaculators to make because it often fits in with the underlying cause of their problem. The man must think of putting his penis in the vagina as being an extension of foreplay. In this way he uses his penis instead of his hands or mouth to stimulate the woman. This gives him the impression of being in control of himself and he now finds that he can last for as long as he wants or even not ejaculate at all on any one particular occasion.

By using one or more of the many techniques suggested here, many premature ejaculators can be performing to their perfect satisfaction (and that of their partner) within weeks.

**Problems with erection**

An erection in the presence of a woman is a biological compliment to her but both men who want to have intercourse and those who unconsciously want to avoid it can have problems. Sometimes no erection is possible or it may be insufficiently strong to be of any use for penetration. Some men find that their penis becomes very hard during foreplay but that they then lose their erection before intercourse starts or soon after insertion. In some cases the man ejaculates whilst his penis is less than fully erect and, because of the poor orgasm resulting, may scarcely know that he has done so.

The word impotence is often applied to these problems but this is only partially correct as the term also covers and includes problems with ejaculation too. Probably the word is best dropped from use and, like the female equivalent 'frigid', should never be bandied around loosely nor used to attack a partner.

Erection problems can have physical causes. More than twenty types of drug, especially antihypertensives, tranquillisers and antidepressants, can cause impotence, as can alcohol and even excessive cigarette smoking. Diabetes eventually produces impotence in a third or so of affected men, probably by damaging the nerves. Diseases and injuries of the nervous system and diseases of the arteries supplying

Masturbating your partner: *Getting your partner's genitals close to yours in this way lets you see what's happening and makes it easy and relaxing to stimulate them.*

the pelvic region are also causes of impotence. Disorders of the hypothalamus and the pituitary gland, under-functioning testes and an over-functioning thyroid gland can result in impotence, as can surgery carried out on the bowel or the prostate. However, the fact that any of these conditions is present in an impotent man does not necessarily mean that his impotence is solely, or even mainly, attributable to that cause. Psychosexual or sexual therapy can improve the performance of at least some of the men with this problem.

Erection problems which are present only intermittently, or in which a full, hard erection occurs at some stage in the proceedings, can be, but rarely are, of physical origin (unless they are attributable to intermittent medication with an offending drug). Men who can masturbate satisfactorily and who wake with a hard erection or have one during the night are also unlikely to be impotent as a result of a physical cause. However, the fact that a man has erection problems in both masturbation and intercourse does not prove that the cause is physical; in fact it is commonly a result of depression, sexual despair or high levels of anxiety from previous failures in intercourse which have spilled over into masturbation as well.

In couples in whom the problem has persisted or for whom it suddenly starts after a period of adequate functioning, the psychosexual and emotional state of both partners needs to be assessed, as do their personalities and the relationship. In some cases the briefest assessment reveals the nature of the problem, which is usually something along the lines given earlier, and leads to a prompt cure. In others it can be much more difficult.

In general, the couple are best advised to avoid intercourse and return to courtship. Where the basic relationship is sound, most couples take to this happily and usually with much more enthusiasm than in their original courtship. A holiday often helps. Encouraging total communication and then giving each other physical pleasure, perhaps using sensual massage, all helps. The man learns, often for the first time, of his partner's real eroticism. Learning how to read her signs of sexual arousal comes as a revelation to many such men. It is also a good idea to introduce more eroticism into your life generally, perhaps including books and films. If a woman is under-confident or prudish about her body, as some are, her partner will have to persuade her to see it from his point of view. In this way he can make her more confident. Most men are aroused by watching their partner masturbate and this can be incorporated into foreplay. Very often a couple need to be persuaded to set aside time to tease, undress, explore and investigate each other.

Many men with erection problems based on an unconscious desire to avoid intercourse (or their partner) fear having an erection because they think that this will lead to their partner expecting, attempting or even demanding intercourse. Once intercourse has been 'prohibited' by a therapist he is free to erect and does so readily. Confidence in his ability to erect can be increased by the woman repeatedly rubbing his penis, stopping, letting the erection subside and then restoring it. The man's attention can be increasingly distracted from the performance of his penis by encouraging him simultaneously to concentrate on giving pleasure to his wife. A penis which is fearfully watched by its owner never erects, just as a watched pot never boils!

When his secondary anxiety and fears have gone and he is more confident about his penis, the man usually (provided any underlying problem has been treated) begins to suggest intercourse or has a try at it. In collusion with the therapist the partner may have been instructed to avoid it. Eventually the man reaches a point where his desires so exceed his fears that he can tolerate his frustration no longer and he 'forces' the woman to have intercourse. At this point the confidence of both partners greatly increases, the man's for obvious reasons and the woman's because she sees herself as desirable and desired. Most partners of men with erection problems consider, at some point, either that their loss of attractiveness is to blame or that the man has another woman. Usually neither is the case.

In some cases a variety of pills and potions will help if the man thinks they can but none can 'make' him have intercourse. Using Anglo-Saxon words for the couple's sex organs and sexual functioning has an aphrodisiac effect on some men (and women). Sex aids can help as can the woman playing with the scrotum and compressing the base of the penis during intercourse.

Although aphrodisiacs have a bad reputation, in a recent trial in 48 men thought to have psychological impotence, 6 mg of yohimbine were given three times a day for 10 weeks. Nearly half showed at least some improvement after two or three weeks. Men with physical reasons for impotence also improved.

Surgery, or other medical treatment, may relieve impotence from physical causes. A new treatment which is carried out on the penis itself, and can help both physical and psychological impotence, is to inject a substance called papaverine into one of the corpora cavernosa. Men can be taught to do it themselves in hospital and then carry it out at home and have intercourse. This restores confidence and in many cases only a few injections are required. One danger is prolonged erection, 'priapism', and the other warning sign is that the manufacturers of papaverine in the US take no responsibility if it is used for this purpose.

Rigid or inflatable tubes are also now available and can be implanted inside the penis at an operation. They make intercourse possible. They are useful in impotence from physical causes that can not be relieved in any other way. Before going this far a man should consult a sex or psychosexual therapist to see what can be achieved by other means. It is a treatment of last resort.

Although expensive, a device called ErecAid avoids injections and implants and has been shown to help impotent diabetics. Others may benefit too. It works best if the partner is interested and helpful in the treatment. The lubricated penis is placed in a tube, suction is applied to the tube to induce an erection and a constricting band is applied at the base of the penis to retain the erection and permit intercourse. Used in conjunction with psychosexual counselling it can be highly satisfactory but not everyone, perhaps due to underlying marital reasons, benefits. After a few uses spontaneous erections may return, relegating the device to become a reassuring back-up to be used if necessary.

Another, similar, device is called Correct Aid. It is rather like ErecAid but is actually worn during intercourse.

**Retarded orgasm and an inability to ejaculate**

Some men suffer from a delay in reaching orgasm and cannot ejaculate with their penis in a vagina. Some can be masturbated or fellated to orgasm by the woman if they withdraw, whereas others cannot be brought to orgasm by a woman at all, by any means, and may not be able to ejaculate if a woman is even in the same room. Some men who are successfully treated for premature ejaculation then suffer from retarded orgasm and vice versa. The majority of the partners of such men are distressed by it. Some women conclude that they have over-stretched their vagina during masturbation or childbirth and that this is the explanation.

However, the problem sometimes presents itself directly in the form of complaints that the vagina is too large or too wet or that the penis, or some portion of it, has lost its sensation. Some men in this group are discovered to compress their penises tightly during masturbation. They have simply mis-trained themselves and now cannot respond without tight penile pressure. Others complain of intense penile pain, which they naturally want to avoid, at orgasm. In all such cases intercourse or pleasure is being avoided in order to reduce anxiety.

Diabetes and various drugs can be the cause in men who complain of a lack of sensation, but more often their ultimate unconscious need is to deny that they are having intercourse. It is only by doing this that they can function at all. Some, who unconsciously equate genital fluids with excretion, want to avoid soiling the woman and others unconsciously equate the woman with their mother. Their response is not to stop sex with her but not to ejaculate inside her. Others who, it is easily imagined, were rebuked and punished by women – sometimes even by older sisters – for genital activity in childhood, are simply afraid to lose control and reach orgasm in the presence of a woman.

Relatively inexperienced men who have this problem say that at some point during intercourse the whole business loses its excitement and that distracting thoughts enter their minds. The explanation is that as their level of pleasure and therefore, to them, sinfulness, rises, so does their anxiety, so reducing the pleasure. Some maintain their erection and others simply lose it. Although most, but not all, men enjoy intercourse more if the woman also moves her pelvis, this activity or what she says can be the distraction which intrudes into the man's mind. It increases his self-awareness and thereby his anxiety about what he is doing.

Various fears can cause the same problem, although they may only be vehicles for yet deeper fears. These include a fear of making the woman pregnant, a fear of VD or AIDS and fears about other men with whom the woman has had intercourse. Thinking about other men makes him jealous or makes him worry that her previous lovers were better endowed sexually than he or were better lovers.

Treating the underlying cause, together with re-education, a decrease in anxiety, a reduced emphasis on orgasm, and an increase in penile pleasures and eroticism, all with the involvement of the woman, with the aim of increasing the efficiency with which the man responds to her manual or oral stimulation, forms the first stage of treatment. Once the woman can reliably bring the man to orgasm she, without saying anything, can on occasions, when he is near orgasm, quickly get on top of him and thrust rapidly so as to make him ejaculate in her vagina. Usually his perceptions change and his anxiety falls.

## *Sexual problems in women*

The extent of sexual problems in women as revealed by the survey we quoted earlier in the chapter suggests that all the clinics and therapists dealing with them are doing no more than scratching at the surface. When one bears in mind that women are biologically endowed with an enormously greater sexual capacity than are men, the extent of the present situation is impressive and a cause for concern. There are many ways of tackling the problem. The best course, in our view, is prevention, by bringing up children differently. Better sex education for girls is becoming an urgent necessity in an age when men are being increasingly encouraged to perform to their partner's satisfaction and when women have increasing sexual expectations. The discrepancy between what women are capable of and what they can achieve may in itself account for the marked difference between the sexes in the prevalence of emotional illness.

Women would probably perform better if they were able to communicate more to their partners and if men were educated to understand them better.

To say that men suppress women is provably wrong. Their mothers probably suppressed them far more as girls – and much more than they did their brothers. Men often complain that their women undervalue themselves and so underachieve. In fact they tend to see more potential in their women than the women do themselves.

These influences and many others, exert negative influences on female sexuality generally. It could be that human females are designed to be sexually dissatisfied, at least to some degree, so that they have an incentive to have further sexual activity. Human females are, in effect, permanently 'on heat' or 'in season' because humans are capable of rearing their young in any season of the year in which they are born.

Most women seem to be in touch with a deep inner sexuality which they fear because of the consequences which could result if they were really to let go. In fact many sex problems in women are the result of what is called 'reaction-formation' against their own powerful sexuality. They have learned that it is bad to be sexual and then have realised how sexual they are. Thereafter their interests, attitudes, behaviour and pleasures all have to be presented, even to themselves, as the opposite, or a modification of what they really are.

Re-education can rapidly and dramatically alter this situation, especially if the woman's partner is encouraging. Many women are afraid to be themselves for fear of earning condemnation and this is one reason why bold, self-confident and sexually dominant men, who expect a woman to be very sexual, appeal to so many women. Underconfident, shy and embarrassed partners simply make many women feel inhibited as well.

If men were better educated to know about and to accept female sexuality there would be fewer sex problems in women.

**Orgasm problems**

Any woman who cannot masturbate freely and enjoyably proves that, for one reason or another, she is unable fully to accept her genitals, her sexuality and her right to have pleasure. Sex for her is something a man does *to* her. Some such women claim that they have never ever been at all sexual. They deny ever having experienced sexual arousal, sex dreams or desires. While some say they have always been like this, others trace it back to some event such as the loss of a particular partner, a rape, having a baby, and so on. Their genitals are perceived as being totally unpleasurable. Depending on her personality, a variety of strategies such as explanation, education, careful history-taking, clinical examination and so on, can be used by a therapist to demonstrate the fallacy of her belief. Starting from her positive thoughts about what turns her on, however meagre these may be, the therapist then expands her sexual consciousness gradually until she blossoms in a way she never dreamed of. A depressed, drab, under-confident and sexless woman can rapidly become a new person. Such a change is often not as welcome to her partner because he may have chosen her *because* she was so inhibited, and her new self puts him in a dilemma. At this point psychosexual therapy may be necessary for them both.

The next step in helping such a woman to masturbate efficiently is to establish proper masturbation using any device, circumstances, fantasy, erotica or movements which appeal to her. When she has achieved masturbation on her own and is confident, she can then demonstrate her ability to her partner who should encourage and help her, perhaps sharing some of her fantasies with her. Gradually he takes over and learns to masturbate her as well as, if not better than, she can herself. He encourages her to masturbate regularly and shows his pleasure at her success. Intercourse, which has usually been quite deliberately stopped during treatment, is resumed with either partner continuing her masturbation until she learns to have an orgasm with the penis inside her vagina. The left-lateral position is ideal for this.

After this the couple can find the particular positions for intercourse which suit them best whilst being encouraged by their therapist to expand their erotic lives, to experiment, to use whatever sex aids appeal to them and to devise sex games if they want.

In all this it is important for the man to discover or work out as much as he can about the woman's real sexual inclinations and

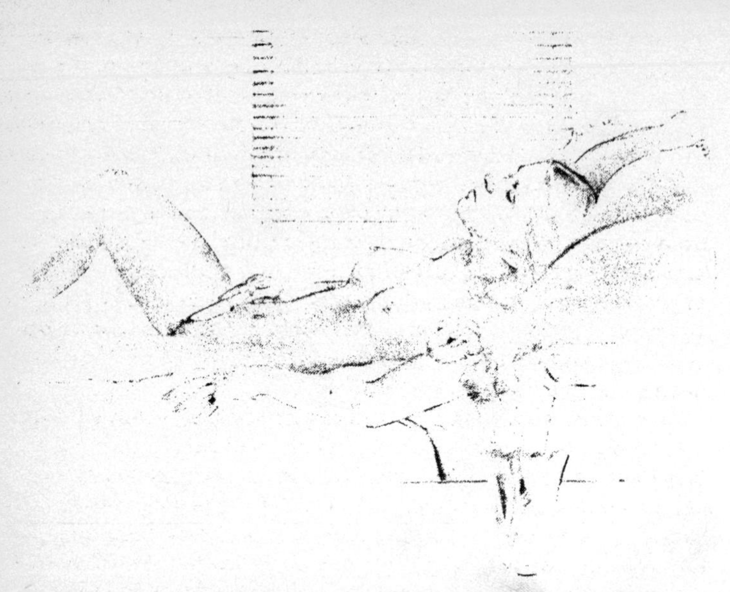

Difficulties with orgasm: *Many women find a vibrator useful when learning to have orgasms. Once they have mastered the art the vibrator is usually abandoned in favour of the fingers.*

wishes whilst unobtrusively monitoring her sexual responses to a variety of situations. Obviously, the above outline is very basic and personal elaborations are endless, but if things go well the man becomes an expert on foreplay *for his partner*, rather than following advice in books, which may work well for other women but not necessarily for her. Since a woman will do almost anything for the man she loves and enjoys giving him pleasure, the scene is set for a deeply satisfying sex life for them both.

These techniques are applicable to all the sex problems listed by women in the survey we mentioned earlier. Occasionally, physical illness such as diabetes or any condition which reduces the woman's level of testosterone can account for some problems and this will need appropriate medical treatment.

**Pain on intercourse**

In the majority of cases the cause of the pain is physical. A woman may have pain or discomfort if she has a vaginal discharge (see page 291); immediately after having a baby; for weeks or months after an episiotomy; for some weeks after a vaginal operation; as a result of internal disorders of her reproductive organs; if intercourse is attempted too quickly, before she is lubricating; after the menopause if there is dryness of the vagina; and for a host of other reasons. Any persistent pain for which there is no obvious cause should be reported to a doctor. If when intercourse is attempted the muscles surrounding the vaginal entrance go into an involuntary spasm, this is called vaginismus. Some women also suffer from vaginismus because, for example, they do not 'accept' their vagina, are guilty about sex, are anxious early on in a sexual relationship or fear the penis or getting pregnant. Latent or actual lesbians may suffer from the same problem when heterosexual intercourse is attempted. Other women experience vaginismus for some time after being raped or after similarly distressing sexual experiences.

Treatment, which can be very difficult and may involve psychosexual therapy, consists of persuading the woman to accept vaginal penetration by, for example, fingers at first and then, perhaps, objects of increasing size or a vibrator. When eventually penile penetration is attempted some woman fare best if they control it by being on top of the man whereas others function best underneath or on all fours. If the vagina is well lubricated and the penis inserted slowly and gently, pausing for a moment if any painful spasm results, full penetration can usually be achieved. One technique which sometimes works well when all else fails is to instruct the woman in the voluntary control of her vaginal muscles. When penetration is attempted she contracts them as firmly as she can momentarily, whilst her man pauses. As she relaxes the man pushes his penis in a little further and so on.

Sex problems vary from a total lack of interest in sex to its inefficient or unenjoyable expression. In general men and women express their sexual inefficiency as performance problems. The inefficiency may only amount to a slight brake on pleasure but in the end the person's interest usually remains fixed on intercourse. Sex is more in the mind than their genitals but the central problem is one of genital inefficiency. Some can overcome their problem and function well if certain conditions, or partners, are available.

For some unfortunate people their desires never exceed the fears and they never function well, or even at all, with another human being, either heterosexually or homosexually. Sometimes the cause is no more than a belief, in a shy and inhibited person, that there is something unacceptably wrong with their body, such as a small penis or different-sized breasts. In some, the feared defect is not even really there, or it is trivial and is simply being used to mask a deeper fear.

Fortunately, more help is available today than ever before and a person with a sex problem can usually find some answers, if not necessarily a complete cure, at a special centre. Addresses of clinics and sex therapy clinics are listed on pages 369–378.

*Chapter 14*

# Contraception, planning a family and infertility

Contraception literally means 'against conception' and any practice, device or substance which prevents conception is said to be contraceptive. So, clearly, abstaining from intercourse is a means of contraception, as is oral intercourse, anal intercourse, mutual masturbation and, for that matter, any sexual activity that does not involve intercourse between a fertile man and a fertile woman. The practice of sterilisation, in which the tubes delivering the eggs or sperms are interrupted, can be used to make either sex permanently infertile. Avoiding intercourse at and around ovulation, or the man withdrawing his penis from the vagina before he ejaculates, are both contraceptive practices. The use of devices which allow him to ejaculate in the vagina but which prevent the sperms reaching the cervix are contraceptive as are those such as the Pill which prevent ovulation occurring. Although abortion is sometimes spoken of as being a form of contraception, it clearly is not and, since it often allows conception to occur, the IUD is probably not really a method of contraception in the strict sense but is included here nevertheless. No one really knows how the IUD forces the lining of the uterus to eject the fertilised egg – it should in fact be considered as a kind of extremely early method of abortion rather than a type of contraception.

We have called this chapter contraception *and* planning a family because the two are rather different. Contraception, is by definition simply a way of preventing the conception of a baby, but family planning may well involve the planned spacing of children. Many women attending so-called 'family planning' clinics are not planning a family at all – they are looking for a 100 per cent successful way of not getting pregnant, often for the many fertile years after they've finished having their children.

If words mean anything, and contraception means 'against conception' then any method with a significant rate of failure is clearly not truly contraceptive. We feel this point is worth making because the topic is often discussed as if there were a wide choice of efficient methods. This is simply not so.

If a couple want to avoid conception but also want to have intercourse freely, the method they use should ideally be 100 per cent effective. To some extent the method they choose will depend on the woman's age since most couples are increasingly less fertile after thirty or so. For the older woman a less efficient method can be used yet still be highly effective because her fertility is less high as a result of her having less intercourse as she and her partner age.

As well as being efficient, the 'ideal' contraceptive method needs to be acceptable and simple. A 100 per cent efficient method which is so complex that only 10 per cent of the population are able enough to use it properly is only 10 per cent effective. Similarly, a 100 per cent efficient method which is unacceptable to 90 per cent of the population because of, for example, religious reasons, medical fears, messiness, or interference with sexual pleasure, is again only 10 per cent effective.

However effective any given contraceptive method is in theory it is only as reliable as the person using it. A major and powerful influence affecting personal efficiency in the practice of contraception is motivation. The essential point to grasp here is that unconscious factors can so easily alter a person's conscious intentions. Many so-called 'method failures' in which the individual woman claims to have used the method conscientiously but nevertheless has become pregnant, are probably caused by an unconscious deliberate mistake. The topic is a large but often ignored one and it is only possible to give a few examples here.

The young are particularly likely to be victims because, although they may consciously believe that they are free from guilt about intercourse, unconsciously they are still strongly influenced by the moral teaching of our culture instilled into them in their childhood. A sexually inexperienced girl may say to herself, out of guilt, after each time she has intercourse, that she is not going to do it again until she is married, so there is no need to go to a doctor or a clinic to get an effective method of contraception. Indeed, to take such a step, she may well think, will only encourage her to 'sin' again. This accounts for the apparent paradox of the girl who will not use contraception until she is 'going steady'. The point is that she has been taught that sex is justified only if you love a man. So before that blessed state arrives she is constantly trying – and failing – to avoid sex by avoiding contraception. It is because of this that many girls reared with excessive and unreasonable moral restraints are among those most likely to have unwanted pregnancies. Such girls often deny to themselves, as much as to others, that they have sexual desires, and so they, unlike girls who can accept their sexuality, never prepare for sex. The all too obvious point that only those who thoroughly accept their sexuality have any hope of controlling it is largely overlooked, both in child rearing and sex education, especially as far as girls are concerned.

Along the same lines, a boy who, for example, doubts his fertility, perhaps because of earlier mumps orchitis (inflammation of the testes) or because he fears his penis is too small, may consciously intend to use the withdrawal method but, because of his unconscious desire to prove himself, is slow in doing so in the unconscious hope that the girl will become pregnant and thus prove his potency.

One of the first things that girls are told about their sexuality in our culture is that they will grow up and one day have babies like mummy. The strong unconscious notion is thus imparted – and later greatly reinforced – that sex is for babies. From this it is a short step to believe that sex other than for babies is sin and that pregnancy is the punishment. This view lurks behind much anti-abortion propaganda.

The consequences of all this for contraception and family planning are enormous. Some women cannot enjoy sex unless there is a chance of pregnancy. This leads to contraceptive fecklessness such as stopping the Pill on the most trivial of excuses. Often actions such as this are rationalised on the grounds of medical fears, or the fear of fatness, for example, but the real underlying fear is that of sin; the woman has not fully accepted her right to sexual pleasure although at a conscious level she may regard herself as completely uninhibited. Eventually her fear of pregnancy will drive her back to the Pill, but she will be vaguely unhappy and may even say her sex drive or her ability to achieve orgasm has gone. In this way she writes off the only 100 per cent effective method and her unconscious desires will have been fulfilled. Other consequences are that such a woman will unconsciously see a pregnancy as punishment, and accept it, even though it does not fit into her plan for her family; for the same unconscious reasons (needing a possibility of pregnancy) a woman may lose all pleasure in sex after she has been sterilised or reaches the menopause.

Other unconscious motives for frustrating contraception whilst consciously trying to 'contracept' are: to escape from a work situation; to punish parents; to provide a dependent baby who will *really* love her (she thinks that no one has *ever* really loved her); to give her partner something to worry about; to compete with a sister, a friend, or a colleague; to prove her fertility (many women fear that small breasts, scanty periods, a previous abortion, or using the Pill have impaired it); and so on.

All this leads us to the conclusion that effective contraception starts with sensible child rearing in respect of sex. Beyond that, and provided that the underlying attitudes are satisfactory, then it is true to say that the only true contraceptive we possess at the moment is the Pill (oral contraception). It is the only method which approaches totally efficiency. Unfortunately, recent evidence has found that there are real, if small, health hazards in women over thirty-five who use the Pill and are fat, have high blood pressure or smoke, so this makes it only suitable up until this age. After thirty-five it is probably best for women to use a progesterone-only Pill (the so-called 'mini' Pill; it is the oestrogens in the Pill that are mainly suspected of causing the problems in older women), or another method. Let us now look at the main types of contraception.

Currently, about 1.7 million UK women use family planning clinics and 2.7 million their GP. For 84 per cent of the latter the Pill is prescribed whereas only 55 per cent of clinic patients receive it. The implication of this is that probably clinics tend to see more patients with problems since the diaphragm, IUD and natural methods are more likely to be prescribed.

Due to costly litigation in the US, the pharmaceutical industry is slowly withdrawing from research into contraception and this, combined with the effects of concern about AIDS, is likely to affect the overall situation in the future. In fact, a world expert has said that things will continue to deteriorate so that at the close of the century we will end up with fewer contraceptive methods than we started the century with.

Girls under 16 require parental consent to their receiving contraceptive advice. Provided her parents are sensible and realistic this is wise. If the girl is really unwilling to approach her parents a doctor can still prescribe for her if it is in her best interests to do so, if she is mature enough to understand and is having, or intends to have, intercourse regardless and may suffer if help is withheld. This also is wise.

## The Pill

In its commonest and most effective form the Pill contains the synthetically produced female hormones, oestrogen and progesterone. Because these two are combined in one pill it is called the 'combined Pill'. The hormones these Pills contain are very similar to the natural ones produced by a woman's body but are different enough to allow absorption from the stomach and intestines. Natural hormones would not be absorbed if taken by mouth. The Pill's constituents are, after absorption, so similar to the natural hormones that they influence chemo-receptors (specialised monitors of blood hormone levels) at the base of the brain in the same way as natural hormones. If they were not identical or nearly so they would not work because chemo-receptors are highly specific. Because of this it is not quite right to think of them as totally alien chemicals, which is how they are sometimes represented. The reason the Pill works so well is that it copies Nature. Its effect is to convince the pituitary gland that a pregnancy has already occurred and in this state the pituitary suppresses the release of the hormones which normally make the ovaries release an egg each month. It is a form of false pregnancy.

It sometimes happens that whilst a woman is on the Pill an egg *is* produced, but conception still does not occur because one effect of the progesterone in the Pill is to make the mucus in the passage through the cervix so thick that no sperms can penetrate it. A further effect of the combined Pill is to prevent the development of the lining of the uterus, the endometrium, so that even if conception were to occur the embryo could not implant and grow there. Although there have been tremendous advances in oral contraception some improvement is still possible.

There are 24 different brands of the Pill available and the principal basis on which one is chosen rather than another is to administer the lowest doses of hormones that suit the particular needs of the woman. In some cases the medical and family history may make the Pill an unsuitable choice. Starting and administration instructions vary. The phased Pills, in which the ratio of oestrogen to progesterone varies throughout the pack so as better to imitate what happens in the natural cycle, are different from the 21 tablet formulations. Instructions about what to do if a pill is taken late or missed, or if it is desired to postpone a period, also vary so instructions for a particular Pill must be followed carefully.

What seems to be a period for the woman on the Pill is not one in fact. It is a withdrawal bleed due to the supply of hormones being stopped.

The Pill's constituents are broken down by the body over twenty-four to thirty-six hours and are excreted via the urine and stools. Some women metabolise the Pill more rapidly and so need higher doses. Others who are on certain drugs such as some anti-tubercular, anti-epileptic, or anti-fungal drugs and some antibiotics also metabolise the Pill more rapidly, as may vegetarians. This could mean that they need a higher-dose Pill to be safe. If these women are on a normal-dose Pill, it, so to speak, 'runs out' before the next one is due. Women who, perhaps for the psychological reasons mentioned earlier, 'forget' the Pill or who are very late taking it are also exposed to the Pill running out. In all of these cases the sign to go by is the spotting of blood or even a full withdrawal bleed. If a pill has only been taken, say, six hours late, spotting is not inevitable, but if it does occur it happens two or three days later. In other words it is a 'mini' withdrawal bleed. The reason why a full bleed does not occur as a rule is that the woman continues to take the Pill. The correct reaction to repeated spotting or withdrawal bleeding at unexpected times, provided it is not caused by interference from other drugs, is *not* to change the Pill you are on, as many doctors and clinics suggest, but rather to be scrupulous in taking it within, say, an hour of when it is due.

The Pill is a very safe and efficient contraceptive but problems can and do sometimes occur. Problems mostly arise in those who are found on psychosexual investigation to have unconscious difficulties about accepting their sexuality, as we mentioned earlier. These should be cleared up before a change in method is seriously considered, simply because all other methods are less efficient. Depression, irritability, and bad dreams can be due to unconscious self-detestation for Pill-taking and depression often results in a loss of sex drive, a failure to have orgasms, and over-eating, leading to the marked weight gain sometimes reported on the Pill. This is not to say that *all* Pill symptoms are emotional or psychological but many are and can be prevented or cured by psychosexual counselling alone. It is interesting that in studies in which women were given a dummy tablet yet were told it was the Pill, the women had Pill-like symptoms which went on until they stopped taking the tablets!

Medically the Pill has both advantages and disadvantages. It is thought that statistically the former outweigh the latter. Although it can (rarely) lead to blood clots and may or may not (the evidence is conflicting) increase the chance of breast cancer and cancer of the cervix, it reduces benign breast disease, produces a two to three fold reduction in the chance of having an ovarian or endometrial cancer and, in older ex-Pill takers, protects against osteoporosis. Its lesser benefits, such as reducing pains associated with menstruation thereby, perhaps, reducing the consumption of pain relievers which can be harmful in themselves, are very considerable.

Obviously careful medical supervision is advisable because this ensures correct usage, is reassuring for the woman, provides an opportunity to disentangle psychosexual factors which may greatly benefit the woman and her partner in other ways, and provides a basis for regular health checks including cervical smears. Most of the things which are found to be wrong when doctors carry out routine Pill checks are nothing to do with the oral contraceptive.

## Other hormonal methods

### *Progestogen-only Pill*

This contains only the progesterone component and in lesser dose than is used in the combined Pill. Although regarded as very safe medically it is less effective than the combined Pill, having a failure rate of 2 to 3 per 100 woman years, but since fertility effectively declines with age, women of 40 years and older are likely to be well protected. The big snag is that cycle control is poor and excessive, irregular or no bleeding may occur.

### *Depot progesterone injections*

These are more effective than progestogen-only Pills and are given by injection once every 8 or 12 weeks. They are reserved for special situations such as waiting for the man's semen to clear of sperm after a vasectomy; for older women with menstrual problems; and in some very hairy women. Once given they can not be removed; they may lead to problems with bleeding; and the return of fertility may be delayed after their use.

### *Morning-after Pill*

If, as a result of unprotected intercourse or a condom bursting around the time of ovulation, fertilisation may have occurred, two pills (Eugynon 50 or Ovran) can be taken within 72 hours, but preferably 48 hours, of exposure followed by two more 12 hours later. Pregnancy is now unlikely to occur.

However, a pregnancy test must be carried out 3–4 weeks later and a barrier method of contraception should be used in the meantime. There is a risk, however theoretical, that if the woman *is* pregnant and continues, the foetus may be damaged by the pills. Your GP or any clinic can provide the service. (Some clinics remain open even over the Christmas holiday for this purpose). Alternatively an IUD can be fitted and has the same effect.

## *Male pill*

Hormones as well as other substances such as gossypol, discovered by the Chinese, and D-propranolol, a drug normally used to reduce blood pressure, have been tried in Pills for men. Since a man makes 100,000 sperms per minute, compared with a woman's one egg a month, it is a tall order and all formulations have problems in practice. Whatever is possible technically though, one survey of over a thousand women found that two-thirds would not trust a man who said he was taking a male Pill.

## *Anti-progesterones*

These substances block the body's progesterones. One such product, RU 486 (mifepristone), is undergoing trials. It can be given by mouth, vaginally, or by injection. If given in the second half of the cycle or early in pregnancy it usually results in menstruation occurring. In this respect it is similar to an IUD.

## Sterilisation

Next to the combined Pill in efficiency is sterilisation. One could be forgiven for thinking that sterilisation should be 100 per cent effective since it involves an operation. However this is not so because there is a measurable failure rate for the operation in both men and women. Overall, sterilisations fail in less than 1 per cent of cases but, of course, one partner being sterile does not prevent the unsterilised one from being involved with a third person.

Around 90,000 women are sterilised each year in England and Wales and around the same number of men have a vasectomy. Before the operation counselling is advisable so as to make sure that some other method might not be more suitable. Also the doctor has to be certain that the couple realise that some small risks are involved, that the operation may be irreversible, and that there is a failure rate. Most doctors also like to discuss the reproductive plans of the couple to ensure as far as is possible that there will be no regrets later and to discuss their sex life. A further consideration is to discuss which partner is to be sterilised. Vasectomy is cheaper and less prone to complications than is female sterilisation but many women cannot face up to their man being sterile and 'over-persuading' them is likely to lead to psychological or marital problems later.

Both male and female sterilisation procedures can be carried out on a day-care basis but more usually women stay one night in hospital.

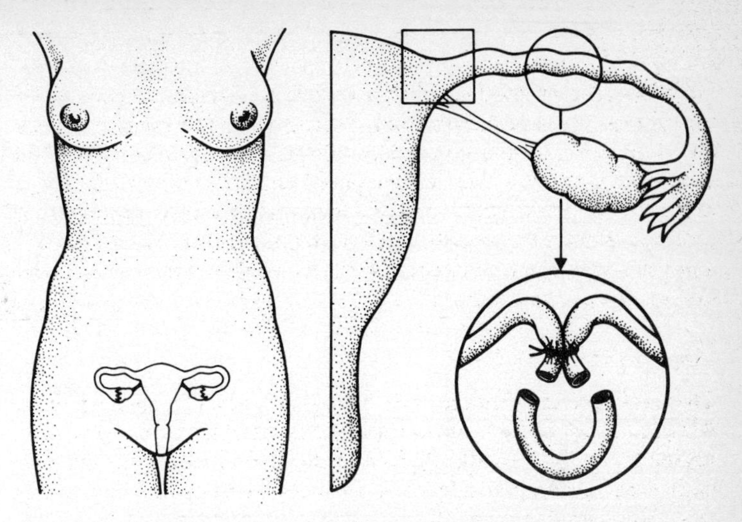

Diagrammatic representation of one form of female sterilisation: *In the diagram on the right the fallopian tube on one side has been severed and tied.*

If the man is brave enough, and most are, a vasectomy can be performed under local anaesthetic. Through two small incisions at the top of the scrotum the vas deferens is located and cut on each side. To reduce the chance of the cut ends joining up again later a length of tube may be removed. Heavy work should be avoided for a couple of days afterwards and sex can be resumed when comfortable but contraception must be continued until the semen is clear of sperm. This can take many weeks and must be tested for. Problems can arise from infection and bruising and the operation can fail altogether if the surgeon thinks the vas had been found but it has not. After the operation both male hormones and semen, which is normal in appearance, are still produced.

When sterilising a woman the abdomen can be opened and the fallopian tubes found and cut but it is much more usual for the laparoscopic method to be used. Usually, but not always, under a general anaesthetic two small incisions are made in the abdominal wall and a device like a thin telescope (a 'laparoscope') is inserted. Through another incision a device is introduced either to apply an electric current to each tube thereby destroying a portion of it or to apply a clip or ring to each tube. As in the case of vasectomy, the surgeon may fail to identify the tubes correctly so that they are not

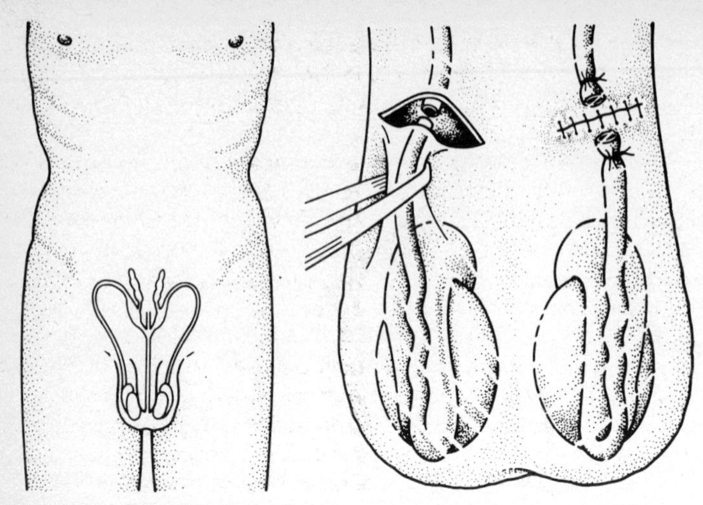

Diagrammatic representation of vasectomy: *The diagram on the left shows the spermatic pathways in a man and on the right the point at which the vas deferens is severed and tied.*

obstructed and the woman is not sterile, or the ends can join up again. A failure, in the form of a pregnancy, is more likely to be apparent in the first year after operation rather than later.

There is some risk of stones forming in the kidney after vasectomy and of abnormal menstrual cycles or even a mini-menopause in women following sterilisation.

Family circumstances or reproductive intentions may change and either sex may seek to have the operation reversed. Success is more likely in women if a ring or clip has been used and in men if a large length of vas has not been removed. Reversal rates of between 40–90 per cent success can be achieved in women, depending on the method of sterilisation used, and in good hands the same can apply to men. Lower success rates are usual 10 or more years after the original operation.

## IUD (intra-uterine device; coil; loop)

Although it has its fans the IUD is less satisfactory than the Pill, especially in young women who have not yet had a baby. The method probably works by dislodging an embryo which arrives in the uterus. Because of this it is really a type of early abortion – not a method of preventing conception.

Before an IUD is fitted the woman should have sufficient information about other methods in order to make an informed choice. She also needs to know the advantages and disadvantages of an IUD.

The advantages include the fact that nothing contraceptive needs to be done at the time of intercourse. Secondly, except at the time of insertion, it requires no motivation. Thirdly, if she is symptom-free and does not object to its presence, as some women do, it is an acceptable method; and finally, it does not disturb the hormones in the body as does the Pill.

The disadvantages are that the device is expelled in 2–10 per cent of women perhaps unknown to the woman herself. Although recent designs minimise this risk, the IUD has a failure rate which is about the same as the progestogen-only Pill. An IUD can produce menstrual disorders with resultant anaemia and also inflammation of the fallopian tubes, with the risk of subsequent infertility, if an infection with organisms such as chlamydia (p. 295) is present. This eventuality, and pregnancy, occur most commonly in the early months after the device is fitted but manufacturers recommend removal and the fitting of a new one every 2 or 3 years. If the woman is allergic to copper then devices containing copper should not be used and neither should the IUD be used in women with valvular heart disease or those on corticosteroid drugs. Furthermore, at the time of insertion or later, the device may pass into or through the wall of the uterus.

IUDs do not increase the chances of cancer of the cervix or uterus but deaths do occur from it at the rate of 3 to 5 per million users per year. Overall it is as safe from this point of view as other methods and safer than using no contraception.

With all this in mind the method is best used by older women who have completed their families and in whom sexual life style is fairly settled.

There used to be a variety of IUDs but choice is now more limited because of manufacturers withdrawing products from the market as a result of litigation, especially in the US. The Multiload Cu 375 gained a favourable report from the World Health Organisation. High hopes also exist for the Novagard/Nova-T which releases progesterone and can be left in position for 5 years. A failure rate of 1 per hundred woman years is claimed and it is associated with less menstrual pain and less blood loss.

For a variety of reasons the success of an IUD is associated with the fitting of the device by a doctor who has some enthusiasm, but not too much, for the method and who has a lot of experience in fitting them and caring for the patient afterwards. This factor appears to influence success more than the actual device fitted.

## Chemical methods

Various substances kill sperms and, if put into the vagina before intercourse, reduce the chances of conception. Vaginal foams and pessaries are probably the most effective but any of the chemical methods can cause irritation. A possible advantage of these methods is that as well as killing sperms they may kill gonococci and other organisms.

The effectiveness of such chemical methods is increased by using them along with a barrier method, such as a condom (sheath, rubber, protective) or a cervical cap (diaphragm) all of which are intended to prevent the sperms reaching the cervix.

## Barrier methods

There are several barrier methods and more people are using them than in the past.

### *Condoms*

The commonest is the condom. The male version may burst and the correct method of usage to reduce this hazard is shown in the diagram. The advantages are that it cuts down the risk of infection, is widely available, is available free from clinics, and requires no prescription. It causes impotence in some men but can prolong the performance of premature ejaculators. For the same reason some men say that it is like wearing a wellington on the penis and some women object to it as being 'unloving'. Women with a fear of semen can find its use an advantage. It should be used from the commencement of sexual proceedings and if the woman puts it on the man it can become an enjoyable part of foreplay. It is usually lubricated. One brand provides a pessary of nonoxynol-9, which kills both sperms and HIV (see page 298), along with the condom. The pessary is placed in the vagina and thereby provides additional protection. The condom is far from foolproof but with careful and conscientious use failure rates can be brought down from the usual 14 to 1 or 2 pregnancies per hundred woman years.

Clinical trials are under way with the female condom. It amounts to a plastic bag, about three times wider than a male condom, sealed

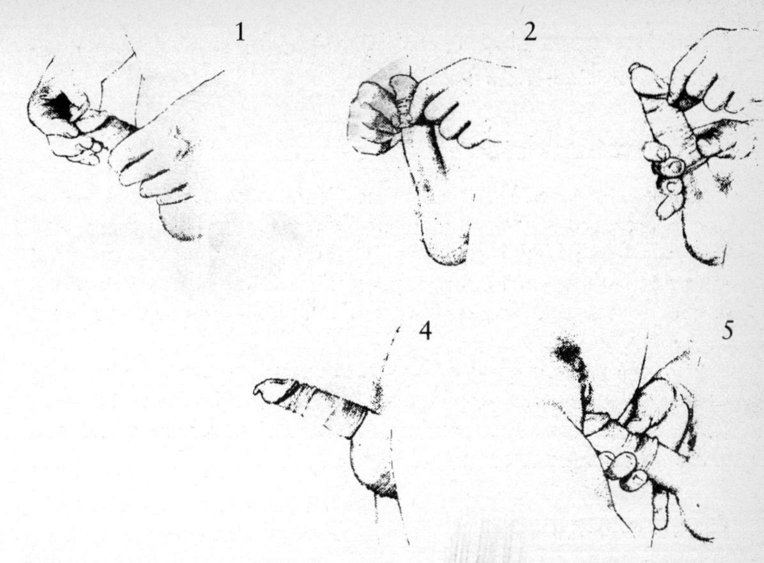


The use of a sheath: *Used carefully, a sheath can be a very safe method of contraception.*
*1) Squeeze air out of teat and apply sheath to penis after placing a few drops of spermicide inside.*
*2) Unroll the sheath along the length of the penis 3) using other hand to ease it back towards the head of the penis.*
*4) When the sheath is on completely it should be totally unrolled and the packing rings should still be visible.*
*5) Withdraw shortly after orgasm keeping a finger or two on the base of the sheath as you withdraw.*

at one end and with a springy plastic ring at the open end. The closed end is put in the vagina and another loose ring is inserted to keep the device in place. The ring at the open end prevents this from slipping into the vagina. Men say they prefer it to the male condom and some women say that it improves their orgasm – perhaps due to the outer ring rubbing the clitoris.

## *The diaphragm*

This can look awesomely large to some women and is shaped something like a section of a tennis ball. The correct size for the woman has to be selected by her GP or clinic and the woman has to be trained how to use it. A spermicidal substance is applied to both sides prior to insertion. After sex it must be left in place for six hours. The failure rate is similar to that of the condom.

A woman with a prolapse may find it hard to fit but the new arcing diaphragm helps overcome this problem. The diaphragm is non-hormonal but requires high motivation for consistent use. It can cause some complaints of loss of sensation especially for the woman whose most sensitive part is her front vaginal wall. This is almost entirely covered by the rubber of the device. To some extent it protects against sexually transmitted diseases and cancer of the cervix but it cannot be relied upon to protect against AIDS. Urinary tract infections are more common in diaphragm users and the method is unsuitable for women who are habitual cystitis sufferers.

### *The sponge*

This modification of an ancient method is enjoying something of a revival since it is easy to insert and does not need to be fitted by a doctor. One such product consists of a 50 mm × 25 mm dimpled polyurethane sponge impregnated with 1 gram of nonoxynol-9 spermicide. There is a ribbon on one side to facilitate removal. The sponge must be moistened before insertion. Its failure rate is about 10 pregnancies per hundred woman years so, whilst better than nothing, it is probably best suited to the older woman with declining fertility or the couple who wouldn't mind much if pregnancy occurred. Attempts to perfect it could be rewarding.

## Natural methods

By 'natural' we mean the absence of pills, potions and devices. Several methods are available. They are all best regarded as inefficient for the woman who is determined not to get pregnant, but they are useful for the couple who is not too worried about having another baby or for those who are really meticulous about their use.

A simple method is for the *man not to ejaculate*. Provided the woman knows this is his intention she can still enjoy intercourse and even have an orgasm. The method suits many older men who enjoy vaginal stimulation of the penis but do not necessarily want to ejaculate every time they are aroused. Once the man has made up his mind to use this method it is easy to master if he is determined. It can allow intercourse to continue for as long as the woman wants and makes it possible for the man to have intercourse more often. On occasions when he does want to ejaculate, of course, contraception must be used.

Having said all this it must be remembered that there are sperms present in the pre-ejaculatory fluid (the few drops of liquid that emerge from the tip of the penis before a man climaxes) and that this might, rarely, get a woman pregnant. Because of this, the method has some danger for a fertile couple.

## *Withdrawal*

This is a simple method but it can be frustrated by, or frustrating for, either partner. The man withdraws his penis during the interval between his orgasm setting in and ejaculation starting. Since his instinct at this time is to thrust his penis deep into the vagina he may fail to withdraw in time. As the first few spurts of semen contain most of the sperms this is potentially dangerous. Some women so much hate the thought of withdrawal that they try to prevent it in the heat of the moment. This is a very unsafe method and can be emotionally unpleasant for the couple.

## *The rhythm method*

This essentially consists of trying to predict when ovulation occurs from a study of the woman's menstrual cycle. To do this properly she has to have an accurate record of her periods over the preceding year. Only then can she see a reliable time pattern. Going by what has happened over a few months is simply not accurate enough. The first day of the cycle is taken as being the day menstruation starts and the last day is the day menstruation next commences. The life of the egg is thought to be one to two days (although it may be as short as twelve hours) and that of the sperms in the tubes two to three days. Adding a day either side for safety means that intercourse has to be avoided for seven days around ovulation. This means that you cannot have intercourse between the eighteenth and eleventh days before your next period starts. To allow for variations in cycle length, the first unsafe day is calculated by deducting eleven from the number of days in the longest cycle. After every cycle the numbers should be worked out again so as to cover the last twelve cycles. This is important because very few women are regular as clockwork and many things, such as stress and illness, can alter cycle length. If you work on the assumption that your cycle is twenty-eight days long all the time you will definitely expose yourself to getting pregnant.

## *The temperature method*

In this the body temperature is taken daily, first thing before getting up, by inserting a thermometer into the mouth, rectum or vagina. The result is plotted on a chart. The temperature recorded like this is seen to rise over the two or three days after ovulation to a plateau about 0.4°C above the temperature recorded in the early days of the cycle. After the temperature has been at this plateau level for three days intercourse can be resumed. If intercourse is avoided for four days (the longest reasonable life of a sperm in the female reproductive tract) before the predicted date of ovulation (as calculated from several months' charting of your temperature or doing a kit test) and resumed at this later point in the cycle, the method can be reasonably effective.

## *The mucus method*

As menstruation stops the vagina is usually 'dry' for some days. This is followed by a phase in which vaginal mucus is found to be thick, whitish or yellowish, opaque and sticky. Before ovulation the mucus becomes clear, slippery and watery, like the white of a raw egg and you have to stop having intercourse unless you want to conceive. In the next stage the mucus changes and becomes tacky and opaque and the feeling of vaginal wetness diminishes. The last day of the clear, watery, slippery mucus is peak mucus day and intercourse is not allowed until four days after that day. In practice this turns out not to be a safe guide if used alone so the method should be combined with the temperature method and intercourse resumed when three consecutive daily temperatures have been above the level of those on the previous six.

## *Ovulation predictors*

This method is also known as 'traffic light contraception'. Urine tests are available which detect the rise in luteinising hormone that immediately precedes ovulation and the colour changes either allow or bar intercourse. They are costly, and inefficient because sperms may still be surviving in the fallopian tubes from intercourse which occurred before the colour change suggested that sex was inadvisable.

# Planning a family

Having a baby is nothing like buying a TV set or a car and a couple's urge to produce a baby should ideally be controlled until the man and woman know they are secure together; that they can cope with the bad times as well as the good; that they want a baby for the baby's sake only and not to please themselves, to keep up with the Jones's, improve their own self-esteem and so on; and until they can provide for it without undue sacrifice on their part.

Producing another human being who may well live for eighty or more years is becoming an increasingly awesome undertaking. Most couples are having fewer babies and having them later. This is surely responsible. An increasing proportion of couples (up to 10 per cent) are choosing to have no children at all for various reasons and others are unable to do so because they are infertile.

The ideal way to space a family is not known. Nature's way, which depends on long-term, unrestricted breastfeeding, ensures that babies are born at intervals of about two and a half to three years. This is not acceptable to most Western couples who do not want a baby every three years throughout their reproductive life, but can be useful between their first and last babies.

If children are born too closely together the mother may be over-taxed, but longer intervals can increase rivalry between the children. Spreading them out with very long intervals means the family is committed to child rearing for years on end, but this suits some women who feel most fulfilled when caring for babies. Longer intervals also reduce the severity of the economic effects of having children on the family. Small families tend to be more favourable to the intellectual development of the children than large ones.

Whatever plan is adopted it has to be related to contraception. One reasonably effective plan is for a highly efficient contraceptive method such as the Pill to be started before the couple first have intercourse. The woman continues taking the Pill until about six months before the couple want to conceive their first baby. At this time the Pill is stopped and a condom or other barrier method used to allow time for the Pill's effects on the body to wear off. After about three months the couple can start having unprotected intercourse, but it is important to remember that many couples do not conceive at once, whether or not the woman has been on the Pill. A woman having intercourse on an unrestricted basis and not protected by any contraceptive takes an average of 5.3 months to conceive. Twenty-five per cent of couples will have conceived in the first month, 63 per cent by the end of six months, 75 per cent by the end of nine months and 80–90 per cent by the end of one year.

If a couple decides to have a second child but timing is not too important then relatively ineffective methods such as vaginal foams, a diaphragm, or one of the natural methods such as relying on unrestricted breast feeding could be used. If no further children are wanted at all, the Pill can be used again until the woman is about thirty-five years old. Alternatively, one of the partners could be sterilised. After the age of thirty-five less reliable methods can be used, such as the progestogen-only (mini) pill.

Contraception needs to be continued until about a year after the periods end at the menopause, but as fertility is falling rapidly by this age in most women less efficient methods can be used.

## Infertility

Infertility afflicts about one couple in 6 or 7 but nevertheless lies somewhat outside the scope of this book. Because so many abortions are being done fewer babies are available for adoption so the topic is becoming one of increasing importance. With the constant coverage of 'test-tube' methods in the popular press infertility, once a taboo area, is now widely discussed.

For conception to occur, a sperm capable of fertilising an ovum which is capable of being fertilised have to meet and fuse, and for a baby to grow normally the fertilised ovum has to develop efficiently and the woman's body has to provide for it and protect it efficiently.

For all this to happen a man has to be capable of producing sufficient sperms of adequate quality and has to deliver them to the top of the vagina. Male genital malformations causing infertility are increasing for unknown reasons and sperm counts have been falling consistently since 1960, at least in the US. Increasing stress may be a reason since sperm counts in students, for example, fall when their examinations are due. Another related reason may be that intercourse rates are falling, according to some researchers. Some men

*Some abnormal sperm forms which can result in difficulties in conceiving.*

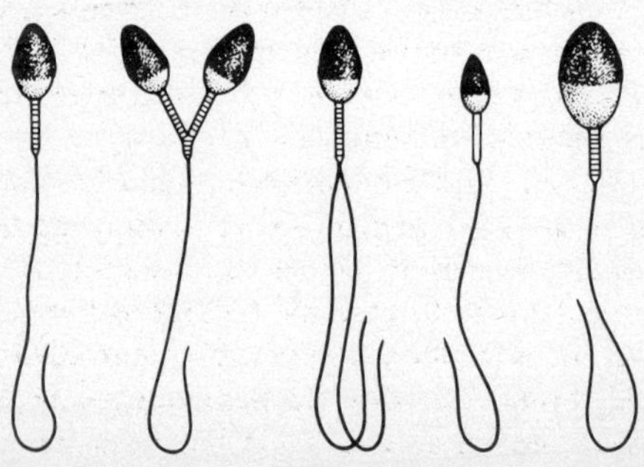

produce healthy sperms in the testis but by the time they are ejaculated large numbers have lost their tails and look moth-eaten under the microscope. The presumption is that the sperms are being damaged in the epididymis. If ejaculation rates are raised sperms spend less time between testis and penis and so might be less damaged. Getting such men to ejaculate twice a day does in fact improve sperm quality.

One way in which these sperms might have been damaged is by the man's body making antibodies to his own sperms. Normally this does not happen but it can do if sperms reach the blood stream because of an injury to or obstruction of the tubes through which they pass. One way round the problem is to obtain an egg (by stimulating the ovaries hormonally and then retrieving the eggs laparoscopically) from the partner, wash the sperms free of antibody and bring about fertilisation in a test-tube. A woman's body may also make antibodies to her partner's sperms but this is not common because sperms usually have the ability to suppress such a response. The same test-tube technique can be used to overcome this problem but another way that is being explored is to place semen in the woman's peritoneal cavity in the hope that sperms will enter the fallopian tubes without being interfered with by antibodies. Evidence that antibodies may be the problem can be obtained by studying what happens when the sperms encounter the mucus in the canal through the cervix. The sperms may be immobilised or destroyed.

Male causes are responsible for infertility in about 30 per cent of couples and sperm defects probably account for a quarter of all cases of infertility. Low sperm counts, provided over half the sperms are mobile when looked at under the microscope, are not as serious a cause of infertility as was once thought. Some such couples can also be helped by the test tube method. Failure to ejaculate sperms is a much less common problem and can be due to the testes failing to produce them or a blockage in the vas or other tubes. One cause of this is a chlamydia infection of the epididymis. In this respect the situation is the same as chlamydia infection leading to later blockage of the fallopian tubes in women.

If sperms are absent and the blockage cannot be relieved, all that can be done is to advise artificial insemination using semen from a donor. Hormonal causes of male infertility are rare.

In the female this is not the case and failures to ovulate account for about a fifth of all infertility. Thanks to recent advances the vast majority of such women can now be made to ovulate. In fact care is needed to ensure that excessive ovulation does not occur. If the fallopian tubes are blocked an attempt can be made to repair them surgically but if this proves impossible the test tube technique can be tried.

Returning to the sperm, actual sperm counts are of less importance these days then they used to be. A few good quality sperms can fertilise an egg but even quite large numbers with some sort of defect may not do the trick. The sperms can look all right and move under the miscroscope but still lack a capacity to fertilise an ovum. Oddly enough this, and other vital properties of the sperm, can be tested by mixing them with hamster eggs and seeing how the sperms perform. In a similar way to sperms, a woman's eggs can be defective but at present very little is known about this.

Varicose veins adjacent to the testis, a condition known as varicocele, used to be thought to be a cause of male infertility and enthusiastic claims were made about the effects on fertility of treating them. More scientific investigation indicates that it is not a common cause of infertility. Similarly, until recently, endometriosis was thought to be a common cause in women but treating it does not greatly increase the chances of conception so the relationship between the two is not a simple one. However, the test-tube method often results in success with these cases.

A newer variant of the test-tube technique is called GIFT (Gamete Intrafallopian Transfer). Provided the woman has at least one unblocked tube it can be used. The aim is to copy what happens in Nature in which fertilisation occurs at the outer end of the tube. A number of eggs are placed in the fallopian tube along with a prepared sample of sperms. In a third of cases fertilisation occurs and the eggs are slowly wafted along the tubes to the uterus and implant on the uterine wall, as happens when things are left to Nature. The technique is used particularly in cases of infertility for which no explanation can be found and where the test-tube method has failed.

Another technique used is insertion of the husband's semen into the cervix or into the uterus but this is controversial.

No reader of this book should be surprised to learn that psychotherapy and psychosexual counselling have their successes in cases of otherwise unexplained infertility since the psyche has such a profound effect on the body that some cases of infertility must be due to disturbances between them. From this point of view persuading couples not to become obsessional about their problem but to learn how to enjoy sex can result in apparently dramatic cures. One part of the explanation could be that if the woman learns to have orgasms in intercourse semen may be sucked into her fallopian tubes, thereby increasing her chances of fertilisation. That there is a formidable psychic component to infertility can be judged by the finding that a substantial minority of women conceive after seeing an infertility specialist even long before any treatment is instigated.

Overall, only a minority of infertile couples can be helped. Private specialist clinics can often be of more assistance than the NHS but may be costly. The longer the problem goes on the more the chances of success diminish so it is reasonable to consult your doctor if after a year of trying pregnancy has not occurred. However, there are things you can do to help yourselves.

## Helping yourself

Masters and Johnson found that simple advice on and attention to technique, such as in the list below, provided the answer for one in eight of their so-called 'infertile' patients.

### *Sex technique*

To have the best chance of getting a woman pregnant a man's penis must penetrate her vagina deeply and he must ejaculate while it is there.

### *Timing*

For most sexually active couples it does not much matter how often they have intercourse, because if they do so often enough then by chance alone they will soon hit the time around ovulation and the woman will conceive. However, if a man is a shift worker or works away from home a lot, if either partner is ill, or if for any other reason they do not have intercourse often, their chances of the woman getting pregnant are greatly reduced. The best time to have intercourse in order to stand the best chance of pregnancy is around ovulation. The rhythm, temperature and mucus methods of contraception can obviously be put to use for conception since all aim to foretell ovulation as do the ovulation predictor tests.

### *Frequency*

As we have seen, there is no 'normal' number of times a week to have intercourse. However, if you are having intercourse very infrequently you stack the odds up against yourselves very heavily when it comes to conceiving a baby. Many of the couples attending infertility clinics are having intercourse once a month or less. Given that the couple having intercourse about two or three times a week will on average take 5.3 months to conceive, once a month is not giving yourselves a fair chance.

For many couples low intercourse rates are what they want and trying to increase the frequency can produce all kinds of problems in the marriage. Such couples may benefit from professional help. Some couples worry about saving up sperms to produce a better quality ejaculation and so increase their chance of conceiving. There is some truth in this because sperm counts are reduced in a man who ejaculates every day, but there is no point in 'saving up' for more than two days.

## *Sex positions*

If you are fertile it does not matter in what position you have intercourse, but if you are sub-fertile it can make all the difference as to whether or not you will conceive. The first thing to try is to put a pillow under the woman's hips so that the pool of semen ejaculated into the top of her vagina does not run straight back out again. The woman lies down after intercourse for half an hour and should not get up to pass water or to wash. Ideally, she should go to sleep in this position, but this may be inconvenient.

For a woman whose uterus is retroverted (tipped backwards), raising the hips takes her cervix out of the pool of semen in her vagina and so makes a pregnancy less likely. These women are more likely to conceive if they use an 'all-fours' position for intercourse. The woman kneels on the bed with her elbows and forearms on the bed. This allows exceptionally deep penetration of the penis and bathes the cervix in semen.

Generally speaking, if you are having difficulty in conceiving you should use the positions that give the deepest possible penetration. If deep penetration is painful you should see your doctor.

## *Exercise*

Excessive exercise and jogging have been associated with subfertility and so should be moderated.

## *Y-fronts*

To function effectively the testes need to be cooler than the rest of the body so it is sensible not to wear Y-fronts which prevent the testes moving downwards when hot.

## Miscarriage

Even if fertilisation and implantation are achieved the foetus may still be lost. In fact up to three-quarters of all conceptions are lost, usually without the woman even knowing she had conceived.

Loss of the foetus later on is a more obvious miscarriage and has a much more profound effect on a woman and her partner. Ironically, even though Nature seems to reject so many foetuses we humans too add to the number by electing to terminate unwanted pregnancies. The active process by which we do this is called abortion – and this is the subject of the next chapter.

## Causes of infertility

| Female Conditions | Cause | Treatment |
|---|---|---|
| **Ovulation problems** | Usually unknown | 80% of women ovulate with the drug clomiphene. |
| | 'Normal' – most women don't ovulate every month. | None |
| | Poor quality egg as woman ages. | None |
| | After coming off the Pill | Time usually cures |
| | Hormonal dysfunction | Sort out causes |
| | Certain tranquillisers | Stop drug |
| | Psychological stress or shock. | Periods return spontaneously but clomiphene can be used. |
| **Fallopian tube** | Blockage secondary to STD. | |
| | As a long term result of the coil (IUD). | Use surgical techniques to unblock fallopian tubes; replace them with a transplant or remove pelvic adhesions where present. |
| | After an abortion | |
| | Any pelvic inflammatory disease causing blockage of tube (appendicitis, for example). | |
| | Deliberate damage to sterilise a woman. | |

| Female Conditions | Cause | Treatment |
|---|---|---|
| **Endometriosis** | Unknown | Pregnancy<br>The Pill for 1 year continuously<br>Male hormones (Danazol)<br>Surgery |
| **Infections of the genital and urinary systems** | Gonorrhoea causing blocked tubes. | Treat gonorrhoea but surgery usually necessary too. |
| | T-mycoplasma | Tetracycline |
| | Thrush/trichomonas | Treat vaginal infections |
| | Urinary infections | Treat infections with drugs |
| **Cervical factors** | Cervical infection | Drugs and/or local minor surgical treatment. |
| | Narrowing of the cervical opening. | Dilate it under anaesthetic (D & C); if unsuitable can have AIH. |
| | Thick cervical mucus | Oestrogen therapy |
| | Hostile cervical mucus | Use condom for 1 year to allow antibodies to sperm to disappear or use drugs that suppress the body's immune mechanisms. |
| **Abnormalities of the uterus** | Inborn abnormalities | May be none |
| | Fibroids | Surgical removal |
| **Polycystic ovaries** | Unknown | Clomiphene, gonadotrophic hormones or surgery. |
| **Turner's syndrome** | Congenital | None |
| **X-rays** | Usually women working with x-rays. | Remove source of problem |
| **Menstrual back-flow** | Unknown | Surgery to pull up tubes |

| Female Conditions | Cause | Treatment |
|---|---|---|
| General diseases | TB<br>Diabetes<br>Any severe illness<br>Severe malnutrition<br>Severe depression<br>Anorexia nervosa<br>Gross obesity | Usually only temporary cessation of ovulation. |
| Vitamin B12 deficiency | Unknown | Give vitamin B12 |
| Stress | Many | Cure cause or use tranquillisers if necessary. |

| Male Conditions | Cause | Treatment |
|---|---|---|
| Varicocele | Varicose vein around testis. | Surgery, results can be good. |
| Testicular failure | Mumps | None – few men permanently infertile as a result. |
| | Klinefelter's syndrome | None |
| | Accidental knock or trauma during surgery. | Sperm count returns to normal with time. |
| | Twisting of testis | If caught early, sperm count not permanently harmed. |
| 'Glandular' | Usually unknown<br>Thyroid gland underactive. | Treat if possible |
| Obstruction of vas deferens | Vasectomy | Can be reversed in about 50% of men. |
| | TB or gonorrhoea | Relieve blockage of vas deferens by surgery. |
| Poor semen volume | Unknown | Use small volume for AIH |

| Male Conditions | Cause | Treatment |
|---|---|---|
| **Ejaculation problems** | Sperms go into bladder not down penis. | Retrieve urine and separate out sperms which are then used for AIH. |
| | Premature ejaculation | Man 'comes' too soon and sperms never get into vagina. Sex therapy useful. |
| **Undescended testis** | Developmental | Surgery or drugs in little boys but no treatment satisfactory in men. |
| **Sperms agglutinate** (clump together) | Immune disorder | Wash sperms in laboratory and use for AIH. |
| **Necrospermia** (man produces dead sperms) | Unknown | None |
| **Genito-urinary infections** | TB<br>Gonorrhoea<br>Colon bacteria | Treat infection |
| **Zinc deficiency** | Many. Usually poor dietary intake. | Give zinc tablets |
| **Drug allergies** | Sensitive to drug | Stop drug |
| **Ageing** | Normal | None |
| **Stress** | Many | Remove cause |
| **Severe malnutrition** | Usually enforced | Give nourishing food |
| **Heat** | Tight underpants, frequent hot baths/showers. | Wear boxer shorts, bathe scrotum twice daily in cool water. |

| Male Conditions | Cause | Treatment |
|---|---|---|
| **Drugs** | Many drugs dangerous to sperm production – ask doctor. | Stop taking offending drug |

| Joint Male/Female Conditions | Cause | Treatment |
|---|---|---|
| **Sex at wrong time of month** | Ovulation around day 15 – must have intercourse around then. | Have intercourse every other day from day 11 to day 18 of cycle. |
| **Sex too infrequent** | Many | Have intercourse more frequently, especially around middle of cycle. |
| **Poor positions** | Woman gets up after intercourse and 'loses' all semen. | Woman stays lying down for ½ hours after intercourse with hips on pillow. |
| | Uterus tilted backwards. | Intercourse in rear-entry positions. |
| **Lubricant jellies washing/ douching etc.** | Obvious | Stop all these practices – they can kill sperms. |
| **Sexual performance problems** | Many – see doctor or marital therapist. | Treat individual sex problem. |

*Chapter 15*
# Abortion

Abortion is an emotive and therefore a controversial subject. By removing the embryo (which is the name given to the fertilised egg in the first eight weeks of a baby's life) or the foetus (which is what it is called thereafter), a potential life is lost.

However, Nature also makes use of abortion. In some unknown way, a pregnant woman's body 'inspects' an embryo and if it is defective it is likely to be rejected without the woman even necessarily knowing she has conceived. It is thought that a half to three-quarters of all fertilised eggs are lost like this. Later, when the pregnancy is recognisable and established, a further 10 to 15 per cent of pregnancies fail, mostly between the second and third months. Many such foetuses are found to be visibly defective. Sometimes, the woman may be hormonally deficient or may have an abnormality such as fibroids. All such naturally occurring abortions are labelled 'spontaneous' and the public calls them miscarriages. Not all imperfect babies are spontaneously aborted. Around 2 per cent of babies are born with congenital defects, but most of these are slight. Nature may be a little more 'strict' in her scrutiny of female embryos, in that they are probably rejected earlier than male ones. This may account for the preponderance of male births of around 104 male to 100 female.

Abortions which are caused by human intervention are called induced abortions. They can be self-induced, criminally induced, or therapeutically induced (by doctors). One effect of the passage in Britain of the Abortion Act of 1967, which legalised therapeutic abortion, has been to eliminate almost entirely the first two categories.

The Abortion Act allows abortion provided that it is carried out in places approved for that purpose and is undertaken by a medically qualified person, and that two medical practitioners certify that the pregnant woman's existing children or her own physical or mental health would be at a greater risk if the pregnancy continued than if it were terminated. If there is a substantial risk that the child would be born handicapped then abortion is also legally allowed. By and large the medical profession increasingly supports the Act because it means that women no longer have to become unwilling mothers or be abandoned to the dangers of illegal abortion. Understandably some obstetricians and gynaecologists are somewhat reluctant about the Act because it is they who have to carry out the operations when their training and orientation is towards helping women to have live, healthy babies safely.

In an ideal world no woman would become pregnant unless she wanted a baby for its own sake and was able to provide an emotional and physical environment in which it could prosper. But there is evidence that up to a quarter or so of all babies born are not wanted in this positive way although, we should add, they may not be completely *un*wanted.

Women who have abortions are sometimes represented as being unnatural or frivolous, but there is another way of looking at the subject. The age group which has most abortions is the late adolescent and young adult one. There is no evidence to suggest that these women are trying to avoid pregnancy *altogether*, only *this* pregnancy. Presumably, a strong motive for seeking an abortion is that they cannot provide properly for a child at the particular time and so want to defer pregnancy until they can. From this point of view having an abortion is a responsible act.

The younger generation, contrary to appearance perhaps, is the one which encounters the most problems arising from psychosexual conflicts and confusions. Many long-married women with families have abortions because they cannot face another baby for a whole range of reasons. Whether or not such women should be 'allowed' to use abortion as a form of birth control is a debatable subject, which we do not want to go into here, but some women only come to the decision after much heart-searching and agonising. Almost all women are disturbed by the event.

As a result of various difficulties, the National Health Service in the UK is able to undertake abortions in only half of all cases. The remainder have to make private arrangements, usually at a private hospital specialising in the operation. Such specialist organisations are usually very efficient because of the experience they acquire in doing the operation. There are also both National Health Service and private counselling services which help women decide whether or not to have an abortion and then help them practically. If an abortion is the decision, then good counselling can reduce anxiety, guilt, misapprehension and the possibility of depression later. An experienced counsellor may also be able to detect unconscious motivations, a knowledge of which may prevent the woman starting another unwanted pregnancy. Pregnancy bureaux or advisory services exist and carry out immediate pregnancy tests. They provide counselling, advice and help in connection with abortion and have to be licensed with the Department of Health to ensure their competence.

Over the years the techniques used to carry out abortions have become more refined and safer. In ordinary, uncomplicated, early cases, an abortion is safer than having a baby, even though having a baby is itself now a very safe process.

## Methods

Usually a general anaesthetic is given but local anaesthesia is sometimes used. In most cases the vacuum aspiration method is used, by which the embryo is sucked out. The canal through the cervix does not have to be stretched very much during this technique, unlike older methods in which the canal was opened wider so as to introduce instruments. Overstretching the cervix can result in it becoming loose, which increases the chances of a spontaneous abortion in any subsequent pregnancy.

If the pregnancy is further advanced (14 to 15 weeks and beyond) the prostaglandin method is the one usually used. The prostaglandins, which are introduced into the uterus, encourage it to go into labour prematurely. The contractions slowly enlarge the passage through the cervix, in the same way as in labour, and the foetus is eventually passed. This slow enlargement of the passage does little or no subsequent harm to the cervix.

Apart from making the cervix incompetent the other potential physical complications of abortion are infection and/or haemorrhage. The first can lead to infertility but both are relatively rare when the operator is skilful and experienced. Similarly, the uterus may be perforated by the instruments used, the operation may fail and there are risks, however small, from an anaesthetic. These are infrequent occurrences in skilled hands, but they do occur occasionally. Failure to remove the embryo is understandable when one bears in mind how small it actually is in early pregnancy. Having the operation between the seventh to tenth week after the first day of the last period is best for this reason. Also, the operation is not done under direct vision but by touch. Some women have a double uterus or twins and these again can occasionally mislead the operator into thinking the operation has been successfully carried out when in fact a foetus remains.

Late abortions carry more risks, and unfortunately are common among the young who often 'deny' they are pregnant and not uncommonly even deny having had intercourse. It is only when the woman faces reality that an abortion is sought. Another situation which leads a woman to go for an abortion very late applies to older women. Since the chances of Down's syndrome and other genetic defects rise with increasing maternal age, some obstetricians use the technique of amniocentesis to obtain cells for culture to discover whether the foetus is abnormal and then offer the woman an abortion if something is wrong. Since culturing the cells and then studying the chromosomes takes a long time such women tend to come for an abortion late. Many clinics limit abortions to before twenty weeks but legally they can be carried out until twenty-eight weeks although in practice twenty-four weeks is the limit.

A unique study was started in the 1960s in Czechoslovakia comparing the development of a group of wanted children with a group of those who were not wanted. At birth both groups were the same but as time went on it emerged that the unwanted group were less likely to be breastfed, received medical care for acute illness more often, had more minor accidents, were more likely to be admitted to hospital, were more often overweight, and were more likely to be described by their mothers as naughty, stubborn and bad tempered. At school they were less diligent, more excitable and more likely to be rejected by classmates as friends. Boys were more adversely affected than girls but the problems of both increased with time. Many left education early and by the early twenties were still showing a greater tendency to have social problems.

No woman has an abortion for pleasure and nearly all feel anxious and guilty. If a woman really wants her baby but has an abortion because of her circumstances or ill health she often gets depressed afterwards. However, the majority feel that an enormous weight has been lifted off their minds and some even feel a little guilty about their lack of distress. A woman's relationship with her partner not infrequently improves because it is an adversity shared and surmounted. Contrary to what is often said, her partner sometimes also feels guilty about the situation in which the woman has been placed and by enduring it she earns a new respect from him. Sometimes the relationship collapses. This is especially likely when either partner made the pregnancy happen in an attempt to secure the relationship.

*Chapter 16*

# Pregnancy and childbirth

There are numerous books about pregnancy and childbirth which cover the day-to-day events in detail, and we cannot hope to include this sort of information in a book like this. What we will look at in this chapter is the couple as a sexual unit. Let us start by looking at why women have babies, because understanding the real motives for having a baby helps one understand the feelings, emotions and problems that can arise.

## Reasons for having a baby

The first reason to consider is the cultural pressure to do so. The majority of people do get married and a large proportion of them have one baby or two. Our culture is still 'pro-natalist' – that is it reveres babies and makes them seem desirable objects. This is, of course, healthy and normal because the human race has to continue. However, even if we in the West stopped having babies the world's population would still continue to rise alarmingly. Most people feel it is reasonable to have up to two babies to 'replace themselves' but in worldwide population terms this is no longer necessary or desirable. Increasing numbers of couples (about 10 per cent) are choosing not to have children.

Couples have babies for all kinds of different reasons, many of them quite unconscious. Some have them to prove to themselves and the world that they are grown-up and adult people. A person doing this usually has a poor view of him- or herself sexually or as a personality, and wants to do something the world cannot ignore. This motivation is fairly common in teenage marriages. Some couples have babies to secure a relationship. Before marriage a girl sometimes gets pregnant to make a man marry her but this is increasingly uncommon.

Within marriage some people have a baby to 'save' the relationship, thinking – usually wrongly – that a baby will mend their problems and bring them closer together. Many women have a baby inadvertently – it does not matter too much if they have one so they do not use contraception seriously and as a result get pregnant. Such a baby may not be positively wanted or planned but is eventually welcomed nevertheless. Some young women have babies to keep up with friends.

An unfortunate motive, closely linked to the last one, is that a baby is sometimes seen as the next milestone in life – often under the influence of parents. For some women having a baby is a sign that she really loves her partner and for others it proves her female status. Bringing another person into the world to 'prove' such things is irresponsible.

There are many other reasons why couples have babies. There are, for example, genuine failures of contraception. Also, some – perhaps most – women have babies because of an innate drive to do so. It is almost impossible to say how important this latter reason is because the cultural pressures are so enormous. Many people, including some doctors, believe that a woman is not a 'real' woman until she has had a baby and that deep down all women really want babies. Some doctors even go so far as to claim that women *ought* to have babies. We cannot agree with any of these sentiments.

Ideally every baby should be positively wanted and it is the duty of every engaged couple to discuss carefully their views on the subject. There is little point in getting married to someone crazy about babies if you cannot stand them or want only one or two. Every couple should carefully evaluate their motives for having a baby and unless they both agree on them they should not have one. A baby is not a thing; he or she is a person who is probably going to live for scores of years and starting that process off is an awesome responsibility.

## Preparing for pregnancy

Most of us go into parenthood unprepared. Culturally we are led to think that it is a blissful state in which we will have endless joys, with a text-book baby that sleeps and eats regularly and smiles and gurgles the rest of the time. Preparation for parenthood should start *before* a woman gets pregnant. Most parents minimise the hardships of child rearing when talking to the young about babies. Then when a young girl has her baby she is perhaps fearful, disappointed, amazed, anxious, depressed, lonely and a host of other things because she imagines she must be at fault, since everyone else seems to be coping so well, and that she is a failure.

So during preparation for pregnancy young parents-to-be should be told that babies are tyrannical; do not care for your feelings; tire you out; leave you with little or no time to think, let alone do anything else; wake you at night; get ill; seem ungrateful; act irrationally; and can be generally fairly annoying. A first baby can put tremendous strains on even a good marriage, but a shaky marriage can crumble completely. This is the reason why it is best to leave having a first baby until the relationship is really sound and has proved its strength and capacity to cope with the bad times as well as the good.

Ideally every couple should attend a pre-conception clinic, where they would not only be given all kinds of medical advice but would also have an hour or two with insight-trained counsellors who would look at their personalities and psychosexual development, to help them to decide whether they were really ready for children.

Some people say they wish they had never had children and knew all along, deep down, that they did not want them, but felt they ought to have them. Unfortunately, having children is not like having the flu – you cannot have 'a touch of it'! Of course being pregnant and having babies can be a wonderful, fulfilling and enjoyable experience but we have not played on this aspect because there are plenty of books and magazines that stress these aspects of pregnancy and childbirth.

The 'ideal' mother is at ease with her body, has a strong view of her body image and is not 'uptight' about her figure. She has an active, happy sex life, enjoys orgasms and enjoys her breasts being played with by her husband. She has intercourse rather than copulates, is at ease with her genitals and lets her husband see them and play with them.

Psychologically the woman who is best prepared for motherhood has a good relationship with *her* mother and accepts both her negative and positive feelings about her. Most women have some negative thoughts about their mothers, even though these feelings are held in their unconscious for much of the time. It is an interesting fact that many women tell their own mothers last of everybody that they are pregnant. This may date back to the childhood repression of their sexuality when they were told off for touching themselves and showing an interest in boys. Such a woman joyfully tells everyone else that she is pregnant but her mother she informs with some guilt because it so obviously confirms that she is sexually active.

Lots of women, as pregnancy advances, begin to fear that the baby will be abnormal, that it will be born dead, or that they will die while giving birth. Others worry about the pain of birth. Pregnancy is also a worrying time for women who have, or imagine they have, family diseases or abnormal traits. The time to get these worries sorted out is before getting pregnant. If, for example, you are concerned about spina bifida in your family, ask your doctor to refer you to a genetic counselling service. The vast majority of non-physical family traits are environmentally caused.

All of these fears are perfectly usual, yet according to one survey of women who had various anxieties during pregnancy, fewer than half ever discussed them with anyone, even their husbands, perhaps for fear of appearing silly or even unmaternal. Only later, once they were confident enough in themselves as mothers, could they bring themselves to admit that they had the fears.

A less common but not totally dispelled fear is that of producing a baby of the 'wrong' sex. Although most women say that the first time round they do not much mind whether they have a boy or a girl as long as it is normal, the picture changes for later children, when parents have stronger opinions as to the sex they would like. Surveys have found that the average woman wants two children, 1.3 of whom should be boys! Although social pressures are changing, the picture tends to suggest an in-built desire to have a boy first, and a girl second. The historical family and cultural reasons for having boys are now all but gone (families no longer need many hands to work in the family business, to farm, to produce food or to fight) yet there is still a slight preference for boys. In some parts of the USA, amniocentesis is being used to discover the sex of the foetus, with abortion if it is the 'wrong' one.

Some parents 'choose' the sex they want their child to be on the basis of their obsession with themselves or based on their fantasies of life as it 'should' be. A man may feel (unconsciously) that he will love a boy better than a girl because a boy is more like him. Other fathers (and mothers) fantasise that they will do all kinds of male (or female) things with a same-sex child and that this will make up for things they themselves never did as children.

## Unwanted pregnancies

The majority of babies are born to married couples yet between a quarter and a half are not wanted or are unplanned. In addition to these unwanted babies within marriage a sizeable minority are born outside marriage. One study of the blood groups of children and their parents in a South London suburb found that about a third of the children could not possibly have been their father's and an analysis of the statistics shows that nearly half of all married women attending one major abortion centre in the UK claimed that the baby they were having aborted was the result of extra-marital intercourse. Given that more than half of all women admit to an extra-marital affair (and some have several), and that over 90 per cent of people are sexually active before marriage, there is a very considerable chance of extra-marital pregnancies occurring. The unmarried girl has very different problems.

Some research shows that women having abortions are psychologically just like other women but have simply taken more risks or have used inefficient contraceptive methods. Other research suggests that this is too simple a view and that most of the women get pregnant to prove their love for their man, to add satisfaction to a relationship, or to secure a failing one. Some women were found to have got pregnant to punish themselves for sexual misdemeanours or for a previous abortion. Sometimes it is to replace a dead child or a lost boyfriend. On investigation most of the 'bad luck' category can and should be re-allocated to other causes. Some of these include:

**Uncertainty over sexual identity.** A few women have to prove that they are really female by having a baby.

**To punish their parents.** A teenage girl often wants to punish her repressive parents, especially if they have implied that she is promiscuous when she isn't. Some of these girls also see having a baby as a way of getting away from home.

**Trying to trap an unwilling or hostile partner.** This is much less common than it was.

**Wanting some fun and freedom before 'settling down to middle age'** is not an uncommon story in older women who have an extra-marital pregnancy.

**Deliberate non-contraception** is remarkably common. Many women either don't like the method of contraception they are using, or really want to get pregnant, however unsuitably, or follow a moral or religious code that bans contraception.

**Personality problems.** Women who seek abortions are found to have different views on sex compared with those who go through with their pregnancies. Abortion seekers often don't see themselves as instrumental in their unplanned pregnancy.

**Changes in circumstances after conception** – for example the collapse of a relationship.

**Partner factors** are not all that common but must be considered. Some men deliberately get their partner pregnant to test their own fertility; to try to secure the relationship; to give themselves added personal status; because of an inability to keep away from intercourse during unsafe periods; because of weak personality development; or because of a refusal to let the woman use oral contraception (a virtually 100 per cent safe method), supposedly on religious or medical grounds but really because they fear her fidelity or the demands for sex she might make on them, and so on.

**Psychosexual problems.** As we have said, sexuality is simply one aspect of an individual's personality and women who get pregnant when they know they shouldn't often have some kind of psychosexual problem of which they may be unaware. The types of psychosexual disorder involved are numerous but a few of the commoner ones are: a woman who believes that reproduction is the only justification for sexual pleasure. Such women may have had several babies yet deny that they are interested in sex. A second category includes those women who unconsciously believe that sex is sinful and that pregnancy is a punishment for their sin. This means that there must be a risk of pregnancy if they are to enjoy sex. Other women believe that sex is something done to them by a man and is therefore something for which they have no responsibility, so they don't bother with contraception because to do so would be contradiction. Many young women who believe that love is the only justification for sex, refuse contraception until they are sure of the man and then get pregnant in the intervening time. Some women who don't accept their sexual drives deny them consciously yet unconsciously try to indulge them (by getting drunk, losing control and then getting pregnant, for example). A small proportion of women can't tolerate any sort of contraception because they feel guilty enjoying any form of sexual pleasure. Some women are so filled with shame about their sexual drives that they don't seek contraceptive advice.

Another common fear is that to accept effective contraception is to open the floodgates to promiscuity. Such women (especially when they are unmarried), refuse all contraception and then get pregnant. Some women are unconsciously incited to pregnancy by their mother (who wants a baby for herself) and then regret the conception when it has occurred. And lastly there is the teenage girl who has just started having intercourse. Such adolescent girls frequently refuse to accept that their status has changed and even though they are *not* virgins can't bring themselves to accept the fact and continue to live with the fictitious belief that they *are* virgins. Many such girls say that they are better able to keep up the lie to their parents, and themselves that they are virgins if they don't use any contraception. Such a girl believes she is still a virgin (albeit a part-time one) and for this reason doesn't really need contraception. Such a delusion in a part-time virgin unfortunately leads all too often to unwanted pregnancies.

Many of these reasons for being unwantedly pregnant can be prevented with professional help and better sex education but parents certainly ought to be aware of them if they are to help their daughters both before and after marriage.

## Pregnancy

For most women who want to be pregnant and who have no particular fears or anxieties, pregnancy can be an enjoyable time. The first three months produce most of the classic pregnancy symptoms and during the middle three months most women find themselves well and content. Increasing research has shown how important the psyche is in pregnancy and there is little doubt that many pregnancy symptoms are produced or made worse by a woman's psychological state. Psychoanalysis of women with strange cravings (for eating coal, soap and so on) for example, or excessive vomiting shows that these women may have deep psychological problems at the heart of their troubles.

One of the most interesting psychological phenomena of pregnancy is the 'phantom pregnancy' (pseudo-cyesis). This is a condition in which a woman believes she is pregnant, and even has pregnancy symptoms, when she is definitely *not* pregnant. She may have a swollen abdomen and can even produce milk. This phenomenon is also seen in animals. In women it is found both among those who desperately want or do not want a baby.

At the other end of the scale are the many psychological and emotional causes for miscarriage. But this raises the question about how a woman knows she is pregnant – many women think they are pregnant and are having a miscarriage when in fact they are just having a heavy period. As so many women worry repeatedly about whether or not they are pregnant we will discuss the subject in some detail here.

Every day there are lots of women who worry about whether or not they are pregnant. A doctor cannot tell with certainty by physical examination whether you are pregnant or not until eight or more weeks after the first day of your last missed period, though many women know within days or at the latest in a couple of weeks, especially if they have been pregnant before.

There is one easy and cheap way to find out – unless you are prepared to wait and see – and that is to have a pregnancy test which is carried out on a specimen of urine. This can be done by a general practitioner, a hospital pathology laboratory, with a do-it-yourself kit from a pharmacist, by a pharmacist himself, or – most reliably – by a pregnancy consultation or advisory centre or service. (All major cities have at least one. They go under various names – look them up under Pregnancy Test Services in the Yellow Pages.)

Today's tests are generally positive a few days after the first day of your missed period, and the newest tests are positive even before this. The secret of getting an accurate result is the careful collection of the specimen of urine. Be guided by the following rules:

1 Don't drink any fluid after 6pm the night before the test.
2 Collect the specimen properly. Sit at the back of the lavatory seat with your legs one on either side. Use clean tissues soaked only in water and wash your vulva from front to back once only with each clean piece of tissue. Separate your inner lips with the fingers of one hand and then start to urinate. Once you have a good stream don't stop but collect a small bottleful of urine as you continue to urinate. Cap the bottle, and if you are doing the test yourself write your name on it, the date of your last period and any drugs you are on. If you have been on the Pill in the last three months the test can be difficult to interpret and other drugs could interfere with the pregnancy test too.
3 Carry out the test or send or take the urine sample to the testing place.

## Sex during pregnancy

Pregnancy can be a wonderful time for a couple sexually, especially if the baby is wanted. In the first three months many women have unpleasant pregnancy symptoms, but after this things greatly improve. Some women enjoy sex more when they are pregnant than at any other time, possibly because there is no need for contraception and because deep down they know that sex can now be for pleasure only. In general though a woman's sexual interest falls as pregnancy progresses.

Most men enjoy their wives being pregnant and find many of the body changes (rounded figure, larger breasts, fuller face, shiny hair, better skin condition, no periods and so on) more attractive. Some men with a poor opinion of their masculinity now really come into their own because they have achieved a tangible landmark as a man that no one can argue with. This makes them more at ease and less anxious about their sexuality. Many women say that from the twelfth week or so onwards they feel more cuddly and physical than usual (though not necessarily wanting more intercourse), and many women want more breast and clitoral play than intercourse, perhaps because they fear that intercourse will harm the baby. There is no truth behind this fear unless the pregnancy is already unstable for some reason.

Intercourse during pregnancy does no harm either to the mother or her baby (except possibly very late on, as we shall see) and we think it actually does the couple good for a number of reasons. First, a couple who are enjoying a lively sex life will be preparing themselves as a partnership to be good parents. Remember that a substantial proportion of all men who ever have an affair do so when their wives are

Sex in pregnancy: *In this restful position the woman can be massaged and masturbated even very late in pregnancy.*

Sex in pregnancy: *In this position provided deep penetration is avoided, both partners can enjoy a lot of pleasure with no risk of harm to the baby.*

pregnant or soon after. This suggests that such couples might not be being as attentive to one another as they might be. During pregnancy, as at all times, married couples need to release each other's sexual tensions.

The second reason why sex is good during pregnancy is that an orgasm is actually a mini-labour, so frequent orgasms may help to increase uterine efficiency and blood flow to the area. It has been suggested that such an increased blood flow might help the development of the baby's brain but this is speculative.

Up until the last few weeks have intercourse in any position you feel comfortable with – you will find the spoons position (see page 238), the various rear-entry positions and the woman-on-top positions most easy to get into and most comfortable when the woman's abdomen enlarges. However, avoid any positions that cause the woman pain or discomfort.

When it comes to the last six to eight weeks, it is probably best to go a little more gently because research has shown that intercourse may possibly cause the baby distress, though this does not cause any real medical problems as far as is known. During this time it may be preferable for the couple to masturbate each other. Oral sex and swallowing semen late on in pregnancy and especially very near term (delivery) can possibly start off labour because of the uterus-contracting substances in semen called prostaglandins. If your general practitioner or ante-natal clinic doctor tells you to avoid sex for a particular medical reason, then of course it makes sense to follow their advice. Also, be sure not to have intercourse if you have vaginal bleeding during pregnancy.

If you have had a previous miscarriage it is probably best to keep off intercourse for the first twelve weeks and especially around the time when your period would have been due, but you could discuss this with your obstetrician.

## The birth

Birth, like the love-making that started it all off, is primarily a sexual event. Unfortunately, with ante-natal care which treats women like objects on a conveyor belt and with delivery rooms like operating theatres, much of modern obstetrics has lost sight of this fact.

From an emotional point of view there is little doubt that it is most pleasant to have a baby at home, but hospital is safer in some cases for both mother and baby. The difficulty in choosing whether to have a baby at home or in hospital lies in the fact that apart from the group of predictable high-risk births, it is impossible to know whether any one labour, particularly a first labour, is going to need urgent medical attention or not. A book like this is no place to go into all the detailed arguments for and against home and hospital deliveries, but wherever the birth takes place the couple should be allowed to be together if they want to all through the labour.

Assuming the woman has a normal birth, there are some guidelines that can make the whole thing more enjoyable.

We favour natural birth situations that involve the minimum of intervention unless medically necessary (when all available help should be at hand) but such methods are, unfortunately, not widely available yet. Ideally the woman should be able to walk around for as long as she wants to and should adopt the positions that are most comfortable for her during each stage of the birth. The majority of women around the world, given a choice, do *not* choose to lie down. Giving birth flat on your back in the 'stranded beetle' position is a modern Western notion that most women accept because it is what they have been conditioned into believing is right. Most women around the world, given the choice, crouch or kneel down and let gravity help the baby come out more easily. Using such methods research has found that less pain relief (if any) is required; that Caesarean sections are rare; that episiotomies are hardly ever needed; that the babies are better oxygenated (have a better blood supply); that labours are shorter; and that the mothers enjoy the birth more. During the whole of the birth the man should be able to be present if he and the woman both wish but if the 'business end' upsets him he can stay up the head end and talk to, cuddle and massage his partner. If the woman and/or the man prefer the man not to be at the birth, the woman should be encouraged to have another trusted and well-known person with her as well as the professional birth attendant.

Immediately after the birth many couples enjoy being together with their baby, relaxing, enjoying each other's company and getting to know the baby. Assuming that mother and baby are both well there is no reason why they should not leave the hospital within twenty-four hours or even less, if the woman wants to – then the couple will be at home again with their baby in their own nest. This is important for the success of breastfeeding and enables the man to be with his partner and the baby. Many couples may not be able to arrange this but it is becoming increasingly possible and is even encouraged in more enlightened centres.

Having a baby is not an illness – it is a normal physiological event. What is needed is more home-like privacy within hospitals, where expert staff and equipment should be available if needed. Unfortunately, many medical and nursing staff have been trained into thinking they are essential even for the average, normal labour and birth and so find it almost impossible not to intervene with one 'essential' procedure or another. Unnecessary intervention can disrupt the couple's inter-personal relationship; infantilise the woman at a time when she, obviously, feels vulnerable, and even possibly harm the mother or the baby.

Most women find the idea that giving birth could be a sensual and even sexual experience rather strange or even impossible to believe, but there is plenty of evidence that it can be these things. A few women describe labour as the most exhilarating orgasm they have ever had! Some women have clitoral enlargement during childbirth, some feel pleasantly sexually aroused when breastfeeding and some even have orgasms. None of this should come as any surprise to a reader who has come this far in the book because pregnancy and childbirth are simply manifestations of a woman's sexuality. All of this sexual behaviour is modified (if not actually caused) by oxytocin – the 'love hormone'. When a woman has an orgasm, is breastfeeding, is in labour, or gives birth, her blood oxytocin level is raised.

## Sex and breastfeeding

There is now no doubt that breastfeeding is best for a baby, yet few babies are still being totally breastfed at one month. It is true that more than half of mothers breastfeed their babies in hospitals in most of the Western world today, but as soon as they get home 'problems' intervene and the babies are soon on the bottle.

Men are well known to influence their partners' choice of feeding method and successful breastfeeding is much more likely if the man is supportive. Breastfeeding counselling experience indicates that breast feeding is not so much a matter of nutrition as of sex; most women think of their breasts as having a sexual function first and a nutritional one second. Many men and slightly fewer women feel that a woman's breasts (and therefore her sexual attractiveness) may be permanently affected for the worse if she breastfeeds. Research shows that this is not so. It is pregnancy with its breast enlargement that causes sagging, if it occurs at all, and not breastfeeding.

Letting the breasts become stretched and over-full (engorged) is probably detrimental too. It is sensible to wear a well-fitting bra in the last few months of pregnancy, even at night, so that the breasts' natural supportive tissues are given some help, and to wear a bra all the time whilst nursing.

Many men are jealous of the baby being at their partner's breasts so much and some create a real fuss. The woman herself, the man and their baby can all enjoy them. In fact a lot of women feel more sexy and breast-centred when they are breastfeeding than they ever usually would and this can be to the man's advantage.

Making love while lactating needs a few words. Many women's breasts become tense and uncomfortable when they are full, especially if squeezed or played with sexually. The answer is to express some milk or feed the baby before making love so as to reduce the tension. This also makes milk leakage less likely if the woman has an orgasm. One answer is to encourage her man to suck her nipples while making love. There will be plenty of milk left for the baby. Intercourse positions have to be chosen so as not to squash full breasts but this is usually no problem for most couples.

One important thing about breastfeeding from a sexual point of view is for the woman to encourage her man to fondle her breasts, even if he is reticent or shy. This helps prevent him from feeling completely left out.

## After the birth

If you go home early you will be back in your own bed and able to cuddle each other and be especially loving towards the baby. Breastfeeding often proceeds more easily with the baby in bed and you will have fewer broken nights than you would getting up to get bottles ready. Many women who feed their babies in bed hardly wake up at all – they usually turn on to one side and the baby feeds on and off all night in the early weeks. This is also pleasant for the husband who does not lose his wife to another room for half the night. He can cuddle his baby too. You should not take a little baby into bed with you if you are very obese, or if you are drunk or on sleeping pills or other narcotic drugs. In any of these circumstances you could suffocate the baby. The vast majority of people around the world have their babies in bed with them and no doubt always have done.

If you are in hospital, be sure to see plenty of your man and cuddle up to each other and to the baby as much and as often as you can. Look after your baby all the time and keep him with you twenty-four hours of the day, in your bed if you are allowed to.

The return to sex after birth is very much a personal matter. Some women who have had no stitches (an episiotomy can leave a woman sore for many months) can go back to sex in two weeks, but most do not feel like intercourse this early. Breastfeeding makes a woman's sexual organs return to normal more quickly than would be the case had she started to bottle-feed, and totally breastfeeding women return to intercourse earlier.

By about six weeks the majority of women feel ready for intercourse again but if there is any pain you should talk to your doctor or obstetrician at the post-natal check up. While waiting for intercourse to be comfortable again you can enjoy other types of love-making. Many women want to return to having orgasms a few days after birth and there is no harm at all in this. In fact it is probably positively beneficial because it seems to help the uterus return more quickly to its normal state. But whenever you return to sex be sure to be well protected with contraception. Whilst you would be unlucky to conceive in the first month or two after birth it can and does happen. Women who breastfeed exclusively and on demand, whenever the baby or they want and who have no long gaps, night or day between feeds, on average do not ovulate for about fourteen months after the birth, but the bottle-feeding mother and the woman who breastfeeds on a restricted basis can do so within a few weeks. Talk to your doctor at the post-natal check-up about which form of contraception would be best.

## Parental reactions to pregnancy and childbirth

Having a baby puts a new mother and her relationship with her man to the test. It tests her maturity; the strength of her identity as a woman; her ability to be dependent and independent; her capacity to cope with anxiety; and her relationship with her own body. Quite understandably many women find all this too much and do not enjoy their first baby as much as they could.

Even a woman who really wants a baby may become anxious and depressed early in pregnancy. Most husbands today are willing to understand and help their wives during pregnancy but the majority do not do as well as they could because they are not sufficiently well informed about the real fears and anxieties of pregnant women. Virtually all men regard the pregnancy as very much their concern and nearly all want to learn how to help. Unfortunately, they are often excluded by health professionals and have only fairly recently been admitted to the labour ward, for example.

About one in ten expectant fathers produce symptoms during pregnancy for which no physical explanation is found. These include abdominal pain, nausea and vomiting, toothache, and so on. These problems are psychosomatic, though no less real, and are known as couvade. The symptoms occur most in the early months but recur at the end of pregnancy and end with delivery.

As the birth approaches most women seem to regress psychologically to a child-like state of dependence. Whether this is natural or a result of the way the culture and health professionals treat them is hard to say. If a woman is adequately prepared psychologically her understandable anxieties will be under control by now, which will help to reduce any pain or distress during labour. Obviously, expectations are important and here again both the culture to which she has been exposed since childhood and the professionals around her have an effect.

## Baby-blues

Three or four days after delivery more than 80 per cent of women develop the 'baby-blues' with weeping, anxiety, confusion, and fears of incompetence. This temporary stage of post-natal depression is probably more common in women in hospital than in those at home and is thought to be less common among mothers who breastfeed on an unrestricted basis from birth. Usually it is short-lived and could be partly due to the dramatic hormonal changes following delivery.

Although some mothers seem to fall in love with their baby at first sight, others question their feelings, waiting to no avail for the overpowering love our culture has taught them is felt by all 'normal' women. Women who have had a baby of the 'wrong' sex may take time to adjust and those whose child has any blemish, no matter how slight, may blame themselves in some way. These doubts may contribute to a feeling of depression. All this is hardly surprising when one remembers that the average woman is emotionally vulnerable immediately after the birth and that for as long as she stays in hospital she is often not treated as the baby's responsible mother – the midwives are. Once home she is in charge and can handle and cuddle her baby more. This is undoubtedly one reason why early depression is less common after a home birth.

## Baby battering

If the pressures on the woman from the baby, from herself and from those around her are considered and if we bear in mind that her relationship with her baby is a straightforward inter-personal one rather than an overwhelming instinctive form of mother-love, then baby battering becomes easily understandable. Increasing research is now suggesting that the way a baby behaves influences its mother's reactions and not just the other way round. The way a baby responds to what its mother does greatly influences the way she in turn behaves. So, as in any inter-personal relationship, both parties influence the actions and reactions of the other. In contrast to the typical picture of an indifferent, neglectful mother, the battering mother is often one who *does* care. She desperately wants the baby to love her but it may seem to her not to do so. It cries inconveniently or incessantly after she has done her very best for it and this she may see as rejection and criticism. Babies are designed to cry instinctively to ensure their survival and though experienced mothers are very sensitive to these calls the inexperienced mother can have real problems recognising them or knowing what to do.

As far as prevention is concerned it is known that anything which fosters the inter-personal relationship is protective for the baby. Keeping the baby with its mother all the time right from the birth is important, as is encouraging her to experience maximum physical pleasure from it. Both of these things help the bonding process between them.

Because of our cultural attitudes battering parents are far more likely to be punished than helped – especially if they are men. Often the circumstantial odds are so stacked against them that at the particular moment when they resort to battering, they seem to have no other option. Parents Anonymous (address and telephone number on page 370) is a self-help organisation run by parents who have been in this position, for others who fear they might batter or who actually have battered their babies.

## Men's role

The arrival of the first child signals a tremendous change from the man's one-to-one relationship with his partner and is the start of increasing detachment from her unless they both work hard at keeping emotionally close. Alternatively, the man may compete with the baby or may try to form an exclusive relationship with it so as to have it for himself.

Obviously a woman who makes her man feel unwanted or pushed out by the baby is foolish, not only because he will feel bad but because she is at a time when she needs a friend and someone who cares for and loves her. Having a baby is a joint affair – it is not something a woman does on her own.

First-time parents-to-be have fantasies, fears and concepts of 'ideal' parenthood which influence their attitudes towards their new baby and all that surrounds it. These areas are rarely investigated or even acknowledged by those caring for the pregnant woman but they need to be discussed fully by the couple and problem areas taken further with a professional where necessary. When this advice is followed the couple can anticipate problem areas and do something about them, so enhancing their enjoyment both of the events and each other.

## A final word

Pregnancy, childbirth and motherhood all suffer from culturally inspired fears, myths and expectations. Good sexual attitudes and satisfactory sexual practices are the background, preparation and key to happy pregnancy, childbirth and especially to good mothering. Women not only have a spiritual bond with their babies – they also have a powerful biological one. The damage we do to girls by ignoring the physical and biological side of mothering is enormous and leads many of them to get less out of pregnancy; birth; and motherhood than they could. This is not simply of academic interest, though, because it deeply influences how they behave to both their partner and their baby and the way they view themselves.

*Chapter 17*
# Teaching children about sex

## Sex education

Unlike animals and some human communities, we in the West do not allow children to learn about sex from direct observation of adults in action. Whatever the merits of this course of action, it can expose our children to misunderstandings, misleading fantasies, misinformation and a general state of ignorance and confusion. It also raises questions about the age at which children should be taught, what they should be taught, by whom and how, and what rights, if any, parents should have in deciding these issues.

Some people believe that the child or adolescent should not be taught anything at all but that they should be left to find out for themselves – after marriage, of course. Their underlying fear is that if children are taught anything before marriage they will go straight off and do it. Others, more realistically, believe that it is impossible to keep knowledge about sex secret from the unmarried and that the best course is to try to inculcate a sense of responsibility, along with accurate information and knowledge of contraception and the hazards of sexually transmitted diseases, before it is too late. Reason is on their side because ignorance is more likely to lead to sexual irresponsibility or incompetence than to provide a firm basis for prevention.

The term 'sex education' is a woolly one. In this chapter we are dealing with formalised sex education in the teacher-pupil sense – although the teacher may of course be a parent. The vast majority of 'education' about sexual matters occurs informally in the very earliest years of life – in fact sex education starts in the cradle.

That harm can come from sex education is indisputable. Individual children can be generally disturbed by it but this is not usually the case. Such vulnerability may spring from problems unique to a particular child and may be associated with his or her rearing, but sex education may not be the best way of helping the child at a particular time. In any case, education about sex, like education on other topics, can be done well or badly, and sensitively or insensitively. It may not be done at all, as happens especially for boys. This is illogical because when it comes to sexual behaviour the human male depends more than the female on learning. Sex education is more common for girls and its covert aim is usually to deter them from sexual activity. In some schools sex education is so vague that the child does not realise it has been given.

Even before a child starts school his or her psychosexual development is well advanced. The child will have seen how his or her parents show affection (or do not) and he or she will have been rebuked or restrained over sexual matters many times. Attitudes about sex, which will affect sexual behaviour later, have already been instilled into the unconscious mind, largely from the unconscious minds of the child's parents.

There is considerable discussion among sex-educators as to the best age to start formal sex education. Various ages are suggested. A favourite choice is some time in the junior-school years when the child is in the stage of latency and therefore unlikely to become obsessed with the topic. However, such discussions overlook the fact that the foundations for sexual attitudes in subsequent life were laid years earlier. The parents, unwittingly or unconsciously, have already established the basis of a moral code in the child. The fact that this may be unsound in that it sometimes adds negative emotions to sex is discussed in Chapter 1. A sound programme of sex education might try to establish more rational attitudes, but the difficulty or impossibility of achieving this in formal teaching situations will be understood by everyone who realises that it is the unconscious rather than the intellect which largely governs sexual attitudes rather than the intellect.

However, this raises two points. First, any realistic sex-education programme should be based on the establishment of insight. To explain to the young what has basically happened to them during their psychosexual development and what will happen in future is to provide them with a powerful means of self-control. If they can also be given insight into the opposite sex they will be better placed when it comes to partner selection and entering into marriage.

The point that self-control is only possible through insight and knowledge is proved by research. Much of the United States is prudish about sex and sex education is, as a result, often of a restricted nature. This could be one of the reasons why there has been such an adult reaction against sexual restriction especially on the West Coast. The teen-age pregnancy rate is 96 pregnancies per 1000 teenagers per annum in the US. The Netherlands, on the other hand, has a very matter-of-fact acceptance of teenage sexuality. Formal and informal sex education is freely available to this age group and so is contraception. Their teen pregnancy rate is the lowest in the Western World at 14 per 1000 per annum. England and Wales, which are fairly restrictive countries, have a rate of 45 per 1000.

The second point is that formal sex education should not be thought of in the context of school alone. Most mothers want to do their very best for their babies and guidance on sex education as a part of ante-natal classes would be less controversial than sex education in schools and would be aimed at the one segment of the community who really are in a position to influence the next generation. Moreover, even at a factual level mothers themselves often benefit from such education. Surveys of the knowledge of simple anatomical facts have revealed appalling ignorance.

A recent survey of 127 working girls aged sixteen to twenty-one showed only minimal knowledge of contraception and over two-thirds had run the risk of pregnancy. Obviously the sex education they had received was ineffective, insufficient, or both, and required supplementation.

This, however, points to a further difficulty in sex education. Those girls who *have* been given adequate contraceptive information may choose (unconsciously) not to incorporate it into their body of knowledge. This ineffectiveness arises from the fact that, because of attitudes instilled during rearing, some children do not want to know about some aspects of sexuality and even when told in a clear and pleasant way repress what they have been told. Studies have found that many children shown sex-education films in the morning cannot say what they were about later the same day. Clearly their unconscious minds have suppressed the information.

Another problem with sex education is that a child's perception of the individual who is putting across sexual information affects his or her readiness to accept it. A teacher who is open and friendly is likely to be more effective than one who is moralistic and religious.

Perhaps the best solution would be to train specialist teachers who would move from school to school to give lessons in the presence of the usual class teacher who would then be involved in the subsequent discussion. Perhaps 'sex-education classes' could be established independently of the formal education system. Probably many parents, and teachers, would welcome such a development.

A great proportion of sex-education material, even for adults, let alone for the young, treats the recipients as if they were fools. The consequence of treating people like fools is that they are likely to behave foolishly. On these grounds alone sex education should be fully factual and should use photographs or films whenever possible. Such material can easily be labelled obscene but with care suitable illustrations can be found. Obviously it should not be shocking. Some films of childbirth, for example, are fully realistic but manage to be more reassuring than frightening. Others put some girls off childbearing for life and frequently make both girls and boys faint. Some teaching materials about sexually transmitted diseases and publicity about AIDS are so horrific that the children are frightened off the opposite sex. This is totally inexcusable. Surely the idea of sex education in the widest sense must be to encourage the sexes to think well of each other and to enjoy each other. Shock-horror propaganda will never do this.

The knowledge given should match the stage of development of the child to whom it is addressed and should aim to deal with myths and the false fantasies that arise in that particular stage of development. For example, pre-pubertal children, especially girls, are interested in relationships and mating. A simple but complete overview of sex and the man-woman relationship should be given in these years and sex set in a biological perspective. Early-adolescent children need to understand the changes in their own bodies and in those of the opposite sex. These should be illustrated with photographs. The guilt which arises at this age about masturbation needs to be recognised and ideally eliminated, but masturbation also needs to be placed in perspective. The romanticism of mid-adolescence can be expanded so as to place sex in relation to emotion but should be combined with warnings about the dangers of using loving feelings to justify sex. Contraceptive information is likely to be well received at this age (although the age at which some girls now become pregnant raises the possibility that it should be taught earlier), but it should be clearly stated that intercourse at this age can harm subsequent personality development.

The young will listen to good, sensible-sounding advice but frequently reject moral prohibitions and judgements. Encouraging the young to take responsibility for their own sexual behaviour tends to instil a sense of caution and removes rebellious motives from sex.

Late adolescents, most of whom have left school before reaching this stage, require, above all, practical advice on how to seek, establish and maintain relationships which are suitable for them. Fuller details of sexual communication and techniques are best left to this stage, although an outline idea of intercourse as an act should first be mentioned in early adolescence. This is essential to combat the many harmful and misleading myths and sexual jokes that abound amongst early adolescents. Although the topic of venereal disease should have been discussed earlier, but without being used as a deterrent, it is in late adolescence that the young person really needs to know how to suspect the presence of sexually transmitted diseases both in himself or herself and in a potential partner.

## Questions children and parents ask about sex

Once children get to school they discuss sex just as they would anything else. Both during this and the later phases leading up to puberty we feel that a child's parents are the best people to give information because they know the child and what he can cope with day by day and year by year. Parents also have the advantage over formal systems in that they can take opportunities as they arise and use them to talk about sex in an informal, unplanned way. Satisfying a child's curiosity is ideally done in a spontaneous way and the old notion of saying nothing until you sit your child down to talk about 'the birds and the bees' is not only unfashionable but far less pleasant for both child and parent.

There is so much in daily life that raises questions about sex that can be dealt with a low-key, matter-of-fact way that the average child can end up very well sex-educated without ever realising it. TV, shopping, the people a child meets and his or her mother's experiences with carrying, bearing and rearing a baby can all lead to questions which are best answered simply at the time.

### *Some general guidelines about answering children's questions about sex*

**Don't say too little.** This is a common mistake. The child then becomes even more confused but will probably never be able to verbalise his confusion, especially if you have been dismissive or made it all sound so simple that he or she feels they *should* have understood what you were talking about. On the other hand:

**Don't take the opportunity to deliver a lecture on the subject.** Most children are simply looking for a straightforward, uncomplicated answer to what seems to them to be a very simple question. By going on at too much length you will confuse them, especially young ones. Gauge your replies according to what you know the child can cope with intellectually and emotionally.

**Try very hard not to colour every answer with your personal views and hang-ups.** We all have some negative or downbeat views about sexual subjects and it takes a real effort to try to counteract them for the sake of our children.

**Ask the child a question in return and use the answer to teach on.** When a child asks where babies come from you could, for example, ask, 'Where do you think they come from?' The child might say, 'from the tummy button' and you can use this to teach the true facts and to dispel false beliefs and notion, so killing two birds with one stone.

**Always answer sex questions at the time and do so spontaneously.** Never put off the answer or the child will imagine there is something strange going on and that you cannot answer straight away.

**Bear in mind that a sex question from a young child simply does not have the same overtones and connotations it would have coming from an adult.** If an adult were to ask you, 'What's a homosexual?' your answer would be very different from the one you would give to a six year old, yet the question is exactly the same.

**If you don't know – say so.** This raises the general question of honesty. We feel parents should never lie to their children about sexual matters. Children look to us as sources of trustworthy information on most things in life and we owe it to them not to lie or mislead them with half-truths.

## *Some questions young children ask . . . and some suggested answers*

**Where do babies come from?**
They grow in mummy's tummy after daddy puts a seed in there.

**Where does daddy get the seeds from?**
They grow inside his body in the things that hang down behind his penis.

**How do they get into mummy's tummy?**
Daddy and mummy cuddle together and he puts his penis into her vagina and the seeds come out inside her.

**Can I watch you do it?**
Well we'd rather you didn't because we like to be alone when we're doing it – it's nicer for us to be undisturbed.

**How does the baby come out?**
Mummy's tummy pushes it out down the same way that daddy's seed went in – down the vagina.

**Why haven't I got a penis?**
Because you're a girl and girls have a vagina instead. There has to be a place for the daddy's penis to go to get the seeds inside the mummy. If they both had penises there'd be nowhere to put the seeds and she couldn't grow a baby.

**Does it hurt having a baby?**
Yes it does for some women, but some have no pain at all and if the pain is too bad then midwives and doctors can help.

**How does a baby breathe inside you?**
It doesn't breathe because there's no air inside mummy's tummy. It gets all its food and everything it needs to grow down a cord that joins it to mummy inside.

**What's a tummy button for?**
When a baby is inside mummy it's joined to her so that it can live. When it's born it comes out with this tube still attached to its tummy. The tube is cut near the baby's tummy but this doesn't hurt. After a few weeks the tube drops off the baby and leaves a mark called the navel, tummy button or umbilicus.

**Do you have to be married to have a baby?**
No you don't but if the mummy is all alone she might have difficulty getting enough money to look after herself and the baby. It's really best if there's a mummy and a daddy because then they can look after each other and the baby.

**Why do you have to go to hospital to have a baby – I thought only people who were ill went to hospital?**
Yes, it's usually ill people who go to hospital but when a baby comes out of a mummy's tummy it's best to have a midwife or doctor there just in case anything goes wrong with the baby or the mummy. Most mummies have their babies in hospital though some choose to stay at home.

**Why don't men have babies?**
Because you have to have a thing inside you called a uterus which is where the baby grows. You also have to have a vagina so that the baby can come out. Men don't have these things. They have a penis so that they can put seeds into mummy's tummy to start the baby. Daddies start babies off and mummies have them. Then they both look after the baby together.

**When a daddy puts his penis inside a mummy does he do a wee inside her?**
No he puts seeds inside her.

**Does it hurt when a daddy does that to a mummy?**
No – in fact they both like it a lot.

**Where do you and daddy do it?**
Usually in bed because it's warm and cuddly there but we could do it anywhere when we're on our own and quiet.

**How old will I be before I have a baby of my own?**
Well you could have a baby when you are a teenager but it's best to wait until you are married so that the baby has a mummy and a daddy to love it and look after it. After all, you like having a mummy and a daddy, don't you?

**Can I have a baby with daddy (mummy)?**
No, mummies and daddies have babies together but brothers and sisters and parents and their children mustn't have babies together because the babies might not be normal. Mummy and daddy love you but they love each other in a slightly different way. Anyway, its best to have a baby with someone you're married to and you can't marry your mummy (daddy) or brother (sister).

## *Questions parents ask*

**What should we do if the children burst in when we're making love?**
This depends on the age of the child. Babies and toddlers cannot be expected to look after themselves safely so you cannot make love when they are awake anyway. Pre-school children may have to have some attention paid to them before you ask them to go and play while you cuddle, but older children can be handled more firmly and kindly. Very young children can mistake a man on top of a woman as an act

Sex education: *Children learn about sex education in many more ways than most parents realise. With parents like this children will grow up to be physically affectionate.*

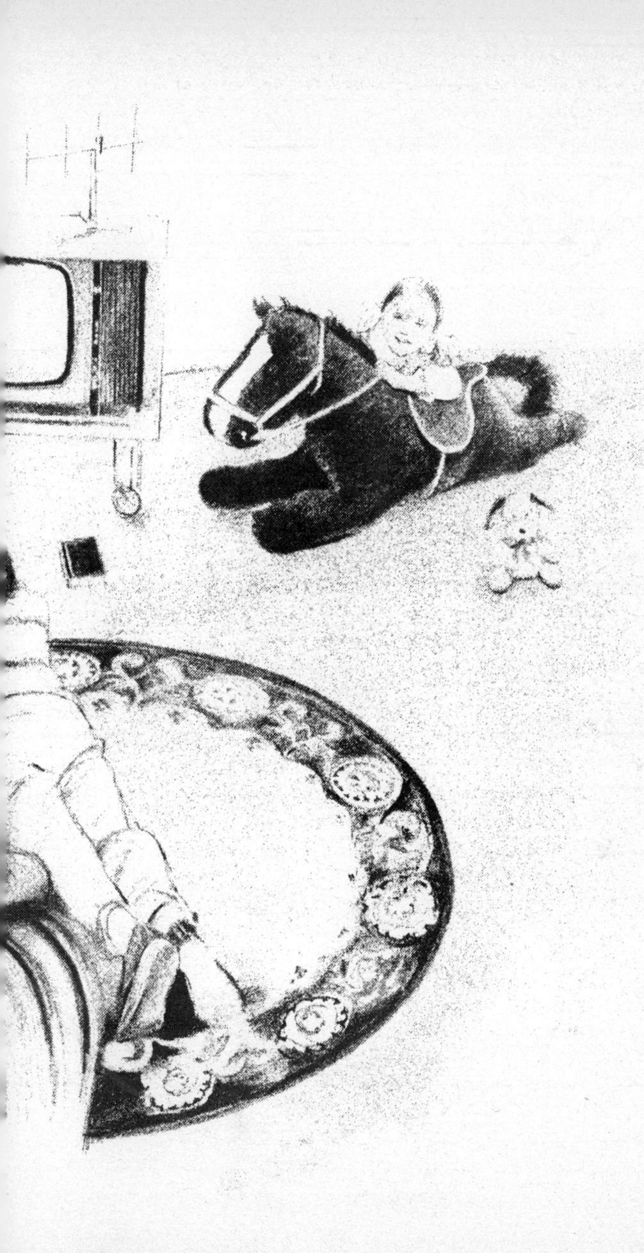

of brutality, especially if she is noisy when having orgasms. Older children who know that you are having sex can be quietly and firmly asked to go because you are making love.

Most parents are embarrassed, shocked or angry but this is not the child's fault. If you are likely to react in this way lock the door beforehand so that you don't take your feelings out on the child. Explain as soon as you can afterwards why you were cross and don't make him or her feel bad about it.

**Is it true that some people use their children as an excuse not to have sex?**

Yes, it is and this is especially true of women. Ideally a woman should discuss with her husband why she does not want sex or get help from a professional. Keeping quiet and making the children an excuse is damaging to the relationship and makes the man resentful about the children.

**Why should I tell my children anything about sex at all?**

Because if they do not hear from you in a loving, caring, balanced way they may hear from someone else in a much less attractive and informative setting. Parents greatly underestimate the misconceptions children have about sex and leaving the subject unmentioned actually does more harm than good. Research has shown that a part of the body that does not have a label (the sex organs, for example) are thought by the child not to exist. Just think how extraordinary it would be if a child grew up having no word for his feet. The sex differences between men and women (and boys and girls) are so compelling that children have an insatiable desire to learn about them and all that results from them. Many of the subjects in the sex area are baffling and amazing to adults; so imagine how much more so they must be to children, with their natural curiosity and delight in the unknown.

**What age should we start sex education?**

Sex education begins at birth. From the cradle until mature adulthood children need information, a source of dependable reference when told nonsense that frightens or alarms them and a haven of love on which they can rely no matter what. In addition to all this they need to see a close, loving relationship at work in their parents' lives because the parents are their most important models for the future.

**What if they don't ask questions?**

If the child is young leave the subject alone rather than force discussion on matters that he or she couldn't care less about. In time most children want to know and they will ask you or someone else. Unfortunately, so much of our sex-negative thinking comes across unconsciously to our children, just from the way we react or behave, that they feel sex is a 'no-go area' and so do not feel like asking questions. A child's questions may have been discouraged by a parent or even another adult, or he or she may have been fobbed off in the past and now does not know how to ask about something that obviously upsets his or her parents.

A lot of parents find that bringing up the subject under some other pretext works well but if you do this, don't make the mistake of taking any spark of interest the child shows as an indication that he wants a full-blown medical prize-winning lecture on the subject. Some children are naturally more shy than others and others are less inquisitive about everything; others think they know it all anyway (even a seven year old may say the subject is boring and that he knows all about it). The main thing is to encourage and reward curiosity.

**Why can't I just leave it all to the school or someone else?**

You can if you want to and many parents do. But if you do, don't then get upset if what they tell your child is not what you would have said. If you have specific ideas about any area of sexual knowledge you should ensure that your children understand your position, even if one day they choose to reject it. Young people will eventually make up their own minds about sexuality just as they do about everything else, but if you want to influence them because you care for and love them it is silly to leave the imparting of sex information to others – they simply will not understand, love or care for your child in the way you do.

Of course there is no reason why the two options should be mutually exclusive. Start off by answering all your children's questions when they are young and then help them to understand what they hear at school and discuss it with them if they want to do so.

**Are pets any help?**

Yes. By having pets and watching them mate and have their young, children of all ages can learn a great deal about sex in a gentle, natural way. Of course, watching rabbits teaches nothing about human inter-relationships but it helps get the plumbing sorted out in their minds and this in itself is a help. Research shows that country children are much more at ease with physical sexuality and that this is probably because their experience of animal sex has made them see the whole thing as natural and normal, which it is.

**How useful are books for children?**
That depends on the book and the child. Some children are happier to learn from books than from adults, so for them a good book can be just the job. There are lots of good books around for children of all ages, but be sure to read any book first so that you know what your children are learning. If there are things you do not like about the sex-education books they use at school, take up the subject with the head teacher. There are books available for parents to read with their children and this can be a very good way of handling the subject.

**How do we handle the dirty jokes from school?**
When children are about six or seven they start to giggle at 'dirty' words like 'underwear', 'penis' or 'naked'. Early dirty stories do not necessarily have a sexual component but the child gets a kick out of telling them. The next stage is to find excretion and sexual functioning hilariously funny. There are now some sexual overtones. Swear words become incorporated in the stories and even the unfunniest of stories causes the child to fall about with laughter. It is interesting how little dirty jokes have changed over the years. Today's nine year old laughs at exactly the same things as his grandparents did and for the same reasons. Dirty jokes are an early sign of the child's growing independence and preparation for the adult world. Sometimes the jokes are defiant and rebellious but most often they are geared to shock the 'stuffy' adults around him. Often they laugh because everyone else is laughing (it is simply a social pursuit) even though they may not really understand the joke. All of this is a part of growing social confidence and enjoyment and acceptance of becoming part of a peer group.

With all this in mind it is possible to stay calm and to put dirty jokes into perspective. By all means enjoy a joke with your young children, if only to show them that you know what they are on about and that you are not dead from the waist down. Dirty jokes, if they are not actually harmful or worrying your child, are simply a passing phase and will do no harm.

**What should I do if I find them playing doctors and nurses?**
Young children are learning all the time and are naturally curious. They particularly like the differences between male and female bodies and explore everything. Part of this involves exploring their own and

other children's bodies. Unfortunately most parents are so anxious about children showing each other their genitals that they do not cope very well and so pass on negative attitudes to their children. Almost all children undress in front of the opposite sex and play 'doctors and nurses', 'bottoms', 'mothers and fathers' or something similar, and no harm comes of it. They are all ways in which little children try to mimic the sex roles of adults, if only for a few minutes. They also enjoy the exciting feelings it produces.

What *is* harmful is the guilt the child feels if his parents are cross or make him feel wicked. Lots of children, realising that it is not what their parents want them to do, try to get caught so that they *have* to stop what they are doing. This sense of wanting to be caught because of the 'rudeness' of it all is made far worse by heavy-handed telling off.

Some control may be helpful in certain circumstances because young children get excited and alarmed by the feelings of excitement (even though it is not usually genital excitement) that such play can sometimes arouse and they need to know that their parents can cope with the situation and control it. These are big feelings for young children and they need help in handling them. Often a child will be far more guilty-looking and embarrassed than the true nature of the sex games warranted.

A very few children's sex games are a sign of a disturbed child, but such games are usually imposed on other children rather than enjoyed mutually, and the other children tell their parents. Such disturbed children need professional help as do children for whom sex games have gone wrong and caused distress. Apart from keeping an eye open for any negative effects sex games may be having, also make sure that the children are not doing anything dangerous to one another. A young child who has had its temperature taken rectally may, for example, introduce other children to things being pushed up their bottoms and this should be discouraged because of the possibility of physical damage.

Sex games among young children are simply a prelude to other much more sexually explicit discovering 'games' they will be playing ten years later, so it is just as well to come to terms with your curious, enquiring child because this is the first step on a long ladder and if you worry and fuss at every rung you will both end up anxious and neurotic over sex.

**What are the commonest misconceptions children have about sex?**

Children (like adults) have all kinds of strange ideas about sex, mainly because they feel it is a 'no-go' area, about which they cannot ask, or that if they do they will not get an honest answer.

Here are some of the most common misconceptions, so that you can work them out before they come up. (They are arranged approximately in order of the child's age.)

A woman gets pregnant by swallowing a man's seed.
Babies come out of eggs like chickens.
You can buy a baby at a shop.
Babies come out with urine from a woman's body.
Babies are born from a woman's anus.
Babies come out of the navel.
Even if a man and a woman only kiss they will have a baby.
Every time a man and a woman have sex they have a baby.
Girls used to have a penis but it was cut off for some reason.
Men have nipples so they must be able to breastfeed.
All fat women are pregnant.
Only women who are married can have a baby.
Only women who love their partner can have a baby.
The only time a man and a woman have sex is when they want a baby.
Masturbation will make you homosexual.
Masturbation will give you spots.
Girls can keep your penis in their vagina and even cut it off in there.
Girls who have just started having periods cannot have babies.
The only time a woman can have a baby is when she is 'on heat' (menstruating).
A girl cannot get pregnant unless she has an orgasm.
You can only get VD from toilet seats.
French kissing can get you pregnant.
Orgasms can make you pregnant.
Being in love means you ought to have sex with someone.
Sex is the best way of proving you are in love.
Parents cannot possibly begin to understand what you are going through because they are too old-fashioned.
No mothers masturbate and they are too old for sex.

## Aims for ideal sex education

Sex education should prepare the young for the conflicting and difficult emotions they are about to experience (or actually are experiencing) and should help them cope with them.

An ideal sex-education programme would undo previous harm,

correct tendencies towards perversions, and detect children who need more personal education and care or perhaps even therapy. Through insight it would simultaneously maximise both the child's potential and control. These, surely, are sound educational aims whatever subject is being taught.

# *Chapter 18*
# Masturbation

Masturbation is an inexhaustible subject of increasing public interest. The reason for this is that it is, in one form or another, universal, but because of centuries of religious opposition it came to be regarded as sinful, shameful, harmful, and secret. The removal of the veil of secrecy has led to the altogether healthy increase in interest.

It is widely agreed that almost all men masturbate, but statistics gained from surveys purport to show that masturbation is less common in women. This is because female masturbation is very difficult to define. It is infinitely more variable than in men and all that can be said with reasonable confidence is that it consists of some recurrent psychological and/or physical activity, undertaken consciously or unconsciously, resulting in signs of sexual arousal (signs which in themselves might not be recognised by the woman) and perhaps resulting in an indefinable orgasm. This highlights another area of difficulty. Male sexual arousal is easy to recognise but female arousal is not obvious to an observer except on close inspection. This is probably why boys are said to masturbate more than girls in childhood.

The next problem when considering the subject is to account for the diversity of female masturbation and its relative inefficiency in some women. The answers can be found by considering three related phenomena. The first is the greater parental suppression of genital activity in girls than boys. Parents of both sexes are more tolerant of genital handling in boys than in girls. Because they are more affection-dependent, girls may also be more willing to try to conform. They may, as a result, find ways of masturbating that do not lead to easy detection. Instead of lying on their backs, opening their legs and touching their vulvas, many routinely adopt other postures such as lying face down, lying on their side, sitting, or even standing. Muscular contractions or rubbing the vulva against an object (including the heel) may be substituted for direct touch methods. If genital stimulation is not abandoned altogether, as it is in some girls, it can occur through clothing, or a whole variety of objects may be used as a substitute for the girl's hand.

Alternatively masturbation may become attached to 'legitimate' pursuits such as washing the vulva or even urination. Although many women claim to be able to masturbate by more than one method, women who carry into adulthood, as most seem to, any of the less obvious methods mentioned above can find themselves unable to reach orgasm except in that position or by that method. As a result they claim they never masturbate.

Man masturbating woman: *A position in which a man can comfortably pleasure a woman. This is a particularly good position for helping her to experience orgasms from the stimulation of her clitoris yet leaves her feeling unthreatened.*

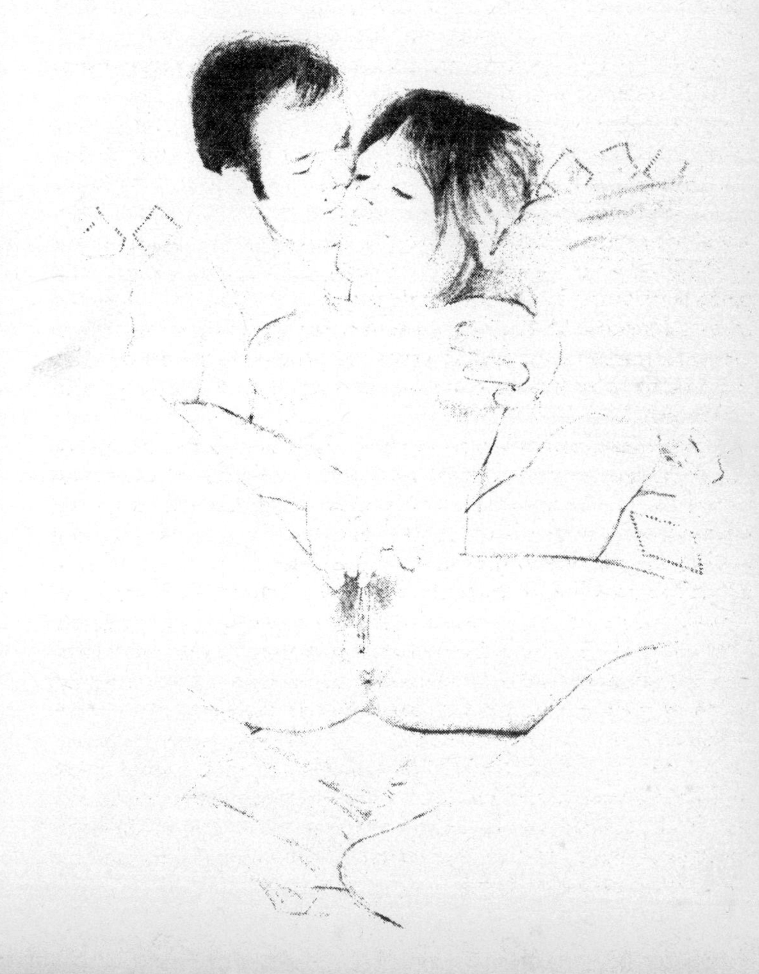

The second explanation of the diversity of female masturbation lies in the fact that the female body can respond sexually to stimulation in almost any anatomical area. This also happens in pre-adolescent boys. Movements such as rotating the pelvis, rhythmically contracting the vaginal muscles or making thrusting movements with the pelvis can bring on an orgasm in some women. Being rocked about on buses, bicycles, motorcycles and trains, for example, can lead to orgasms in others. Even movements of the vulva against underclothing is reported as being arousing to the point of orgasm by some women.

The third reason is that female orgasms are very variable in intensity. One factor here is the number of throbbing muscular contractions which occur during an orgasm. If there are only a few of these contractions it is experienced as only a mild sensation and if the woman has been taught that sexual pleasure is rude, naughty or sinful, the anxiety associated with the act may stop the contractions entirely. Something similar can happen in anxious men. Similar muscular contractions to those which women enjoy at orgasm eject semen in men and under some circumstances ejaculation can be reduced to a few little dribbles. Since most definitions of masturbation refer to orgasm as the end-point, a woman who when

A pleasant way for a woman to masturbate a man: *With both man and woman comfortable this can be pleasant and stimulating for them both. It is relaxing for the woman as her hands are in a restful position that she would use to masturbate herself.*

masturbating only can achieve a minor sensation may think of herself as not masturbating at all.

The point here is that the anxiety earlier instilled into her gives her an unconscious incentive to play down her responses so as to avoid too much guilt. Similarly, the women mentioned earlier who use somewhat obscure masturbation methods are using less than the best method (direct stimulation of the genitals) to get an orgasm and as a result are inefficient. Unfortunately, for these women, direct methods would arouse anxiety to a point where it would be impossible to have an orgasm at all.

Men, of course, or some of them, have the same difficulties. Men who have been strictly reared with regard to masturbation (parents sometimes even make them promise never to do it) masturbate the way many other men do yet can block off the consciousness of orgasm and although they ejaculate they still claim not to masturbate. Although older men often rub their erect penis with no intention of reaching orgasm (which according to most definitions would not amount to masturbation, though it clearly is), some guilty young men do so too and later have a nocturnal emission (wet dream). These men also deny that they masturbate.

Guilty women will, in a similar way, confine their masturbation to the twilight state between sleeping and waking (or vice versa) and so deny masturbation on the grounds that it does not occur when they are fully conscious. Some women who deny masturbation do so on the basis that they do not fantasise while doing it. However, they often have a rich fantasy life which simply does not coincide with when they stimulate the vulva.

A substantial minority of women claim never to have masturbated, as do a tiny percentage of men. When the factors outlined are taken into account, however, it can be seen that the denial does not necessarily amount to a deliberate lie. In clinical experience, at least, and regarding those people in whom it is important that the subject of masturbation be clarified, it is true to say that virtually everyone masturbates in some way or another.

The less direct the method used, the more the individual shows that a difficulty exists about sexual expression. It could be argued that the less direct methods have been learned by chance and have then become fixed in preference to more usual methods. Such an argument does not fit in with clinical experience which shows that unusual masturbation methods are almost always associated with a difficulty. This is serious because learning to masturbate bears the same relation to intercourse as does learning to speak to conversation.

As well as being a form of sexual training, masturbation, or rather its associated fantasies, helps to bring images of the bodies of the opposite sex and of intercourse with them to mind, especially in the young. This is a learning process and is a kind of sexual rehearsal for the adolescent. Some males of all ages, but especially younger ones, rely on girlie magazines to get clear images for their fantasies. Learning to masturbate is simply a part of what a growing man has to learn. Girls and women may also be aroused by girlie magazines because they identify with the girls in the pictures but they commonly find the stories more of a turn-on.

Amongst adults today, married men are often found to be more reluctant to talk about their masturbation than are their wives. Less well-educated men are particularly likely to regard it as an abnormal and juvenile habit. However, it has a real place in married life because it allows differing sex drives to be accommodated without looking outside the partnership. This may be the reason why, on average, surveys report that women who masturbate do so more frequently than men. Also, a man can either have intercourse or masturbate, but not both in a short space of time, unlike a woman. In fact, women are perhaps, other things being equal, more likely to want intercourse after masturbation because sex is in their minds. This is useful clinically in women who have lost their sex drive. Encouraging them to masturbate can rejuvenate their sex lives.

Clinical experience with large numbers of couples who are happily married and enjoy sex with each other shows that on average the wives masturbate about as often as they have intercourse, whereas only every fourth orgasm in the husband is produced by self-masturbation. One value of masturbation in marriage may be that material from the accompanying fantasy may then be available for incorporation into marital sex. Even the fantasy itself may be used during intercourse because many women and particularly older men need to use fantasy to sustain their arousal and have an orgasm. Some people with deviant sexual needs can function satisfactorily in intercourse only by using an appropriate fantasy.

Women say they masturbate to relieve emotional tensions and some boys and men use masturbation to blot out anxieties in the same way that alcoholics and drug-takers do. This is really a misuse of masturbation. Other men find masturbation more gratifying than intercourse – this is a sign of the presence of an inhibiting anxiety. Women, especially young ones, tend to get more satisfaction from masturbation than they do from intercourse and frequently display greater physiological body changes during orgasm induced by masturbation. This may come about because they can stimulate themselves in their favourite way during masturbation whilst fantasising a scene that arouses them. This does not necessarily mean that such women prefer masturbation to intercourse – they like both.

Some men, on the other hand, routinely masturbate and never attempt to have intercourse with a woman. Due to reasons already discussed (Chapter 13) women make them so anxious that it spoils the pleasure.

## How men masturbate

How men use the hand to rub the penis is described in Foreplay (Chapter 11). Some men use the other hand to play with their scrotum or, less commonly, their anus. Many stop occasionally during the act and others stop for a while before orgasm and then restart, so as to prolong the pleasure. Variants of this behaviour consist of lying face down and then using the flat of the hand to press the penis on to the mattress whilst making copulatory movements. Objects such as a pillow folded over or even aids from sex shops may be used to form an artificial vagina. Some men masturbate sitting down, pushing their penis down between their thighs, crossing them and then stimulating the penis by moving the thighs and trunk towards and then away from each other. Unusual methods such as these seem frequently to be associated with difficulties in intercourse and undue guilt about sex.

More worrying signs of trouble are where the adolescent boy (or man) dresses in female clothes to masturbate or reduces his level of consciousness by over-breathing, taking alcohol, glue-sniffing, using drugs, or by other means. Individuals of both sexes who are guilty about masturbation or intercourse sometimes express their guilt by having bouts of sexual anxiety interspaced with longish periods of abstinence. Another sign of difficulty in either sex can be elaborate rituals, sometimes based on washing, after masturbation.

## How women masturbate

Unusual practices, although less bizarre, are more widespread amongst girls and women, as we pointed out earlier. The most basic pattern though is to lie in the normal female intercourse position and stimulate the vulva directly with the hand. The variations thereafter are immense. For example, the whole vulva may be massaged or one specific area of the side of the shaft of the clitoris lightly stroked. The edges of the inner lips may be specifically rubbed or they may be trapped between the fingers. A vertical or circular motion may be used. Some women press so hard that their knuckles turn white. This may be because their clitoris has fewer nerves than average. On reaching the plateau stage of sexual response many women change their type of stimulation. As orgasm approaches the area stimulated may be well away from the clitoris. Intermittent stopping is characteristic, although guilty women may race to have an orgasm as quickly as possible to get it out of the way.

Intermittently, one, but more commonly two, fingers may be inserted into the vagina and rotated rather than moved in and out. Since only the entrance of the vagina is very sensitive the purposes are to delay progress to orgasm, simply for the pleasure of it and, frequently, to act out a fantasy of penetration. Objects may be used to stimulate the vulva and are sometimes inserted into the vagina. The commonest object used like this today is probably the battery-driven vibrator, but in the past a huge variety of objects has been used if articles which have had to be medically removed from women's vaginas are anything to go by.

Women are more reluctant to admit that they do anything to their vaginas when masturbating than they are to massaging and caressing the vulva. Some women use only the vagina when masturbating. It is in masturbation rather than in intercourse that women demonstrate their greater sexual capacities than men – although of course they may not fully use them. Women have been known to obtain fifty and (many) more orgasms in a single session. Such sessions are sometimes repeated frequently, especially if a vibrator is used. Clinically such women are no more likely to be 'neurotic' or 'obsessional' than other women (as has been suggested by 'experts' over the years), nor are they more likely to show over-growth of the inner lips or clitoris than are other women (as some women fear). Such an over-growth, which many women attribute to masturbation, is probably part of the normal anatomical variation between individuals. During early adolescence the labia may be more vulnerable to such enlargement.

In later life many women who have nothing physically wrong with their uterus or their hormones, but who nevertheless menstruate so heavily and so frequently that they are likely to end up having a hysterectomy, are, on psychosexual investigation, found to be poor and inadequate at having orgasms when masturbating and during intercourse. They often express strong opposition to masturbation. Psychosexual therapy designed to reverse the opposition to indulgence in sexual pleasure can sometimes bring the situation under control without a hysterectomy being needed. The underlying cause of the bleeding is possibly the continuous congestion of blood rarely relieved by orgasm.

## Fantasies

Masturbation is a psychosexual act which incorporates both fantasy and physical stimulation. Some men and women claim never to fantasise during masturbation. As a rule they seem to fare as well as anyone else both in masturbation and intercourse, so the deficiency is apparently not usually serious. Presumably their fantasy is unacceptable to their conscious mind and so is repressed into the unconscious. The dissociation of the act and the thought is presumably the result of guilt and sometimes the point of the repression appears to be to avoid a particular situation or homosexual or incestuous thoughts. Fantasies are, of course, a rich source of information about the sexuality of an individual and can be of tremendous importance in the treatment of sexual problems.

Allowing for the shame people feel about discussing fantasies they regard as unusual, the range of sexual fantasy is enormous. The same fantasy theme may be used for a period of time but is usually varied slightly. Reliving previous sexual experiences, possibly in an elaborated form, is a common source of fantasy material. Most fantasies can be grouped into people fantasies and practice fantasies. In the first, the fantasy is of sex with someone the person knows or members of the opposite sex in photographs or stories. In the practice type of fantasy the person concentrates on the sexual activity rather than on any particular partner.

In men with sexual problems the fantasy often ends in foreplay activities and no penetration is involved. Often the fantasy is of being fellated. In people fantasies, men who are scared of women often use either schoolgirls or much older women. This is commonplace in adolescent boys who want intercourse but are still at the stage where their fears are greater than their desires. Passive men who have not fully resolved their early attraction to their mothers often have fantasies of being in total control of the woman. Deviations and perversions reveal themselves in fantasy. Sometimes they only show their presence in a sudden change in fantasy as orgasm approaches. Some individuals, more often men than women, see someone else instead of themselves performing sexually in their fantasies. This usually points to excessive anxiety about intercourse, which may be the basis of voyeurism.

To generalise from large numbers of individuals it seems that

Male sexual fantasies: *In general men seem to be less ingenious than women in their sexual fantasies and seem, oddly, to stop short of intercourse.*

women fantasise more extensively but less deviantly than do men. In spite of the oft-made claim that women's sexuality can be expressed only in the context of a loving relationship, this certainly does not seem to be the case, to judge from their fantasies. Adult women usually start the fantasy with themselves naked in the presence of the man without 'explaining' how it came about.

Adolescent and pre-adolescent girls may find fantasies of being

Female sexual fantasies: *These are many and varied but many women inhibit them because of their feelings of guilt and shame.*

naked exciting and often use stripper fantasies. In their fantasies women often portray themselves as being overwhelmed. This is evidence of their residual guilt about sex and reduces objections from their conscience. In this way fantasies of being forced to have sex; the use of restraint; of being had by many men; and of being a slave-girl commonly arise. As well as these fantasies many, if not most, women also have fantasies about one or more men they actually know.

## In perspective

It is difficult to escape the conclusion that if masturbation, in the full psychosexual sense, proceeded with less difficulty in adolescence, then intercourse would be improved to the benefit of the man-woman relationship. Opposition to masturbation may have made sense to some people in the past as a control against sexual expression becoming rampant, but there is no justification for repressing it today. In fact the reverse is the case; those individuals who are most accepting of their sexuality in all its forms are the ones who are most responsible about its expression.

*Chapter 19*
# Sexual morals

## The historical background

It is characteristic of human beings to have beliefs about how they and others around them should behave. This leads to concepts of what is right and what is wrong; what is good and what is bad; and the way we 'ought' to behave in general. One workable definition of a nation or a culture is 'a group of people who share the same moral codes'. Morals are simply codes of behaviour that a given nation or sub-group within a nation agrees are acceptable. Such codes differ greatly around the world today and have probably been even more different over the centuries. Morality does not only cover matters to do with sex, of course. People make moral judgements about the upbringing of children, the conduct of business affairs, matters of government, and gambling and financial matters, among other things. Often the morals in such circumstances can be agreed upon fairly readily and adhered to or not according to the individual. When it comes to sexual morality the story is rather different because our sex lives put such urgent pressures on us that exceptional codes of behaviour are called for if we are to run a tolerably pleasant community.

Over thousands of years people have considered various sexual practices 'immoral' but it was not until the coming of Christianity that *all* such practices were forbidden. Throughout history, societies have usually condemned adultery; have sometimes condemned homosexuality and abortion; and have never condemned masturbation. The Christian Church declared all these pursuits to be immoral and, what is more, sinful. Not only did they, it was agreed, have adverse effects on society but they also offended God and cut the offender off from his maker until he repented. In the first few centuries after the death of Jesus, early Christian thinkers virtually outlawed any form of sex other than that within marriage for the procreation of children. Some of the greatest Christian proponents of these ideas could hardly bear to accept that men and women had to have intercourse to keep the race going, so fervently anti-sex were they. Most of these moral rulings had little or nothing at all to do with the teachings of Jesus, but were an embellishment of basic Judaeo-Christian thinking by over-enthusiastic authorities such as St Jerome, St Augustine and, to a lesser extent, St Paul.

Jesus, perhaps surprisingly, said very little about sex (though he specifically condemned adultery and divorce) and was loving and forgiving to those who broke the moral codes of the day. The Church over the years since his death has reinterpreted much of what He said, often to suit its own ends. This has resulted in the Church having basically negative and prohibitive views on sex and sexuality, though views vary considerably from sect to sect within the Christian Church world-wide. Even among members of some Christian denominations (for example Catholics) there is a considerable breadth of interpretation among both clergy and laity.

This had led to a situation in which Western cultures usually discuss morality solely in relation to sex. A woman can be a wonderful mother, never steal, cheat or lie and be a good housekeeper, but if she is unfaithful to her husband, then she is immoral. On the other hand as long as she is faithful to her husband, she can be a slut, a spendthrift, a poor mother and never out of the courts, yet she will not be labelled 'immoral'.

The earliest moral rules were aimed at providing four main things. First, they were aimed at maintaining and increasing the numbers of the nation. From this real need arose rules that forbade any form of sex that did not result in children (such as homosexuality, masturbation and, of course, contraception). By going against these rules the person not only did himself 'harm' but also damaged the group or the race.

The second aim of traditional sexual morality was to strengthen the family unit because the family was the main structural unit of society. Marriage developed as a way of giving the children resulting from sexual intercourse a secure base from which to grow up and this tended to have a stabilising influence on society generally. At this time, most women died in their thirties or forties, not long after their procreative function had ended (the menopause was earlier in pre-Christian times). This meant that women saw their sexual role as inextricably linked with childbearing from when they were sexually mature until they died. This led to the view that all forms of sex that did nothing to promote family and marriage were 'wrong'. Sex outside marriage was therefore 'wrong' as were all types of sex (such as homosexuality) that took men away from their main duty in life – that of supporting women within a family.

The third area of traditional morality is not so practically or socially based but involves the philosophical concept of asceticism. The argument runs as follows: given that sex is so pleasant, is it not 'better' in moral terms to prove to yourself that you can do without it and that it does not rule you? The acceptance of this principle led quite understandably to the state of affairs we have already discussed in which sex was ideally to be avoided at all costs. The early Christians were particularly influenced by this line of thought because they had seen the sexual excesses of the Roman empire which, they argued, had led to its downfall. After such a libertarian system people all over Europe were ready for something more sober. As a result Judaeo-Christian asceticism over sex came at the right time and the seeds fell on fertile ground. People had seen the terrible problems of libertarianism and did not want to pay the price themselves. The emerging Christian Church, like any other clever political institution, saw the advantages of taking this line, latched on to it and promoted it.

The fourth aspect of Christian sexual morality has occurred more recently in Christian and Marxist writings. It is suggested that too great an emphasis on sex is bad in a purely practical way because it takes people's eyes off the production of material things for the community (in the Marxist version) or God (in the religious version). So either way sex 'gets in the way' of the real business of living and is therefore to be avoided.

For hundreds of years these attitudes were so ingrained in society that they became accepted as essential for all human beings – a view which is patently nonsense. Other societies all over the world have developed very different sets of morals, all of which are perfectly acceptable to them, yet many of their 'norms' are quite unacceptable to societies based on Judaeo-Christian principles. Clearly, then, morality in sexual matters in any one society is not necessarily based on concepts of absolute 'rights' or 'wrongs'. Sexual morality, like all morality, is based on practical considerations, the origins of which are often forgotten as the centuries pass. New codes of behaviour are constantly emerging and in a highly complex society such as ours in the West today there are many sub-groups whose concepts of sexual morality are developing at a different rate from those of others.

What then is happening today in the Western world? Quite simply, although we live in a notionally Christian society, few people adhere to Christian principles to any degree and as a result a secular collection of 'morals' has developed by common consent. This in itself would be fine but unfortunately things are not as clear-cut as one might think because, although most people do not follow Christian precepts, they have an uncomfortable feeling, deep down, that they should do, because our culture is inextricably tied up with individual religious affiliations. The problems arise when new or different concepts of morality, no longer based on the traditional ones, start to conflict with what we have been brought up to believe are unshakeable truths. If for all of your life you have been brought up to think of masturbation as immoral or sinful (for the historical reasons we have outlined), it is not going to be easy to unlearn this programming and suddenly to accept it as OK.

We live in a changing world in which many traditional morals are being questioned. This does not mean that the new morals are necessarily right, or that we are necessarily any happier because of this questioning, but it is undoubtedly happening and is producing all kinds of problems. The old objectives of traditional morality seem mainly irrelevant to many today, when population growth is, if anything, anti-social; when marriage is frequently a short-lived undertaking with a decreasing success rate; and when asceticism is a very unfashionable concept. Today's moral principles seem to be based more on the increasing of pleasure for the majority and, perhaps even more important, on the *right* of each individual to express him- or herself in the best way he or she can. Because sex is an important form of self-expression it has become a very important part of this way of thinking.

These ideas have taken root and grown all the more quickly because we live in a world in which we no longer need so many children and in which we have effective contraception and abortion. These changes have freed us to have intercourse without worrying about what was, until very recently in human evolutionary terms, the inevitable outcome – children. Now that babies are no longer the inevitable outcome of intercourse, sex has taken on a new function which traditional moralists did not have to face. Add to this the fact that in today's society women (perhaps with the help of the state) can support themselves and it becomes relatively unimportant for them to marry men in order to be supported. This has led to concepts of more temporary support and even to a reversal of the roles with some women supporting their partners.

Only a tiny minority of even so-called 'religious' people today adhere strictly to traditional Judaeo-Christian morality in all its detail, and the law of the land certainly no longer upholds such morals as being essential for the maintenance of the fabric of society. Adultery, homosexuality and prostitution, for example, are not *illegal*, even in so-called Christian countries. What we see is a situation in which even religious people (a small minority of the whole population) adhere only to those parts of traditional morality that they choose. Clearly the average man and woman in the street are running their lives according to a set of moral codes that they have to some extent defined for themselves individually. Morality has thus become 'privatised' to a great extent. But even such a private system of morals is passed from generation to generation.

## The Christian code

The Bible is a large and complex book, compiled from many different sources originating long ago. It is therefore subject to dispute about the exact meanings of many of the words originally used. It is possible, by out-of-context quotation and misquotation, to support almost any point of view. Biblical 'authority' has been used by some Christians to create a system of sexual tyranny, complete with punishments both in this world and the next. Historically this inspired fear amongst many largely illiterate populations who could not read the Bible for themselves. Even today some Christian moralists try to find ways of bringing individuals they see as sexual transgressors before the courts in the hope that the law can be used to punish them.

It is little wonder that the negative attitudes and moral self-righteousness lying behind such behaviour eventually appeared repellent to many. Some of the attitudes were so unrealistic and so extreme that they led to an equally extreme response on the opposite side. The extreme moralist and the extreme anti-moralist are but two sides of the same bad penny. The truth lies elsewhere and in Christian terms is based on unconditional acceptance of the full human sexual and other potential belonging to ourselves and to each other.

Individuals who find extremes unattractive and return to the Bible itself to see what it actually says find that it is not against sex. In the book of Genesis the Bible says, 'The man and the woman were both naked, but they were not embarrassed.' The Songs of Songs in the Old Testament contains some of the most beautiful and erotic love poetry ever written. Throughout the Bible there are positive comments about sex and in St Paul's writings in particular there is a good deal of helpful advice. Paul sees marital love as an art which can be taught (just as many marital therapists do today). He suggests that both partners behave in such a way as to create a relationship of openness, sharing and caring, in which each is seen as part of the other. Paul recommends regular sex and also tells husbands to be as concerned about their wives' sexual enjoyment as the wives are about that of their husbands. The Bible mentions the fun of sex and stresses that marriage is first and foremost for companionship and only secondarily for procreation. Nowhere does it forbid *any* form of sexual behaviour between a man and a woman who are married to each other, although over the centuries the Church has sought to regulate even sex between husband and wife.

Imagine what would have happened if the extremists in the early Church had not been so influential and a different path had been pursued. If, instead of the populace being treated like children to be terrified into obedience, sex had been regarded as something infinitely precious to be constantly enjoyed, and if masturbation had not been condemned, then today a situation could have existed in which individuals, and especially the young, might have listened and acted upon advice as to how to maximise sexual pleasure. At this point we would argue that the tenor of this whole book, and 'traditional' Christian advice can be reconciled into a pattern of behaviour which might well suit many individuals.

If positive attitudes instead of negative ones were instilled into the unconscious minds of children then most of them would enjoy the capacity for full sexual expression on achieving maturity. Youngsters brought up in such a way would stand a better chance of reaching true maturity and would thereby be more capable of supporting a mature relationship.

Emphasis on the point that intercourse is an inter-personal and not solely an inter-genital, activity would tend to reduce the Church-inspired preoccupation with genitality and direct attention towards a more 'Christian' concern with relationships. Advice to avoid full intercourse until marriage and then to confine it to marriage, which is, in essence, the Christian code, could then be put forward in its own right, not solely as a moral issue, but as an important option for everyone. It is interesting that the sexual freedom accepted by many in the West today does not seem to have led to any *more* happiness or personal fulfilment; in fact the opposite could be said to be the case.

This is not to say that a return to a repressive sexual code would be a good thing, but just that there is a middle path which may be inherently better for us.

# *Chapter 20*
# Maturity

All parents bringing up their children want to see them grow up to become well-balanced, mature adults, and much of what parents do for and with their children has this end in view.

When it comes to concepts of physical maturity definitions are relatively easy. A person can be said to be physically mature when he can reproduce himself or when bone growth has stopped. These two ages do not coincide in man, so even physical maturity is not a simple concept.

But if physical maturity is difficult to pin-point, emotional and psychological maturity is nearly impossible to define. All of us eventually mature physically but many people never fully mature emotionally and psychologically – they remain as children in certain respects all their lives and often this is to their disadvantage.

Two interlinked themes are involved in the concept of emotional maturity. One relates to the development of the individual as such and the other is concerned with the way he or she relates to others. So clearly, any definition or concept of maturity has implications both for the individual and for society at large.

Central to the personal aspect of maturity is the comparison between a child and an adult. A very young child is totally dependent on its parents, particularly its mother: it takes rather than gives; consumes rather than produces (except for noise and body-waste); is unreasonable and unreasoning, being governed solely by instincts; is intolerant of discomfort and frustration; is egocentric (being concerned only with its own feelings and having no concern for the welfare of those around it); and is prone to outbursts of rage and anxiety. Yet within this young child lie blueprints for physical and psychological development and under the influences of these blueprints the child gradually progresses from childhood to adulthood.

From the biological point of view the function of an adult is to reproduce and rear children. Obviously, a child cannot fulfil these tasks. The process by which he or she becomes fitted to do so is what we call maturation. It is widely thought that children are best produced and reared by a mature man and a mature woman who love each other and have a sense of commitment to each other and to their child. For such a state of affairs to come about, the two individuals obviously have to have the necessary confidence and social skills to attract a mate in the first place; sufficient inter-personal skills to keep him or her; a sufficient degree of emotional development to love and be loved; and sufficient sexual skills to have intercourse. In order to continue the relationship in a reasonably happy and efficient way they, as a rule, need to be able to give and receive support and love and they need to be reasonably independent, so as not to overburden each other or anyone else, and yet be capable of asking for help when they are confronted with situations which are beyond their capabilities.

As far as their child is concerned, they need to be able to provide for it, protect it, accept its independence and not to have unrealistic expectations of it. They should be sufficiently close to each other not to want to make a special love-object of the child or to use it as a weapon against each other and not to take out on the child the anger they may occasionally feel towards each other. Each must accept that they have responsibility for it and that in this respect, over the years, the father's role is no less important than the mother's. They should be sufficiently secure to allow the child to be, within reason, itself and not to try to turn it into some form of apostle for, or replica of, themselves.

The child's interests, which are not necessarily synonymous with the child itself, usually need to be placed first and foremost, especially when he or she is very young and, above all, the child needs to be loved not because it is good and pleases its parents, but because of itself.

However, another set of factors influences progress towards maturity. A child is exposed to his or her family and to the experiences of life. Such exposure affects personality, psychosexual, emotional and other development. The topic is vast but a few examples might help by way of illustration.

Being born largely unwanted and subsequently being less than adequately loved exposes a child to feelings of inadequacy and uselessness which undermines all other development, even physical. Children who are severely neglected emotionally, or are unloved, do not grow physically the way they should, boys being worse affected, at least physically, than girls. The situation is complicated because the child may not obviously lack for anything: in fact it may be spoiled by the parents out of guilt. As adults such people may be less than mature because they demand rather than give love. Frequently they become 'neurotic' about love, perpetually demanding proof of it, and watching the partner for any sign of what they regard as evidence of not being love. Most commonly they are depressive, self-critical and generally unable to love themselves adequately. They may be suicidal or promiscuous.

Where a mother or mother substitute is generally unmotherly, it is thought that schizophrenia may result in the child, as may alcoholism. A boy reared in this setting, for example, may subsequently fear all women or hate them overtly or covertly and children of either sex may later display 'mother-hunger' or 'father-hunger' in which they seem to try to revert to childhood to be loved by a woman or a man as a parent. All shades of such effects can occur and in some instances the child's perceptions of reality are governed by rivalry with brothers and sisters more than by any defect in its mother or father. On the other hand, over-close, over-demanding, over-indulgent, seductive, remote or rejecting parents of either sex can distort the psychological development of a child of the opposite sex.

Parents who refuse to allow their child to grow up and treat him or her perpetually as if he or she were younger than his or her years, who oppose independence and, in an effort to meet their own needs, encourage the child to cling to them, run the risk of producing an immature adult who will always want to be dependent on his or her spouse or anyone else (perhaps including those from the social services or psychiatrists). Such individuals regress to childhood as soon as they encounter any difficulty in life.

In a household in which rules are few and lax, children remain impulsive and self-indulgent and in one in which they are over-harsh, they become inhibited and anxious. Where the rules are inconsistent the children become indecisive and confused.

Attitudes are conveyed in a similar way. Thus a child may, for example, be taught to fear failure, ill health or a lack of money more than anything else. Alternatively, he or she may be trained to have excessive fears about the opinions, real or assumed, of others, or may develop an undue fear of or contempt for authority.

In a similar way a child may learn that sex is excessively private, dirty or sinful, and so on. If children develop serious inhibitions about sexual matters they may later lack sufficient drive to overcome their fears, which will impair their social and emotional as well as sexual development.

A child's capacity to experience anxiety, which has a natural survival value for the human species, is probably over-utilised by most parents in child rearing. It is very easy to do this, especially if the parents were reared this way themselves, but it is a real disadvantage to the child, who will grow up to become anxious about almost everything.

Instead of inducing anxiety, try to give positive reasons why your child should or should not do things. If you are always threatening ill effects as the result of various activities it will be hardly surprising if the child actually believes that most behaviour produces a negative outcome and then grows up to fear or be anxious about most things.

In the same way parents can teach their children to be hostile to others, but even more commonly they fail to deal adequately with the hostility that arises in their children towards their brothers and sisters and even towards themselves. Behind this is probably the failure to deal with fear, especially the fear of the loss of love. On the other side of the coin, many parents threaten to stop loving their child if he or she does things they do not approve of. This is especially harmful behaviour. Whatever the child does, especially a young one, he or she needs to know that he or she is loved and to threaten to withdraw that love – or to do things which make the child feel it has been withdrawn – is a form of psychological torture which is harmful if frequently repeated.

These and similar concepts obviously have implications for society and inter-personal relationships within it. A lack of maturity damages the individual, the institution of marriage, parenting and society in general. Emotional immaturity is often the root cause of criminality, social inadequacy, disruptive politics and extreme religious fervour. At the same time we have to admit that emotional immaturity can sometimes be a spur to achievement which is creative rather than destructive.

In one sense we never grow up – we simply become more elaborate. The child is present in every adult as it was in childhood. A truly mature individual is still in contact with the child within him – or herself and can allow it out to play occasionally without becoming childish. Retaining the child-like capacity to experience total pleasure, to be free of all criticism of someone who is loved, to be full of curiosity and excitement and to retain a sense of wonder are all, paradoxically, elements of maturity. Presumably too, progress towards maturity involves the shedding of the unpleasant results for the personality of the bad aspects of one's rearing.

Apart from hatred and envy, already mentioned, and an undue fear of condemnation by others or God for natural behaviour which is harmless to others, senseless shame, especially about sex and inappropriate guilt need to be controlled. The tendencies to tell lies to avoid trouble, to denigrate others out of fear or jealousy, to be spiteful over minor wrongs, to be unduly suspicious over the motives of others and to need to obtain love and approval from all, thereby leading to insincerity, should ideally be eliminated. A capacity not only to accept failure without disintegration or discouragement but also to learn lessons from it and to be stronger needs to be developed especially in a culture such as ours in which the middle classes at least give children the impression that what they achieve is the true measure of their worth.

## Characteristics of a mature person

Bringing these strands together then, the characteristics of a mature person could probably be said to be that he or she:

Is reasonably independent but not excessively so.
Is capable of giving as well as receiving – emotionally as well as in other ways.
Is free of undue aggression and competitiveness and is able to put such feelings to constructive use.
Is productive as a member of society.
Is cooperative.
Is mainly realistic and is not too much governed by self-deception, fantasies and unrealistic perceptions.
Is largely free of childhood feelings of inadequacy, self centredness and inferiority.
Is capable of controlling impulses and converting the energy they contain to more socially acceptable ends when necessary.
Can tolerate frustration for a reasonable period of time, or even for ever, by coping with it in another form.
Is flexible and adaptable, not responding neurotically to changes in circumstances.
Is, eventually, fairly well aware of his or her true capabilities, and faults, neither unduly exaggerating nor minimising them.
Is capable of dealing with individuals as individuals and not as if they belonged to stereotyped categories.

# Chapter 21
# Homosexuality

## What is homosexuality?

The word 'homosexual' has nothing to do with the Latin word *homo* (man) but comes from the combination of the Greek work *homo* (same) and the Latin-based word 'sex'. So it means sexual activity between people of the same sex. This can take many forms, just as sexual activity between people of the opposite sex does.

Current research suggests that there are about 2 million adult homosexual men and women in the UK today. Below the age of 16 such behaviour is not counted as homosexual. A recent survey showed that two in three people condemn homosexuality but that women are less inclined to do so than men.

## Why are some people homosexual?

The short answer is that no one knows. As we have seen, the vast majority of boys go through a developmental stage around puberty during which some degree of homosexual behaviour is normal. Some experts believe that most adult homosexuals have remained frozen at this stage of their development.

Recent evidence has found that a specialised area of the brain (the hypothalamus) that controls all the hormones of the body is 'cycled' in its activity in all young foetuses. In male foetuses it normally becomes uncycled but in some male homosexuals it may remain cycled. Perhaps this points to something happening early in pregnancy that prevents the developing male foetus from becoming a typical male.

Some young people and, indeed, adults of any age, have problems with narcissism – that is, they are attracted only to someone like themselves. They are consequently predisposed to choose a sex partner from their own sex.

Many people deprived of sex with the opposite sex for long enough (for example in prison) will turn to some kind of homosexual activity, even if it stops short of intercourse. Some women turn to homosexuality after bad experiences with men and many more at least consider doing so. These homosexuals often return to the heterosexual life once the balance of their lives returns to normal again.

Sometimes homosexuality arises in a man because he is so tense with women that he cannot relax and so never has satisfactory sexual relationships with them. Such men turn to other men and find that they have better quality, more enjoyable orgasms with them. The 'cure' here must surely be to ensure that boys are not brought up to fear women, as too many are. Thankfully this is less true today than it was in the past. A similar situation also lies behind some lesbianism – some women can relax more with another woman and climax more easily.

Lastly, experimentation in sexual matters has become a feature of the current scene and experimenting with homosexuality is sometimes simply a part of this. Some youths, frightened of getting girls pregnant or simply wanting to sample both sides of the fence before deciding, try a homosexual relationship. Unfortunately, there are real dangers in this because, at this young age, a boy can become locked into the homosexual sub-culture all too easily and so does not get a chance to develop his heterosexuality. An extension of this type of homosexuality is that in which a rebellious teenager uses homosexuality to punish his or her parents and rebel against society.

If all of these 'causes' seem to point to a clear, black and white picture of homosexuality, this would be wrong. Certainly, about one in twenty-five adult men choose to be exclusively homosexual, but there are many others who have fleeting homosexual experiences.

Broadly speaking, homosexuality can be latent (beneath the surface) or openly expressed. Many people are latently homosexual and with very little provocation demonstrate their homosexual side on occasions. (Incidentally, the fact that many people, men and women, find anal stimulation erotic does not make them homosexual.) Overt or expressed homosexuality is less common and is unfortunately plagued with unhelpful stereotypes in many people's minds.

## What do homosexuals do?

Male homosexuals most often use one or more of the following sexual techniques when making love: reaching orgasm by rubbing their bodies against each other; masturbating a partner; being masturbated by a partner; sucking the other's penis (fellatio) or having their own sucked; and performing or receiving anal intercourse. According to one study almost all homosexuals indulged in at least five of these practices in any one year and about a quarter will have done them all.

Women homosexuals' practices, according to one survey, are mainly: reaching orgasm through body rubbing; masturbating their partner; being masturbated; performing cunnilingus (licking the clitoris of the partner); and receiving cunnilingus. Most female homosexuals experience masturbation (both doing it to their partners and having it done to themselves) more commonly than other physical practices. The thing they like best (according to the above survey), is cunnilingus.

## Is my child going to be homosexual?

As was pointed out earlier, it is perfectly normal for young people to go through a homosexual phase during their sexual development. This should not be seen as a prelude to a lifetime's homosexuality but as a safe way of discovering about one's own sex.

The stages differ in boys and girls, so let us look at them both briefly. Girls go through this stage in their pre-pubertal stage (thirteen to sixteen). Girls will play dressing-up games, which include undressing and perhaps smacking each other's bottoms; kissing 'like a boy'; putting a finger in a friend's vagina; or playing with each other's breasts. Rarely though, do girls teach others to masturbate.

Boys talk a lot about sex; have competitions as to who can ejaculate first; have mutual masturbation sessions, compare penis sizes; count hairs and so on. Boys of this age usually do all these things with boys of their own age and as long as this happens all is well. When older boys or men are involved there are legal and personal problems and such contacts should be vigorously discouraged.

Many girls at this stage, and later, have a crush on older girls or school teachers. Such homosexual crushes are rarely overtly sexual in content (except perhaps in the girl's fantasies). They usually fulfil an unconscious need the girl has to identify with a woman she sees as likeable or successful in a quite non-sexual way.

All this means that it would be harmful and pointless to punish a child found enjoying homosexual experiments within these age bounds. Two girls aged sixteen found mutually masturbating for example, *should* be a cause for concern though because, unless it is a one-off game, it could well mean that one or both will have problems in relating to men.

The problem often starts when teenagers declare to their parents that they think they are homosexual. Over 80 per cent of parents are upset and understandably find it difficult to know what to say other than to be negative. The best way to handle this problem is for the parents and the child to discuss it fully and then to get professional help if there is still concern. The best place to start off is probably with the family doctor or Relate Marriage Guidance counsellor locally. Either of these will hopefully provide a relatively unbiased approach to the subject. By going straight to the many homosexual organisations a young person runs the risk of being welcomed with open arms and their homosexuality confirmed and celebrated. We feel this is bad for the young person, who might well just be going through a temporary phase in his or her development and because it might preclude or hinder heterosexual development in the future. Only if it is clear that the young person seems convinced of and is happy with his sexual orientation does it makes sense to contact a homosexual group so that he or she can start off his or her sexual life prepared for the problems and able to meet like-minded people. Until homosexuality becomes totally acceptable (which is still a long way off), this sort of situation will always be a terrible dilemma for the average parent.

## What to do if you think you are a homosexual

Obviously if you have chosen to follow a homosexual life-style as a mature adult, it is your choice and you should be allowed to live with it. The problems arise for those men and women who find themselves turning towards same-sex partners without being happy about it. This can happen for many reasons, as we have seen.

Very few spouses can cope with the thought of their partner being or becoming homosexual, so the best place to start is probably your general practitioner or local Relate Marriage Guidance counsellor. You do not have to be married to go to the latter. Some basic help from such people will often put your mind at rest, but if you need more detailed or specialist help you can contact a specialist psychosexual therapist either throughout the marriage guidance organisations or through one of the organisations listed on pages 000-000.

There are thousands of men living secretly with their homosexuality within marriages and the going can be very tough without outside help. Once you have had some professional help you (or your therapist) may suggest that you discuss it with your spouse. How this is done will vary greatly from couple to couple. Some perfectly happily married couples continue to run a normal and happy family life with one of them conducting a secret homosexual love-affair, but they are few and the stresses usually tell in time. The odd homosexual encounter (especially for women) may not threaten a marriage but anything more serious will need professional help. Remember too that many male homosexuals have or have had a sexually transmitted disease and that if you have a homosexual affair you run a considerable risk of giving such a condition to your wife. All of this is more worrying today with AIDS which is, of course, very much more common in the male homosexual community.

*Chapter 22*
# Sex-related diseases

Let us now look at the sexually transmitted diseases in turn. But before doing so let us consider vaginal discharges because they can cause such confusion and worry.

## Vaginal discharge

The normal, healthy vagina produces a whitish secretion with a characteristic odour. The amount of this fluid produced varies considerably from day to day and with the stage of the menstrual cycle. This discharge is different from the lubrication which occurs during sexual arousal, when all healthy women produce clear fluid. Normal vaginal secretions have a very characteristic smell which turns many men on sexually. Unfortunately, the advertising industry has done its best to portray the vagina as needing frequent cleaning and many women believe they should wash out their vagina with a douche, on a bidet, or mask their natural odour with deodorants. None of these is necessary. Simply wash the outside regularly and leave the inside to take care of itself. If you think you have too much of the normal secretions, or if the secretion smells unpleasant or makes you itch, see a doctor.

Two common diseases produce a vaginal discharge. One is thrush (moniliasis or candidiasis) and the other trichomoniasis.

### *Thrush*

This is a fungus which infects humans. A woman can get it in her vagina where it causes intense itching, soreness and a thick, curdy, white discarge. A doctor can confirm the diagnosis by taking a swab and examining it under a microscope. In a man, thrush may produce no symptoms or there may be slight soreness or redness of the penis but your doctor may wish to take swabs from him if you are infected.

Thrush is often but by no means always caught venereally (from other people's sex organs). Quite a lot of people carry thrush fungus in their bowels and finger nails but have no symptoms. Women who are pregnant, on the Pill, on antibiotics, or who are diabetic, are especially prone to it. If you have thrush time and again it is wise to have your urine checked for sugar just in case you have become diabetic.

Treatment is fairly simple. For a first attack a pessary, cream or capsule may be prescribed which has to be inserted at the top of the vagina. With luck this single treatment will result in cure. For recurrent attacks, which are common due to reinfection from the woman herself or her partner, pessaries, creams or tampons may be prescribed and have to be used for up to three weeks. During the treatment, or for 10 days, intercourse should be avoided or a condom used, especially if swabs show the man to be infected. He is likely to be given cream to apply under the foreskin. Regular washing, avoidance of tight underclothes, and wearing cotton knickers all help, as does the avoidance of perfumed soaps and bath additives.

If you get thrush, don't assume that your partner has been unfaithful – you have probably caught it from yourself, from your own bowel infection or nails.

## *Trichomoniasis*

This is the second most common cause of an abnormal vaginal discharge and it has been estimated that 180 million women suffer from it world-wide. It is a protozoan infection that is carried without symptoms by many people (one survey suggested that 23 per cent of women carry it), so do not jump to conclusions about venereal spread. In women the infection causes a painful and irritating discharge of a yellowish-green bubbly fluid. It is sometimes offensive to smell. The vulva is usually bright red from being inflamed and intercourse is unpleasant because of the pain. The doctor will take a swab but the condition can be difficult to diagnose.

In men trichomoniasis can produce a slight irritation in the urinary passage (urethra), but usually the partner of an infected woman carries the infection without knowing it. This means that a woman with trichomoniasis must ensure that her partner is treated if she does not want him to reinfect her.

Treatment is simple and effective. Both parties are given a course of a drug called metronidazole (Flagyl) as tablets to be taken three times a day for a couple of weeks. Flagyl can cause sickness and headaches, especially if combined with alcohol. The couple should avoid sex until the treatment is over. Other newer drugs which are effective more quickly are now available. Flagyl is also used to treat

*Gardnerella* infections in which the resultant discharge often has a fishy or 'high cheese' odour. It is estimated that a third of women carry the organism but in many it does not lead to discomfort and discharge.

## *Foreign body in the vagina*

This is the third commonest cause of an abnormal vaginal discharge. Usually it is a forgotten tampon. Other things put into the vagina can also be forgotten and cause a discharge. Such discharges are usually yellow and smelly and need to be sorted out by a doctor if you cannot easily get the foreign body out yourself.

## *Disorders of the cervix*

These are a fairly common cause of vaginal discharge and there are many of them. The fluid tends to be brown or blood-stained, and slimy. Any such discharge *must* be seen by a doctor at once. Many a simple condition can be diagnosed and dealt with by out-patient treatment.

# Gonorrhoea

This is the second most common of the 'real' venereal or sexually transmitted diseases (STDs). It is in sharp decline due to the AIDS scare leading to safer sex in homosexuals and to a lesser extent in others.

Gonorrhoea is caused by a germ called a gonococcus which is mainly transmitted by sexual intercourse. It is possible to catch the disease via infected towels and other household items and this is the way babies and young children sometimes catch it. The bacteria grow in and on the sexual organs but they can also grow in the throat (after oral sex) and rectum (after anal sex). Homosexual men are very likely to get gonorrhoea. If you have sex with someone who has the disease you stand a 70 per cent chance of getting it, but the risk is greatly reduced if the man wears a condom. If a man urinates *immediately* after intercourse with an infected woman he stands a fair chance of escaping infection.

The symptoms differ considerably in the two sexes. In men they are usually fairly obvious. A few days after intercourse with an affected woman or man the man has a severe burning pain when passing urine and then develops a yellow discharge of pus from the penis. These symptoms must be taken seriously, so go to your doctor or local clinic at the hospital at once. Early treatment will not only cure the disease and stop it spreading to anyone else but will also prevent longterm complications of the disease, such as eye trouble, arthritis, painful swelling of the testes, or a narrowing of the urethra (urinary passage).

Unfortunately, as many as half of all women with the disease have no symptoms and as a result may infect others unknowingly. This is why gonorrhoea is such a widespread disease and is so difficult to eradicate. Others get the same sort of symptoms as men but the gonorrhoea also affects the fallopian tubes and ovaries. These can also become inflamed and produce lower abdominal pain, fever, menstrual irregularities and a vaginal discharge. Later still the fallopian tubes may become blocked off and the woman is then infertile.

Treatment is relatively simple and effective and if started early prevents the long-term effects we have outlined. It is really best to go to an STD clinic or to your doctor if you have any suspicion that you have this disease or if you have had intercourse with someone you suspect could have it. Simply ring your local hospital and ask for the 'Special Clinic'. Such clinics maintain absolute secrecy and discretion, and your partner or parents (if you are a teenager) will never be contacted without your permission. There is no need to give a false name as many young people do. If you have any symptoms that could be gonorrhoea, don't have sex of any kind until you have been checked over by a doctor. Almost every infection caught early can be cured.

## Syphilis

This used to be an extremely common disease until the coming of penicillin in the 1940s, but is happily less common today. In the past, when treatment was poor, the long-term effects (both physical and mental) were atrocious. Today such effects are extremely rare.

About a month after having sex with an infected person (often a homosexual man) the contact gets a chancre (pronounced *shanker*) at the site of the infection. This can be on the penis, vagina, nipple, finger tip, or lip. A woman may not know that she has it because it could be deep inside her vagina. The sore goes away after a few weeks. This stage is called primary syphilis.

The second stage starts with a copper-coloured skin rash produced as the germs spread through the body in the blood-stream. There is also a fever, sore throat, swollen glands and loss of hair. These symptoms go away too.

The third stage is a hidden one that can last for years. There are no symptoms but the germs are working their way into almost every organ of the body.

The fourth stage of syphilis which affects about a third of all cases is the one described in historical records with such horror. This stage damages the nervous system, along with most of the other organs of the body, and the person can be paralysed, go blind, go mad and eventually die.

A woman who is pregnant and has syphilis can pass the disease on to her baby who will be born dead or diseased. This disease can be detected easily by taking a swab from the sore and blood tests can help too. Treatment with antibiotics is effective, especially in the early stages. Any long-term changes that have occurred in various organs cannot, of course, be reversed.

## NSU (non-specific urethritis)

This is now the commonest of all sexually transmitted diseases and can be very difficult to treat. It is mainly a disease of men (women can certainly carry it but often do not show any symptoms). There is considerable medical debate as to what organism causes NSU but whatever it is it can be difficult to find.

NSU develops seven to ten days after having sex with an affected person and the symptoms are similar to those of gonorrhoea. The discharge may be white, yellow, green, grey or streaked with blood and must be reported to your doctor. The first sign may be pain on passing water.

The STD clinic will do tests to rule out other types of venereal infection and you will be given a long course of antibiotic tablets. Repeated courses may be necessary as the disease can take months to clear. This makes it very wearing to suffer from as repeated visits to the clinic are essential.

One cause of NSU of increasing importance is Chlamydia but the organism is difficult to detect. In women it can inflame the cervix leading to bleeding after intercourse and occasionally to a discharge, but the infection causes no symptoms in two-thirds of women. In some, however, it leads to attacks of pain similar to acute appendicitis or gall-bladder disease. It can reach the tubes, especially if the woman has an IUD, leading to pelvic inflammatory disease (PID) with resultant damage which can cause ectopic pregnancies or even infertility. It is a more frequent cause of PID even than gonorrhoea.

As with trichomoniasis it is very important that if the man is diagnosed as having NSU his partner should also be treated. Otherwise, the detection of the infection depends on the GP suspecting its presence from symptoms and/or the appearance of the cervix. Unfortunately, men can carry the organism but have no symptoms. Treatment is with tetracycline or erythromycin by mouth.

## Genital herpes

Until the seventies the existence of this incurable condition was hardly known to the public. It is caused by a virus (the cold-sore virus) which produces painful, burning, fluid-filled genital blisters. There may also be burning pain on passing urine and painful lumps in the groin. The sores can become infected. About 30 per cent of sufferers have other symptoms such as tingling pain down the legs, back pain, a fever and swollen lymph nodes (glands). The blisters may recur several times a year and some people have as many as twelve bouts a year with stress and menstruation seeming to act as triggers.

Genital herpes is caused by the herpes simplex virus which is closely related to the virus that causes cold sores. Of babies infected during birth (as they come down their mother's infected vagina), about half die or are severely retarded – so it is a serious disease for them. In women, recurrent attacks are thought to increase the risk of cervical cancer five- to eight-fold and sufferers are advised to have a smear done every six months.

Probably the most unpleasant thing about the disease is the terrible psychological and emotional effects it can have. These have been aggravated by exaggerated propaganda about the disease. However, the thought of having to declare that one has an incurable venereal disease before having intercourse with someone is a tremendous strain and carries an enormous responsibility. In the US so great is the problem that special self-help herpes groups have been formed. A new drug (Acyclovir) is available to help treat the disease but has to be given intravenously which means a short stay in hospital. Various other treatments including diets, locally applied yoghurt, whisky and ether have been tried but have proved ineffective.

## Genital warts

Of the new cases attending STD clinics in 1976 genital warts were found in twenty-two and a half thousand. By 1985 the number had increased to nearly 54,000 and has risen further, especially in women, since then. The condition is important because the organism which causes it, human papillomavirus, has now taken over from the herpes virus as being the chief suspect as causing cancer of the cervix. The worry arises from the fact that after declining for years, the number of cases of cancer of the cervix is rising, especially in young women.

Warts are transmitted venereally and appear after quite a long incubation period anywhere on or in the genital and anal areas. At first they take the form of hard lumps in the skin but they soon turn into typical warts which can be more prolific than those which appear elsewhere on the body. They can be treated with substances such as podophyllin or be removed by other means. Talk to your GP about them or go to a Special Clinic.

## Pubic lice (crabs or nits)

These parasites live in pubic hair and suck human blood to live on. Their eggs are called nits and look like small white blobs attached to the pubic hairs. Infestation makes the pubic area itch like fury. You cannot wash out the eggs; you need a chemical which can be bought without a prescription from any chemist. Chemical preparations are also available from your doctor or STD clinic. They kill off the tiny crab-like insects and the nits, and cure the condition. The infestation is caught by being in contact with someone who has the condition or from close contact with infected bedding, clothing, towels, or even a lavatory seat.

Unfortunately it can take some time to kill every last nit, so while this is happening wash all your clothes, underwear, towels, flannels, sheets and so on and don't have sex until you are completely in the clear. Be sure to see that all your close physical and sexual contacts are treated.

## Scabies (the itch)

This is an infestation with tiny mites which usually cause itching, often in the webs of the fingers, around the waist, on the wrists and under the armpits. Tell your doctor or special clinic – treatment is simple and effective.

## Hepatitis B

This is a viral disease which, it is strongly suggested, can be transmitted via saliva, semen, menstrual flow and other body fluids. To this extent it can probably be transmitted sexually. Homosexuals are more likely to be affected than heterosexuals and the disease is important because it can cause chronic damage to the liver. Having said this, the majority of infections are symptomless and self-limiting. Unlike with other types of venereal disease there is no way of detecting carriers of the disease nor is there any way one could suspect a potential partner of having it. A vaccine is now available against the disease.

## The AIDS virus (HIV)

AIDS is caused by the *human immune deficiency virus*, always referred to as HIV, of which there are two types – HIV I which causes most infections and HIV II which is found in parts of Africa. The latter appears to be more benign.

Where HIV came from is not known but it made its appearance in the US and Europe in the mid '70s. Recent evidence suggests that it existed in monkeys in Africa before this but in a form harmless to man. Some people think that some 15 to 20 or more years ago it changed its properties, that is, mutated, and acquired its present capacity to infect and harm humans.

One reason why an effective vaccine against the virus is not likely to be available for many years is that the virus still mutates rapidly and so may well elude any vaccine devised.

The virus is not very infectious and is passed from one person to another only by infection either through the skin, as in drug abuse, blood transfusions or cuts; or through vaginal or anal penetration. Once it is securely established in the body it begins to reproduce but this provokes the body's defences to take steps against it. One of these is the eventual production of antibodies which destroy the virus. However, some of the viruses avoid these defences, probably by hiding away in the bone marrow and brain. These hidden viruses then gradually destroy the body's immune system, hence the name of the virus and the disease. As the immune system is destroyed, the victim loses the capacity for defence against all kinds of infections with other organisms which are usually dealt with easily. The infected person is often well until this final stage is reached, which takes several years and sometimes it is only when things get this serious that it is realised the individual was infected with HIV years before. It is this illness which comes in the final stage, when the immune system is immobilised, which is called AIDS.

## *Progression to AIDS*

So, when the signs and symptoms of AIDS finally appear it is usually impossible to know exactly when the HIV was originally acquired because initial infection with the virus causes no upset. However, in those cases due to transfusion with infected blood it is possible to work this out and in one such investigation it was found that in women the average time from infection with HIV to the development of AIDS was eight and a half years. In men it was five and a half years. Progression was faster in people over 60 at around 5 years on average but in children under five it was less than 2 years.

Insurance companies calculate that a 30 year old man can expect to live another 47 years if he is not in an at-risk group for AIDS (see below) and is not HIV infected. If he is in a risk group he can, on average, expect to live 27 years. If actually HIV infected this falls to 8 years and if he has developed AIDS it is only one and a half years.

## *The tests*

The antibodies to HIV, mentioned above, take an average of 8 weeks to appear after infection. The tests used to find out whether someone is infected with HIV depend upon detecting the presence of the antibodies. If tests are carried out before antibodies appear the results are negative – the individual seems to be free of infection. If a donor gives blood during this period the blood will be used because the tests carried out on it (since 1985) are negative although it contains HIV. Therefore the Blood Transfusion Service asks those who are 'at high risk' of carrying HIV not to volunteer to give blood. These high-risk groups include men who have had sex with another man since 1977; people who have injected drugs under the skin or into the blood stream since 1977; people who have had sex, either homosexually or heterosexually, in Africa, south of the Sahara, or Haiti since 1977; and the partners of members of any of these high-risk groups. These groups are also asked not to carry organ donor cards and the men are asked not to donate semen. The reason for all these precautions is that HIV antibody tests may be negative but the individual still carries the HIV virus.

The wisdom of these rulings has been illustrated by the arrival of a new test which depends not on detecting antibodies but actually detects the HIV itself. Using this test it has been found that in some people antibodies do not appear for three years or more. The test is not yet ready for routine use but what it tells us is that some people disseminate the virus for 40 or more months whilst the standard antibody tests remain negative.

## *How are they used?*

The antibody tests are now very accurate and anyone can be tested by asking their GP; going to a Sexually Transmitted Diseases (STD) Clinic which can be found in the phone book under STD or VD clinic; or to a private test centre.

However, before a test is carried out counselling will be given. This is wise for two reasons. First, it offers the opportunity to discuss sexual behaviour and receive advice on how to cut down risks and second, it begins to prepare the individual for the fact the test *may* come back positive.

Although most people who are HIV-positive (those who have antibodies thereby showing they are carrying the virus) are well until AIDS starts, it is not known how many people are carrying the virus. One way to find out would be to test everyone compulsorily. The British government is against this.

Blood is taken from thousands of people every day for all manner of tests and another way would be to test such samples for the presence of HIV antibodies without telling the patients. This is known as involuntary testing but the snag is what to do if the result is positive. Do you tell the patient or the spouse? Some people commit suicide when told. It was found in New York that actual AIDS patients are 66 times more likely to commit suicide than are other people. Once told, the individual will have difficulty in obtaining life insurance honestly and may even be refused a mortgage. In one survey 14 per cent of people in the UK said that they would refuse to work with anyone who was HIV-positive so if the news leaks out the individual might lose his job. In consequence this method is not being used.

A variant of involuntary testing is to do anonymous testing on the routine blood samples mentioned above. In this form of testing the blood samples have the name of the patient removed. The idea is that this will give us some idea of how the virus is spreading in the community which would be useful in planning prevention. Many members of the medical profession are against this form of testing.

So it comes down to voluntary or, as it is called, 'informed' testing. Obviously anyone in the high-risk groups mentioned above, if they can face up to it, should ask for tests. The British government plans to ask pregnant women to agree to be tested, partly to find out if HIV is spreading in the heterosexual population and partly so that anyone found to be positive can be advised about the pregnancy. Women's Health Concern say that they are being inundated with requests for tests from women who are worried because they have had many partners; because they have been with bi-sexual men; or because they are planning a pregnancy. If everyone were as sensible as these women we would be much better informed about the spread of the virus.

## *How widespread is HIV?*

As must now be clear, no one knows. Outside Africa it still seems to be largely confined to homosexuals and drug abusers. Some people think it will remain that way but the British government wisely has doubts. The virus is often transmitted sexually so it could spread from homosexuals, bisexuals and drug abusers to heterosexuals. Because it takes years to develop AIDS, infected heterosexuals could spread infection without anyone knowing and an epidemic could be with us before it was realised. In consequence health education programmes on both sides of the Atlantic are aimed at persuading everyone, not just homosexuals and drug abusers, to cut down risks. This is so sensible as to be beyond question but the authorities are being attacked for it.

An example of how spread to heterosexuals could happen is provided in Scotland which contains 10 per cent of the UK population. However, 20 per cent of all British people known to be HIV-positive live in Scotland and 60 per cent of these are drug abusers. By sharing needles they spread the infection between themselves and as a result many women (500 in Edinburgh alone) become infected. To support their expensive habit many resort to prostitution. Professional prostitutes usually make clients use a condom but some men are prepared to pay more if the woman does not insist. The drug abusing HIV-positive prostitute needs as much money as she can get and so agrees to sex without a condom thereby risking the spread of HIV into the heterosexual population.

The World Health Organisation estimates that there are between 5 and 10 million people who are HIV-positive in the world of which one and a half million are in the US and 50,000 in the UK. Most are unaware that they are carrying and spreading the virus. Another indication is that up to February 1987 tests on new blood donors in the UK showed that one in 55,500 were HIV-positive.

## *How common is AIDS?*

The total number of cases of AIDS in the UK; how the infection was originally caught; and the number of deaths so far (end of May 1988) is shown in the table.

| How infected | Males | Females | Total | of which have died |
|---|---|---|---|---|
| Homosexual/bisexual | 1279 | — | 1279 | 718 |
| Drug abusers | 21 | 6 | 27 | 17 |
| Homosexual drug abusers | 25 | — | 25 | 11 |
| Haemophiliacs | 97 | 1 | 98 | 63 |
| From blood transfusions | 19 | 11 | 30 | 21 |
| Heterosexuals | 35 | 18 | 53 | 24 |
| Baby from mother | 6 | 10 | 16 | 7 |
| Not known | 11 | 2 | 13 | 7 |
| Totals | 1493 | 48 | 1541 | 868 |

These numbers are not very horrific compared with say, injuries and deaths from road accidents but it must be remembered that the people these figures represent were originally infected with HIV some years ago. The statistics are history. People infected now will not appear in these statistics until well into the next decade. There is also evidence that the figures may well underestimate the number of AIDS deaths not all of which are identified as due to AIDS or notified even if so identified. Even if the HIV mutated itself out of existence now the number of AIDS cases will rise for some years to come.

The World Health Organisation estimates that there are now 150,000 cases of AIDS in the world although only 94,000 have been notified to it. Of these 69,000 are in North and South America; 12,000 in Europe; and 11,000 in Africa. It expects 150,000 new cases in 1988.

## *What actually happens?*

As we have pointed out, the actual first infection causes no immediate symptoms. As the antibodies begin to appear some people have a short glandular-fever type illness with such symptoms as sore throat, enlarged glands, muscle pains, diarrhoea and vomiting. Many conditions can cause such symptoms so the fact it is due to HIV infection is not likely to be realised unless, perhaps, the patient is in a high-risk group. Many sufferers might not even see their doctor.

It is thought that most people who have the virus – who are HIV-positive – are highly infectious about this time but thereafter that infectivity declines until they develop the signs and symptoms of AIDS. In the meantime they may appear fit and well. Some, however, continue to be infectious and may be troubled by persistent enlarged glands. In others symptoms occur intermittently and these include feeling unwell, fevers, night sweats, arthritis, weight loss, candida infections of the mouth (thrush), and diarrhoea. Such people are referred to as suffering from AIDS related complex (ARC).

Currently available evidence suggests that around 75 per cent of people infected with HIV will eventually develop AIDS. The disease can present itself in many different ways including heart disease or mental symptoms (such as an inability to concentrate; a loss of memory; or even schizophrenia). Most commonly the first symptoms are a special form of pneumonia and purplish patches on the skin known as Kaposi's sarcoma. Once AIDS has started death is inevitable but progress to AIDS and AIDS itself can be slowed down by treatment with a drug called Zidovudine. Many other drugs are being researched but it is thought that it will be a long time before a drug *cure* is found.

## *How can I avoid catching HIV?*

Considering what has been said above this is the only sensible question to ask about AIDS.

One answer is to avoid both sex and injecting drugs. For most the former would be considered worse than AIDS. So the answer is to have safe, or rather, saf*er*, sex. This means restricting yourself to one faithful partner or avoiding all high-risk group partners. But even in a stable relationship it is not always possible to know with certainty what risks our partner might have taken previously. Women would be wise to note that about a third of all heterosexual men have had some sort of homosexual experience and that 15 per cent of homosexual men have had heterosexual intercourse in the previous year. Some couples now insist that each has a test before they become intimate in a relationship. In some States in the US testing is compulsory before marriage.

However, the risks of actually picking up the virus from intercourse with even a casual heterosexual partner who is not in a high-risk group are small. One estimate puts it at 1 in 50 million.

Because the HIV is not easily transmitted and because, as we have said, many go through a stage of low infectivity, the risk of catching the virus from a partner who is HIV-positive are calculated to be only 1 in 500. If a condom is used the risk is estimated to fall to 1 in 5,000 which assumes a failure to protect in condoms of 10 per cent. Having said this it must be remembered that some people draw the short straw and records show that women have become infected during a single act of intercourse and from receiving donated semen. The chances are affected by such things as the infectivity of the partner; the health of the recipient; whether blood is drawn or not; and the actual sexual activities involved.

Arising from research, mainly in homosexual men, sexual activities can be classified by the risk involved:

| | |
|---|---|
| *No risk* | Self masturbation<br>Massage of partner away from genitals |
| *Low-risk* | Dry kissing<br>Body rubbing<br>Mutual masturbation |
| *Medium-risk* | Wet kissing<br>Water sports<br>Sucking penis (especially to climax)<br>Cunnilingus<br>Licking anus<br>Vaginal intercourse with condom |
| *High-risk* | Any sex act drawing blood<br>Sharing sex toys and drug needles<br>Stretching of the anus with the fingers or hand<br>Vaginal sex without condom<br>Anal sex without condom |

Risks fall with safer practices, fewer partners, and the use of condoms. Risks can be further reduced by using condoms lubricated with nonoxynol-9 which kills HIV. It is reported that in sex clubs in the US so called 'teasing' has been developed to cut down risks. By such means as stripping, inspecting genitals, blowing on them and rubbing bodies, the participants safely work each other up and then watch each other masturbate. Thin sheets of latex, called 'dams', are also used to fix over the vulva to make cunnilingus safer. Specially thick condoms to make anal sex safer are also available, even in the UK.

The results of adopting safer sex practices have been dramatic amongst homosexuals in San Francisco where 21 per cent of them became HIV-positive in 1982 compared with only 0.8 per cent four years later in 1986. A local health education programme 'Stop AIDS' has closed down as there is no more work to do!

## *How effective is the safe sex campaign?*

When asked if AIDS has altered their sexual behaviour people in the UK tend to say 'no' but the evidence says otherwise. According to Virgin Healthcare, condom sales had been increasing by 4–5 per cent a year but in 1986 increased by 20 per cent. Hepatitis B virus is transmitted in very similar ways to HIV and in 1987 only 800 cases were notified – the lowest figure since statistics were first collected in 1974. Methods used to make sex safer also reduce the chances of getting syphilis or gonorrhoea. Expressed as a percentage of all new cases these two diseases have fallen from 16 per cent in 1976 to 7 per cent in 1986.

## *Mothers and babies*

HIV-positive women carrying the virus can infect their unborn baby. The number of women attending ante-natal clinics who are so infected is not known since many refuse to be tested. Sketchy evidence suggests it may be 0.3 per cent in London. If the pregnant woman is well, pregnancy does not seem to hurry progress towards AIDS but if she has symptoms these are likely to be worsened. As far as the baby is concerned it looks as if a quarter to a half will catch the infection from the mother but whether this occurs whilst in the womb, at delivery, or through breastfeeding is not known though the first route is thought to be most likely and the last very unlikely. Women who show signs of not being well due to infection with HIV are thought to be particularly likely to infect the foetus and they are usually offered a termination of the pregnancy. Current government advice in the UK, which is contested by some, is that HIV-positive mothers should not breastfeed for fear that if the child has not already been infected it may become so via the milk. However in third world countries it may be much safer for the baby of an HIV-positive mother to be breastfed.

## *Other matters*

The evidence strongly suggests that HIV is not spread by insect bites but in one case it seems to have been caught from a human bite.

Lesbians are not a high-risk group (although 80 per cent have had heterosexual intercourse). However, one case of female-to-female spread might have arisen. For example, lesbian activities in the presence of menstruation might increase the risk of transmission but what actual sex took place is not known in this particular case. Woman-to-man spread has certainly occurred and in one instance after only two sexual episodes.

Lavatory seats are an unlikely source of infection with HIV but theoretically the water in the toilet could contain HIV if the previous user was infected. Water splashes have transmitted trichomonas to the vulva. Since most women crouch over rather than sit on a strange toilet there is not much risk but as a precaution the toilet could be flushed *before* use. Acupuncture could transmit infection but there should be no risk if a professionally qualified acupuncturist is used. Tattooing, at least theoretically, could be risky, as could activities involving body piercing.

Why HIV disease and AIDS are largely heterosexual diseases in Central and East Africa, especially in the towns, but not in the West is not known but suggestions have been made that the practice of circumcising girls may be important since they can then perhaps be infected more easily. Many of the prostitutes in these areas are infected and patronage of prostitutes is high. The fact that women are as likely, and in some cases more likely, to carry HIV than men is a major source of worry to those concerned with prevention in these areas. The question is could it happen here? The evidence seems to say that it could. The more people who are infected in the world the more likely is the virus to spread here, so helping other countries to control AIDS is a way of helping ourselves.

Although it is repeatedly said that no health worker has caught HIV from a patient this is not true. Health workers are at some small risk. However, some doctors, dentists and nurses have become neurotic about it and may even refuse to treat a patient they know or suspect is HIV-positive. This is understandable but reprehensible. Recently prisoners working in a prison laundry refused to wash the underclothes of an HIV-positive prisoner although there is no risk. The Governor, to make a point, washed them himself by hand. This sort of episode points to the fact that many people form an unreasonable fear of AIDS which is sometimes referred to as FRAIDS.

Because many male prisoners become involved with homosexuality in prison the World Health Organisation has recommended that they be supplied with condoms. In the UK there are about 70 prisoners known to be HIV-positive. Both the UK and the US

Governments have refused to go along with the WHO suggestion for fear of it increasing homosexual behaviour. Since many men in prison behave homosexually from need (or 'persuasion' by other prisoners) and not choice, they revert to heterosexuality on release and so may help to spread HIV.

If possible drug injectors should cease or change their habits but if they cannot needles should not be shared. In respect of blood transfusions the safest blood to receive is your own. Some centres now offer a service whereby one's own blood is removed and stored before an operation which might require blood is carried out.

Finally, in a way the outbreak of AIDS reinforces the message of this book which is to try to find a compatible partner with whom a happy, fulfilled life is possible, to develop the relationship fully, and to stick to them.

## *Further sources of information*

- Local health education department
- Local sexually transmitted disease clinic
- Special AIDS line 0800-555777
- Healthline telephone service: 01-981-2717, 01-980-7222, 0345-581-151
- Health Education Authority, 78 New Oxford Street, London WC1A 1AH, 01-631-0930
- The Terrence Higgins Trust, BM/AIDS, London WC1N 3XX Helpline 01-833-2971 (7 pm–10 pm everyday)
- The Haemophilia Society, PO Box 9, 16 Trinity Street, London SE1 1DE 01-407-1010
- SCODA (Standing Conference on Drug Abuse), 1–4 Hatton Place, London EC1N 8ND
- Welsh AIDS Campaign, 0222-464121
- Scottish Aids Monitor 031-558-1167
- Northern Ireland AIDS Line, Belfast 0232-226117
- Foundation of AIDS Counselling, Treatment and Support (FACTS)

*Chapter 23*
# Prostitution

The Cynthia Payne case and the almost continuous revelations in the press concerning relationships between prominent men and prostitutes show that the topic arouses enormous public interest. Male patrons of female prostitutes are usually married and so the topic is of interest here.

## What is a prostitute?

A prostitute is a person, male or female, who, in part or in whole, makes a livelihood by gratifying the sexual desires of other individuals, either male or female, within transient relationships, in return for remuneration. Although male prostitutes and even brothels exist to satisfy women and although homosexual and lesbian prostitutes are available to members of their own sex, by far the most common form of prostitution is that in which a man pays a woman.

Most prostitutes do the job to make money – and it can be very lucrative. Sometimes it may pay for the woman's drug habit. More basic reasons for going into the profession include a lack of training for anything else, boredom, loneliness, being drawn into it by friends, and sexual gratification (this latter is usually, but not always, strenuously denied by the prostitute). A woman prostitute may be punishing her mother or taking revenge on her father who she felt could not possibly love her. Some may not have resolved the problems associated with releasing the childhood bond they had with their father, and for them taking money from men is a symbolic, child-like way of taking love.

Some prostitutes think they can meet 'better' men than would otherwise be possible and some hope for a marriage to a rich and powerful client. Others who feel, or used to feel, unattractive as women can get repeated boosts to their morale which seem to them to prove they are desirable. A number of prostitutes who work heterosexually (with men clients) are lesbian and yet others may be latently lesbian and use heterosexual prostitution to ward off the tendency.

Women prostitutes who cater for both sexes are becoming increasingly common.

Most female prostitutes have an understandable willingness to satisfy most clients' demands, if only to ensure their return (because most prostitutes like a regular clientele), and possibly have a greater capacity to undertake and even enjoy a diversity of sexual behaviour than does the average woman. This is fortunate because many prostitutes say that the majority of their clients want something in addition to, or even in place of, normal intercourse. A prostitute may have to dress up in special clothes, provide special equipment, utter special words, undertake special acts, and be prepared to bring her client to orgasm by a whole variety of means. Of these, oral sex, carried out by and to her, is increasingly popular. The customer might simply want to look at her (she need not necessarily be naked) whilst he masturbates himself (sometimes he will not even want to do that) or ejaculate on her. More commonly he wants her to carry out these acts on him. Some men ask prostitutes to have anal intercourse with them using a dildo or a vibrator. Yet others may only want, they claim, to reform or rescue her, whilst others brutalise her out of a hidden religious motivation or in symbolic revenge against all women. As a result of these many, often strange, requests, the average prostitute has to be able to look after herself and to remain in control of the situation. This she can do very well because as a matter of professional pride she only occasionally gets 'carried away' by what is going on and she knows exactly where to draw the line. Even so, prostitutes are open to danger from their more weird clients and this is a danger of which they are only too well aware.

Some prostitutes specialise in particular areas of sexual behaviour, common examples being humiliation, bondage and flagellation, all of which are much more widespread than is generally believed. A variant of this is the 'mistress' type of prostitute who has an on-going relationship with her submissive clientele which may even be carried out through the post. Others specialise is using pornography to arouse and excite the man. More specialist set-ups also exist such as saunas and massage parlours where the clients are eventually masturbated, the euphemism for which is 'hand-relief'. In others the clients are in separate rooms and look at naked women through a window. Other prostitutes may be specialised in the way they get their clients. Call-girls and women who work through an escort agency are two common examples.

Male homosexual prostitutes, who are usually young, are said to pay more attention to the physical appearance of would-be clients than do their female counterparts. Like the latter they usually deny any desire for sexual pleasure themselves and they also often deny that they are actually homosexual. Nevertheless, they erect and ejaculate with male clients and, it is said, usually pursue a homosexual life-style when they have to give up prostitution. Although some dress and behave effeminately, most try to emphasise their masculinity.

## Clients of prostitutes

The clients of prostitutes are said to come from all walks of life but increasingly come from the older segment of the community because free sex, it is said, is more easily available to the young today than in the past. Older men, especially if they are concerned with their respectability, are often unwilling to make advances to women of their acquaintance and may be happier to patronise prostitutes. Older husbands are more likely to be sexually bored with their partner than are younger men and are often less willing to run the risks of emotional entanglement with a non-prostitute. Men with more 'deviant' needs, with physical handicaps, or with a penis they regard as unusually small, may all be more attracted to prostitutes rather than face rejection, or exposure, by a non-prostitute. If you are paying the woman (they argue) she cannot refuse you. This is not in fact true and prostitutes will refuse clients with whom they do not feel safe or who do not fulfil other criteria.

Because prostitutes are available in all age groups and in all variations of body-form and colour, the patron of prostitutes can choose what he wants, as opposed to picking from what happens to be available in the non-prostitute population he meets. Some men who have been reared to believe that sex is unacceptably sinful can only get normal sexual pleasure when with a prostitute and some men who are emotionally immature may prefer prostitutes to other women.

## Some arguments against prostitution

Various arguments are put forward against prostitution. Some of them are listed here:

- It is sinful, immoral and promotes fornication. It may lead to divorce.
- It degrades and misuses women solely to satisfy male lusts.

- It is an exploitation of the weaknesses of men by women and would not occur if women did not offer the temptation.
- It tends to be associated with crime and criminals.
- It affects certain areas of cities reducing property values and making life miserable for non-prostitute residents. (The Sexual Offences Act 1985 aimed at preventing curb crawling has done something to help in this respect.)
- Due to ignorance or lack of care, the prostitute may harm the performance especially of young men by, for example, hurrying them and so conditioning them to become premature ejaculators.
- It spreads disease. This does not appear to be particularly true, at least for London prostitutes, and similar reassuring reports have been published from Copenhagen.

In the main, London prostitutes now insist that new clients wear a condom. The main concern there is the tendency for condoms to burst. Fifty prostitutes examined in 1985 were all clear of HIV. Women working in the San Francisco sex industry are no more likely to be HIV-positive than other sexually active women there. Elsewhere, especially in Africa and Haiti, prostitutes *are* a source of HIV. However, there are grounds for concern. One in five London prostitutes allows regular customers to have unprotected intercourse and nearly all fail to use condoms with their boyfriends and pimps. A more recent survey found 3 HIV-infected London prostitutes in a group of 150 but two were also drug abusers. Furthermore, several had infections with gonorrhoea and chlamydia probably caught from boyfriends. Although customer sex with London prostitutes is fairly safe they could become a source of spread of HIV in the future.

## Some arguments for prostitution

- Men who might otherwise be troublesome because of their inability to attract a sex partner might be able to satisfy themselves with a prostitute.
- Men with deviant needs whose regular partners might not indulge them may be able to satisfy themselves from time to time with a prostitute and thereby sustain a happy rather than a frustrated and bitter marriage.
- By patronising a specialist prostitute men with sexual needs which could result in harm to non-consenting women and girls can be kept under control.
- Prostitution may be an alternative to divorce for men married to

women who for one reason or another cannot, or will not, have intercourse.

- Some men may benefit sexually by the prostitute in effect training them to a better performance.
- Some men have no partner for a variety of reasons, including perhaps travelling a lot or working away from home for much of the time.
- In one sense some prostitutes are almost 'sex therapists' and can help some men overcome their sexual problems.
- Married men who feel the need for a variety of partners are probably in less danger of provoking a divorce by patronising prostitutes than they are by having affairs.

Although this country is said not to be officially against prostitution, in fact much police energy, time and public money is devoted to controlling the trade. The imprisonment of prostitutes for soliciting has recently been abandoned but a prostitute can still be fined. Her male consort, who may not be a pimp and indeed may even be ignorant of her true activities, or any other man who may profit from her activities, can be charged with living off immoral earnings. Anyone, male or female, can be charged with controlling the movements of prostitutes or of running a brothel.

*Chapter 24*

# Am I odd?

## *A brief look at some more unusual aspects of sex*

Unbelievable though it might seem to many people, there are individuals, lots of them, who believe that any form of sexual expression other than putting the penis into the vagina is a perversion, and for some women, to enjoy sex simply for the pleasure it gives them is near perverse.

Such notions still underlie our cultural heritage. Unconsciously, many people, including those who think of themselves as sexually liberated, believe that any indulgence in sexual pleasure is likely to bring punishment from God, perhaps in the form of mental illness or disease. Our laws and customs also reflect the view that sex is sinful and harmful.

Our sexualities work against this suppression imposed in childhood and adulthood. But the desires and instincts that are blocked may have to find an outlet in some closely related form and this, by definition, is a deviation. However, our sexualities are as various as our personalities, so some people all of the time and all of us some of the time are going to be attracted to activities, either as a prelude to intercourse or as a substitute for it, which do not conform to the basic cultural norms of copulation. Because there is often so much shame attached to the desire it may not be admitted to the individual's partner. Even if it is, some partners cannot cope with the request for what to them is very odd behaviour and sometimes use a deviation like this as a reason for divorce.

Because the whole subject is so shrouded in secrecy the public's knowledge of what 'normal' people do or would like to do sexually is poor and it is easy to denounce the sexual behavior of others as abnormal, deviant or perverse. Such condemnation used to be very prevalent, but many activities that used to be thought of as unusual or perverted are now known to be widespread and well within the range of acceptable and 'normal' behaviour. Oral sex (fellatio and cunnilingus) is an example and is dealt with in the chapter on foreplay.

Today the topic of oral sex has been so widely discussed that it has become a positive fashion. Most couples use it simply as a sexual enhancer before actual intercourse and so long as it remains a form of foreplay to arouse or an occasional change from vaginal intercourse it is acceptably normal but a person who can have only orgasms as a result of oral sex probably needs professional help.

Cunnilingus is probably increasing and the main explanation other than the fact that inhibited women can often succeed in having an orgasm only with oral sex, may be that the male population collectively is losing its self-confidence with regard to penile performance and is increasingly depending on the more reliable tongue, which does not lose its erection or come too quickly. In the end, though, we are mammals and mammals suckle their young. So our first physical pleasure in life is oral and this involves sucking another person. It would be surprising if orality were not important in our sexuality – it certainly is in some other mammals. Its practice in the past has been denounced as a perversion simply because it seemed to lead to 'pleasure sex' rather than furthering copulation as a reproductive duty.

What we have said about oral sex can be used as a model to discuss almost any sexual activity other than basic and unadorned copulation. Nearly all the activities involved can be used as a part of foreplay (as a sexual enhancer), as an occasional alternative to penis-in-vagina sex, or as a more or less perpetual substitute for it.

In foreplay we tend to re-enact not only our psychosexual development but also the stages through which most young people progress from first sexually kissing a member of the opposite sex to first having intercourse. So foreplay usually contains elements of pre-genital behaviour (oral, anal and phallic) and to this extent could be (wrongly) regarded as perverse. Good foreplay also contains an element of courtship too. Everyone, or nearly everyone, unless they repress them into the unconscious, has sexual fantasies which they, or others, would think of as perverse. Foreplay can be the way in which couples, especially younger ones, both express and contain their perverse thoughts and fantasies. This explains why young couples tend to experiment more sexually and this is good because they should in this way slowly evolve a pattern of sexual behaviour which suits them both. In general, a sensible rule is that anything which helps one's partner to greater arousal and better quality orgasms and satisfaction is not only permissible but welcome. So voyeuristic, exhibitionist, oral and even minor sadistic and masochistic acts as well as bondage could well be involved.

## What is perversion?

The word perversion should only be used, if at all, where heterosexual intercourse is consistently bypassed in favour of other sexual activities. Perversions can, rarely, be the result of a personality disorder, mental illness or disease of the brain but apart from these causes, perversions are in theory caused by one of two things.

First, the person's psychosexual development may have gone ahead more or less normally but, because of previous experience or suppressive rearing with regard to intercourse, intercourse causes too much anxiety for it to be really pleasurable. This can result in sexual dysfunctions of various kinds or a tendency to go off at a tangent from intercourse into activities which approach it, purely for pleasure. In this way, a man may be willing to have intercourse but in fact enjoys orgasms more when mutual masturbation or oral sex is involved. Many cases of non-consummation of marriage fall into this category. 'Deviation' seems an appropriate word because the aim is right yet it slightly misses or deviates from its target.

The other basic cause of perversions or deviations are distortions in psychosexual development (see Chapter 1 for more details). In these types of perversion the person grows up fixed at a certain stage of childhood sexual development or returns to it because progress to a later stage involves too much fear, guilt, anxiety or pain. After a difficult time with a member of the opposite sex an individual may return to an earlier stage. Usually, he or she recovers rapidly but the examples show how we can move up and down the ladder of psychosexual development. When psychosexual development goes awry like this the individual is a good distance away from heterosexual intercourse and the term perversion is probably more appropriate. We think that it is important to point out that the word applies to a perversion of *development* rather than the actual practice involved.

Apart from the most commonplace deviations or perversions there are several real disadvantages to being locked into non-intercourse sex as your main or only means of sexual release. First, many of the opposite sex will find you strange or unacceptable; second, you will have difficulty finding suitable sex partners; and last, you could get drawn into all kinds of sub-cultures in society, many members of which are unusual or unacceptable in other ways.

Deviations and perversions are usually thought of as being the almost exclusive preserve of men but the causes from which they spring apply to both sexes and, in our culture, even more to women.

Women may, because of their nature, be less prone to respond to the damage inflicted on them during rearing by becoming deviant. They simple become less sexually efficient. Alternatively, they may be more ashamed of the need and so repress it more, or they may be better able than men to meet the need in fantasy during intercourse and masturbation. Men also have more to learn about sex than do women and as a result are more vulnerable to *mis*learning.

One theory of perversions in men attributes it to repeated masturbation while fantasising perversely during adolescence; the resulting orgasm acts as a reward and reinforces the tendency to enjoy the thought of the perversion. Because perverse fantasies are common in adolescence but perversions in adults are comparatively rare the theory is unlikely to hold true for the majority, but it can be applied in reverse when treating deviants. In this technique, which is applied to both men and women, the individual is advised to masturbate frequently to their usual perverse fantasy but to change it at the last moment to a fantasy of normal intercourse. By association with orgasm the heterosexual fantasy increases in strength and erotic power. Gradually it is extended backwards in masturbation so that, eventually, the whole of the associated fantasy is of intercourse and the interest in the perverse activity fades.

The characteristics of a full-blown perversion are its compulsiveness and its fixity. The person *has* to do it and cannot easily stop doing it. He cannot overcome it by reason, fear, shame, threat of punishment, or even exposure. Lesser degrees, which can be described as borderline cases of perversion, exist, particularly in women.

## Sado-masochism

In sado-masochism there is an erotic association between pain and sex. The sadist inflicts pain and perhaps humiliation and restraint on the partner and the masochist pleasurably endures it. The accepted generalisation is that men are sadistic and women masochistic. Whilst it is undoubtedly true that many women enjoy having intercourse in a brisk, no-nonsense way which brooks no objection and some claim to like rough treatment, which may include having their bottoms smacked, there are probably reasons involved other than masochism. The main one is guilt reduction. A woman who has been brought up to think of sex as dirty and sinful, yet really enjoys it, gets most pleasure when she is 'forced' to have sex because it takes her actions out of her own hands and this excuses her otherwise inexcusable (to her) behaviour.

Many woman find it flattering and exciting to have their desirability confirmed by being wanted urgently and passionately, especially if they have been married a long time and think their husbands may be going off them. Many women say that sexual situations are the only ones in which they enjoy being subordinated entirely to a man's will. Most hope that their partners will do something new to them and many say that it is best if it just happens to them, without their being notified in advance. This state of affairs arises more because of passivity than masochism and it could also be a consequence of the way our culture shames women, which results in their being inhibited in expressing their more unusual needs. However, women may tease men or provoke them to anger, perhaps in the hope that they will end up being treated in a rough way and then 'forced' into intercourse.

The subject is highly complex but a simple way of thinking of true sado-masochism is to think of sadists as being afraid of retaliation by the opposite sex so that they feel that their partners have to be controlled and punished. The masochist is afraid of his or her own sexuality and so hands over the control of it to someone else. In most cases, for the sadist really to enjoy the act, the masochist must enjoy it too.

Sadism may have its origin in the anal stage of development but it may also be due to a fusion of sexual and aggressive forces. Symbolic aggression expressed in a sexual form can impart a degree of ardour to a man's love-making. Masochism is thought to be, amongst other things, the reversal of sadism or the eroticisation of submission. Sado-masochistic desires are frequently combined in the same person and couples who practice sado-masochism frequently change roles. The ability to do this is not present in the true pervert.

## Putting objects in the vagina

Many women when they masturbate, or couples when making love, put objects other than their fingers into the vagina, and many wonder if this is safe.

The vagina is fairly tough but anything which might break whilst inside, scratch or be difficult to retrieve afterwards should be avoided. Penis-shaped objects such as brush handles, suitable bottles, fruits, candles and much else, as well as vibrators, are all used. Persistent use in self-masturbation sometimes suggests a higher-than-average degree of guilt about the sex act. Some women even destroy the object after use.

None of this can be regarded as perverse unless masturbation itself is so regarded. More questionable are insertions designed to inflict pain (and orgasm).

## Sex aids

These have been used for thousands of years and are now widely available through marital-aid and sex shops, either directly or by mail order. Almost all sex aids are sold to couples to enhance their foreplay and to increase the pleasure they get from intercourse. The biggest-selling sex aid by far is the vibrator and it is used on the male or female genitals and in the vagina or anus. A word of caution is necessary about using vibrators in the back passage. Quite a lot of people enjoy having a vibrator in the anus when masturbating or even during intercourse and this is fine provided it does not *then* get put into the vagina where it could cause a troublesome infection. Anything that has been in the anus should be washed thoroughly before being put into the vagina. The second problem is that by putting the vibrator too deeply into the anus it can get lost and this is very dangerous because it will have to be removed surgically.

Sexy underwear and various types of condoms (sheaths) are probably the next best-selling lines in a sex shop but both are, of course, available elsewhere too. These are purely for fun and can do no harm but there is a word of warning about putting rings and other things around the penis. When the penis is limp it will obviously be easy to put a ring around it, but when it is erect the ring may be impossible to remove.

Other available sex aids include dildoes, strap-on penises, implements and clothing for sado-masochistic games, preparations which might help erection or delay male orgasm, and other things, all of which amount to sex toys for adults. For more solitary use are sex dolls for both sexes, artificial vaginas, which some couples find useful in training men to prolong intercourse and penis enlargers which probably help to maximise erection so making the penis seem larger. For those who have no partner or whose partner is unavailable such aids are an alternative to plain masturbation, an affair, or a prostitute.

Much hostility is unreasonably directed against sex-shops but provided their window displays are not offensive, they could be regarded more as an assistance to at least some couples, to enhance their erotic value to each other. Anything which helps men and women to love each other more should not be condemned out of hand. Insofar as they may assist harmful, perverse behaviour, they are more questionable.

## Anal sex

Technically, anal sex is illegal between a man and a woman but not between two men of the required age and by mutual consent in private. Until 1861 anal sex was punishable by death in England and it is still illegal in some states of the US.

About two in five married couples admit to having tried anal sex (although the actual figure is undoubtedly higher than this) and historically it has been widely used as a form of contraception and at times when the woman was menstruating or had a vaginal infection.

Anal intercourse is perfectly acceptable medically with a few provisos. First, the man will have to take things gently if he is not to hurt the woman. A couple who want to have anal sex should spend some days preparing for it. Start by gently inserting a well-lubricated finger tip into the woman's anus while she masturbates or while you are having intercourse. Over the next few days insert another finger or two, never causing pain, and then eventually – with plenty of lubrication – try to use the penis.

The only real problem with anal sex is that it is easy to transfer bowel germs from the anus to the vagina and this can cause troublesome infections. If a penis has been in the anus it should be thoroughly washed before being put into the vagina, or indeed anywhere else. Of course a condom can be used.

Due to AIDS, anal intercourse is best avoided with partners who might have been exposed to HIV injection (whether in a homo- or heterosexual context). It is twice as risky in this context compared with vaginal intercourse.

## Exhibitionism and voyeurism

The accepted generalisation is that women are more exhibitionist (like to show their bodies) than men but less voyeuristic, while men are more voyeuristic (wanting to look at women) and less exhibitionist. This seems to make biological sense given that in the western culture our notion of beauty is based, at least to some extent, on the female body. So, in general, women enjoy displaying themselves and men like looking at them. The female body in itself is quite capable of producing an erection in many men, especially if it is scantily clad or naked. In the West women are allowed to show off their bodies (albeit not entirely naked) whereas the law intervenes if a man put his genitals, legally called his 'person', on public display.

Exhibitionism becomes a perversion when it is a person's preferred sexual activity, leading to his greatest sexual pleasure. It is most common in timid young men who frequently best enjoy the activity if the selected victims, usually pubescent girls, look at them just as their masturbation has reached the point of ejaculation. Such acts are not intended to be seductive and if the man has a partner of his own, (some are married) he does not usually want intercourse. Such men

*The sultan/sultana game: The male voyeur' responds to the exhibitionist behaviour of his partner—usually as a prelude to intercourse. Such games enable the woman to take control in foreplay as she teases her man and confirms the power she has to arouse his passion.*

are basically harmless but other types of exhibitionists certainly are not. Some alcoholics, psychotics, criminally sadistic paedophiles and brain-damaged people may exhibit themselves occasionally but this may not be the limit of their activities. Similarly, disturbed women may exhibit their genitals and perhaps masturbate in public. Some mentally deficient people exhibit themselves too, probably to attract attention rather than for any overt sexual pleasure.

Survey evidence suggests that nearly a half of all girls and women can expect to be the victim of male exhibitionism or, as it is called, indecent exposure. A third or so of these will tell no one, but if they are under the age of sixteen or so they can be very upset by the episode. The young girls who are subsequently most disturbed are those who tell their parents who then over-react, perhaps involving the police, as happens in a fifth of cases.

Few members of either sex would fail to watch nude members of the opposite sex or a couple having intercourse if the opportunity presented itself, especially if there were little chance of detection. Inhibited people of either sex who have been fitted with an eye-camera, and who therefore know that the experimenter knows what they are looking at, will look anywhere except at the nude body of a member of the opposite sex with whom they are confronted. When looking is allowed, as at strip shows, which are now available for both sexes, or on nude beaches, the inhibition recedes. Probably we are all reared, by others if not by our parents, to believe that it is 'dirty' to look at the genitals or sexual behaviour of others.

Whilst this is voyeuristic behaviour it is not really voyeurism in the true sense of the word. Voyeurism is a condition in which the person usually, but not invariably, takes deliberate steps to watch others undressing or copulating and so gets his or her kicks from witnessing 'realistic pornography'. Some conceal themselves in bushes, creep on knee pads, drill holes in walls, or climb ladders in pursuit of their peeping-Tom activities. Some homosexuals spy on their own sex and some specialist voyeurs concentrate on watching women urinate. An occasional voyeur such as a psychopath may assault the woman he is watching but the vast majority of peeping Toms are harmless.

## Fetishism

Fetishism is usually, but wrongly, said to apply only to men. It can take many forms and can merge into transvestism or even sadism. Usually the affected person becomes 'hooked' on a particular object and cannot have a successful orgasm unless the conditions are just right. Some men have fetishes about women's shoes or underwear, for example, and others are equally affected by fur, leather, or other fabrics and textures.

In a book of family love and sex the subject is worth discussing because some fairly convincing but controversial evidence suggests that an individual's mother may be the cause of such fetishes. Treatment of the adult fetishist is difficult, although effective, so prevention is obviously very important. A few words of explanation are necessary before proceeding, because they will help explain in general how a person's rearing can deeply affect his sexual functioning as an adult.

As it grows, a baby passes from a totally self-centred stage (see Chapter 1) to a stage at which he or she relates to others around him or her and most of all to the mother. At the stage when the child moves from self-centredness to the development of an object-relationship with the mother, he or she may fix on an inanimate object, such as a doll or a piece of cloth, which the child then treats as a comforter. The main difference from the mother is that the comforter does not have to be shown the same consideration as a love object. Such articles are called 'transitional objects' and quite a lot of insecure and lonely children get considerable solace and comfort from them. In certain cases an attachment to such things can become pathological and far from helping the child to form relationships with people, they can form relations only with their transitional objects.

Whatever the contributory factors which go into making a fetishist, the affected person responds erotically only to the fetish object, usually stockings, gloves, shoes or underclothes, all preferably permeated with a body odour. Newly purchased objects are of little interest but stolen ones are especially valued. The fetishist handles and kisses the object, perhaps ejaculating or masturbating during the process. Even the thought of the object can lead to sexual arousal. In the infinitely more common form the fetish object may not be inanimate but can be a part of the body such as the buttocks or the feet. Whatever the object the fetishist homes in on, it stands for the whole person and the individual relates to the partner through the object. The object has to be present for maximum sexual satisfaction. In a sense, it is like a talisman which has to be present in order to ensure a good performance, although this type of fetishist is usually able to undertake less than satisfactory sexual activity in its absence. Some such men are impotent.

## Transvestism and transsexualism

These are rare forms of sexual perversion but ones which can and do often affect otherwise happily married, family men, so they are worth looking at here. Transvestites get sexual pleasure from wearing the clothes of the opposite sex. They usually look at themselves in a mirror and are excited by the signs of sexual arousal in themselves. Masturbation is usually the result. Sometimes a woman partner will be involved, some being willing to provide female attire and make-up. Either intercourse or masturbation may then be the outcome.

Some cross-dressers do not become sexually aroused but describe a sense of peace and contentment which comes over them. These are probably not true transvestites because there is no arousal. Both, however, no doubt reflect some disturbance in the early relationships with their mothers. Around four years of age many boys go through a stage of putting on their mother's clothes, presumably because their softness symbolically represents the mother's skin. However, there is evidence that more mothers of transvestites would have preferred a girl than other mothers and some even treat their little boys like girls for some years.

Where a transvestite responds to only one article of clothing, such as knickers, the distinction between him and the fetishist is difficult to make. More commonly, the transvestite will put on his wife's, or his own, female attire when she is out. His general interest in other sexual activities, including intercourse, is usually low.

How common transvestism is in women is an open question and some experts believe it does not occur at all. This is improbable and some causes of orgasm problems in women may be due to its presence. Psychotherapy can be an effective treatment for tranvestism.

Most transvestites indulge their interest only occasionally, although some need to expand their activities so that they are dressed as the opposite sex most of the time. They do not usually want to change sex: as one said, 'I'm just a cock in a frock', but he nevertheless had a female name for himself in the role.

Where there is a desire to change sex (the individual believing he or she is a member of the opposite sex trapped in the wrong body), the condition is known as transsexualism. As well as wearing the clothes of the opposite sex, these people want to be rid of the body they have and replace it with one which resembles that of the opposite sex. As a result they seek hormone therapy and surgery. Women want testosterone so as to grow a beard, break their voice and, perhaps, enlarge the clitoris, and surgery to have their breasts and their uterus removed. Men want oestrogen to create breasts, reduce beard growth and make their contours more rounded and surgery to remove their genitals and construct a vagina. Most seem to be more sexually inhibited than sexually expressive and their preoccupation with their sex-change is obsessional. However, they can subsequently regret and resent the change. If frustrated in their quest, however, the transsexual can become depressed and suicidal. Although transsexuals may be homosexual, the problem is not basically one of which sex they are orientated towards sexually but rather one of gender-identity. They have identified their gender incorrectly. Mothers of male transsexuals (like those of transvestites) also more commonly wanted a girl than other mothers and it is said that they feminise the boy from childhood onwards. The father does not rescue the child and is usually distant. These mothers are often said to be unfeminine and disappointed tomboys themselves.

Transsexuals say they have always known that they were of the wrong sex and need to belong to and be accepted by everyone as a member of the opposite sex. At school such boys usually relate only to girls and girls become their reference or peer group. They put on female clothing and continue to do so in spite of any rebuke or punishment. They may even say they want babies. Successful attempts have been made to rescue boys from a future of transvestism or transsexualism by therapy administered before puberty. The justification is that gender-role disturbance (an incomplete or unsatisfactory acceptance of the masculine role in boys or the feminine role in girls) or cross-gender identification (the belief that one belongs to the opposite sex) leads to so much disorganisation and unhappiness that it should be prevented if at all possible. Girl transsexuals can be treated successfully even in adolescence. In their cases it is usually the mothers who have been neglectful and the fathers who have taken care of them and encouraged masculine tendencies. The fathers perhaps wanted boys, or wanted to exclude the mothers from their relationships with the girls.

Again, as with all these perversions and deviations, often the child's rearing has so scarred his or her development that he or she is trapped into believing and feeling the way he or she does. For the families of the individual involved things can be very difficult and professional assistance is almost always needed. Self-help groups can be a great help. See pages 369–378.

## Incest, child abuse and child sex abuse

Although different, incest, child abuse and child sexual abuse are frequently related in practice. Obviously, not all cases of incest involve children and not all instances of child sexual abuse involve a blood relation. Neither are children subject to abuse necessarily also involved in child sexual abuse but all these can be conveniently considered together for our purposes since all represent a breakdown of family harmony, social taboos and, except in cases of adult incest, a failure of child care.

Incest means intercourse between family members considered legally too close to marry. Child abuse, as defined by the World Health Organisation, is any intended or unintended act or omission which adversely affects a child's health, growth or psychosocial development, whether or not regarded as abusive by the child or adult. The most commonly used definition of child sexual abuse is the involvement of dependent, immature children or adolescents in sexual activities they do not fully comprehend, to which they are unable to give valid consent and which violate the social taboos of family roles. Child sexual abuse is regarded as existing in one of four forms. First, exposure such as being allowed to view sexual acts, seeing pornography or witnessing exhibitionism; second, molestation or fondling of the child's or adult's genitals; third, sexual intercourse – an ongoing activity which involves the child's mouth, vagina or anus; and finally, sexual intercourse in which the child is obviously assaulted – rape.

Incest, child abuse and child sexual abuse all cause social outrage and can all lead to court proceedings and imprisonment. In consequence they are often difficult to detect and can be hard to prove; the cases which do come to light are thought to be a minority and all three offences are said to be more widespread than popularly believed. Estimates of child sexual abuse in some parts of the world range up to 1 child in 3. In all child sexual abuse surveys women are twice or more as likely to say they have been sexually abused in childhood than are men and the same holds true of incest surveys where in one, for example, 5 per cent of women but only 2 per cent of men reported this experience. Child abuse, especially in the forms of neglect, non-accidental injury and emotional deprivation, is even more widespread and is most likely to occur in families in which the couple are young and immature; in which pregnancies are unplanned; or in which the mother is young and unsupported. In Western countries the perpetrators of both child abuse and child sexual abuse are parents or step-parents in 70 to 90 per cent of cases.

Since all three conditions are thought to be widespread and detection is difficult, some professionals, such as social workers and doctors, have become carried away with their enthusiasm to root out such problems. Several enquiries have condemned social workers for incompetence or slothfulness in instances of child abuse where the child has eventually died, thus illustrating, yet again, how easy it is to be wise after the event. The purpose of such enquiries is to avoid repetition but one consequence seems to be that in their eagerness not to err again social workers have now become over-zealous to the extent that their departments are so overwhelmed with cases they have identified as being possible abuse that real abusers are even less likely to be detected and helped.

Again, some hospital paediatric departments are fully examining, including genital and anal examination, all children brought to them for whatever reason (such as, for example, an eye examination) in their keenness to detect child sexual abuse. This may upset children, may be a form of abuse in itself, may deter parents from seeking medical help for children and may make it less likely that a sexually abused child will ever be brought to them. Whatever the justifications and they are cogent, it is ill-advised for the medical profession to risk forfeiting public trust by using blundering methods of unnecessary examinations. Yet again, over-zealousness has misled some doctors into diagnosing abuse or sexual abuse when the signs and symptoms in the child were caused by some other medical condition or were even normal, thus undermining public confidence. Worst of all, some professionals when interviewing children suspected of child sexual abuse have used extremely unwise methods, language and techniques which draw their own motivations into question and deprive the alleged perpetrator of any right to innocence.

Yet all this zeal, which involves only a minority of professionals, is justified by such individuals on the grounds that children are defenceless and must be protected. However, all parents must now face up to the fact that a new hazard of parenthood is that they may be, justly or unjustly, accused of abusing or sexually abusing their children and their innocent explanations of illness or injury may not be instantly accepted. This is a heavy price to pay for the protection of children but it may be worth it if it really leads to the detection of children in danger.

To any reader who has reached this point in the book little of all this will come as a surprise. Relevant points to consider mentioned elsewhere include the tendency of love and sex to go together but the need to suppress sex in inappropriate relationships; the tendency of alcohol to diminish inhibitions; the attractiveness of children; the intensity of the heterosexual love for the opposite sex parent in the Oedipal stage which can colour the subsequent recall of events when interviewed as an adult; bad or frightening memories being repressed into the unconscious and thus unavailable for recall; the normal curiosity about genitals between brothers and sisters (and other children); the fact that not all marriages are between mature people and such marriages often produce children early; and that not all children are wanted. Important too are the points that children who have been exposed to violence and sexual abuse, later, as adults tend to become similarly involved; one partner in a marriage may become over-involved emotionally with a child because of defects in the marital relationship; and not all marriages are sexually well-adjusted, leaving one partner frustrated.

Further points to consider are that older children and adolescents may tell lies for their own ends and several accusations of sexual abuse have been shown to be fabrications. Mothers may unconsciously collude in sexual abuse or are sometimes the perpetrator or assist the perpetrator.

Some parents now report that they are limiting their physical contact with their children so as to avoid possible accusations of abuse and say they have stopped undertaking activities which could be misreported or misunderstood, such as allowing children to see them in the bath or dressing. Even loving displays between some couples are now being curtailed in the presence of their children. This is unreasonable and probably harmful to children. Whatever is done, provided the presence or participation of the child is not an additional erotic gratification for the adult, then sexual abuse is unlikely to be occurring. Wise parents should heed the possibility that their children may let sex-play reach the point of incest and should reduce the opportunities for it to occur. They should also consider whether others in contact with their children might sexually abuse them and take steps to reduce opportunities for this to happen. Grandparents, baby sitters of both sexes, teachers, neighbours, older children and so on have all been perpetrators.

The cultural tendency of parents to exercise more control over the movements of girls seems to be justified by their greater likelihood of being sexually abused. If parents detect in themselves any tendency to abuse their child, sexually or in other ways, they should discuss it with a professional and together try to devise ways of controlling the situation. Once abuse is discovered professional help must be sought because it is almost always impossible to deal with it in the family alone. Confidentiality when approaching a professional is obviously a major concern and this may be refused but obviously if the parents are trying to help themselves and there is no immediate danger to the child most professionals will be only too willing to do everything in their power, including obtaining assistance from other professionals, to help and are most unlikely to take steps which could harm the parents. Virtually everyone would regard this as an ideal outcome to a potentially harmful situation.

The political response to child sexual abuse is to set up teams of paediatricians, GPs, police surgeons, psychiatrists, gynaecologists, psychologists and social workers so as to take a broad view of possible cases and also to curb the zealots. Whether a committee of this type is the right way to go is open to question but we shall see. The most fundamental means of prevention is to carry out research on cases and families so as to devise preventive strategies, advise parents and generally become better at case detection. The involvement of psychiatrists, family therapists and psychotherapists is therefore to be welcomed.

Although the child or its mother may report abuse, as may family friends, GPs, social services and so on, teachers rarely report it. Nevertheless they, along with sensible parents, have a role to play in teaching children to be wary, to say no, to scream and get away if abused, and not to feel bound by promises of secrecy where wrong-doing is involved but to tell an adult they trust at once. Obviously, too, teachers and the school medical service are in a good position to detect neglect and abuse in schoolchildren whereas health visitors can help with its detection in younger ones. Since child abuse can be inadvertent this is an area where parents might see intervention as being helpful and be glad of it if the situation is creatively handled.

Just as child abuse may come to light through fractures, burns and bruises so incest may be revealed by pregnancy, and sexual abuse through pregnancy, genital warts or VD. Genital signs, such as an enlarged hole in the hymen may show the presence of vaginal intercourse in incest and child sexual abuse and damage to the anus may indicate that anal intercourse is occurring. Most sexual abuse starts at around 8 years of age and incest perhaps even later. In both these and in emotional forms of child abuse psychological symptoms may predominate. The child may be ashamed, sad, guilty, depressed, withdrawn, regressed, isolated, untrusting, failing to thrive and have eating problems or academic problems at school. His or her behaviour may be sexually precocious or show other abnormalities.

Long term consequences for the child are related in some degree to the amount of trouble which results from the situation. In girls long continued sexual abuse by the father seems to be particularly harmful and an introduction to homosexuality in a boy may fix his sexual preferences, perhaps for life. Psychiatric illness or sex and relationship problems later in life may all follow from childhood abuse. Difficulties in relating to the opposite sex and a difficulty in obtaining a partner are often seen later in cases of brother-sister incest. A report from Australia on the examination of victims of child abuse several years later showed they had fewer friends, were less ambitious, had poor self-esteem and more behaviour problems than non-abused children.

Once detected the treatment of all three conditions must be to stop the incest, child abuse or sexual abuse, to prevent a recurrence and to repair the damage. Medical treatment may be necessary, especially in child abuse but individual, group and family therapy are most used to cope with other aspects. Strengthening the marital relationship and improving the parents' sex-life can bring child sexual abuse to an end with a degree of ease. Psychotherapy to promote maturity, including psychosexual maturity in the parents, can also work wonders in child abuse as well as child sexual abuse. Helping the victims of incest, child abuse and child sexual abuse to deal with what has happened and particularly to help them deal with the guilt many of them feel seems to limit the chance of future distress.

Where repair of the situation seems to be unlikely, impossible or has failed, or where the gravity of the offences is thought to demand punishment, the professionals and courts may, unhappily, put children into care and perpetrators into prison. Since few parents, or even step-parents, set out with the intent to harm children, it is a sad outcome to be avoided if possible because children may end up worse off than before.

The subject of child sexual abuse is vast and the reader is referred to specialist books on the subject aimed at parents, for further information.

## Paedophilia

No perversion, apart from rape, arouses such public outcry as does paedophilia, the condition in which an adult or older adolescent takes an erotic interest in a child under the age of fourteen. Even hardened criminals cannot tolerate this crime and paedophiles often have to be isolated in prison for their own safety.

In heterosexual paedophilia the victims are usually seven to ten-year-old girls who are sometimes harshly treated or even killed. Usually a paedophile wants the girl to show her vulva, to look at pornography, or to handle his penis. He may fondle or smack her, or attempt to have intercourse with her. How parents can rear girls so as to avoid such individuals without encouraging them to fear all men or become discourteous to men who are being socially pleasant towards them is a real problem and there are no easy answers. On balance it makes sense to teach children never to go anywhere with strangers without first asking permission from their parents and children should never take sweets or anything else from people they do not know unless their parents are there. It is upsetting to think that we have to bring up our children fearing anyone they do not know but one has to be realistic and child molesters can be dangerous.

Oestrogen, anti-testosterone drugs and castration have been used in attempts to control paedophiles and rapists but the best course must be prevention. Usually men and women show a tendency to consort with individuals corresponding to their own stage in psychosexual development. Heterosexual paedophiles are immature, scared of women of their own age and often revengeful against them. They masturbate a lot to vivid fantasies of little girls, concentrating perhaps on their buttocks or even on things such as the ankle socks they wear. Whatever the precise cause, clearly the psychosexual development of the heterosexual paedophile has not prospered and he needs professional help.

The more common form of paedophilia is that in which men are attracted to young boys. To say they are homosexual may overstate the case since many, although not too attracted to it, do have heterosexual intercourse. Many are married. Their love of small boys is probably self-centred since what they really love is the image of themselves when young. They often shave off their pubic hair and watch themselves masturbate in front of a mirror. They are fascinated by boys, especially nude.

A number of people who are mentally disordered also commit sexual offences against children.

## Other perversions

There are many other perversions. For example, there are some people who get their best sexual pleasure from masturbation and prefer it to other activities. Rapists sometimes claim in their defence that pornography led to their condition, but as erotic and pornographic material is widespread and rapists are not, other factors must be involved, even if the original statement is true as far as it goes. The use of alcohol is probably a much more common precipitant factor in a rather inadequate individual who is basically afraid of women but hostile towards them. Some rapists find that the struggle and the power they feel enhance their sexual drive, so perhaps they should really be considered perverted. Others can scarcely perform at all. Certain types of rapist are deterred if the woman fails to struggle or if she gives in. Psychopathic men may displace anger with one woman on to another and generally manage to convince themselves that the woman deserved what she received.

In general the conclusion which emerges from studying perversions is that there are components of them in most of us, but in most people they are integrated into the overall pattern of their sexuality and certainly do not dominate it. If they are to be at all useful, theories as to what causes them have to be sufficiently precise to allow parents to prevent their formation in the first place. Insufficient research has been carried out on this subject. The main dilemma such research would try to explain is why some individuals exposed to fairly similar situations in childhood and beyond as those experienced by deviants and perverts should develop normally or fairly normally. Some individuals are able to control their tendency towards a perversion, but may become neurotic and produce other physical and psychological symptoms.

On the whole psychiatry has been woefully inadequate in investigating perversions and has very little to say about their prevention. Another body open to criticism is the Home Office. If the Home Office made clinical histories of sex offenders available for study, together with the prisoners themselves, if they were willing, much light could be shed on the subject. Whilst prisoners should not be deprived of any rights, many would be willing to involve themselves in serious research aimed at uncovering the real causes of their plight, as opposed to the ones offered publicly in court, especially if it led to the establishment of preventive programmes.

A more immediate solution may be to establish walk-in clinics on the same lines as VD clinics, where even the names of those attending need not be taken. In such clinics help, advice and treatment could be offered to those who suffer from, or think they might have, a problem. Many know something is wrong before they commit an offence and some would be sufficiently motivated to seek help if it were available.

Looking at the problem more generally, anything which promotes happy and fruitful man-woman relationships, better marriage and healthier, more rational attitudes towards sex would help. Parents and teachers need to be better informed about normal sexual development and, with increased knowledge about what is normal and what is not, should be able to get professional help for their children before things go too far.

Although many readers may be put off by the subject matter of this chapter, feeling that most of it is totally foreign to them, it must be seen as a part of human experience. Though we have tended to present the many facets of unusual sexual expression as simply as we can and in somewhat 'barn-door' ways, it should be realised that they also exist in lesser and less easily recognisable forms in most of us.

Rather than condemning the individuals whom this chapter describes, it perhaps behoves all parents to think critically about the impact of cultural restraints and excitations upon their children and to reflect on the long-term harm that can result from thoughtless actions.

*Chapter 25*

# Sex and health

## Good or bad for your health?

As mentioned in Chapter 10 there is some hard evidence that sex promotes health but it has to be admitted that some people seem to manage perfectly well and live healthy and happy lives without it. Possibly they find satisfaction in displacing, or sublimating as it is called, their sexual energies into other activities. Others are unable to do this and become miserable without a regular sex life.

Most definitions of good health include a reference to the need for a loving relationship and sexual expression. A good image of oneself as being sexually desirable and a confidence in the ability to function efficiently with the opposite sex is an important component of the morale of most people.

Another way of looking at the matter is to realise that depression and severe illness diminish sex drive and excessive anxiety reduces its value.

Sex, of course, can also be associated with ill health through guilt, STDs, complications of pregnancy and childbirth, and so on. It can do harm through disturbed individuals committing sex-related crimes such as rape, child molestation, jealous assaults, or sex-murder. This sort of trouble arising from sex has helped to give sex a bad reputation in our culture.

To be more positive and to give us all something to aim for, it is not possible to do better than to look at the World Health Organisation's observations on sexual health. They say it has three elements: a capacity to enjoy and control sexual and reproductive behaviour in accordance with a social and personal ethic; freedom from fear, shame, guilt, fake beliefs and other psychological factors inhibiting sexual response and impairing sexual relationships; and freedom from organic disorders, diseases and deficiencies that interfere with sexual and reproductive functioning. They conclude that the purpose of sexual health care has to do with the enhancement of life and personal relationships – not merely with counselling and the treatment of infertility and STDs. The WHO have also pointed to the contradiction between having to plan contraception rationally and the desire to experience sexuality spontaneously. How right they are!

## Some things that can go wrong for women

### *Smoking*

In addition to the well known risks of lung cancer and diseases of the blood vessels women smokers are said to be more hairy and more prone to cystic ovaries, infertility and ectopic pregnancy. Also, if pregnant, smoking and alcohol are known to endanger the child.

### *Retroverted womb*

Usually the womb lies on top of the bladder at a 90° angle pointing forwards towards the front of the body. If the womb is tilted backwards instead of forwards it can produce pain on intercourse. This position of the womb is found in 15 per cent of women, though not all have pain on intercourse.

### *Prolapse*

The womb can also fall down into the vagina and in some cases can appear at the opening of the vagina. There are several reasons for a prolapse. A few women have weak supports to the womb from their birth. Others have their natural support mechanisms severely weakened by childbirth, lifting heavy weights, or by repeated straining to pass hard bowel motions. There is a swelling and a sense of fullness in the vagina and the womb feels as though something is coming down inside. There are often urinary symptoms, backache, heavy periods or a discharge. If you have any of these in combination see your doctor at once.

### *Hysterectomy*

This is an operation to remove the womb. Once the scars are healed, the operation does nothing to impair intercourse but women say that it alters their orgasmic sensations, which is hardly surprising since the womb contracts during an orgasm. Because of this (amongst other reasons) some surgeons try to keep the cervix and lower part of the womb if possible and to remove the upper part only. Some women are so pleased to be rid of the heavy periods, or whatever caused them to have their womb removed, that they see the whole procedure as entirely welcome. Others mourn the loss of the organ and become depressed.

Hysterectomy is a very common procedure (about a quarter of a million women a year in the USA lose their uterus) and many operations are done unnecessarily. One advantage to having a hysterectomy is that contraception is no longer a concern. Periods cease, of course, but ovulation continues as normal (if the ovaries have been saved) until the menopause.

## *Sex and the bladder: honeymoon cystitis*

Sex can affect the bladder in a number of ways. One, widely known, upset is referred to as 'honeymoon cystitis'. This refers to the fact that the tissues around the entrance of the vagina are tight in women who have not had a baby and tend to push the thrusting penis towards the front wall of the vagina so 'bruising' the urethra and bladder. Urination may be painful after intercourse and cystitis, a true infection of the bladder, may follow. Organisms are milked up the urethra by the penis and because the female urethra is so short the germs soon reach the bladder where they multiply and eventually begin to irritate and inflame it leading to cystitis. Passing urine immediately after intercourse may overcome the problem by washing out the germs. Some women, however, find this difficult.

### *post-menopausal women*

Because the wall of the vagina thins after the menopause it makes it easier for germs to get into the urethra on intercourse leading to pain on passing water, urgent desires to pass water and infections of the urinary tract.

### *urinary tract infections (cystitis)*

Passing urine frequently and painfully is a sign of an infection of the urinary tract. Such infections are common in women and many are related to intercourse. Washing the vulva before sex, passing water after intercourse and less vigorous intercourse, perhaps in a new position, may help prevent the condition. Large quantities of fluid may also help cure an attack. Some women have similar symptoms in the absence of organisms in the urinary tract. Emotional or sexual factors may also be involved.

## *Incontinence (involuntary passage of urine)*

This is regarded as an embarrassing topic by women since leakages of urine can occur in intercourse. Up to a quarter of women are said to be affected at some time in their lives. Of these two thirds pass urine on penetration and one third at orgasm. This latter observation raises the question as to whether women can really ejaculate as the G-spot enthusiasts claim, or could it just be urine? Recent research in which tampons blocked off the vaginal opening and fluid was meticulously collected from the urinary passage showed that the vast majority of women who ejaculate do not lose urine. The liquid is very like prostatic fluid.

Some cases of urine leakage are due to stress incontinence and others to so-called detrusor instability – a local muscle weakness. Both conditions exist and give trouble at other times as well as during intercourse. Some of the sufferers are utterly miserable and anxious as a result of the symptoms.

**Stress incontinence** Some women leak a little urine when coughing, laughing or undertaking physical effort. The reason is that the circular muscle, at the base of the bladder, which is like a rubber band, is incompetent and when pressure rises inside the abdomen, as it does when doing these things, the muscle cannot prevent the flow of some urine from the bladder to the urethra. Various operations exist to relieve the condition. A tampon inserted before strenuous activity can prevent stress incontinence and pelvic muscle exercises can cure it.

**Detrusor instability** Learning to be dry in infancy consists of establishing the control of the conscious mind over the reflex tendency of the bladder to empty when it is full. Urination then occurs only at socially convenient times and places. In detrusor instability this control is lost and the urgent and frequent passage of urine results along with symptoms of stress incontinence in some women. Bladder retraining is used to relieve the condition. The woman keeps a urinary diary for a week showing when and where she urinated. She is then taught to delay emptying her bladder by initially encouraging her to wait for half an hour between pees. Gradually she is encouraged to wait for 3 to 4 hours. Various medicinal drugs may have to be used, especially for those in this group who are incontinent at orgasm.

More generally, it seems that urination does, or can, have more significance for women then men, at least in our culture. Reasons advanced by women to explain the situation have included the fact that the act is less 'tidy' in women than in men; that our culture makes female urination into a bigger secret and a greater shame than male urination; and that even in childhood girls begin to feel inferior because they are taught to pull down underclothing and crouch to urinate. Correspondence magazines such as 'Forum' have recently included many letters from women discussing the pleasures of standing to urinate, the delights of knicker wetting and the modifications necessary to male type urinals to make them suitable for use by women. Whilst all this may revolt some women it does suggest that, perhaps, the emotions attached to female urination are weakening – if only in a tiny sub-fraction of the population. If so more women with problems might feel able to come forward for treatment instead of putting up with them out of unnecessary shame.

## *Hairiness*

Western women spend millions of pounds and hours in removing hair they believe to be unsightly. Hair on the upper lip, on the limbs, around the nipples and up the abdomen and extensions of the pubic hair to the top of the thighs are all common but sometimes unwelcome. Men and women have about the same number of hairs – the real difference is in the type of hair at different locations and its visibility. Hairiness in women is occasionally the sign of the presence of disease but is mainly genetic in origin. Some men prefer hairy women and claim they are more sexy than others. Apart from electrolysis or periodic plucking of unwanted hairs, shaving is probably as good a solution as any for these women who are upset by the hair. Chemical depilatories are also very widely used. Indeed, female body hair removal is a multi-million pound business.

## *Monthly check-up*

Most women are understandably afraid of contracting breast cancer and it makes sense to detect a breast lump as early as possible so that it can be treated. It is best to feel your breasts for lumps regularly each month using the same routine a day or two after your period has stopped. Get to know how your breasts feel during other times of your menstrual cycle too and always report any suspicious lumps to your doctor. A delay could make treatment more difficult.

If you have an IUD pop a finger into your vagina each month the day your period stops to check that the tail of the device is still coming

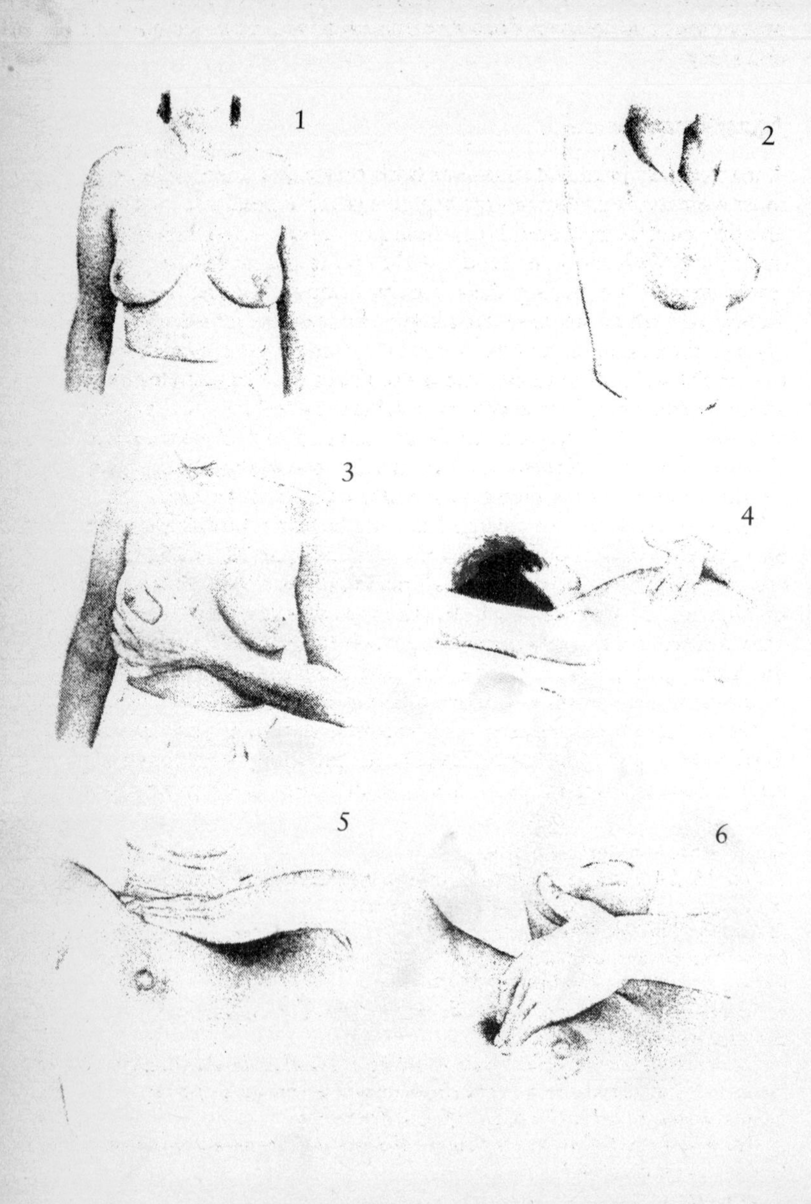
1
2
3
4
5
6

out of the cervix. If you can't feel it, take other contraceptive precautions and see your doctor at once to have a new one put in if necessary.

## *Mastectomy*

A mastectomy (removal of one or both breasts) is a major blow to most women's sexuality but the negative psychosexual effects can be greatly reduced by careful psychological preparation before the operation. With modern trends in the treatment of breast cancer fewer women are having their breasts removed so the problems associated with mastectomy are likely to be seen less frequently.

Once the operation and its immediate after-effects are over, worries about sex and sexuality often dominate a woman's emotions about mastectomy. Many women say that they feel less of a woman and the natural reaction in the early days is to feel unsexy and undesirable. Some women even feel strongly enough to say that they would rather have kept their breast and lived a few years less.

The one key factor to emerge from the large amount of research into this subject is that the role of the woman's partner is absolutely crucial. This is true of women of all personalities and of all levels of intelligence and education. Ideally, the woman's husband should be actively involved through the whole process right from the time when the lump is discovered. In this way the woman feels she has the support she needs and so fares much better.

There is no reason why sexual intercourse should not be resumed the day the woman gets home. There is no such thing as too much sex after a mastectomy and as long as the wound area is not hurt there are

Stages of breast self-examination:
*1) Stand in front of a mirror with your breasts bare. Look carefully to see if there is any change from your normal appearance.*
*2) Raise your arms and see how your breasts move. Are there any dimples or bulges that change their outline? Does each nipple point in the same axis as its breast? Is there any puckering of the skin?*
*3) Gently squeeze the nipples. If more than a drop of colourless fluid emerges, see your doctor.*
*4) Lie down on your back with a small pillow or towel under the shoulder of the breast you are feeling and work slowly round the breast, section by section, feeling with the tips of your fingers for lumps.*
*5) Don't forget to feel at the very edge of the breast tissue which can extend high up on the chest and*
*6) under the arm*

no problems. It is a matter of trial and error to find a position that is comfortable for the woman and then to use it until healing is complete.

Some women are afraid that their partners will leave them – the underlying fear being that a woman with one breast is not able to attract and keep a man. The facts are that men are no more likely to leave their partner after a mastectomy than otherwise and that most worry a lot about how to be supportive and helpful. Although most women try to hide their chests from their partners (especially in the early days), most men are not as upset by the loss of the breast as their women think they will be.

Some couples approach mastectomy with considerable existing psychosexual and relationship problems and for them the mastectomy may be the last straw. That this is unusual can be seen from one study which found that two-thirds of post-mastectomy women judged their emotional state to be excellent or very good. Women who fared best had been married longer, had found their partners (and doctors) more supportive and were pleased with the response from their children and the hospital staff.

Strange though it may seem, most women say that the worst time emotionally is immediately after the lump is discovered. Only one in seven women in one study found the immediate post-operative period the most difficult. Although most women have thoughts about mutilation, loss of femininity and death, several studies have found that the good news outweighs the bad. One study, for example, found that 71 per cent of women rated their husband's reaction to the mastectomy as extremely or very understanding; 76 per cent felt that the loss of the breast made no difference or had a positive effect on their sexual satisfaction or their ability to be orgasmic; and 60 per cent rated their overall post-mastectomy adjustment as 'very good'.

Many women have married after a mastectomy. If you are still having periods, you may find you will get the same sort of discomfort on your mastectomy side as you previously had at this time of the month.

Remember that talking about it with your husband, family and friends is bound to help. Slowly they will all come to terms with your new condition.

## Some things that can go wrong for men

### *One testicle instead of two*

Often a man who has two perfectly normal testes will appear to have only one. The other one will simply have popped into the canal above the scrotum and can be popped back down again just as easily. If a man has never had a testis down on one side he needs medical advice because experience shows that cancer is commoner in an undescended testis than in one which is down in the scrotum. If you can't feel two testes in your baby boy it is probably best to get an opinion from your doctor or baby clinic, but most doctors do not worry about an undescended testis much before the age of four or five.

### *Hydrocele*

This is a fluid-filled swelling around the testis and epididymis. It can be present at birth but is much more commonly found in older men. A torch held behind the mass makes it glow red and a doctor can drain it with a special needle or operate to cure it permanently. It rarely causes any sexual problems – other than discomfort during intercourse because of its size.

### *Priapism*

This is the medical name given to an erection which is painful and will not subside. It is rare and needs medical attention urgently. More common (but not commonplace) is the man who is repeatedly woken at night by a painful erection if he has already had intercourse or has masturbated. Repeated intercourse or masturbation does not seem to help. Time is the healer and no other cures are needed.

### *Phimosis*

This is a condition in which the foreskin is very tight in an uncircumcised boy or man. It can be caused by parents forcibly retracting and tearing their baby's foreskin, which then rejoins, with the formation of scar tissue, so tightening up the whole area. Infection behind such a foreskin can cause troublesome *balanitis*. Anything other than a moderate degree of phimosis needs treating (by circumcision) because intercourse can be painful.

## *Peyronie's disease*

This is a distressing condition the cause of which is unknown. It comes about as a result of a layer of fibrous tissue being laid down in the penis. This abnormal tissue can be felt as a firm plaque on the top surface of the penis. The man has painful erections with angulation of the erect penis itself. Intercourse is difficult and painful for the man or may be impossible. The pain usually passes off in a year or so and then surgery can be used to straighten the penis. Many other treatments such as vitamin E have been tried and may help.

Although men have fewer problems with their genitals than do women, a monthly self-examination is recommended. It is best carried out after a bath or shower in the standing position. The foreskin, if present, is fully retracted and the penis, including the opening of the urethra, inspected for any signs of discharge, ulcers, spots, inflammation, warts, or other lumps. Next, the scrotum is similarly examined and then each testis in turn by placing the thumb on top and the index and middle fingers below. By rolling the testis between them any lumps or changes in size, shape or tenderness can be detected. If any abnormality is found, consult your GP.

## *Prostate problems*

There are several conditions that can affect the prostate gland. It can become inflamed or cancerous but the commonest condition is a non-cancerous enlargement. This is very common in elderly men and produces a feeling of discomfort in the pubic area. Over some time it becomes difficult to empty the bladder fully, involving the man in frequent trips to urinate. This can be especially troublesome at night.

Eventually the bladder mouth can become shut totally off with a complete inability to pass water. This requires urgent medical attention.

If ever a man has any of the following symptoms it makes sense for him to see his doctor: difficulty in passing water, or a poor stream once he does start; a chronic sense of bladder fulness; impotence or premature ejaculation; pain on ejaculation; erections that occur spontaneously and without any cause; blood in the urine or semen; low back pain; getting up at night to pass water; and pain in the testes.

Modern research suggests that nutritional imbalances are at the heart of at least some prostate problems. It is worth trying Vitamin E, magnesium and zinc supplements, and reducing your intake of coffee and sugar.

## The effects of illness and drugs on sexual function

In our society we tend to equate sex with health and youth and assume that the ill and the handicapped are sexless. This simply is not true. Only during the most acute of illnesses do people go off sex, and increasingly doctors are realising that couples continue their sex lives wherever possible if they have chronic illnesses.

### *Heart disease and high blood pressure*

During intercourse the heart rate may double, as may the breathing rate, and the blood pressure rises too. There is considerable public concern that sexual activity with heart disease or high blood pressure is dangerous or even possibly fatal. Such deaths are in fact very rare and when they do occur they do so more commonly during extramarital intercourse.

Advice about sex after a heart attack varies enormously but it is

Intercourse after a serious illness: *This man is recovering from a heart attack. His wife is taking most of the initiative and is playing the active role.*

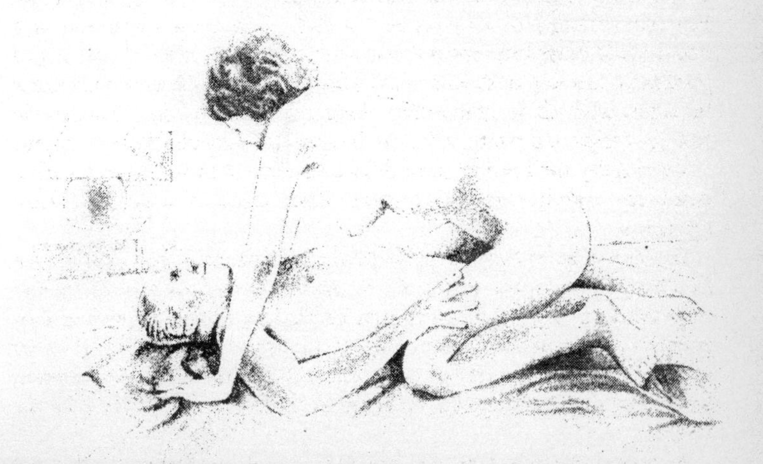

probably safe to resume sexual activities five to ten weeks after the heart attack unless the attack was exceptionally severe. One way to tell if you are ready is to see how you feel after a quick walk or after going up a couple of flights of stairs.

People with angina should take a tablet before intercourse and should ideally avoid sex immediately after a meal.

Even if one of these conditions makes one wary of returning to or carrying on with intercourse there are several half-way houses that can be tried which stop short of actual intercourse and its exertions.

Mutual masturbation relieves sexual tensions but is less strenuous. The next stage can include woman-on-top positions – when it is the man who is recovering – in which the woman makes most of the physical effort. Slowly a couple affected by heart disease can wean themselves back to normal sex life.

## *Drugs that alter sexual performance*

Many drugs are now known to alter the sex drive of both men and women but the most dramatic and well-proven effects are usually only noted in men because a woman can have intercourse even if she is not highly aroused.

Alcohol in moderation is said to enhance sexual responses, but is in fact a common cause for a temporary loss of potency.

These lists summarise some of the known sexual side-effects of drugs:

**Drugs interfering with ejaculation**

*Antipsychotic drugs*
Thioridazine (Melleril)
Perphenazine (Fentazin or Triptafen)
Trifluoperazine (Stelazine)
Haloperidol (Serenace)

*Antidepressant drugs*
Pargyline (Eutonyl)
Imipramine (Tofranil)
Amitriptyline (Tryptizol)
Clomipramine (Anafranil)

*Antihypertensive drugs*
Reserpine (Serpasil)
Guanethidine (Ismelin)
Methyldopa (Aldomet)
Debrisoquine (Declinax)
Bethanidine (Esbatal)
Guanoxan (Envacar)
Guanaclor (Vatensol)
Phenoxybenzamine hydrochloride (Dibexyline)

*Other drugs*
Heroin
Methadone

**Drugs interfering with erection**

*Antipsychotic drugs*
Fluphenazine (malicate)
Thiordazine (Melleril)
Benperidol (Anquil)
Chlorpromazine (Largactil)

*Mood-modifying drugs*
Lithium
Imipramine (Tofranil)
Protriptyline (Concordin)
Tranylcypromine (Parnate)
Desipramine (Pertofran)
Clomipramine (Anafranil)
Phenelzine (Nardil)
Amitriptyline (Tryptizol)

*Antihypertensive drugs*
Methyldopa (Aldomet)
Guanethidine (Ismelin)
Clonidine (Catapres)
Reserpine (Serpasil)
Guanoxan (Envacar)
Guanoclor (Vatensol)
Spironolactone (Aldactone)
Bethanidine (Estabal)

*Other drugs*
Clofibrate (Atromid-S)

**Drugs that interfere with female orgasm**

*Antidepressant drugs*
Phenelzine (Nardil)
Clomipramine (Anafranil)

Few drugs are known to affect female orgasm but common sense dictates that many that affect men could well affect women too.

## *Diabetes*

About half of all diabetic men eventually become impotent but this may not happen until their seventies or eighties. However, for the unlucky few, impotence is the first sign of diabetes. A middle-aged man who suddenly becomes impotent for no apparent reason should have his urine checked for sugar in case he has become a diabetic. A diabetic's sex drive is usually normal; it is only the ability to erect that is the problem. When caught early, careful management of the diabetes can improve things but in more serious cases a mechanical prosthesis may be needed. Diabetic women also experience sexual dysfunction and, as with men, there is no link between the severity of the disease and the onset of their sexual dysfunction.

Vaginal thrush is more common in diabetic women and this can cause uncomfortable sex or even an avoidance of sex altogether.

Some diabetic women find that their insulin requirements are raised when they become sexually active.

## *Brain damage*

Certain specific kinds of brain damage affect the sexual functioning of the brain and certain tumours can alter a person's sexual behaviour but this is rare.

## *Blindness*

This is, of course, no bar to sexual expression but it can be difficult for the blind to learn about their bodies and sex generally.

## *Arthritis*

As we grow older our chances of suffering from some kind of arthritis increase and osteoarthritis of the hip can severely impair a person's ability to have pain-free intercourse. About two-thirds of sufferers have intercourse difficulties. A hip replacement, of course, remedies the situation all round. It is interesting to point out here that many couples find that regular intercourse actually lessens their arthritic symptoms, though no one knows why. If you have a problem in this area talk to your doctor and see if he can get the pain better controlled with drugs if you cannot have an operation or while you are waiting for one.

Arthritis affecting other parts of the body (except the knees) usually has no effect on sex.

## *Colostomy, ileostomy and bowel surgery*

Having major bowel surgery and ending up with a colostomy or an ileostomy can have major psychological effects on the sex life of the individual and his or her partner. As well as this there are often very real neurological problems caused by the removal of key nerves along the bowel. Impotence and sexual dysfunction are very common after the removal of lower bowel cancers but surgery for non-malignant conditions produces far fewer problems.

An American study found that men were more supportive of their wives after such surgery than the other way round, but that women are more afraid of being unacceptable to their husbands. There are now 'ostomy' (stoma) nurses in most large hospitals who can advise those about to undergo such surgery about the problems and how to overcome them right from the beginning. There are also 'ostomy' clubs in most Western countries whose members have seen and heard it all before and can be very helpful and encouraging.

## *Sex and the handicapped*

The handicapped need love, affection and a chance to express their sexuality just like the rest of us. Sex education in the special schools that deal with various handicaps is at last beginning to take the sexuality of the handicapped seriously. Until recently it was a subject ignored even by those involved with the handicapped. Unfortunately, a lot of handicapped people live in situations or institutions where privacy is in short supply and this makes life even more difficult for them.

Girls who are physically handicapped (and especially the completely paralysed) start to menstruate very young (often as early as eight). Men with multiple sclerosis may become partially or completely impotent (60 per cent have an erection problem). Women with multiple sclerosis often have problems with orgasms because they feel tired and they may be advised against pregnancy because relapses are so common shortly after having a baby.

The mentally handicapped also have rights in this area and some are keen to be sexually active. With the trend towards community-based living (rather than hospital care) for the less severely handicapped, this demand will undoubtedly rise over the years. IUDs are the best method of contraception for mentally handicapped women whose intelligence level or unsatisfactory motivation would make other methods too risky.

## *Chronic diseases*

Any long-term (chronic) disease can exhaust the individual as can long-term drug therapy, hospital visits, treatment and so on. All of these can adversely affect the most sex-centred person, as well as those who were content with very infrequent sex before their trouble began. Many diseases actually cause a loss of libido (sex drive), as do many drugs; so if you think your sex life should be better, and you are suffering from a long-standing illness, discuss it with your doctor in case the two could be linked.

## *Strokes*

Far too little is known about the sexual problems of stroke patients, of whom there are many thousands in the UK alone. The trouble is that a stroke is a very complex business and results not only in physical weakness and loss of sensation but in mental and psychological changes too. This raises all kinds of anxieties about sexual performance and the physical problems often make physical sexual expression difficult even if the heart is willing. All of this can alter the way a couple relate to each other after a stroke, but physical closeness, other manifestations of love and sexual activities which are not genital-to-genital can work well. Loss of bladder and anal control is very upsetting, but many couples who really want to can find ways around these practical problems. Sex therapy can greatly help stroke sufferers and it can be useful to experiment with sex until the couple finds a way of living with the disability.

*Chapter 26*
# Sex in old age

Any account of ageing is bound to seem like a catalogue of physical decline but, as at all ages, a person's psychological state, flexibility and previous experience all affect the situation. Every age has its opportunities and there are people of both sexes who do not reach their full sexual potential until their fifties, sixties or, in some cases, even later.

Again, as at all ages, ill health can dominate the picture and is more common, though by no means inevitable, as age increases. The notion of remaining healthy and active, perhaps with medical assistance, as age advances is increasingly accepted as the norm. A continuing sex life is also seen as a part of this healthy and active life.

Although we could hardly claim that the services and money provided by the community for the care of its ageing population are over-abundant, poverty and a lack of suitable accommodation are not problems any longer for the majority of old people. Because of early rearing influences, some pensioners voluntarily enforce poverty on themselves by unnecessarily trying to economise and save, but this is often a manifestation of their personality rather than a necessity. Others, because of misguided pride, will not accept state help to which they are entitled and so are worse off financially than they need be. Some fail to take adequate care of themselves which could be a late expression of hidden rebellion against over-strict training during childhood or an expression of emotional despair.

Men who have lived for work or women who have lived their lives only in terms of their close emotional relationships may begin to feel that there is nothing left to live for when these come to an end.

Preparation for old age starts in childhood with the development of the capacity to accept and enjoy life. This involves keeping interested and interesting. Boredom kills. Productivity can continue, but perhaps in forms other than paid work. Some ageing people take up entirely new pursuits in fulfilment of long-held wishes – pursuits that the pressure of other work and family commitments prevented earlier in life. Many say they are busier in their sixties and seventies than ever before and that they enjoy life more as a result.

However, there are problems. One is our cultural attitude towards old age. At some point society sets the ageing individual aside from its main stream and a lifetime of experience, knowledge and wisdom can count for nothing or even be regarded as foolishness. The older generation is now an untapped and unrecognised national resource of great potential value to society although at the level of the family this may not be quite so true. Grandparents often make an essential contribution to child rearing, but because the world is changing so fast many feel out of touch with current views and practices in this field and this reduces their own feelings of value.

Another of our cultural attitudes that may cause problems is that towards sex. Many older people retain an interest in sex but fail to indulge it because they feel ashamed. Sex belongs to life, and its harmless expression, in appropriate forms, at all ages should be welcomed and accepted as normal.

One problem in this sphere is that even if ageing people escape the cultural pressures against sex and retain an interest in it which they want to express, they may not have a partner who is available, willing or able to indulge. As a result of higher death rates among men than among women of all ages, there is an increasing surplus of women as age advances.

It is all very well talking positively about sex in old age, but very substantial numbers of people (many more women than men) simply do not have the opportunity for any kind of sex life – and this can go on for twenty years or more. No other age group would tolerate it, so why should the elderly?

A part of sex education should be developed aimed at encouraging the younger generation to accept that the older generation are sexual, if only to prepare the young themselves for old age. The retention of sexual prowess and pleasure in old age helps to maintain a person's self-respect and morale and should be encouraged by all. In a society with sensible attitudes towards sex it would not be necessary to say any of this – it would be taken for granted.

The presence of all these complicating issues makes it difficult to disentangle psychological from physical effects influencing sex in the elderly, especially as the two interact anyway.

As at all ages, among the elderly it is the man who mainly controls the level of sexual intercourse, if only for the obvious reason that if he does not have an erection intercourse cannot occur. Information about the sexual behaviour of older men is somewhat sparse.

Although this curve looks a little gloomy, it has to be remembered that the figures are averages and there is a considerable variation

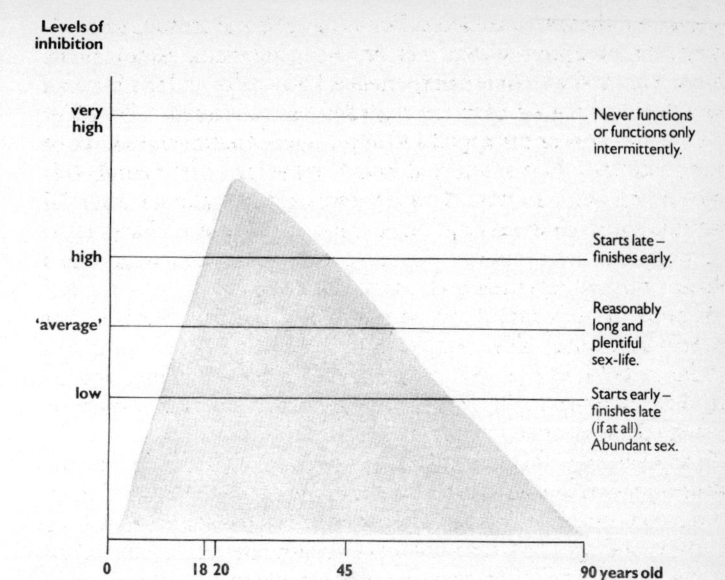


*Male sex drive through the years.*

either side of the mean. For example, one man of seventy was experiencing over seven orgasms a week. Also, there are signs that other factors influence the situation. One might be sexual boredom with the partner. A new partner or a new technique usually results in increased sexual activity, at least for some months. Of Kinsey's sample of over 6000 men almost 70 per cent had had experience with prostitutes. For the older men as a group, prostitutes were important in replacing other sources of sexual satisfaction. This may be a bit misleading because prostitution, at least in the USA, was as much a social as a sexual activity in the earlier years of this century.

Morning erections tend to continue, although with decreasing frequency, for years after the onset of impotence and this suggests that the man could have intercourse if his perceptions or circumstances were different. A further sign that elements of frustration may be involved is the fact that a third of fifty-year-olds were still experiencing occasional 'wet dreams' as was one man of eighty-six!

A more recent survey of over 1000 Danish men, who may not be representative of men in other countries, found that although a third of those in their nineties said they had an interest in sex and a third said they had morning erections, only 3 per cent had had intercourse in the previous year. The investigators found a considerable degree of reluctance to answer questions about masturbation, from which they deduced that guilt about it is widespread but about a quarter of men seventy-five to ninety-five years old did admit to it. So this survey again demonstrated that intercourse rates decrease faster than those of other sexual activities.

A recent in-depth investigation of nearly 200 men aged sixty to seventy-nine in the USA more or less confirmed these findings. It also confirmed the great differences between individuals. As a measure of sexual behaviour in the past it is interesting to note that for the whole group, the average age at first intercourse was around twenty-two years, with marriage at around twenty-seven and the numbers of sexual partners before the age of forty, three or four. Only a small percentage of the men regarded their partner as being sexually unattractive and the great majority regarded their marriage as being highly successful. Of the men who were least active sexually, some reported difficulties with erection and premature ejaculation, and this could be taken to prove that they wanted, no matter how unconsciously, to avoid intercourse. This could have led to a lack of interest on the part of their wives but, on the other hand, a lack of interest in sex on the part of the woman could have been the cause of the man's sexual problem in the first place.

What emerged from the findings was that those men who had been most sexually active in their early years remained the most active in their later ones. The most sexually active men still responded to the sight of nude women and were the least tolerant of prolonged sexual frustration. However, if men are not in contact with women their interest in sex slowly declines. A further interesting finding was that many men in the least sexually active group who had problems did not report much in the way of reduced self-esteem. A comparison of the most sexually active men with a group of men aged fifty to fifty-nine showed that many older men are as sexually vigorous as those fourteen to twenty years their junior.

It is worth commenting in passing that the sex life of older couples can be assisted or enhanced by the use of sex aids. Some devices have a physical benefit, while others have more of a psychological one, but either way they are worth considering as a means of overcoming declining interest, decreasing pleasure and some minor sex problems. Vibrators, and devices to help with erections may be particularly useful. Sex shops could do more to encourage the older generation to patronise them.

From about the age of forty, the hormone-producing cells in the testes decrease in number, so less of the male sex hormone testosterone is produced. Although there is a considerable variation between individuals, even in extreme old age, the amount of testosterone actively available in the body is around a third to a half of that in young men. The testes themselves become somewhat smaller and fewer sperms are produced. Nevertheless, men of almost any age can father a child if they can perform sexually. As age advances, the angle the erect penis makes with the trunk increases and erection is slower and needs more help from the partner. Pre-ejaculatory secretion decreases and ejaculatory spurts have less force.

## The menopause

For women, the sexual situation can be complicated by the menopause. This is another area in which physical and psychological factors interact. Some women welcome the menopause because it liberates them from the fear of pregnancy but its approach is viewed by many as the end of their sex life. Those who really believe that sex is only for babies often suffer badly, as do self-centred women who measure their personal worth by their sexual attractiveness.

Because the menopause often coincides with the departure of children from the home, a woman who has invested all her energies in loving and caring for her children loses her role at the same time as her sex life (in her view). As her husband, who on average is three or four years older than she is, may be becoming sexually uninterested or seeking new partners, additional stresses are added. If her husband is successful in his career, he may be even more involved in his work than in previous years and will be less available just when she needs him most. Understandably some women become anxious, critical and unhappy, which tends to alienate their partners and perhaps discourage them from sex.

Any social, personality and temperamental differences between the couple become more pronounced and some such couples divorce once their children have left home. Unless a woman takes steps to counteract it even her circle of women friends diminishes as they lose the common experience of rearing children. In such a state of mind her preoccupations are more likely to turn inwards and menopausal symptoms assume an importance greater than would otherwise have been the case.

A woman's ovaries begin to 'shut down' from her mid- to late thirties. The supply of available eggs gradually becomes exhausted and their quality declines. The pituitary gland increases its secretion of sex hormones in an effort to stimulate the ovaries but, when egg production finally stops supplies of oestrogen and progesterone fall.

Some women report a loss of sex drive after the menopause. In some this can be explained by the modest fall, of around 25 per cent, in testosterone (the sex-drive hormone of both sexes) but in others depression, a deteriorating relationship with her partner, sex-avoidance by him, or the belief that her sex life should have ended, may also be involved. There may be pain on intercourse, resulting from vaginal dryness and thinning of its lining, and this too can put a woman off sex.

As the menopause approaches, some women experience an increase in sexual interest and pubescent fantasies of the rape and prostitution type may occur. Extra-marital intercourse is not at all uncommon at this stage if a woman sees it as her last chance. Many women say that they have less intercourse than they want at this period of their lives. Masturbation rates often peak as the inhibitions taught in early life recede but in general, as with men, women tend to continue the habits of earlier years. However, although the intensity of sexual arousal may decrease around the time of the menopause orgasmic capacity in intercourse certainly does not. In fact, some women first experience orgasms in intercourse at this time of life.

Around the time of the menopause and afterwards women may be more likely to suffer from heart attacks. This is probably due, in the main to the reduction in oestrogen levels which previously protected them. But there are certainly other factors too. In a survey comparing 100 women who had suffered a heart attack (and survived – those who died were obviously not available for questioning) between the ages of forty and sixty with a similar group of women who had not, it was revealed that 60 per cent of the heart-attack group had either not been able to have orgasms during intercourse or no longer had intercourse because of their husband's incapacity, compared with only 24 per cent of the second group.

Similar evidence is available from studies of men suffering from heart attacks. Around two-thirds have been found to have had significant sexual problems before the onset of the attack.

From this and other research it seems reasonable to conclude that to the established practices for the avoidance of heart attacks – such as not smoking – we should add, for both sexes, the establishment of a successful sex life. Some investigators have also concluded that a good sex life in later years wards off mental deterioration.

Some older people with arthritis, which is increasingly common with age, find that their condition improves after intercourse. There is now some evidence to suggest that people who continue to practice and enjoy sex tend to live longer, but it is not possible to claim that sex itself makes for a longer life because it is equally possible that whatever factors promote a full sex life also promote a longer life.

The average age for the menopause is now around fifty. Those who start menstruating late tend to finish early: around 4 per cent do so in their early forties. Women of fifty-two and fifty-three have given birth to live babies – sometimes after a year or two without periods. Because of this, it is advisable to use some form of contraception for a year after the periods stop. The menopause lasts for between six months and three years.

Although all manner of symptoms are attributed to the menopause they fall into three groups, *vasomotor* leading to perspiration, hot flushes and night sweats; *metabolic* due to falling levels of oestrogen and resulting in thinning of the vaginal wall, a dry vagina and skin changes; and *psychological* including the loss of sex interest already mentioned, depression, lassitude, insomnia, loss of concentration, and irritability. Two more hidden consequences are the effects on the heart, mentioned above, and on the bones. Not all women experience a difficult menopause but it tends to be worse in smokers. For example, around a quarter of women are troubled by vasomotor symptoms.

The adverse effects on the vagina can be offset by oestrogen preparations used in the vagina and by using the vagina more in intercourse and/or masturbation. One small difficulty is that the partner can absorb oestrogen through the penis and in rare cases this can be sufficient to make his breasts enlarge. However, a side benefit of vaginal oestrogen is that the urinary problems which are common in older women are often relieved.

However, all the troubles can usually be controlled by hormone replacement therapy (HRT) which, as the name suggests, aims to make up for the reduction in production of female hormones. The topic is controversial but medical opinion is now turning towards the more extensive use of HRT. Tablets, usually, are taken by mouth and the oestrogen in them relieves the symptoms. However, there is a risk of cancer of the endometrium (lining of the womb) and to control this progesterone is added for 10 or more days each month. The progesterone also has a mild sedative effect and relaxes muscles. Women who cannot take oestrogen for one reason or another may be given progesterone only. Problems are that withdrawal bleeding (see page 203) usually occurs and appears to be like a normal period but does not indicate a return of fertility. Fluid retention and breast discomfort may also occur. Regular medical checks are necessary.

The psychological problems of the menopause are often alleviated as a result of increased self-esteem and happiness as the physical symptoms recede.

Most doctors believe that HRT, if used at all, should be restricted to the year or two after the menopause but some now believe the benefits to be so great that it should be continued to 65 or even older.

One benefit is the reduction in bone loss (osteoporosis) which occurs rapidly in the years immediately after the menopause. It afflicts a quarter of women between 55 and 65 and half of those between 65 and 75. The problem is to know which women will be affected. Women of short stature, with small bones, who had an early menopause, who are lean, or who have a family history of osteoporosis may be especially vulnerable.

Apart from causing the bend in the upper spine known as a dowager's hump, osteoporosis leads to bones being fractured easily and this is serious. Hip fractures (45,000 a year in the UK) are the most serious. They are increasing in frequency and a fifth of women suffering them are dead within six months. Oestrogen stops or reverses bone loss. For women not on HRT, increasing calcium intake, for example, by drinking more milk, does not help but those on HRT do benefit from extra calcium. Exercise is beneficial and post-menopausal women, whether on HRT or not, should make considerable efforts to keep fit and not fall into the trap of becoming inactive. Exposing the skin to sunlight also helps.

Women on HRT are a third less likely to die than women of their age not on HRT, but other factors may affect this statistic. Their chances of heart disease are reduced by two-thirds and of cancer of the endometrium by half. Cancers of the breast and ovaries may also be reduced. Women, after years of being on the Pill, might not want to face a fresh bout of pill taking at the menopause and at the moment their GP is unlikely to raise the topic. The benefits, though, are so great that more women than at present are likely to be asked to consider HRT in the future. Oestrogen has the added effect of maintaining pre-menopausal skin and body characteristics.

Although the topic is the subject of considerable debate and controversy, it is now widely agreed that men can also have a menopause. It is thought to affect around 15 per cent of men. A few even have not flushes. Psychological factors can also afflict men in their fifties and sixties as they realise they are not going to live for ever, that they have not fulfilled their earlier ambitions and dreams and that younger men can beat them in many ways. Obviously if both partners are suffering from bruised egos at this stage of their lives they can either mutually support each other or blame each other.

**The best sexual advice for ageing couples is as follows:**

1. Try to establish a good sex life before the effects of ageing set in.
2. Try to avoid losing the habit of intercourse as can happen so easily, for example after a period of enforced abstinence because of illness.
3. Be resourceful and imaginative in finding ways round problems as they arise, for example, with arthritis.
4. Continue having lots of physical contact even if you do not want to have intercourse as often as before.
5. Indulge in mutual genital stimulation.
6. Do not expect the man always to have an orgasm in self- or mutual stimulation or in intercourse.
7. Overcome any shame about the possible use of erotica and sex aids, which can add a new dimension at this time of life.
8. Expect some failures and do not be demoralised by them.
9. Seek medical advice for any condition that makes intercourse difficult or painful.
10. Ignore what people say about sex being only for the young.

*Chapter 27*

# Love

Although love and loving behaviour are common themes throughout this book, nowhere have we isolated them from their surroundings and looked at them separately. In a sense this fragmentary approach is inevitable because love is indefinable, means different things to different people (and even to the same people at different times of their lives) and subtly affects many of the areas of life we have covered.

## Mother and child love

Clearly there is a bond of vital importance between a young mammal and its mother, especially in the earliest days and weeks. This is true of human infants, though research into the subject is very difficult to carry out in an ethically acceptable way. But enough work has been done with babies who have been separated from their mothers in non-experimental situations for us to gauge the effects.

A baby must be cared for in order to survive and, like certain other animals, human mothers are genetically programmed to respond to their new-born offspring's behaviour. A baby continually tries to attract the mother's (and later the father's) attention to make sure that she is aware of his or her needs. As she cares for him or her in response to these needs, she'll talk to him or her, smile, cuddle and play. In return the baby will stop crying, listen intently, gaze at her face (and eyes in particular), keep quite still or sometimes kick in a certain way, and smile or coo at her.

At around three months, it is clear that the baby recognises his mother. He or she has an extra special smile for her and within a few months will cry when she leaves him or her, or if a stranger approaches. The baby is said at this stage to be 'attached' to his mother and treats her in a special way, clearly liking her more than anyone else. He is now in love with her and responds very badly to losing her as his love object. If his mother does not look after him or her, the baby becomes attached to whoever does. Whoever brings them up, babies form an attachment to one person in particular (if given the opportunity to) by between six and twelve months. Babies brought up in institutions by many caretakers can become confused and even emotionally deprived. This is why it is always best for one particular person to be responsible for a baby for much of the time.

It is well known that a baby can become attached to people other than his mother. Babies can, in fact, form multiple attachments. This is obvious, but can be forgotten when one talks in psychological jargon. However many people a baby is attached to, there is always a favourite (usually the mother). If she is not there, someone else will do and the baby will turn to the person next on the list of his own personal hierarchy – it may be his father, sister, granny or nanny, for example. Although they are 'second best' in his or her attachment league they are still very important to him or her.

When babies or young children are with several people to whom they are attached, they automatically choose to be with the one they are most attached to. For instance, if a baby is tired or falls over and both his or her mother and nanny are there, he or she will want to be comforted by the mother if he or she is most attached to her. One thing is certain and that is that a stranger will not do. A baby does not become instantly attached to someone new but takes time to get to know them.

It is the emotional aspects of the baby's attachment experience that are most important and this is true of all love-bonds. One person may take physical care of him or her – feeding, washing and keeping him or her warm, for example – but if another person is the one who mainly reacts in a loving way (even if only for a short time each day), the baby will become attached to that person. Active and responsive interaction with a baby is what counts and sensitive responsiveness to the quality most likely to further attachment. Usually of course, the person who gives a baby this also meets his or her physical needs, besides comforting him through anxiety, fear, illness and tiredness.

It is through a baby's first love with the person to whom he or she is attached that he or she learns to love other people. The more adequately the emotional needs are met, the better able he or she will be to respond lovingly to others in turn.

A child can become attached (or remain attached) to someone even though he or she may treat him or her very inconsistently or even harshly. This explains why a baby or young child who is sometimes physically or emotionally hurt by the mother will still cling to her when in the company of others. It seems that it is better for children to have someone to be attached to, however he or she treats them, than to have no one special to call their own.

Almost all of this attachment form of love arises because young babies rely totally on their mothers (or other close people) to answer their needs and cravings. This makes it very important, in our view, that such needs are met lovingly, unconditionally and promptly by the attached adult figure, so that the baby thinks well of the world from day one of life. Although it is extremely difficult to prove what the effects of poor mother-baby love are in later life, and there is little doubt that even quite severe harm in this area can be repaired in later childhood, we feel safe in stating that a really responsive, loving relationship must be the best way of starting off life.

It is fairly obvious that babies can either grow up knowing they are loved and loving someone else or they can grow up with feelings of anger, resentment, frustration and sadness because they have not experienced such love. This is a totally dependent form of love and one which most people can easily understand. It also raises another important concept when discussing love and that is *caring*.

One way in which we can recognise love (even if we cannot define it) is to watch people's behaviour. This shows that whatever they love, they care for. It matters to them what happens to it. They are prepared to make sacrifices for it. They jealously guard it in the face of threats and they want the best for it. So it is with mother-love. A mother knows all these feelings and recognises them as a part of the complex emotion we call love. The baby cannot, of course, realise such things but knows, even before he can express himself, what love means to him.

Every love experience in life to some extent takes us back to our first childhood experience. Indeed, it is the very aspect of love that many people find so difficult. In every adult loving relationship there are seeds of child-like love, yet many adults fight them, thinking that adult love, linked as it so often is to genitality, is something apart.

## The evolution of love

Most people are quite happy with concepts of mother-baby love and have no difficulty accepting such notions. However, love clearly does not stand still – it changes and matures. In the mother-baby relationship love is both given and received by both parties, to their mutual satisfaction. This clearly has to happen biologically or mothers would not feel sufficiently motivated to put up with the real and provable problems of rearing a totally dependent little baby or young child. Babies are, at first, totally self-centred – all they want is to have their needs satisfied. This changes, though, over the first few weeks and months, so that the mother and baby become a mutually rewarding love unit.

In the Oedipal phase of young childhood, this love is vested in the opposite-sex parent, at least to some extent, until eventually in early adolescence the opposite-sex parent is de-loved as teenagers invest their loving feelings in themselves. There is abundant clinical experience to show that if the teenager does not negotiate this stage successfully he or she can never truly love another person of the opposite sex and this can lead to the disturbed man-woman relationships we have described elsewhere (such as the mistress-madonna syndrome).

In late adolescence teenagers seek an emotional object to love and in our society combine this with a sex-object. So it is that love and genital sex start to grow together. Now the masturbating, self-centred kind of love gives way to a more mature type of love. Around this time many adolescents experience a generalised kind of love.

## Generalised love

This is an immature, late-adolescent phenomenon but one (like the others) which can last throughout life in certain people. Some never get beyond it at all. Such love is almost totally idealistic (not romantic) and is sometimes centred around good causes, concepts of freedom, political ideologies, and similar concerns. At this stage a youngster will throw a brick through an embassy window to protest at a country's treatment of whales or whatever. His or her sense of outrage on behalf of the underprivileged knows no bounds, and in the name of love all kinds of unloving acts are possible.

The late adolescent loves everybody – this is probably why there is such an interest in socialism at this age. Social wrongs are seen as totally unacceptable and the young person sets out to put the world to rights.

One way of looking at this not-altogether-amicable phenomenon is to see late adolescents as groping to find a way to express their love and need for love in relation to others. Because they are still insecure in their capacity to give and receive love they generalise it to any individual or group who seems oppressed. Because such love is not inter-personal (as adult love is) the adolescent is freed from the dangers of rejection, yet able to convince him- or herself that he or she is a decent, loving person. Unfortunately, elements of hatred also intrude and those who are perceived as the oppressors are attacked to show how loving the late adolescent really is. This is probably the stage in life when love and hate are most poignantly felt, but by no means are these reactions solely found in adolescents.

Love is an ambivalent business and most psychiatrists and psychoanalysts find that hate is never far from loving feelings. The very fact that we protest our love so much often underlines feelings of hate we cannot cope with.

Out of all these complex emotions of late adolescence grows love for another individual.

## Love for another individual

It is this that most people call love in everyday speech but clearly true love is much more complex. Love at this adult stage brings together a love-object and a sex-object. This needs a little explanation. An 'object' in psychological jargon is a thing with which an individual is able to indulge his instinctual needs. A mother can therefore be a love-object to a baby and a wife a sex-object to a husband. When adults are in love, if they are mature, their love-object and their sex-object is one and the same person.

However, for many these two are separate. Some men, for example, cannot have a meaningful sexual relationship with someone they love (their wife, for instance) because they see her as untouchable. Such men (and there are many of them) will be able to have perfectly enjoyable sex outside marriage but not within it. Most, if not all, of this attitude is, of course, in the man's unconscious – he does not realise that it is happening unless it is pointed out to him. Others see their partners purely as sex-objects and have little or no love-object relationship with them. Such a couple can be happy loving their children, their home, their possessions, or whatever, and enjoy each other purely as sex-objects.

The ideal marriage blends the two in perfect harmony to satisfy both the childhood craving for love and the adult craving for sex.

The thing to remember is that, whatever sex books may suggest, sex alone is never enough. We all need loving 'rewards' in life from one source or another. Psychologists call such rewards 'strokes' and say, quite rightly, that we all need 'stroking' throughout our lives.

Adults who love each other stroke each other (physically or metaphorically) as much as they need and a good relationship is built up of physical and psychological strokes that demonstrate the partners' love for each other. This begins to explain why people have such different ideas of what loving someone means. Many people with marital problems say, 'If he (she) *really* loved me they would/

wouldn't do . . .' But the partner may not realise that this is the definition of love to which they are supposed to be adhering.

Communication is vital within any loving relationship because each of us is unique and we all need to get our strokes in different ways. Some want all their strokes to be physical and require an active sex life as a proof of the other's love. Others want praise, outward signs of affection, practical signs of love, and so on, as their sources of strokes. In a short chapter such as this we cannot possibly do anything more than scratch the surface of this subject, but interested readers should examine their lives to see what they like best in the form of strokes and then discuss with their partners why they are not getting them – if they are not. The giving and receiving of strokes is the hallmark of mature adult love.

The final stage of love expands one's love for an adult to a love of all mankind.

## Love of all humankind and the whole world

The Ancient Greeks saw this as the highest plane of love. From the security of having been loved as a baby and child, from loving oneself and being confident that one is lovable, and from having a mature love for another adult comes the ultimate – the maturity of love that enables an individual to extend all these feelings to mankind in general. This is no longer an adolescent 'change the world' form of love but one forged from the experience that life cannot and will not go the way you want it to; that everyone has their rights and points of view; and that yours have to fit in with those around you. At this stage you can love those that persecute you; you can turn the other cheek and no longer retire hurt or angry when the world refuses to go your way. Such love is the Christian love of the New Testament in which one loves one's neighbour as oneself. People in this stage of love really *do* change the world and contribute to it. The mature adult at this stage expresses his or her general love in specific ways – often with powerful effects.

## Displacement of love

As we grow through our teens and early twenties we may think at various times that we are in love with or even 'love' several members of the opposite sex. Sooner or later we realise that we and this particular person are not right for one reason or another, and we part.

This causes real grieving on occasions and certainly most of us feel unhappy or depressed, at least temporarily.

It is a vital part of growing up and maturing psychosexually that we *do not* marry our first love object after puberty – it would usually be disastrous if we were to do so. This then implies that we have to be able to accept the loss of a loved one and live to fight another day. This, of course, applies not only to love-sex objects but also to the loss of relatives, parents, or even pets. Throughout life people's love-objects are withdrawn from them (by death or divorce for example) and most grieve their loss. At this time the affected person says to him- or herself, 'I'll never have another husband/dog daughter/ mother like that again', and of course they are right because each person and animal is unique. However, Nature heals this wound over some years – depending on the individual's personality and the nature of the relationship involved – and they are soon on the way to investing their love in someone else.

In a sense the original love for the love-object is displaced on to the new one, because, as we have seen, we all need to love and be loved. This primitive, instinctual drive leads many people to rush into the search for a new love-object after the loss of their original one and such people often choose someone very similar to the last one. In this way the lost love-object never dies (or disappears, in the case of divorce) – they live on in the remaining person's memory, yet may be related to through the 'new' love-object.

Those who have invested an enormous amount of love in a person who subsequently dies or leaves often tell how they never really get over the loss but simply put on a brave face for the world and even to a new partner. Such a reaction can become troublesome to some people because they hanker after one *perfect* love-object (even if during the object's time with them things were far from perfect), idealise the past and they cannot step into the future because they fear that no one will ever match up to the lost love-object.

But where does all this leave the kind of love that story books talk about? We have looked at romantic love in Chapter 6. Let us look here at 'being in love'.

## Being in love

'Falling in love' or 'being in love' are strange experiences with which most of us have at least a passing acquaintance, and they do not necessarily have anything to do with the types of love we have already been discussing.

The person who is 'in love' has a fairly well recognised collection of signs and symptoms – in fact, some people have likened the condition to an illness and speak of people being 'sick with love'. The signs of the 'illness' are restlessness, agitation, an irregular heartbeat, a raised blood pressure and pulse rate, clammy palms, sudden flushes, a loss of appetite, poor sleep, an inability to think straight, extreme mood swings, and even hallucinations.

Is it any wonder that the newly in-love feel so strange and confused? Such feelings are commonplace, especially in the young whom we condition to expect them.

Although women tend to fall in love earlier and to have more 'attacks' before the age of twenty, once past this age men continue to fall in love while women seem relatively immune. In one survey women were found to consider it quite reasonable to marry an otherwise suitable partner without being love-sick. Another study found that women are much tougher than men when it comes to breaking up (they 'de-love' men quicker than men 'de-love' them); and that they were much more likely to report nostalgia, depression and loneliness afterwards. Also see Chapter 12.

The most vulnerable time for falling in love is during adolescence and teenagers whose parents are divorced, those at odds with their parents or authority in general and those with poor self-esteem are most at risk. In later life wars and other socially stressful events tend to make people profess love for each other, perhaps as a bid for reassurance or biological survival.

Falling in love is more common in men during the mid-life crisis, in women just before the menopause and in those facing retirement or redundancy. In fact research has found that situations that increase the body's adrenalin make people more inclined to attach themselves to each other.

Unfortunately, in our Judaeo-Christian culture, 'being in love' has become a cultural essential for intercourse. We would certainly be happy to go along with any argument that linked intercourse to real love, but not necessarily to 'being in love'. Unfortunately, for the young, the three are almost indistinguishable. They think true love is what they are feeling and, whatever their parents say, by way of guidance, love-sickness clouds their judgement and hampers rational decisions. If only we could separate falling in love from copulation and intercourse the world might be a happier and more stable place but several hundred years of cultural conditioning cannot be undone overnight.

## Jealousy

It is impossible to think of love without jealousy – a wholly negative emotional state in which the sufferer becomes anxious, suspicious and angry in response to real or imagined threats to the love-bond between him or her and another. Some degree of sexual jealousy is probably normal and it has been extensively studied and copiously represented in literature over the centuries. Such normal jealousy probably plays a part in holding couples (and their families) together and probably stops errant partners from indulging their sexual whims more than they otherwise would. It can, of course, work the other way and turn homes, in the words of one expert, 'into hells of discord and hate'. Marital sexual jealousy can be very dangerous indeed and men are more dangerous than women because of their greater physical strength and aggressiveness. Sexual jealousy affects both homosexual and heterosexual couples and can drive people to commit crimes of violence and even murder.

Jealousy is a strange emotion because it has a large component of self-pity and selfishness to it. In jealousy there is often more self-love than love. Any situation that makes one of the partners feel at a disadvantage in the struggle to obtain or keep a mate predisposes the handicapped person to sexual jealousy. Impotence on the part of the husband and frigidity on the part of the wife and a marked disparity between the sexual appetites of the couple are often predisposing factors.

There are perfectly well-recognised psychological and medical causes for sexual jealousy too. For example, some forms of mental subnormality and certain sorts of brain damage are known to cause it. Drunkenness makes people jealous; as do cocaine and amphetamines. During pregnancy, in the post-natal period and around the menopause women often feel jealous even when there is no reason for them to do so. This could be hormonal in origin but is more likely to come about because at these times women feel disadvantaged in the sex market in comparison with other women.

Often jealousy is a sign of inferiority in the complaining (jealous) partner. He or she is threatened because of the possible loss of his or her spouse's love. This often means he or she has no confidence and sees every man or woman as a threat to the relationship.

## Love and commitment

Although we can love many things and many people, most of us put our one-to-one love relationship on a rather special pedestal and try to preserve it. This is important because it is probably the most powerful emotion in our adult lives and is the glue that holds the family unit together. We see all around us what happens when this glue gets weak – families fall apart in fragments. Although most of us would like to see our one-to-one relationship as the perfect blending of love-object and sex-object, for all but a minority this simply is not a reality. In our society we are 'allowed' lots of love-objects but only one sex-object within marriage. This creates problems for millions of people who do not want to threaten their love-bond for their spouse yet are not content with only one sex-object. So what can they do?

There are no simple answers but discreet adultery has always been *an* answer. There are, needless to say, considerable dangers to this approach and many people prefer to relate to their sex-objects in fantasy during masturbation rather than in reality. Clinical experience shows that people who have multiple fantasies of different members of the opposite sex are more likely really to enjoy the opposite sex than are the bedroom cowboys who misuse the opposite sex in reality. Everyone wants to be happy, to love and to be loved, but every deal in life has a price and marriage is no exception. Other men and women exist in the world around the loving, married couple and they have to be dealt with. Each individual will have to find his or her own way of coping with this problem and we have given several hints and tips in the book. Most women want and need clear lines of commitment and are very sensitive to any signs of withdrawal of love. Women appear to be much more love-dependent than are men – even little girls demonstrate this – and this makes them vulnerable to losing love. True, they can build up the 'strokes' they need from other sources, including their children, but deep down most women want a loving, secure relationship at the heart of it all.

Many marriages get to the stage in which the individuals are separately counting the cost of their loving commitment to one another. The one who receives too few strokes is vulnerable to an extra-marital affair.

Unfortunately, many people look for unattainable and unrealistic perfection within their marriage, demanding perfection of their spouse when they are not themselves perfect and forgetting the simple fact that everybody is a package deal. You cannot buy life in units of perfection – life is really only a heap of things that have fallen together in a particular way that you are trying to make the best of.

From the point of view of attachment, a mature adult is one who can both give and receive love. Life, to be successful, depends on maintaining a balance of dependence on and independence from others.

A mature person can ask for love when he or she needs it and, knowing he or she will get it, feels confident to give love to others. It is difficult and probably impossible to extend love to others in a mature way if one has not received it or is receiving none oneself. To this giving and receiving of attachment love, genitality is added in adulthood and this further deepens and strengthens the loving bonds.

There is no more an 'ideal love' than there is an ideal marriage. We are all complex, ever-changing beings whose ability to give and receive love varies from day to day and from year to year. What a shame it is that more couples do not realise this as they cast around the sexual arena, or go for professional help in an effort to improve their lot when in reality what they already have is potentially pretty good.

Perhaps the final thought should be along these lines.

*In matters of love – and for that matter, sex – don't commit the grievous error of making the best the enemy of the good. Remember that the ideal doesn't exist in this world.*

# Useful addresses

All the addresses and telephone numbers on the following pages were checked at the time of going to press, but it is quite possible that some of them will have changed by the time you read them. If you have difficulty in contacting a particular organisation discuss the matter with your local Citizens Advice Bureau who will be able to suggest an alternative organisation or might even help you with a new address and telephone number.

## General help and advice

**Association of Sexual & Marital Therapists**
c/o Dr C. M. Duddle, Student Health Centre, University of Manchester, Manchester M13 9QS.
A multi-disciplinary professional organisation which, if you send an s.a.e. will tell you the name of your nearest sex therapist or clinic.

**British Association for Counselling**
37A Sheep Street, Rugby, Warwickshire. Tel 0788 78328
Will provide a list of local counselling and advisory centres that can help with sex, drugs, accommodation and other problems. Send £1.50 to above address.

**Citizens Advice Bureaux** (CAB)
These can be found in most towns and cities. Telephone numbers in local phone books. They give free, confidential advice on all kinds of subjects and will tell you where to find other specialist organisations in your area.

**National Council for Civil Liberties**
21 Tabard Street, London SE1. Tel 01 403 3888
A vigorous group that campaigns to safeguard the rights and freedoms of the public. Gives free and confidential advice on many areas including drugs, sex, homosexuality, dealing with the police, legal aid and so on.

**Parents Anonymous for Distressed Parents**
(Life Line) 6 Manor Gardens, London N7. Tel 01 263 8918
A self-help organisation run by parents who have battered their babies, for those who fear they might batter or who actually have battered their babies.

**Release**
1 Elgin Avenue, London W9. Tel 01 377 5905; 24-hour emergency service 01 603 8654
Provides free advice and information on birth control, abortion, single parents, marriage, legal, personality and personal problems. Can also help with names and addresses of organisations local to you.

**Samaritans**
An organisation mainly to help the lonely, desperate and suicidal. Look up local branch in telephone directory. Telephone advice and counselling in complete confidence.

## Education

**Advisory Centre for Education (ACE)**
18 Victoria Park Square, Bethnal Green, London E2. Tel 01 980 4596
A valuable source of information about all educational matters. Will help if you are pregnant and under school-leaving age, if you are expelled from school etc. Advice free. Phone or write.

## Health

**Community Health Councils (CHCs)**
Usually on your local high street in or over a shop. Look up telephone number in local directory. Will advise on your medical rights, how to complain about the Health Service, where to go for help on abortions, contraception, VD and drug problems, among other things.

**Health Education Council**
78 New Oxford Street, London WC1. Tel 01 631 0930
The country's main source of health education information, research and materials. Has free leaflets on VD, personal hygiene, sexual development, contraception, drugs and many other interesting areas. Look up local branch in your local telephone directory or contact the main address above.

**Patients' Association**
18 Charing Cross Road, London WC2H 0HR. Tel 01 240 0671

A pressure group which acts for patients who have complaints against the Health Service or for those who want to know where to get medical treatment for a specific illness. Many useful leaflets and books.

**Sexually Transmitted Diseases Special Clinics**
For address of local VD clinic talk to your general practitioner; look up in phone book under venereal disease or VD, or phone your local hospital and ask for the Special Clinic. Sometimes these clinics are now called STD clinics.

**Women's National Cancer Control Campaign** (WNCCC)
1 South Audley Street, London W1. Tel 01 499 7532
Provides information on cancer and its treatment. Free leaflets on checking for breast cancer and other interesting topics.

## Sex Therapy Clinics in the UK

**Many of these clinics are funded by the National Health Service or are supported by charities. A few of them are private clinics, so it is wise to check the fees before making an appointment. Hospital clinics will want a referral letter from your doctor.**

**London Area**

Ante-natal Tower Block, North Middlesex Hospital.
Tel 01 807 3071

Caryl Thomas Clinic, Harrow Weald. Tel 01 863 7004

Cassel Hospital, Richmond. Tel 01 940 8181

Charing Cross Hospital, W6. Tel 01 748 2040

Family Planning Clinic, Stuart Crescent Health Centre, N22.
Tel 01 889 4311

Hammersmith Hospital, W12. Tel 01 743 2030

The Institute of Behaviour Therapy, N2. Tel 01 346 9646

Lincoln Memorial Clinic for Psychotherapy, SE1. Tel 01 928 7211

London Centre for Psychotherapy, NW3. Tel 01 435 0873

London Institute for the Study of Human Sexuality. Tel 01 373 0901

Margaret Pyke Centre, W1. Tel 01 734 9351

Marie Stopes Clinic, W1. Tel 01 388 0662

Marital Difficulties Clinic, Royal Free Hospital, NW3.
Tel 01 794 0500

Marital Sexual Therapy, Croydon. Tel 01 680 1944

Marriage Guidance Council Clinic, Kingston upon Thames.
Tel 01 549 3318

Marriage Research Centre, Central Middlesex Hospital, NW10.
Tel 01 965 5733, ext 2309

Maudsley Hospital, SE5. Tel 01 703 6333

Middlesex Hospital, W1. Tel 01 636 8333

Netherne Hospital, Coulsdon. Tel Downland 56700

Psychosexual Clinic, University College Hospital, WC1.
Tel 01 387 9300

Queen Charlotte's Maternity Hospital, W6. Tel 01 748 4666

Raymede Health Centre, W10. Tel 01 960 0942/3

Rosemary Avenue Clinic, Enfield. Tel 01 367 2095

Psychiatric Research Unit, Atkinson Morley's Hospital.
Tel 01 946 7711

St Mary's Hospital, W2. Tel 01 725 6666

St Thomas's Hospital, SE1. Tel 01 928 9292

West London Hospital, W6. Tel 01 748 3441

Westminster Hospital, SW1. Tel 01 828 9811

The Whittington Hospital Family Planning Clinic. Tel 01 272 3070

Women's Psychosexual Problem Clinic, Elizabeth Garrett Anderson Hospital, NW1. Tel 01 387 2501, ext 219

York Clinic, Guy's Hospital, SE1. Tel 01 407 7600, ext 3425

## Sex counselling for young people

There are Brook Advisory Centres and Youth Advisory Centres in many towns and cities. Check with your local town hall or Citizens Advice Bureau for the nearest centre.

### Brook Advisory Centres

**Birmingham**

City Centre. Tel 021 643 5341
Handsworth. Tel 021 554 7553
Saltley. Tel 021 328 4544
York Road. Tel 021 455 0491

**Coventry, West Midlands**
Coventry and Warwickshire Hospital. Tel 0203 412627

**Liverpool, Merseyside**
Bold Street. Tel 051 709 4558

**London**
Islington. Tel 01 272 5599
Kennington. Tel 01 735 0085 (Wednesdays and Saturdays only)
Lewisham Hospital. Tel 01 703 9660
Shoreditch Clinic. Tel 01 739 8351
Tottenham Court Road. Tel 01 323 1522
Walworth. Tel 01 703 9660

### Youth Advisory Centres

These are charities with teams of trained staff (both medical and non-medical) who see people aged from thirteen to twenty-five with any problem at all. They are usually free if you live in the area.

Battersea YAC. Tel 01 720 9409
Bechenham YAC. Tel 01 650 0125, 7–9 pm
Open Door, Hornsey Young People's Consultation Service.
Tel. 01 348 5947
Westminster YAC. Tel 01 969 3825
Kentish Town YAC. Tel 01 267 4792

## Pregnancy and sexual problems

Many of the addresses given in the section immediately preceding may well also be able to help on pregnancy and sexual problems.

**Association for the Improvement in Maternity Services (AIMS)**
21 Iver Lane, Iver, Bucks. Tel 0753 652781
A self-help, campaigning organisation that believes that childbearing couples should be treated as normal, responsible adults capable of making their own decisions relating to childbirth and that individual parental choices in the matter should be respected. Useful regular newsletter available.

**British Pregnancy Advisory Service**
Austy Manor, Wootton Wawen, Solihull, West Midlands, B95 6DA.
Tel 05642 3225
A non-profit-making charitable organisation offering pregnancy tests, counselling, birth control, pregnancy and abortion advice in many major towns and cities. Geared to young people and their problems. Telephone number in your local book.

**Brook Advisory Centre**
233 Tottenham Court Road, London W1. Tel 01 323 1522
An organisation giving advice on birth control and sexual problems. It also offers counselling services for young people. There are centres in Birmingham, Bristol, Coventry, Edinburgh, London and Liverpool. Consultation and birth control supplies are free at most centres but a fee is charged for pregnancy testing and infection testing at some centres. Contact by phone, writing or by walking in.

**Family Planning Association (FPA)**
27–35 Mortimer Street, London W1. Tel 01 636 7866
Look up in your local telephone book for your local FPA. Provides free and confidential advice and information on birth control, sexual problems, abortion, cervical smear testing and pregnancy testing. Many useful leaflets, posters etc on all aspects of sexual relationships.

**Family Planning Association of Northern Ireland**
47 Botanic Avenue, Belfast, B7. Tel Belfast 325488
Runs twenty-two clinics in Northern Ireland providing the same services as the British FPA.

**Grapevine**
416 St John Street, London EC1. Tel 01 278 9157
A free sex information and advice service for young people. Offers support and counselling for sexual and personal problems and works in schools, youth clubs and community groups.

**Irish Family Planning Association**
15 Mountjoy Square, Dublin 1. Tel Dublin 744133
Provides information and advice on birth control, pregnancy testing and sexual problems. Also a pregnancy counselling service.

**Marie Stopes Memorial Clinic**
108 Whitfield Street, London W1. Tel 01 388 0662
A private Well Women's Clinic giving expert advice on birth control, pregnancy testing, abortion and sexual problems. Also does vasectomies. Modest charges.

**National Childbirth Trust**
9 Queensborough Terrace, London, W2. Tel 01 221 3833
An organisation devoted to improving women's experiences of birth. It also tries to increase women's knowledge about childbirth and related topics and runs classes on breathing in labour, gives friendly advice ante-natally on all aspects of childbirth and breastfeeding and

also offers post-natal support. Trains ante-natal teachers and is active in schools. Encourages fathers to take part. Many useful leaflets and book list.

**National Marriage Guidance Council**
Herbert Gray College, Little Church Street, Rugby, Warwickshire. Tel 0788 73241
Runs clinics for couples over sixteen (whether they are married or not) with sexual, marriage or relationship problems. Will also see the single, homosexual or indeed anyone with personal and inter-relationship problems. Look up nearest branch in local telephone book.

**Pregnancy Advisory Service**
13 Charlotte Street, London W1. Tel 01 637 8962
A London-based charity which provides the same service as the British Pregnancy Advisory Service.

## Adoption, fostering, single parents

**Ally**
Dominican Priory, Upper Dorset Street, Dublin 1. Tel Dublin 740300
A service for single pregnant girls. Runs a family placement scheme so that girls can live with a friendly family which they are pregnant. Free after-care and advice.

**British Agencies for Adoption and Fostering**
11 Southwark Street, London SE1. Tel 01 407 8800
A source of information and advice about adoption and fostering. Useful leaflets and addresses of adoption and fostering agencies in your area. Arranges families for children with special needs.

**Catholic Protection and Rescue Society**
30 South Anne Street, Dublin 2. Tel Dublin 779664
Provides help for single pregnant girls and care for babies in temporary residential and nursery care. Also arranges adoptions. Free and confidential.

**Cherish**
2 Lower Pembroke Street, Dublin 2. Tel Dublin 682744
For girls who want to keep their babies. Also offers pregnancy counselling service advice and accommodation during and after pregnancy.

**Gingerbread**
35 Wellington Street, London WC2. Tel 01 240 0953 (Also at 39 Hope Street, Glasgow G3. Tel 041 248 6840)
A self-help group for one-parent families with 300 branches throughout the UK.

**Life**
Tel 0926 21587 (Head office) or 01 487 4776 (London counselling service)
Offers a free and confidential counselling service to women and girls with unplanned or unwanted pregnancies so as to help them avoid abortion. Life's pregnancy care service extends all through pregnancy, the birth and for as long after the birth as is needed. There are fifty-two 'Life Houses' in the UK, where mothers and babies can be accommodated, and there are forty-three full-time centres.

**National Association for the Childless**
318 Summer Lane, Birmingham, B19 3RL. Tel 021 359 4887
An organisation devoted to helping the childless and supplying information to others on the subject. Useful book list and leaflets.

**National Council for One-Parent Families**
255 Kentish Town Road, London NW5. Tel 01 267 1361
Helpful advice for all single parents. Will put you in touch with organisations, social workers, etc in your area. Also confidential advice for single pregnant girls.

**Parent to Parent Information on Adoption Society**
Lower Boddington, Daventry, Northants. Tel 0327 60295

**Scottish Council for Single Parents**
13 Gayfield Square, Edinburgh EN1 3NX. Tel 031 556 3899
Advice for lone parents and single pregnant girls.

**Single Handed Limited**
Thorn House, Hankham Place, Pevensey, Eastbourne, Sussex. Tel 0323 767507
A private organisation helping single parents find accommodation by introducing them to others who want to share.

## Rape

**Rape Crisis Centre**
PO Box 69, London WC1. Tel 01 278 3956; 24-hour emergency service 01 837 1600

Gives legal and medical advice, counselling and moral support for women who have been raped or sexually assaulted. If you live in London the Centre will organise for someone to go with you to a clinic, doctor, police station or court if you want.

## Sexual identity

**Albany Trust**
24, Chester Square, London SW1. Tel 01 730 5871
A charitable organisation concerned with educational research and psychosexual health. Counselling services for those with homosexual, bisexual, transsexual, transvestite, paedophile or other sexual identity problems. Free.

**Beaumont Society**
BM Box 3084, London WC1.
A charitable organisation offering counselling for heterosexual transvestites.

**Campaign for Homosexual Equality** (CHE)
38 Mount Pleasant, London WC1. Tel 01 833 3912
120 local groups in England and Wales provide social activities and, if you want, a chance to campaign for homosexual women and men of all ages. Free legal advice service.

**Gay Christian Movement**
BM Box 6914, London WC1. Tel 01 283 5165
Groups all over England for all ages of Christian gays.

**Gay Switchboard**
BM Switchboard, London WC1. Tel 01 837 7324
24-hour phone help service for gays providing information on all aspects of homosexual life.

**Irish Gay Rights Movement**
Phoenix Centre, Dublin 1. Tel Dublin 730063
Help and advice for gays in Eire.

**Lesbian Line**
BM Box 1414, London WC1. Tel 01 251 6911
Confidential phone advice for girls who think they may be gay.

**London Friend**
274 Upper Street, London N1. Tel 01 837 3337, 7.30–10 pm; 01 354 1846, female callers only; 01 837 2782

Transvestite/transsexual information. Confidential advice to young people. Free.

**Northern Ireland Gay Rights Association**
PO Box 44, Belfast BT1. Telephone counselling service, Belfast 22023, 7.30–10 pm.

**Quest**
BM Box 2585, London WC1. Linkline 01 373 7819
Roman Catholic gay group.

**Scottish Homosexual Rights Group**
60 Broughton Street, Edinburgh, EH1. Tel 031 556 4049. Lesbian line: 031 557 0751
Several branches in Scotland providing information about social events of interest to sexual minorities.

## Other useful telephone numbers

Brighton Gay Switchboard. Brighton 690825

Norwich Friend. Norwich 503713, 8–10 pm, Mondays.

Liverpool Friend, Liverpool 708 9552

West Midlands Friend. Birmingham 622 7351

Manchester Friend. Manchester 236 6283

# Index